BILINGUAL EDUCATION AND ENGLISH AS A SECOND LANGUAGE

GARLAND REFERENCE LIBRARY
OF SOCIAL SCIENCE
(VOL. 464)

BILINGUAL EDUCATION AND ENGLISH AS A SECOND LANGUAGE
A Research Handbook, 1986–1987

Alba N. Ambert

GARLAND PUBLISHING, INC. • NEW YORK & LONDON
1988

Library of Congress Cataloging-in-Publication Data

Ambert, Alba N., 1946–
    Bilingual education and English as a second language: a research
handbook, 1986–1987 / Alba N. Ambert.
        p.   cm. — (Garland reference library of social science ; v.
464)
    Bibliography: p.
    Includes index.
    ISBN 0-8240-6625-1
    1. Education, Bilingual—United States.   2. English language—
Study and teaching—United States—Foreign speakers.   3. Second
language acquisition.   4. Education literature—United States.
    I. Title. II. Series.
    LC3731.A66   1988
    371.97—dc19   88–16446
                                                              CIP

Cover design by Mary Beth Brennan

Printed on acid-free, 250-year-life paper
Manufactured in the United States of America

To the language minority children
of the world, with hope.

CONTENTS

Part III: Practice

Part IV: Implications

Appendices

Indexes

ABOUT THE EDITOR

Alba N. Ambert is Senior Research Scholar at Athens College, Athens, Greece, where she conducts psycholinguistic and educational research and offers in-service teacher training. Previously, she was Visiting Scientist at the Massachusetts Institute of Technology's Department of Linguistics. As a National Research Council Postdoctoral Fellow Dr. Ambert performed research on the language development and language disorders of Puerto Rican children living in the United States. She was assistant professor and director of the Bilingual Special Education Teacher Training Program at the University of Hartford, in Connecticut. Dr. Ambert has written numerous articles and several books on bilingualism, bilingual special education, and the language development of Spanish-speaking children, including the co-authored book <u>Bilingual Education: A Sourcebook</u>. She has presented her research findings at national and international conferences. She received a B.A. from the Universidad de Puerto Rico and her M.Ed. and Ed.D. degrees from Harvard University with concentrations in language development and language and reading disorders in Spanish-speaking children living in bilingual settings. Dr. Ambert has recently completed a criterion-referenced test to identify reading disorders in Spanish-speaking children.

CONTRIBUTING AUTHORS

Maria D. Alvarez received her Ph.D. in School Psychology from New York University. She is a practicing school psychologist with the Boston Public Schools where she works with children and families of three linguistic groups: Spanish, Haitian-Creole, and French. Dr. Alvarez specializes in the non-biased assessment of language minority groups, in the design of educational planning for children with special learning needs, and in bilingual schooling. Her doctoral research, conducted in Spanish Harlem, was a study of the personal, domestic, and school variables that promote/hinder academic achievement among Hispanic students. Using anthropological methods she has conducted ethnographic research in different cultures, especially in Haiti, where she has studied socialization and health practices.

Angela Carrasquillo is an associate professor at Fordham University, where she is coordinator of the Teaching English to Speakers of Other Languages (TESOL) Program. Dr. Carrasquillo is a prolific writer. She has written two books in the area of teaching reading to the bilingual student and she has authored several monographs on the Neo-Rican. She is nationally known in the area of bilingual education and ESL. Dr. Carrasquillo has degrees from the Universidad de Puerto Rico and a Ph.D. from New York University.

Yvonne De Gaetano is Assistant Director for the Division of Training Evaluation and School Services at Teachers College, Columbia University. She is also Director of the Cultural Diversity Training program for the Division. She has had vast experience in education ranging from teaching in early childhood programs to teaching in graduate school in the United States, Puerto Rico and Italy. She has co-authored <u>ALERTA: A Bilingual, Multicultural Approach to Teaching Young Children</u> and <u>Kaleidoscope: A Cross Cultural Approach to Teaching and Learning</u>. She has also developed and written a training guide, <u>Cultural Diversity</u>

<u>Training for Social Service Staff</u> and many articles on school improvement and training. She has made numerous presentations at national and international conferences.

Jay Heubert is an assistant professor at the Harvard Graduate School of Education, where he teaches education law. He has also taught courses at Harvard Law School. From 1980 to 1985, as a trial attorney in the Civil Rights Division of the U.S. Department of Justice, he litigated cases involving racial discrimination in education. He has also been a high school English teacher and an advisory specialist on school desegregation. He received his B.A. from Swarthmore, his M.A.T. from Duke, and his J.D. and Ed.D. from Harvard. He has coauthored articles on competency testing and higher education desegregation.

Judy Kwiat is a consultant/teacher trainer for the Illinois Resource Center. In this role, she has provided workshops, training and consultative assistance to teachers who work with limited English proficient students in grades K-12. She has planned educational seminars and conferences, authored numerous educational publications and taught graduate level courses for the National College of Education in ESL and bilingual education. She is a Ph.D. candidate in Curriculum and Instruction at the University of Illinois, Chicago. She has a M.A. in Linguistics with a specialization in ESL from the University of Illinois and a B.S. in Spanish. She has been a bilingual, ESL and Spanish and English language arts teacher with the Chicago Board of Education and the Department of Defense Dependents' Schools Europe in Hanau, West Germany.

Andres Rodriguez, Jr. is Supervisor of the Funding Services Unit at the New York City Board of Education, Office of Bilingual Education. Formerly he directed two programs in the Academic Excellence division of the city: the Bilingual Reading Clinic Demonstration Program and the Parent Involvement Project. He received an M.S. and a Ph.D. in reading from Fordham

University.   He has taught   reading and   ESL in
the New York   City   Intermediate   Public Schools
since 1972.   He is currently a candidate for the
Ed.D.   degree   at   Fordham   University   in
Educational Administration and   Supervision.   He
continues to   provide lecture   presentations and
workshops   to   school   systems and organizations
throughout the United States.

Dennis Sayers coordinates the Connecticut office
of   the   New   England   Multifunctional   Resource
Center at the University of   Hartford and offers
workshops to bilingual   educators throughout the
Northeast.   He is the editor of the New England
Bilingual   Literacy   Correspondent.   Mr. Sayers
earned an   M.A.T.   in   ESL from   the   School for
International Training.   The author   of several
articles   and   book   chapters   on   integrating
writing   instruction   with   current   educational
technology, Mr. Sayers is co-author with Dr. Jim
Cummins   of   MicroTrends,   a   book   on   computer
writing networks (in press).   He   is a doctoral
candidate   at   the   Harvard   University Graduate
School of Education in Cambridge, Massachusetts.

INTRODUCTION

A rich mythology on bilingualism and second language acquisition survives in the United States today. Besides answering questions of a religious, philosophical, and transcendental nature, such as Who made the world? and Why are we here?, myths serve an important function in society. Myths are used to account for traditional customs and to justify an existing social system. It is this second function of the myth that is of concern to us in this volume. Numerous myths have evolved to justify the treatment of linguistic minorities in this country. We have heard many of them at one time or another. Hispanic children are slow, Filipino females are submissive, Asians are inscrutable, and so on. In education, these myths tend to perpetuate inappropriate educational programs for linguistic minority children, such as placing normally developing Hispanic children in classes for the handicapped. As myths go, they have no objective, sound basis whatsoever. Yet, attempts are made to shroud these assumptions under a veneer of scientific respectability.

In a recent publication on the cognitive, linguistic, and scholastic development of bilingual Hispanic children in the United States, L. M. Dunn (1987) contends that Puerto Ricans and Chicanos are inferior to members of the Anglo culture in cognitive mapping, linguistic competence, and academic achievement. He argues that racially-bound inherited genetic traits are a contributing factor to the poor performance of these groups on intelligence tests. He describes the racial mix of Puerto Ricans and Mexican-Americans which explain their intellectual inferiority (Mexicans have Indian blood and Puerto Ricans have black blood). He attempts to prove his argument with an impressive display of data, yet his conclusions are not derived from a thoughtful interpretation of the data. This is a glaring example of how myths are used to justify racist treatment of language minorities; myths not only refuse to die, but are perpetuated in the literature. That a well-known educational

publisher should publish such a biased
treatise is a reflection on society's attitudes
towards the minorities in their midst and its
acceptance of subjective, racially motivated
stereotypes as scientifically-based knowledge.
The author of this geneticist view of
intelligence, has adapted a well-known test (the
Peabody Picture Vocabulary Test in Spanish) by
providing separate norms for Puerto Rican,
Mexican, and other Latino children, the very
population the author considers intellectually
inferior!

There are between 3.5 and 5.3 million
limited English-speaking children (aged 5 to 13)
in the United States. Of these, only one third
are receiving appropriate educational services
(Waggoner, 1986). This fact can only illustrate
the lack of commitment in our society to the
appropriate education of language minority
children. To justify and explain the refusal
to provide adequate educational treatment to
language minorities a number of myths have been
created, and despite research evidence to the
contrary, continue to thrive.

The Language Deficiency Myth

The language deficiency myth has been
around for decades, assuming a variety of
rubrics according to the prevalent theories of
the times. Language minority children have been
described as language deficient, verbally
deficient, nonverbal, alingual, and semilingual.
Today, in a particularly perverse twist, they
are classified as language disordered/impaired
and placed in classes for the learning disabled
or in speech therapy. In a linguistic study of
Puerto Rican kindergarten children living in the
United States, conducted at the Massachusetts
Institute of Technology, Ambert (in press)
found that the children studied had a rich
linguistic repertoire. So much so, that she
calls them "language enriched" children who have
the potential of developing a rich native
language along with mastery of English. The
linguistic deficiencies described by educators
appear to exist solely in the minds of

practitioners who lack elementary knowledge about native language acquisition and the process of second language development.

The English Exposure Myth

In this view, opponents of bilingual education claim that children of limited English proficiency require as much exposure to English as possible. Furthermore, instruction in the native language will hinder acquisition of English. Research evidence in the United States, Canada, Sweden, Australia, Mexico and other countries overwhelmingly rejects this myth. It has been found that language minority children who receive instruction in the native language develop the second language more efficiently than children submerged in the second language (Cummins, 1983; Wong Fillmore and Valadez, 1986).

A dramatic example of the positive role of native language instruction in second language acquisition, is provided by the Spanish-only preschool program in the Carpinteria School District (Cummins, 1986) described more fully in Chapter 4 of this volume. Program evaluation results indicate that after participation in the Spanish-only program, the children performed better than Spanish-speaking children enrolled in bilingual programs, in Spanish and in English, on tests of oral syntactic development. Program participants were exposed to less English, but because of their strong native language skills and their increased conceptual knowledge, they were able to effectively transfer these skills to English.

Despite research evidence from all over the world indicating that native language instruction promotes second language acquisition, the United States Department of Education advocates the "structured immersion" approach as an alternative to bilingual education. In this method, a diluted form of English is used as the medium of instruction. It seems that according to this position, it is better to give language minority students a simplified version of content, if in English, than realize the children's cognitive/intellectual

potential with academically demanding tasks
in another language. Proponents of this
approach cite the success of Canadian immersion
programs, although Canadian researchers have
consistently warned that immersion programs
are not appropriate for language minority
children and, in fact, may be detrimental to
their academic progress (Crawford, 1987).
Also, in the Canadian immersion experiments the
second language is not simplified, but follows
the same French curriculum of native French
speakers. In addition, in their efforts to
eliminate native language instruction, United
States Department of Education officials ignore
the findings of the United States General
Accounting Office (1987) which indicate that
native language instruction helps limited
English proficient students learn English.

Native Language Home Use Myth

According to this argument, native language
use at home is a barrier to language minority
children's academic progress. This myth has
been perpetuated to the extent that language
minority parents are instructed by school
personnel to speak English at home. Yet
research in the home use of the native language
indicates that academic performance is not
hindered by native language use at home. On the
contrary, it has been found that students who
switch to English as the main home language
perform poorer academically than children who
maintain the native home language (Cummins,
1986).

The Language Confusion Myth

Exposure to two languages causes confusion
in children. Children in this situation are
unable to learn either language well. This is
another of the resilient myths of bilingual
lore. As long as bilingual education programs
are implemented effectively, children can
function in both languages without any
detrimental effects. On the contrary, research
has found that bilingual children have greater
cognitive flexibility and enhanced metalin-

guistic abilities than their monolingual peers
(Wong Fillmore and Valadez, 1986). The problems
of confusion arise when educational practitioners (who are themselves monolingual) fail to
understand the dynamics of the second language
acquisition process and misidentify normal
developmental factors as language confusion.
Problems also arise when bilingual education
programs are not implemented according to sound
linguistic theory and practice, such as when
teachers use concurrent translations in the
classroom, a counterproductive educational practice which is all too common in bilingual
programs.

The Bilingual Educator Conspiracy Myth

A common complaint of opponents of
bilingual education is that, for some arcane
reasons, bilingual educators support native
language instruction exclusively and have
little interest in children's acquisition of
English. Bilingualism, to the uninformed, is
really meant as monolingualism in a language
other than English. Yet, English language
acquisition is at the core of all bilingual
programs in the United States. If bilingual
educators support the use of native language
instruction, it is because the native language
can serve as a very efficient tool in the
process of acquiring a second language, without
the unnecessary loss in native language and
academic/cognitive development (Wong Fillmore
and Valadez, 1986).

In a recent study done by Monteagle
Stearns, a foreign service veteran, on the
language abilities of foreign service personnel
(United States Department of State, 1987), he
found serious deficiencies in the foreign
language capabilities of foreign service
officers. Similar reports on the foreign
language limitations in the United States have
been widely disseminated in the popular press.
Yet, the United States has a tremendous asset in
the multilingual, multicultural nature of its
people that it is not willing to exploit. Many
leaders in government, business, and education
are saying the country "has been hurt by its

inattention to foreign language, cultures and affairs." (Gruson, 1986). This is the type of paradox bilingual educators have continuously pointed out. It seems contrary to national interests to destroy the linguistic assets of children who are native speakers of other languages and who can acquire English while maintaining valuable fluency in other languages. Opposition to this goal can only be the result of misguided perceptions that reflect a lack of understanding, or unwillingness to accept, the positive nature of bilingualism. To further strengthen the argument for bilingual education as a means of developing foreign language capabilities in all children, bilingual educators stress that bilingual education is not the exclusive province of language minorities, but can be an effective program for native English speakers to learn other languages as well. All children can and should benefit from bilingualism.

Fortunately, we are poised at a very interesting crossroads in bilingual education and English as a Second Language (ESL) research today. Exciting research of high methodological caliber is emerging (as reviewed in this volume) and much of this research is conducted by members of language minorities themselves. The emerging research points to the effectiveness of well-implemented bilingual programs and to the positive effects of bilingualism. It is important that bilingual educators and program administrators become familiar with the latest research results because the gap between research findings and program implementation is still too wide. In addition, if we are familiar with the research findings in bilingualism and second language acquisition, we will be better able to dispel the adverse myths that continue to flourish. Knowledge of these findings will also place us in a better position to advocate for appropriate educational programs for language minority children in our society. This volume of recent research findings in bilingualism and second language acquisition is intended to assist in the process. The purpose of the book is to describe and analyze the research of the past year (1986-87) in different areas of bilingualism and second language acquisition. Each chapter contains a general analysis of the research in a specific area, recommendations for future research, and an annotated bibliography in the area of discussion. The material is relevant to diverse language groups. Although the intention is to describe the most recent research, we have included past research in those cases where it is necessary to grasp the implications of today's studies or in areas where a scarcity of research is available.

We hope the book will be of use to teachers, teacher aides, teacher trainers, supervisors, administrators, parents, child advocates, and other individuals concerned with the trajectory of bilingual education and second language acquisition.

The contributing authors come from a wide range of disciplines in the field of bilingualism and second language acquisition. They have the special insights of practitioners who are aware of the problems in the field and are able to temper research findings with the reality of practical issues. The continued dedication of these contributors, evident in their everyday endeavors, is the backbone of present and future efforts to guarantee quality education for language minority children. Many thanks for their efforts.

I would like to acknowledge   the support of
Garland   Publishing Editor Marie   Ellen Larcada,
whose idea it was to develop   a reference volume
on bilingualism and second language acquisition.
Many thanks for her   superb editorial assistance
and general support   during   the   development of
the volume.   Finally, I gratefully acknowledge
the   technical   assistance   and   support   of
Constantinos Petrinos,   from Athens College, who
generously dedicated   many   hours   to   the final
production of this manuscript.

                              Alba N. Ambert
                              Athens, Greece
                              December 1987

REFERENCES

Ambert, A.N.   Language   Enriched   Puerto Rican
    Children (in press).

Crawford, J.   "Bilingual education: Language,
    learning, and politics." **Education Week**,
    19-50, April 1, 1987.

Cummins, J.   **Heritage Language Education: A
    Literature Review.** Toronto: Ministry of
    Education, Ontario, 1983.

Cummins, J.   "Empowering minority students: A
    framework   for   intervention."   Harvard
    Educational Review, 56, 1, 18-36, 1986.

Dunn, L.M.   **Bilingual Hispanic Children on the
    U.S. Mainland: A Review of Research on
    Their Cognitive, Linguistic, and Scholastic
    Development.** Minnesota: American Guidance
    Service, 1987.

Gruson, L. "U.S. working to close foreign-
    language gap." **New York Times**, p. 1, A24,
    December 2, 1986.

United States Department of State. "Foreign
    service capability must be enhanced, says
    report to management." **State: The
    Newsletter**, No. 296, January 1987.

United States General Accounting Office.
    **Bilingual Education: A New Look at the
    Research Evidence.** Washington, DC: United
    States Government Printing Office, June
    1986.

Waggoner, D.   "Estimates on the need for
    bilingual education and the proportion of
    children in need of being served." **NABE
    News**, IX, 4-5, 6-9, 1986.

Wong Fillmore, L. and Valadez, C. "Teaching
    Bilingual Learners." In Wiltrach, M.C.
    (Ed.) Handbook of Research on Teaching.
    New York: Macmillan, 1986.

Chapter 1

BILINGUAL CHILDREN:
HOW THE LANGUAGE ACQUISITION PROCESS WORKS

Alba N. Ambert

INTRODUCTION

Understanding a child's development of a second language requires close consideration of the language acquisition process in general and the relationships between first and second language acquisition. Is the process of acquiring languages similar, regardless of sequence of acquisition? Are there differences between first and second language development? If so, what are these differences? The purpose of this chapter is to review the theoretical foundations of the language acquisition process in both the native and second languages and describe what the current research reveals in these areas.

THE LANGUAGE ACQUISITION PROCESS

Language is a system of symbols that relates sounds to meanings; these symbols represent real-life referents. There is no iconic relationship between the symbol and the referent; therefore, which symbol stands for which referent is arbitrary. Language development is an essential part of children's growth. Experimentation with language is a source of pride and delight as children acquire the complexities of linguistic structures and progress from simpler to more differentiated grammatical forms. In the process, they acquire the competence to communicate effectively in different social contexts. Given linguistic stimulation, most children acquire language. Linguistic research continues to explore how children acquire language so quickly and effortlessly. How is it that children acquire such a complex system of symbols at an early stage of development? When we examine children's language formulations closely, we

observe a monumental task of acquiring and
expressing grammatical structures that are
saturated by underlying semantic relations and
grammatical categories. A three-and-a-half year
old girl, for example, spontaneously produced
this semantically and syntactically complex
sentence:

> **You know what, Mommy? Yesterday today was
> tomorrow.**
> (de Villiers and de Villiers, 1978, p. 121)

By the time they enter school, children
have a vocabulary of between 8,000 and 14,000
words and are acquiring eight to ten new words a
day (de Villiers and de Villiers, 1978). They
have also mastered basic syntactic, semantic
and phonological structures of their language
(Bryen, 1981). How do children accomplish this
complex and impressive feat regardless of their
cultural and linguistic background? In short,
how does language acquisition occur?

Behaviorist Models

When behavioralism was the dominant
psychological model for cognitive development,
it was proposed that children learned language
through a rigid reflex response to reinforcement. Language learning ocurred as any
other learning and was determined by stimuli
received from the environment. It was through
reinforcement, imitation, and successive
approximations to adult speech that children
developed language. They did so as passive
recipients of environmental stimuli (Bohannon
and Warren-Leubecker, 1985). Language, then, as
the behaviorists saw it, was a system of
reinforcement of verbal behavior. Yet this
theory did not stand up to empirical studies of
language development. First of all, behavioralism does not explain children's utterances such
as "two foots" and "I comed," common over-
generalizations when children are acquiring
language. These are utterances children have
not heard their parents produce, yet they are
very common in children's early speech. Imitation does not account for them. Behaviorist
theories also do not explain how children
acquire meaning. Parents do not explain what

every word means to their children, the children
pick up meanings, making elaborate associations
in their semantic development. The behaviorists'
main problem, though, was their lack of
research in language acquisition. Instead of
conducting   research   specifically   directed
towards language development, they simply
extrapolated results of their research in
cognitive psychology to the language acquisition
process.

Innatist Models

    A thirteen-year-old boy was asked recently
"How did you learn language?"   The boy shrugged
and responded, "I just always knew it." Almost
thirty years ago, Chomsky proposed his
generative grammar theory which in a sense says
just that, children are born knowing language.
Language is an innate ability. Humans are
genetically programmed to acquire language, a
species-specific behavior unique to humans. We
are neurologically equipped for language
acquisition and we genetically transmit this
language acquisition ability to our children.
According to Chomsky, the human brain has
embedded within it a Language Acquisition Device
(LAD). When triggered by the stimulation of
spoken language, the LAD deduces all the
fundamental rules of the language regardless of
external reinforcement or training. That is why
language is acquired and not learned. So
language is embedded in our brain from the start
and comes to the surface as we are exposed to
the spoken word. All we need to trigger the
Language Acquisition Device is exposure to
language. According to Chomsky, it is this
innate language acquisition ability, this
neurological program, that explains the success
and speed of language acquisition. Research has
stressed that all children go through the same
pattern of language development regardless of
the language they are acquiring or the culture
in which they live (Brown, 1973). The language
acquisition process is, thus, a biological
imperative and it is universal (Chomsky 1957,
1965, 1971). Children are born with an innate
linguistic component and given the regularities

of linguistic systems, this component is independent of cognitive development (Goodluck, 1986).

According to the innatist theory, once the language acquisition device is activated through exposure to language, children go through a process of discovering the rules, the regularities of the language and internalizing the rules of the grammar. They then proceed to analyze language at deeper levels until they are able to produce sentences that parallel adult linguistic constructions. A child is exposed to language and little by little internalizes the rules of the grammar forming his or her own rules and modifying them with further exposure to the language. The following conversation between a four-year-old and an adult illustrates this process.

> Child: My teacher holded the baby rabbits
> and we patted them.
> Adult: Did you say your teacher held the
> baby rabbits?
> Child: Yes.
> Adult: What did you say she did?
> Child: She holded the baby rabbits and we
> patted them.
> (The child has not picked up the
> correction.)
> Adult: Did you say she held them tightly?
> Child: No, she holded them loosely.
> (Cazden, 1972, pp. 4-5)

This child has formed a rule for the formation of the past tense based on her exposure to the English language and adds ed to a verb. She is unable to produce the correct form of held because she has not yet internalized the specific exception to the rule. As we can see, she does not imitate what the adult has said. Until she discovers the appropriate rule on her own, by her exposure to it, she will be unable to use it.

According to the innatists, children are active participants in the language acquisition process. By applying the rules of the grammar, they are able to generate an infinite number of original sentences, sentences they have never

heard before. If the imitation theory to
language acquisition were accurate, children
would only be able to use sentences they have
heard.

Chomsky made another important contribution
to linguistics when he proposed his theory of
transformational grammar. In this theory he
states that when we acquire a language we must
analyze not only the grammatical structures that
we hear, as we hear them, but we must go beyond
the surface structure of language to apprehend
meaning. So there is a surface structure and a
deep structure in language and it is only by
analyzing the deep structure that we can derive
meaning. Ambiguous sentences help illustrate
this point.

The following newspaper headline appeared
once:

POLICE HELPS DOG BITE VICTIM

By analyzing the surface structure of this
ambiguous sentence we really cannot determine
its meaning. It can mean that the police helped
the dog bite the victim or that the police
helped the victim who was bitten by a dog.
Chomsky developed a precise procedure of
transforming sentences from the surface
structure to the deep structure of the language
since it is at the deep levels where the problem
of meaning is resolved. The importance of this
is that in order to master a language, we must
master the deep structure of the language as
well as its surface structure. So in the
sentence "Police helps dog bite victim" it is
only through our knowledge of the deep structure
of the language, that is, the syntax, semantics,
and morphology that we can understand its
meaning. One of the drawbacks of previously
conceived structuralist approaches to linguistics was that its emphasis on grammatical forms
alone did not enlighten the process by which
children acquire meaning. In order to
understand a language, we must be able to master
its deeper levels. Persons who speak a second
language may have difficulty understanding some
of the more complex sentences in their second
language because of limitations in their mastery

of the deep structure of the language.   A motel
sign that reads "Kids are on the house" may be
confusing   indeed   to   a   non-fluent   speaker of
English who may have visions of goats perched on
a roof.

Interactive Models

    Language researchers   have   found   that the
innatist models of language acquisition are not
sufficient to   explain   language   phenomena left
unexplained by   simple performance of linguistic
tasks.   They go a step beyond innatist models
and are concerned with the behavior and contexts
involved   when   a   language   act   occurs.   To
function   linguistically children must   not only
know the appropriate   rules   of   their language,
but   also   understand   the   behaviors   that
correspond to language use   (Carrow-Woolfolk and
Lynch,   1982).   They must have the discourse and
strategic competence   to communicate effectively
(Kessler,   1984).   Interactive   models   analyze
language's cognitive dimensions and its behavioral manifestations.   These models emphasize not
only children's comprehension and   production of
language, but also context and intent. In static
linguistic   analysis an implied request   such as
"Could   you   open   the   door?"   could   not   be
explained   without   analyzing   the   inferential
process   a   listener   must   experience   to
understand   that the speaker   is not questioning
the   listener's   physical   ability   to   open the
door.   The listener understands that the speaker
is conveying a request   by   using knowledge   of
the   situation   to   infer   meaning (McLaughlin,
1984).   The   context   in   which   a   speech   act
occurs   is   also important   in interpreting   it.
The   sentence   "John   says   the   Dodgers"   for
example,   makes   no   sense   unless   seen   as
occurring in the context of   the question: "Who
won the   baseball game?"   Language must be seen
as   a communicative act   and   not   simply   as   a
string   of   grammatical   utterances (McLaughlin,
1984).   The   term   communicative   competence
(Hymes,   1971)   is   now   used   to   describe   the
ability to   use language   effectively   in social
situations.   Researchers are also concerned with

the role played by adults in children's language
acquisition process and the role of cognition in
linguistic development

Brown and Bellugi (1964) identified three
factors affecting children's syntactic development: imitation, reduction, and expansion. In
a longitudinal study with two children, ages
18 months and 27 months, they found that
children attempt to repeat what is heard,
although they often reduce adult utterances.
For example:

Adult	Child
Fraser will be unhappy	Fraser unhappy
That's an old time train	Old time train
It's not the same dog as Pepper	Dog Pepper
No, you can't write on Mr. Cromer's shoe	Write Cromer shoe

The authors also found that parents often
expand upon children's utterances:

Child	Adult
Baby highchair	Baby is in the highchair
Mommy eggnog	Mommy had her eggnog
Eve lunch	Eve is having lunch

The researchers suggest that this pattern
of imitation, reduction, and expansion may
facilitate children's internalizing the
structure of the language. Although children
may possess an innate ability to formulate
grammatical rules, there are other factors in
the child's environment that may play key roles
in the language acquisition process.

The role played by caretakers in children's
linguistic development has been studied
extensively (Snow, 1984, 1986). Researchers
conclude that the language addressed to
children, that is, child directed speech, can
contribute to children's language acquisition
in several ways: (1) when it offers semantic
extensions, that is, follows a child's topic
lead and expands upon it; (2) when it asks
questions, passing the conversational turn to

the child; and (3) when these extensions and
questions recur frequently in conversations with
the child. These instances of child directed
speech are said to have a definite impact on
children's language development. According to
researchers, it appears that these techniques
allow children to make inferences and more
effective generalizations about the language.

Most parent-child interaction research has
focused on white, middle-class families in the
United States. Schieffelin and Eisenberg (1984)
review the research on cultural variation in
child directed speech. They found that in
cultures such as the Luo in Kenya, West Samoans,
Japanese, Chicano, Warm Springs Indian, and
Malaysian Tamil, silence in children is a sign
of respect and deference towards adults and, in
most of these cultures, children are not
expected to participate in conversations with
adults. Nevertheless, children from the
cultures observed acquire the language of their
communities, though individual differences
exist in the acquisition of specific elements of
the languages.

In addition to parent-child interaction,
adherents of the interactionist models insist
that a child's language performance must be
analyzed within the context of the
environment in which speech acts occur.
Children use language to communicate and in
order to do so must learn the conventions of
the language, such as conversational
turn-taking, topic introduction, eye contact,
attention, and so on. Ethnographic techniques
are now widely used to describe language in
context. Sociolinguists focus on the social
context and dynamics of language use and the
process of language acquisition and language
usage in diverse social settings, such as
schools and communities.

Individual differences in child language
acquisition have been found to exist, indicating
that there is some diversity in the universal
patterns of language acquisition. Children vary
in the age of onset of speech and rate of
language acquisition, but also in the words they
acquire and the linguistic styles they use. For
example, studies have shown significant

diversity in the types of words that appear in children's early speech (nominals, action words, function words, etc.). Researchers have also found diversity in children's combining of words syntactically to form sentences. It appears that different children can use different linguistic strategies in the language acquisition process. Children categorized as "referential" appear to move as predicted from one- to two-word stages. Their vocabularies consist mainly of words for objects and they use fewer phrases and acquire words faster than "expressive" children. "Expressive" children, on the other hand, use fewer object words, but more pronouns, modifiers, and function words than referential children. They also seem to acquire more expressions, such as "go away," "stop it," "don't do it," and are slower in acquiring new words. Children have also been described as either "code-oriented" or "message-oriented." Code-oriented children use early words to label, repeat, and practice more than to communicate with others; whereas, message-oriented children are said to use language to manipulate the social situation. The variation seen in children's language development may be due to differences in children's cognitive organization, the linguistic input they receive, and the context in which their linguistic development occurs (Goldfield and Snow, 1985).

In Chomsky's (1969) study of the syntactic development of school-aged children, she found that linguistic development was not complete by the time children enter school. It appears that important syntactic structures are in the process of being acquired between the ages of 5 and 10 years. Other studies have confirmed Chomsky's findings. Recent researchers have found that after children enter school they continue developing semantic features of the language as well as phonological features (McLaughlin, 1984). Recent research findings, then, indicate that individual variation

exists in children's language development
and the language acquisition process continues
after children enter school.

Cognitivists

The cognitive/linguistic interface is a
more difficult question posed by researchers in
language development. According to cogniti-
vists, language development is not an
independent innate ability. Rather, it is a
function dependent on cognitive development and
as such results from cognitive maturation
(Bohannon and Warren-Leubecker, 1986). Cogniti-
vist theories of language development are
strongly influenced by Piaget's stages of
cognitive development. It is only when
children's sensorimotor knowledge develops (how
to organize the world, for example) that
language acquisition is possible (Rice, 1984).
For language acquisition to occur children must
first figure out the linguistic devices to use
to express concepts they already have in a
nonlinguistic stage. Maturation is critical and
children cannot acquire language until a certain
level of cognitive development has been
achieved.

Language Development in Non-English Speakers

Although an overwhelming majority of
research on language development has
concentrated on English-speaking children,
attempts have been made to document the native
language development of non-English-speakers.
Montes-Giraldo (1971) studied his four
children's language development from birth to 51
months in Colombia. He analyzed their
phonological development and followed the
chronological emergence of linguistic categories, such as articles, pronouns, possessives,
adjectives, verbs, adverbs, prepositions, and
conjunctions. Slobin (1966) and Berman (1981)
studied the acquisition of the morphology of
Russian and Hebrew, respectively. Gonzalez
(1970) performed a cross-sectional study on the
acquisition of syntactic features and specific

grammatical structures in three Spanish-speaking Chicano children between the ages of two and five years, living in Texas. Gili-Gaya (1974) studied 50 Puerto Rican children between the ages of four and seven years to analyze the manner in which they used language as a communication tool and the syntactic structures the children used in expressive language. Brisk (1972) identified deviant forms of syntax present in seven five-year-old Spanish-speaking children from New Mexico. In another study, Brisk (1976) analyzed the acquisition of Spanish gender in Spanish-speaking children in Boston and Argentina. Belendez (1980) performed a longitudinal study of four Puerto Rican boys living in Boston for a period ranging from three to 20 months to analyze the pattern of acquisition of the Spanish verb system. Tolbert (1978) studied the acquisition of twelve grammatical morphemes in three Spanish-speaking children from Guatemala. Kernan and Blount (1966) studied the acquisition of grammatical rules in Mexican children between the ages of five and twelve years. Other studies have focused on the acquisition of case morphology in German (Tracy, 1986), verb morphology in Dutch-speaking children (Van Besien and Moerman-Coetsier, 1986), gender rules in German (Mills, 1986) and verb inflections in German (Clahsen, 1986). Olarte (1985) studied the comprehension and production of Spanish morphemes. In a crosslinguistic study of the acquisition of Turkish, Italian, Serbo-Croatian, and English, Johnston and Slobin (1979) found that the order of acquisition of morphemes used to express location (such as in and on) was similar in the four languages. Baslis (1981) studied social class differences in the language of Greek children.

A recent research trend in looking at the language development of non-English speakers in the United States consists of ethnographic studies of children's communicative competence. Researchers have turned away from an exclusive analysis of linguistic forms to an analysis of children's pragmatic abilities. These studies have shown that non- or limited English-speaking children living in the United States have acquired important communicative abilities such as turn allocation, that is, taking turns in conversations (Volk, in press); and describe the individual differences in linguistic competence of children who are growing up in bilingual settings (Zentella, in press). In a study which combined linguistic and pragmatic analysis, Ambert (in press) studied 30 Puerto Rican Spanish-speaking kindergarten children living in the United States. In analyzing both the linguistic structures acquired by the children and their communicative competence, that is, use of language for communication, it was found that the children had developed grammatical structures consistent with their age and they had also developed conversational skills that demonstrated their communicative competence in verbal interaction. Although the children were living in the United States, English language influence was insignificant in the native language of the children studied.

Research in the native language development of non-English speaking children reveals that the process of first language acquisition appears to be the same across languages. Although there are individual differences in the rate and chronological emergence of specific grammatical categories, for example, the basic principles of language acquisition occur in all children. They appear to acquire simpler to more complex grammatical structures and they develop the skills to communicate competently.

Research in native language acquisition is confirming the sophisticated knowledge children possess of the structure of language. Although the innate theory of language continues to have its adherents, it is now thought that in addition to innate abilities in language acquisition, other factors such as child-caretaker interaction, imitation, and repetition of linguistic structures, affect this language acquisition ability children are born with by exposing them to the rules of the grammar and facilitating the internalization of linguistic rules. We are also more aware now of individual differences in children's linguistic development and the continuation of the language acquisition process in school-aged children. Because children use language in the context of their environment, psycholinguists are now looking at children's abilities to communicate competently in a variety of settings. Instances of language usage in school, with playmates, with parents, are shedding light on children's ability to use language in diverse settings. Cognitive theories are pointing to the interdependence of language acquisition abilities in children incorporating linguistic development into the general maturation of cognitive skills.

SECOND LANGUAGE ACQUISITION

In studying children's acquisition of a second language, many questions emerge about the nature of the process. Does the process of second language acquisition follow the same stages as the first? If not, how does it differ? Does age play an important role in this process? Do all children learn a second language in the same manner, or do individual differences exist? Are skills transferred from one language to another?

Second Language Acquisition Theories

Two of the most important contributors to the theoretical foundations of second language acquisition and bilingualism are Stephen D. Krashen and Jim Cummins. Their theories, developed over the past fifteen years, have revolutionized research and practice in second language and bilingual education.

Krashen (1982) distinguishes language "acquisition" from language "learning." Language proficiency cannot be learned, it must be acquired. Learning a language requires a conscious mastery of grammar and vocabulary which is not conducive to effective communication. Acquisition, on the other hand, is the incidental, subconscious, effortless process in which speakers interact meaningfully with no concern for the formal aspects of the language. According to Krashen, language acquisition requires "comprehensible input," that is, second-language exposure that is meaningful, yet just beyond the listener's level of proficiency. Through appropriate exposure to a second language children will internalize the rules of the grammar and develop the necessary vocabulary to communicate effectively. The quantity of exposure is not as important as the quality of second-language input. Krashen maintains that subject-matter lessons specifically geared to limited-English proficient students' level of English are more effective than teaching specific grammatical structures. He advocates the Natural Approach to promote second language acquisition in the classroom. The approach emphasizes meaningful interaction, through extensive use of physical and visual clues; tolerance of grammatical errors, seen as natural to the language acquisition process; and communication of messages relevant to the learner's needs and interests.

In Krashen's theory, the learner's native language plays an important role. An "affective filter" is the set of negative influences that can hinder the second language acquisition process. These influences are motivation, self-confidence, and anxiety. By receiving instruction in the native language, while second language acquisition is occurring, limited English proficient children will experience enhanced self-esteem, a low-anxiety environment, and, because of successful learning experiences in the native language, will be more motivated to acquire the second. Native language instruction makes English input more comprehensible. That is, the information and knowledge children acquire through their native language makes English input easier to understand. This explains results of studies in which children who are taught subject matter in the native language tend to acquire more English than children who receive intensive English instruction.

Perhaps the most influential theorist in bilingual and second language education today is Jim Cummins, a researcher at the Ontario Institute for Studies in Education.

Cummins (1979) provides a theoretical framework to describe the different outcomes of bilingual education in multicultural societies. He cites several studies which suggest that early childhood exposure to two languages can accelerate aspects of cognitive growth beyond that achieved by monolingual children. He notes that in these studies bilingualism had the characteristic of additive bilingualism. That is, competency in the second language was achieved with no threat of the second language replacing the native language. By contrast, he cites studies which indicate low-level academic skills in bilingual children when compared to monolingual peers. In these cases bilingualism was subtractive. Subtractive bilingualism is a condition in which a child's native language is gradually replaced by a more dominant second language.

To further explain the different outcomes of bilingual education, Cummins formulates three hypotheses: the threshold hypothesis, the two-threshold hypothesis, and the developmental interdependence hypothesis.

The threshold hypothesis proposes that the development of different patterns of bilingual skills produces different cognitive/academic consequences:

> ...there may be threshold levels of
> linguistic competence which bilingual
> children must attain both in order to
> avoid cognitive deficits and to allow
> the potentially beneficial aspects of
> becoming bilingual to influence
> cognitive growth. (p. 229)

In the two-threshold hypothesis, he suggests that when the child fails to attain the lower threshold; although he or she may appear to be orally fluent in one or both languages, the child may actually be performing at less than native-like capacity. Thus the child will have difficulty in understanding academically-embedded material. Presumably, at the lower threshold level, the child has sufficient cognitive-linguistic control of one language so that cognitive development is equal to that of monolingual children. Once the child has attained the higher threshold level, he or she is able to integrate concepts in both languages so as to accelerate cognitive growth.

The developmental interdependence hypothesis states that:

> ...the type of competence developed in L2 is partially a function of the competence developed in L1 at the time when intensive exposure to L2 begins. (p. 224)

Cummins suggests that for the children whose knowledge of the native language is well advanced, language medium of instruction may be irrelevant. However, native language education for language minority children may be more successful than instruction in the majority language because the children's linguistic knowledge may not be sufficiently developed prior to entry into school.

Another hypothesis proposed by Cummins (1981) describes a child's basic interpersonal communicative skills (BICS) in the native language (L1) and in the second language (L2) which can be differentiated from the cognitive/academic language proficiency (CALP) required for the development of academic skills. The native language and the second language CALPs are interdependent. He has since modified his BICS/CALP distinction and proposes the terms "context-embedded" and "context-reduced" communication (1984) to explain the different language proficiencies children must master when learning a second language. Context-embedded messages are characteristic of communication which takes place outside of the classroom. It is supported by paralinguistic and situational cues. Context-reduced communication, on the other hand, is typical of the messages used in the classroom and relies heavily on knowledge of the language itself. A child, proficient in context-embedded communication, may be less proficient in the usage and understanding of context-reduced messages that are more cognitively demanding and require a certain level of academic proficiency.

In the "common underlying proficiency" (CUP) theory, Cummins argues that languages develop in the same part of the brain. Skills acquired in one language can transfer easily to another language because cognitive tasks are interdependent across languages. Therefore, once a child has learned to read, or more generally, has acquired cognitive skills in a language, transference of those skills to the other language occurs easily and efficiently. Contrary to popular belief, more exposure to the native language will produce greater proficiency in English as students transfer their knowledge to English without having to relearn skills they have already mastered.

Differences in Language Acquisition

Recent research in second language acquisition indicates that acquisition of a second language is similar to native language acquisition, though differences do exist. McLaughlin (1985) and Hakuta (1986) examine the research in second language acquisition of children from different countries and different linguistic backgrounds. It appears that children follow the same developmental sequence of linguistic patterns as children acquiring the target language as a native one. Children tend to acquire simpler forms first and progress to the more complex grammatical forms, even when they differ in age at the time of second language acquisition.

Research evidence suggests some differences between first and second language acquisition, though. Second language learners are more developed cognitively and have already experienced learning a language, so they bring to the second language acquisition process a great deal of knowledge. They build upon this cognitive and linguistic knowledge to learn the second language more effectively. They have also developed important conceptual and social/communicative skills. For example, an eight-year-old Vietnamese-speaking child learning English as a second language, has already acquired the symbolic representational skills of language (understands that a word stands for a specific referent). She also has acquired concepts, such as <u>on top of</u>, <u>bigger</u>, etc., and merely needs to learn the linguistic labels of the second language to express these concepts. Her cognitive abilities have matured, she has a more developed memory span, auditory processing skills, and a better knowledge of the pragmatic aspects of language, than when she was acquiring her native language. These factors will have an impact on her acquisition of a second language and account for the differences observed in the acquisition of her two languages.

According to some researchers (Wong Fillmore, 1985), the language acquisition device (a cognitive device specialized for language acquisition) may operate for first language acquisition, but more general cognitive mechanisms bear more heavily on the learning of a second language. Based on her studies of second language learners, Wong Fillmore suggests that in acquiring the first language a specialized cognitive mechanism may be a more important factor than general cognitive skills. In second language learning, though, the impact of the language acquisition device is weaker than that of more general cognitive mechanisms. In observing learners of a second language, Wong Fillmore argues, one can see these general cognitive mechanisms at work when children use associative skills, memory, inferential skills, knowledge of social contexts, and other analytic tools to learn the new language. Also at work are the language-specific cognitive mechanisms, that is the language acquisition device, whereby children figure out the system of rules by a hypothesis testing procedure until the rules of the grammar are internalized.

Age

The impact of age on the success of second language acquisition continues to intrigue researchers (Krashen, Scarcella and Long, 1982; Harley, 1986). It appears that the left hemisphere of the brain specializes in brain function for the most part. Aphasics, split brain patients, and persons who have suffered hemisphere removals have provided extensive evidence on this left hemisphere function. Aphasics are persons who have suffered trauma to the left hemisphere of the brain and lost their ability to use language. When trauma to the right hemisphere occurs, language function is not impaired. Split brain patients have the hemispheres severed to control life-threatening epileptic seizures and their language performance suffers as a result. Patients whose right hemisphere is removed for medical reasons suffer no language loss, whereas patients whose left hemisphere is removed suffer language impairment. It was believed that based on the critical period hypothesis for language acquisition (Lenneberg, 1967), an optimal time existed for the language acquisition process to occur. It was generally thought that the left hemisphere of the brain became lateralized, or specialized, for language function at the age of two and this lateralization process continued until puberty. After puberty, the brain lost plasticity and it was extremely difficult to acquire language. Lenneberg claimed that automatic acquisition from mere exposure to a second language disappeared after puberty and foreign language had to be learned through conscious effort. Furthermore, the incidence of "language-learning-blocks" increased after puberty (cited in Harley, 1986). For many years this theory confirmed observations of the apparent difficulty adolescents and adults experienced in acquiring another language. An inference frequently drawn from the critical period hypothesis was that younger children learn languages better than older ones.

Recent evidence does not support the critical period hypothesis nor the contention that the younger the child, the better he or she will learn another language (Snow and Hoefnagel-Hohle, 1978; Harley, 1986). Although the left hemisphere of the brain is specialized for language function to a great extent, no clear evidence exists yet on when lateralization for language is complete. Also, studies have shown that older children are more efficient language learners than younger children. It appears that factors such as motivation, greater

cognitive maturity, more developed native
language skills, and a greater need to
communicate orally, influence older children's
superior performance in the linguistic tasks
assigned in these studies. So it may be the
more advanced native language skills and not age
that affect older children's performance in
second language acquisition. This has important
implications for native language instruction in
the early grades, since it appears important to
develop children's cognitive skills so that they
become efficient learners of the second
language.

Variance in Second Language Development

A frequent concern in second language
learning is the degree to which children vary in
the development of a second language. Many
educators expect children to follow the same
rate of acquisition, the same developmental
sequence. Yet, increasingly, the research
reveals that although there is a regularity in
patterns of acquisition, vast individual
differences exist among children learning a
second language (McLaughlin, 1985 and Hakuta,
1986). It appears that individual learning
style, type of linguistic input received,
motivation, and personality, among others,
explain the variety observed by teachers and
researchers in children's acquisition of a
second language. Some children learn quickly
and effortlessly while others proceed
laboriously. Some will insist in understanding
linguistic structures before attempting to use
them. Others will take risks and use speech
formulas, even when they have not fully
understood them grammatically, in an effort to
communicate.

Transfer of Skills

Transferability of skills from one language
to another appears to play a critical role in
second language acquisition. Vygotsky (1962)
maintained that there were two types of
knowledge: spontaneous knowledge which referred
to familiar, everyday concepts and scientific

knowledge which encompassed formal, school-learned concepts. As a result of his research, Vygotsky found that young children would commit more errors when attempting to incorporate spontaneous concepts into familiar everyday situations than when incorporating scientific concepts into technical situations in sentence completion exercises.

In Vygotsky's research, the children would complete the following sentences with the words although and because:

"The boy fell off his bicycle because..."
"The girl cannot yet read, although..."
"Planned economy is possible in the USSR because..."
"If a ball rolls off a table, it will fall downwards because..."

The children were given similar problems dealing with either scientific or familiar material and their solutions compared. This included making up stories from sequential pictures which showed the beginning, continuation, and end of an action.

Vygotsky found that scientific concepts were mastered and understood earlier than the spontaneous ones. Children made more mistakes when completing sentences which dealt with familiar situations than when the sentences referred to learned concepts. For example, the children would respond: "The boy fell off his bicycle because he was taken to the hospital." But "If a ball rolls off a table, it will fall downwards because of the force of gravitation."

Vygotsky argued that scientific concepts are mastered earlier because the teacher has explained, questioned, corrected, and elicited explanations from the child thus bringing these concepts into consciousness. The child, by knowing the concepts, can use and work with them independently. Spontaneous concepts, on the other hand, are not acquired through deliberate instruction. Children are not aware of these concepts and do not use them correctly until they have become conscious. But Vygotsky argued that once a number of scientific concepts are mastered, the awareness of their development spreads to everyday concepts. Eventually, children are able to solve problems involving everyday concepts with the same accuracy as scientific concepts. By the age of 10, the child uses both scientific and spontaneous concepts intelligently.

In applying his transfer of skills theory to learning a second language, Vygotsky states that "success in learning a second language is contingent on a certain degree of maturity in the native language. The child can transfer to the new language the system of meanings he already possesses in his own." (p. 110) Vygotsky goes on to state that when new systems are formed which are similar to earlier ones, such as written language, foreign language, and verbal thought, a transfer or shift occurs in which the later system repeats the course of the earlier one. It is, therefore, suggested that learning one task will affect learning another. In language learning there is an interrelationship which can be strengthened and capitalized.

The St. Lambert experiment (Lambert and Tucker, 1972) is an example of transfer of skills in language learning. A group of Canadian English-speaking children were placed in a French immersion program where children were not drilled in a traditional foreign language teaching technique, but were immersed in a French milieu where the second language was learned through daily interaction with native speaking teachers. An interesting finding in the St. Lambert experiment was that English-speaking children, taught in French, transferred the reading and computation skills learned in French to English without being instructed in English. The children automatically transferred skills learned in the second language into the first.

There may be a "unified underlying system" serving two distinct languages (Baetens Beardsmore, 1986), that is, certain shared rules and linguistic characteristics. If this is so, then the issue of linguistic transfer-ability becomes important because should children think, perceive, classify in fundamentally similar ways, transfer of knowledge from

one language to another could be encouraged and
facilitated, as   long   as   one   knows how   the
process   occurs.   Unfortunately,   this   very
important issue has received scant attention
from   researchers   in   bilingualism.   More
attention has been given to transfer as a
language interference phenomenon, that is, the
transfer of aspects of one language to another,
than as a transference of universal linguistic
characteristics and specific knowledge acquired
in one language to another.   As Kenji Hakuta
eloquently states:

> What is remarkable about the issue of
> transfer of skills is that despite its
> fundamental   importance,   almost   no
> empirical studies have been conducted
> to   understand   the characteristics or
> even to demonstrate the existence of
> the transfer of skills. (Hakuta, 1986,
> p.218)

    Contributing to the transfer of skills
between languages question, Goldman, et al.
(1983) conducted a study to examine children's
use of first language knowledge in acquiring a
second language. Specifically, the researchers
analyzed children's understanding of narratives,
the degree to which knowledge available to the
child's first language is used in understanding
second language input, and the relationship
between knowledge utilization in two languages
as children become bilingual and acquire more
literacy skills. Selections from Aesop's Fables
were used to study the comprehension skills of
students in grades kindergarten through fifth.
Results of the study indicate that the knowledge
used to guide story comprehension in a first
language is also used to guide story
comprehension in the second language.   This
process is contingent upon mastery of basic
auditory or orthographic coding skills in the
second language.   It was also found that
narrative comprehension skills as assessed in
this study were no different for students who
had been learning one language as for those who
were learning in two languages.

Continuing studies, such as this one, are needed to shed additional light on the transfer of skills phenomenon bilingual teachers observe daily in the classroom.

A Second Language Acquisition Model

Although no comprehensive theory of second language acquisition exists as yet (Larsen-Freeman, 1985), it is possible to develop a model of second language learning based on what we currently know about the process. Wong Fillmore (1985) put together a second language acquisition learning model that incorporates research findings in the field. She begins by describing the necessary ingredients for second language learning. According to Wong Fillmore, there are three major components to the process:

> (1) learners who realize that they need to learn the target language (TL) and are motivated to do so; (2) speakers of the target language who know it well enough to provide the learners with access to the language and the help the learners need for learning it; and (3) a social setting that brings learners and TL speakers into frequent enough contact to make language learning possible. (p. 34)

She discusses three types of processes that affect language learning. They are all interrelated. These are: social, linguistic, and cognitive.

Social processes are actions taken by learners and TL speakers to create a setting where communication in the target language is possible and desired. In this setting both the learners and the TL speakers have specific roles. Learners observe how the TL is used by the native speakers in natural, informal settings. They must also make TL speakers aware of their special linguistic needs, yet attempt to communicate at some level. This participation will signal to TL speakers the need to modify, to adjust the language in such a way that communication is possible. TL speakers must be willing to make these accomodations so that successful communication can occur. This provides a powerful incentive for learners (Wong Fillmore, 1985, p. 34).

Linguistic processes are the assumptions speakers have about the target language that cause speakers to modify linguistic formulations for the sake of the learners. Learners, on the other hand, have certain assumptions about the way language works so that they can interpret linguistic information. Linguistic processes involve the interactions between TL speakers and learners. This interaction allows learners to glean linguistic information about the structure and pragmatics of the language which will eventually help them function in the new language in diverse communicative settings. The linguistic data and the social context in which the data exist are called input, that is, the information learners use for acquisition of the language (p. 35). Adequate linguistic input, that is, the language used by speakers in social interactions with learners, must have certain characteristics to be beneficial. It must be selected for appropriate content and adapted in "form and presentation." Learners will also provide input in the form of the knowledge of their first language which they bring into the second language acquisition process. Learners also bring into the process knowledge of linguistic categories and awareness of the uses of language (Wong Fillmore, 1985, pp. 35-36).

Cognitive processes are the analytical, mental operations that learners carry out to acquire a language. That is, learners must figure out the system of rules of the target language and internalize it, they must discover how speech segments are used to represent meanings, and how these units of meaning are put together to relay complex ideas. To do this learners use the cognitive tools at their disposal, such as associative skills, memory, inferential skills, and any other analytical skills they need to figure out the new language (Wong Fillmore, 1985, pp. 36-38).

The social setting that best meets the requirements of second language acquisition processes is the school. Speakers of the target language (teachers and classmates) can facilitate second language acquisition by interacting with learners in a social context, providing the necessary motivation, and adjusting the linguistic input so that the learner can grasp linguistic patterns and internalize them. In this setting, the learner can use general cognitive strategies and the knowledge about language learning he or she brings from the native language to acquire the social and linguistic skills needed to communicate effectively.

CONCLUSION

Language acquisition in the native and second languages appears to share basic patterns. Nevertheless, research studies are increasingly finding individual variation in the way children go about developing language. Factors such as maturation, cognitive organization, learning style, linguistic input, language context, among others, have an impact on the individual child's language processessing abilities. These individual differences are also evident in a child's second language acquisition process. Second language acquisition researchers are now taking into account learner variables such as age; aptitude; motivation; cognitive style; and social, psychological, experiential, and personal factors. They are also looking at the setting in which second language acquisition takes place whether it be a formal classroom or informal environment (Larsen-Freeman, 1985).

Further research is needed in the general area of bilingualism, if we are to make appropriate educational decisions about children who are acquiring a second language.

We need to know more about:

1.   The transfer of skills phenomenon. Bilingual teachers note the ease and apparent automaticity of transference from one language to another.   Why does this occur and how?   Can

we facilitate the transference process by manipulating certain conditions? Do some skills transfer more readily than others?

2.   Individual   differences   in second language acquisition. What are the specific strategies different children use in learning a second language? How are these related to native language acquisition strategies? How are they applicable to a second language learning environment?

3. The status of the native language while acquisition of a second language progresses. Does native language development have a positive impact on second language development? How beneficial is native language maintenance in second language acquisition? In what ways? What happens to a lost language? Can it ever be retrieved?

4. Hemispheric lateralization for language function. How are two languages processed in the brain? To what extent are some language functions processed in the right hemisphere? What can brain studies tell us about the optimal age for language acquisition?

REFERENCES

Ambert, A.N. "The Enriched Language of Puerto Rican Children." (in press)

Baetens Beardsmore, H. **Bilingualism: Basic Principles.** Avon, England: Multilingual Matters, 1986.

Baslis, Y. "A study of linguistic differences." **Journal of the Hellenic Diaspora,** VII, 1-2, 75-80, 1981.

Belendez, P. Repetitions and the Acquisition of the Spanish Verb System. Unpublished doctoral dissertation, Harvard University Graduate School of Education, 1980.

Berman, R.A. "Regularity vs. anomaly: The acquisition of Hebrew inflectional morphology." **Journal of Child Language,** 8, 265-282, 1981.

Bohannonn III, J.N. and A. Warren-Leubecker. "Theoretical Approaches to Language Acquisition." In Berko Gleason, J. (Ed.), **The Development of Language.** Columbus, Ohio: Charles E. Merrill, 1985.

Brisk, M.E. The Spanish Syntax of the Pre-School Spanish American: The Case of New Mexican Five Year Old Children. Unpublished doctoral dissertation, The University of New Mexico, 1972.

Brisk, M.E. "The Acquisition of Spanish Gender by First Grade Spanish-speaking Children." In Keller, et al. (Eds.) **Bilingualism in the Bicentennial and Beyond.** New York: Bilingual Press, 1976.

Brown, R. **A First Language: The Early Stages.** Cambridge, Mass.: Harvard University Press, 1973.

Brown, R. and Bellugi, U. "Three processes in the acquisition of syntax." **Harvard Educational Review,** 34, 133-151, 1964.

Bryen, D.N. **Inquiries into Child Language.** Boston: Allyn and Bacon, 1981.

Carrow-Woolfolk, E. and Lynch, J.I. **An Integrative Approach to Language Disorders in Children.** New York: Grune & Stratton, 1982.

Cazden, C.B. "Suggestions from Studies of Early Language Acquisition." In Cazden, C.B. (Ed.), **Language in Early Childhood Education.** Washington, D.C.: National Association for the Education of Young Children, 1972.

Chomsky, C. **The Acquisition of Syntax in Children from 5 to 10.** Cambridge, Mass.: MIT Press, 1969.

Chomsky, N. **Syntactic Structures.** The Hague: Mouton, 1957.

Chomsky, N. **Aspects of the Theory of Syntax.** Cambridge, Mass: MIT Press, 1965.

Chomsky, N. "Deep Structure, Surface Structure, and Semantic Interpretation." In D. Steinberg and L. Jakobovits (Eds.), **Semantics.** London: Cambridge University Press, 1971.

Clahsen, H. "Verb inflections in German child language: Acquisition of agreement markings and the functions they encode." **Linguistics,** 24, 79-121, 1986.

Cummins, J. "Linguistic interdependence and the educational development of bilingual children." **Review of Educational Research,** 49, 222-251, 1979.

Cummins, J. "Empirical and theoretical underpinnings of bilingual education." **Journal of Education,** 163, 16-49, 1981.

Cummins, J. Bilingualism and Special Education:
    Issues in Assessment and Pedagogy. Avon,
    England: Multilingual Matters, 1984.

de Villiers,   J.G.   and P.A.   de Villiers.
    Language Acquisition.
    Cambridge, MA: Harvard University Press,
    1978.

Gili-Gaya, S.   Estudios de lenguaje infantil.
    Barcelona: Vox Bibliograf, 1974.

Goldfield, B.A. and Snow, C.E.   "Individual
    Differences in Language Acquisition." In
    Berko Gleason, J. (Ed.), The Development of
    Language. Columbus, Ohio: Merrill, 1985.

Goldman, S.R.; Reyes, M., and Varnhagen, C.
    Utilization of Knowledge Acquired through
    the First Language in Comprehending a
    Second Language: Narrative Comprehension
    by   Spanish-English   Speakers.   Paper
    presented at the National Association for
    Bilingual Education Conference, Washington,
    D.C., February, 1983.

Goodluck,   H.   "Language   Acquisition   and
    Linguistic Theory." In P. Fletcher and M.
    Garman   (Eds.),   Language   Acquisition:
    Studies in First Language Development.
    London: Cambridge University Press, 1986.

Gonzalez, G. The Acquisition of Spanish Grammar
    by Native Spanish-Speakers.   Unpublished
    doctoral dissertation, The University of
    Texas at Austin, 1970.

Hakuta, K. Mirror of Language: The Debate on
    Bilingualism.   New York: Basic Books,
    1986.

Harley, B. Age in Second Language Acquisition.
    Avon, England: Multilingual Matters, 1986.

Hymes, D. "Competence and Performance in Linguistic Theory." In Huxley, R. and Ingram, E. (Eds.) **Language Acquisition: Models and Methods.** London: Academic Press, 1971.

Johnston, J.R. and Slobin, D.I. "The development of locative expressions in English, Italian, Serbo-Croation and Turkish." **Journal of Child Language,** 6, 531-547, 1979.

Kernan, K. and Blount, B.G. "The acquisition of Spanish grammar by Mexican children." **Anthropological Linguistics,** 8, 1-14, 1966.

Kessler, C. "Language Acquisition in Bilingual Children." In Miller, N. (Ed.), **Bilingualism and Language Disability.** San Diego, CA: College Hill Press, 1984.

Krashen, S.D. **Principles and Practice in Second Language Acquisition.** Oxford: Pergamon Press, 1982.

Krashen, S.D.; Scarcella, R.C.; and Long, M.H. (Eds.) **Child-Adult Differences in Second Language Acquisition.** Rowley, Mass.: Newbury House, 1982.

Lambert, W.E. and Tucker, G.R. **Bilingual Education of Children: The St. Lambert Experiment.** Rowley, Mass.: Newbury House, 1972.

Larsen-Freeman, D. "Overview of Theories of Language Learning and Acquisition." In National Clearinghouse for Bilingual Education, **Issues in English Language Development.** Rosslyn, Virginia: National Clearinghouse for Bilingual Education, 1985.

Lenneberg, E.H. **The Biological Foundations of Language.** New York: Wiley, 1967.

McLaughlin, B.   Second Language Acquisition in
    Childhood: Volume 1. Preschool Children.
    Hillsdale,   New Jersey: Lawrence Erlbaum,
    1984.

McLaughlin, B.   Second Language Acquisition in
    Childhood: Volume 2:   School-Age Children.
    Hillsdale,   New Jersey: Lawrence Erlbaum,
    1985.

Mills, A.E.   "Acquisition of the natural-gender
    rule in English and German." Linguistics,
    24, 31-45, 1986.

Montes-Giraldo, J.J. "Acerca de la apropiacion
    por   el   nino   del   sistema   fonologico
    espanol." Thesaurus, XXVI, 3, 322-346,
    1971.

Olarte, G. Acquisition of Spanish Morphemes by
    Monolingual, Monocultural Spanish-Speaking
    Children.   Unpublished   doctoral
    dissertation, The University of Florida,
    1985.

Rice, M. "Cognitive Aspects of Communicative
    Development."   In Schiefelbusch, R.L. and
    Pickar, J. (Eds.) The Acquisition of
    Communicative   Competence.   Baltimore:
    University Park Press, 1984.

Rice, M.L. and Kemper, S. Child Language and
    Cognition. Austin, Texas: Pro-Ed, 1984.

Schieffelin B.B. and Eisenberg, A.R. "Cultural
    Variation in Children's Conversations." In
    R.L. Schiefelbusch and J. Pickar (Eds.),
    The   Acquisition   of   Communicative
    Competence.   Baltimore,   Maryland:
    University Park Press, 1984.

Slobin, D. "The Acquisition of Russian as a
    Native Language."   In F. Smith and C.A.
    Miller (Eds.), The Genesis of Language: A
    Psycholinguistic   Approach.   Cambridge,
    Mass.: MIT Press, 1966.

Snow, C.E.   "Parent-child Interaction and the
    Development of Communicative Ability."   In
    R.L. Schiefelbusch and J. Pickar (Eds.),
    **The   Acquisition   of   Communicative
    Competence.**   Baltimore,   Maryland:
    University Park Press, 1984.

Snow, C.E.   "Conversations with Children."   In
    P. Fletcher and M. Garman, **Language
    Acquisition: Studies in First Language
    Development.** London: Cambridge University
    Press, 1986.

Snow,   C.E.   and   Hoefnagel-Hohle, M.   "The
    critical period for language acquisition:
    Evidence from second language learning."
    Child Development, 49, 1114-1128, 1978.

Tolbert, K.   The Acquisition of Grammatical
    Morphemes: A Cross-Linguistic Study with
    Reference to Mayan and Spanish. Unpublished
    doctoral dissertation, Harvard University,
    1978.

Tracy, R.   "The acquisition of case morphology
    in German." **Linguistics,** 24, 47-78, 1986.

Van Besien, F. and Moerman-Coetsier, L. "On the
    acquisition of verb morphology in Dutch
    speaking children."   **Review of Applied
    Linguistics,** 71,19-41, 1986.

Volk,   D. "Communication Competence in a
    Bilingual Early Childhood Classroom."   In
    Saravia Shore, M. and Arvizu, S. (Eds.)
    **Communicative   and   Cross   Cultural
    Competencies: Ethnographies of Educational
    Programs for Language Minority Students in
    Community Contexts** (in press).

Vygotsky,   L.S.   **Thought   and   Language.**
    Cambridge, Mass.: MIT Press, 1962.

Wong Fillmore, L. "Second Language Learning in Children: A Proposed Model." In National Clearinghouse for Bilingual Education (Ed.) **Issues in English Language Development.** Rosslyn, Virgina: InterAmerica Research Associates, Inc., 1985.

Zentella, A.C. "Individual Differences in Growing Up Bilingual." **Communicative and Cross Cultural Competencies: Ethnographies of Educational Programs for Language Minority Students in Community Contexts** (in press).

ANNOTATED BIBLIOGRAPHY

Aaronson, D. and Ferres, S. "Sentence processing in Chinese-American bilinguals." **Journal of Memory and Language**, 25, 2, 136-162, 1986.

Compared the processing of English words by Chinese-English bilinguals with that of monolingual English speakers. Subjects read and rated English words for their contribution to sentence structure and meaning. It was found that bilinguals generally rated English words as contributing more to sentence structure and meaning than did monolinguals.

Anselmi, D. "Young children's responses to neutral and specific contingent queries." **Journal of Child Language**, 13, 1, 135-144, 1986.

Describes a study intended to determine the developmental stage at which children begin to differentiate specific and neutral contingent queries. The study manipulated the familiarity of the adult listener by having each of the 22 children interact both with the mother and with an unfamiliar adult experimenter.

Baetens Beardsmore, H. **Bilingualism: Basic Principles.** Avon, England, Multilingual Matters, 1986.

An introductory work to bilingualism. Includes definitions and typologies, and the topics of interference and code switching, measurement of bilingualism, and problems of the bilingual speaker, as well as theoretical considerations.

Bialystok, E. "Factors in the growth of linguistic awareness." **Child Development**, 57, 2, 498-510, 1986.

Investigates the metalinguistic ability of monolingual and bilingual children between the ages of five and nine years on two language tasks: grammaticality judgment and correction.

Camarata, S. and Lennard, L.B. "Young children pronounce object words more accurately than action words." **Journal of Child Language**, 13, 1, 51-65, 1986.

Describes a study of young children's production of novel words serving as names of objects and actions which were matched according to consonant and syllable structure. On each measure, accurate production of new consonants was greater for the object words, possibly because action words have greater semantic complexity than object words.

Chapmen, K.L. "The effects of feedback on young children's inappropriate word usage." **Journal of Child Language**, 13, 1, 101,117, 1986.

Describes a study which compared the effects of three types of adult feedback (acceptance, correction with joint labelling, and correction with explanation) on young children's inappropriate word usage. Results showed that correction with explanation was more effective than correction with joint labelling. The least effective was simple acceptance.

Chamot, A.U. and O'Malley, J.M. "The cognitive academic language learning approach: A bridge to the mainstream." **TESOL Quarterly**, 21, 2, 227-249, 1987.

Discusses the Cognitive Academic Language Learning Approach (CALLA) designed for limited English proficient students who are being prepared to participate in mainstream content-area instruction.

Cummins, J. "Empowering minority students: A framework for intervention." **Harvard Educational Review**, 56,1,18-36, 1986.

Proposes a theoretical framework for examining minority students' academic failure and for predicting the effects of educational interventions. Analyzes the schools' power relations with minority students in a societal context. Offers four methods of creating an educational context that empowers minority children: 1) The inclusion of students' cultural and linguistic patterns in instructional programs; 2) parental participation in the education of their children; 3) changing instructional programs from transmission models of instruction to reciprocal interaction models, so minority students can actively participate in the achievement of educational goals; and (4) assessing children to "delegitimize" the practice of assessment to locate problems in minority students, but to advocate for changes in the educational system.

Davidson, R.G. "Definitions and definite noun phrases: Indicators of children's decontextualized language skills." **Journal of Research in Childhood Education**, 1, 1, 37-48, 1986.

Assesses the performance of bilingual children on two language tasks in both the children's languages in order to determine whether the profile of skills in the first language was replicated in the second language.

Faerch, C. and Kasper, G. (Eds.). **Introspection in Second Language Research.** Avon, England: Multilingual Matters, 1987.

Presents a solution to a major methodological problem of second language research, the reconstruction of learners' processes of language learning and language use. Based on recent developments in cognitive psychology, the contributors describe how introspective methods, that is, verbal reports by learners about their thought processes, provide valuable information about central areas in second language research: cognitive comprehension, translation and test-taking.

Feller Bauer, C. "Color: A first language skill." **International Quarterly**, V, 3, 34-35, 1987.

Describes techniques to teach colors to children from different language back-grounds.

Fine, J. (Ed.) **Second Language Discourse: A Textbook of Current Research.** Norwood, NJ: Ablex Publishing Corp., 1987.

Presents up-to-date research on second language discourse. Analyzes the develop-ment of writing, memory and interaction in second language discourse. The following topics are included: the role of discourse in second language study, theory of speech behavior and social distance, effects of participation pattern and task variation on second language classroom interaction, sociolinguistic bilingual proficiency assessment, evaluation of student writing in first and second languages, second language comprehension processes, and integration of first language material in second language comprehension.

Fletcher, P. and Garman, M. (Eds.) **Language Acquisition.** London: Cambridge University Press, 1986.

Discusses the language acquisition process from the perspective of different specialists: psychosocial aspects, cogni-tion, linguistic theory, phonology, grammar, and literacy.

Flynn, S. "Contrast and construction in a parameter-setting model of L2 acquisition." **Language Learning**, 37, 1, 19-41, 1987.

Discusses the contributions made by both Contrastive Analysiw (CA) and Creative Contstruction (CC) theories in the field of second language acquisition. The author argues that the parameter-setting model of Universal Grammar (UG) for L2 acquisition provides the scaffolding necessary for an integration of these two components within one explanatory account.

Gaies, S.J. "Research in TESOL: Romance, precision, and reality." TESOL Newsletter, XXI, 2, 21-23, 1987.

Discusses the development of theory and research in second language learning.

Gass, S.M. "An interactionist approach to L2 sentence interpretation." **Studies in Second Language Acquisition**, 8, 1, 19-37, 1986.

Presents results of a study of sentence interpretation by second language learners of English in which L2 learners resolve the problem of competing factors of syntax, semantics, and pragmatics in the processing of L2 utterances.

Genesee, F. **Learning Through Two Languages. Studies of Immersion and Bilingual Education**. New York: Newbury House, 1987.

An up-to-date overview of immersion and bilingual education programs in Canada and the United States. Integrates actual program outcomes, research fingings, and theoretically based discussions and relates these to educational implications for second-language programs. The book includes an analysis of the influence of sociocultural factors on the form and outcome of educational innovations.

Gonzalez, L.A. The Effects of First Language
    Education on the Second Language and
    Academic Achievement of Mexican Immigrant
    Elementary School Children in the United
    States. Unpublished doctoral dissertation,
    University of Illinois at Urbana-Champaign,
    1986.

    Describes an investigation of the effects
    of first language education on the second
    language and academic achievement of
    Mexican immigrant children in the United
    States. The author examined and compared
    the context-reduced and context-embedded
    language skills in both English and Spanish
    of 34 sixth-grade Mexican immigrant
    children in a bilingual program who had
    been schooled in Mexico a minimum of two
    years (Group M) and 38 sixth-grade children
    of Mexican immigrants in the same bilingual
    program who had been totally schooled in
    the United States (Group US). Reading
    comprehension tests were used to measure
    context-reduced language skills in English
    and Spanish. The Bilingual Syntax Measure
    in Spanish and English was used to measure
    context-embedded language skills in both
    languages. Also, communicative competence
    in English and Spanish was tested using
    recordings of the dialogue elicited by the
    Bilingual Syntax Measure. Results of the
    study indicate that: (a) a valid
    distinction could be made between
    context-reduced and context-embedded
    language skills; (b) there was evidence for
    a common underlying proficiency between L1
    and L2 skills of these children; and (c) L1
    development appeared to be positively
    related to the L2 and academic achievement
    of the children.

Graham, J.G. "English language proficiency and
    the prediction of academic success." TESOL
    Quarterly, 21, 3, 505-521, 1987.

Discusses the relationship between English language proficiency and academic success in universities and colleges in which English is the language of instruction.

Hakuta, K. **Mirror of Language: The Debate on Bilingualism.** New York: Basic Books, 1986.

Examines bilingualism and bilingual education from a historical and theoretical perspective. Analyzes recent research in the field and refutes popular misconceptions about bilingualism and bilingual education in the United States.

Hakuta, K. and Gould, L.J. "Synthesis of research on bilingual education." **Educational Leadership,** 38-45, March, 1987.

Discusses evaluation, cognitive and linguistic research in bilingual education and concludes that the research supports the use of the native language in the instruction of language minority children.

Hakuta, K. and Snow, C. "The role of research in policy decisions about bilingual education." **NABE News,** IX, 3, 1-22, 1986.

Discusses evaluation research and basic research in bilingual education in the areas of language proficiency, relationship of the two languages, language and mental functioning, individual differences, optimal age for second language acquisition, social factors, and literacy.

Harley, B. **Age in Second Language Acquisition.** Avon, England: Multilingual Matters, 1986.

Examines empirical studies done on the impact of age on the second language acquisition process. Describes a research study performed by the author with children in early French immersion programs (grade 1) and late French immersion

programs (grades 9-10) in Canada. She
focused on age-related differences in
acquisition of the verb system in the
second language. Results of the study
indicate that the late immersion students,
that is, the older students, had acquired
greater oral control of the French verb
system than the early immersion students in
some, but not all, areas of the verb
system.

Kendon, A. "Speaking and signing simultaneously
in Warlpiri sign language users."
**Multilingual: Journal of Cross-Cultural
and Interlanguage Communication,** 6, 1,
25-68, 1987.

A study of the complex sign language of
the Warlpiri of central Australia used as
an alternative to speech.

Kessler, C. and Quinn, M.E. "Language minority
children's linguistic and cognitive
creativity." **Journal of Multilingual and
Multicultural Development,** 8, 173-186,
1987.

Discusses findings from a study of the
effects of bilingualism on the linguistic
and cognitive creativity of language
minority children proficiently bilingual in
Spanish and English. Two classrooms of
11-year old sixth graders were studied.
One classroom consisted of monolingual
English-speaking children and the other of
Spanish-English bilingual minority
children. Both groups participated in an
inquiry-based scientific program where they
learned to formulate scientific hypotheses
in a problem-solving setting. The authors
conclude that the qualitatively high
scientific hypotheses expressed by the
language minority children using complex
metaphoric language in their second
language, English, indicate that linguistic
and cognitive creativity is enhanced by
bilingual language proficiency.

Kraetschmer, K. "Current trends in neurolin-
guistic studies of bilingualism." **International Review of Applied Linguistics in
Language Teaching**, 24, 1, 1-11, 1986.

Reviews current research in bilingualism
focusing on the role of the brain's right
hemisphere in linguistic development.

Labrie, N. and Clement, R. "Ethnolinguistic
vitality, self-confidence and second
language proficiency: An investigation."
**Journal of Multilingual and Multicultural
Development**, 7, 4, 269-282, 1986.

Describes a study in which ninth-grade
Francophone students living in a bicultural
milieu responded to tests including scales
of ethnolinguistic vitality, attitudes,
motivation, self-confidence, and second
language competence and usage. Results
indicated that contact with Anglophones and
self-confidence with English as a second
language were related to motivation, which
in turn was related to second language
competence.

Lalleman, J.A. "The development of L1 and L2
proficiency in Dutch: A narrative analysis
of a picture-based story, told by Turkish
and native Duth children at the ages of six
and eight." **Language Learning**, 37, 2,
217-245, 1987.

Presents an analysis of the narrative
proficiency of L1 and L2 learners of Dutch.
A group of Dutch native children and a
group of Turkish immigrant children, born
and reared in The Netherlands, were asked
to tell a story from a series of pictures,
first when they entered primary school and
again when they were in the third year of
primary school. Results of the study
indicate that in comparison with their
Dutch peers, the Turkish children exhibited
more or less the same level of narrative
proficiency in Dutch. However, the Turkish
children's grammatical knowledge appeared

to be deficient, according to the author. The author concludes that by using their communicative skills, the L2 learners are able to perform almost as well as native children in a task that is cognitively and contextually easy.

Machida, S. "Teacher accuracy in decoding nonverbal indicants of comprehension and noncomprehension in Anglo- and Mexican-American children." **Journal of Educational Psychology**, 78, 6, 454-464, 1986.

Examines the degree to which Anglo- and Mexican-American first-grade teachers can accurately decode nonverbal indicants of comprehension and noncomprehension. Teachers perceived boys as understanding more than girls. Slight cultural differences were found in children's behavior, but it did not affect teachers' interpretation.

Maple, R. "TESL versus TEFL: What's the difference?" **TESOL Newsletter**, XXI, 2, 35-36, 1987.

Explains the differences between teaching English as a second language and teaching English as a foreign language.

Morley, J. "Current directions in teaching English to speakers of other languages: A state-of-the-art synopsis." **TESOL Newsletter**, XXI, 2, 16-20, 1987.

Reviews eleven current trends in learning and teaching ESL/EFL on the basis of current linguistic research.

Murray, L. and Trevarthen, C. "The infant's role in mother-infant communications." **Journal of Child Language**, 13, 1, 15-29, 1986.

Describes an experiment which tested the infant's sensitivity to the timing of the mother's responses by arranging a video system so that mother and baby each saw a full-face, life-size image of the other on a video screen. Results provide evidence for the infant's active role in interaction with adults.

Olson, S.L. "Mother-child interaction and children's speech progress: A longitudinal study of the first two years." **Merrill-Palmer** Quarterly, 32, 1, 1-20, 1986.

Describes a longitudinal study of interrelations between mother-child interactions and children's developing speech progress, at six, 13, and 24 months of age. Children with large differentiated vocabularies showed superior in developmental progress relative to peers. Vocabulary progress was most closely linked to frequent responsive mother-child language interaction, even when family social class and maternal education were controlled.

Owens, M. **Eithne: A Study of Second Language Development.** Dublin: Centre for Language and Communication Studies, 1986.

Chronicles the acquisition of Irish as a second language in a four-year old child of bilingual parents, attending an Irish-language preschool program in Ireland. Emphasis is given to the characteristic features of her language learning process and the factors determining which language she used with others. The study was based on adult-child conversation transcriptions with a high proportion of question-answer interactions. The distinctive features discussed in detail include the use of the Irish vocative, colors and numbers, use of prepositions and constructions in which the subject is expressed by means of a preposition, sentence complexity, transfer of discourse skills, participation in conversation, and the productive use of questions as a learning strategy.

Pavesi, M. "Markedness, discoursal modes, and relative clause formation in a formal and an informal context." **Studies in Second Language Acquisition,** 8, 1, 38-55, 1986.

Describes a study in which English relative clauses were elicited from two groups of Italian learners: formal learners and informal learners. The results agreed with other studies on the order of acquisition.

Piper, T. "Learning about language learning." **Language Arts,** 63, 5, 466-471, 1986.

Describes the progress of a kindergarten child acquiring English as a second language.

Power, R.J.D. and Dal Martello, M.F. "The use of the definite and indefinite articles by Italian preschool children." **Journal of Child Language,** 13, 1, 145-154, 1986.

Reports on an experiment to check whether the use of articles by Italian preschool children corresponds to that of their English peers. In a second experiment, the authors investigated the probability that subjects might produce the correct response distribution by following a rule based on the speaker's familiarity with the referent, not the listener's.

Pye, C. "Quiche Mayan speech to children." **Journal of Child Language,** 13, 1, 85-100, 1986.

Describes a study of the linguistic modification in speech to children in the Mayan language, Quiche. Evaluated 17 features commonly cited for speech to children and noted seven additional features for Quiche: whispering, initial-syllable deletion, BT formed for verbs, a verbal suffix, more fixed word order, more imperatives, and a special interpretive routine.

Rice, M.L. and Kemper, S. **Child Language and Cognition.** Austin, Texas: Pro-Ed, 1986.

A theoretical discussion of the relationship between language and cognition. After an analysis of different linguistic and cognitive theories, the authors conclude that because of the linkages between cognitive and linguistic knowledge, cognitive development can influence language acquisition and language may affect cognition.

Ringbom, H. **The Role of the Mother Tongue in Foreign Language Learning.** Avon, England: Multilingual Matters, 1987.

Explores foreign language learners' underlying processes, based on data from Finland showing the differences between Finish-speaking and Swedish-speaking Finns learning English. Results of the study show differences between learning a foreign language that is related and a language that is unrelated to the learner's mother tongue.

Ross, G. "Acquisition and generalization of novel object concepts by young language learners." **Journal of Child Language,** 13, 1, 67-83, 1986.

Examines some of the properties of objects to determine whether the number of different examples of an object concept presented to infants influences concept learning and generalization and to discover whether children's behavior and language in relation to new objects influence learning the concept and generalization to new concepts.

Sauders, G. **Bilingual Children: Guidance for the Family.** Avon, England, Multilingual Matters, 1986.

An introduction to bilingualism for parents interested in the bilingual upbringing of children in the home. Offers specific suggestions for the development of bilingualism and biliteracy.

Skutnabb-Kangas, T. and Cummins, J. (Eds.). **Minority Education.** Avon, England: Multilingual Matters, 1988 (in press).

Analyzes policy issues regarding the education of minority students in reversing the pattern of minority students' academic failure. A central theme of the book is that the causes of minority students' academic failure are rooted in the power relations between the dominant and subordinate groups in society.

Trueba, H.T. (Ed.) **Success or Failure? Learning and the Language Minority Student.** New York: Newbury House, 1987.

Describes a research project based on ethnographic methods and anthropological perspectives on the failure of many minority students and educational reforms which could foster success. Examines the relationship between home and school and the intimate connection among language, culture, and cognition.

Wells, G. **The Meaning Makers: Children Learning Language and Using Language to Learn.** Portsmouth, N.H.: Heinemann Educational Books, 1986.

Describes a longitudinal study of the language development of 32 British children from shortly after their first birthdays to the end of their elementary education.

Wong Fillmore, L. and B. McLaughlin. Oral
     Language Learning in Bilingual Classrooms:
     The Role of Cultural Factors in Language
     Acquisition.   Unpublished   manuscript,
     School   of   Education,   University   of
     California, Berkeley, 1986.

     A   study on the effects   of different
     classroom factors on   the oral English
     acquisition   of   Hispanic   and   Chinese
     children. Results of the study indicate
     the children from the two different ethnic
     groups responded well to different types of
     educational strategies.   Hispanic students
     with the poorest initial English skills
     benefited more from interaction with peers
     in English while   the Chinese students
     derived   the   most   benefit   from more
     interaction with the teacher.

Woods,   A.;   Fletcher,   P.; and Hughes, A.
     Statistics in Language Studies. London:
     Cambridge University Press, 1986.

     Describes the uses of statistical analysis
     in   studies   of   language   acquisition,
     language variation, and many aspects of
     applied   linguistics.   Examples   are
     presented to   demonstrate   the   use of
     statistics in summarizing data in the most
     appropriate way, and then making helpful
     inferences from the processed information.
     Each   chapter   gives   a   step-by-step
     explanation of particular techniques using
     examples from a number of fields and
     followed by extensive exercises. The first
     part of the book provides an explanation of
     probability and statistical inference and
     then progresses through methods such as
     chi-squared and analysis of variance, to
     multivariate   methods   such   as cluster
     analysis, principal components analysis and
     factor analysis. A grasp of mathematics,
     other than algebra, is not required.

Zepp, R. "Common logical errors in English and
     Chinese." **Educational Studies in Mathema-
     tics,** 18, 1, 1-17, 1987.

Describes test of logic using implicational
and disjunctive sentences given to Chinese
and English speakers.   No differences were
found   on   "if-then"   sentences, but differences were found on "or" sentences.

Chapter 2

RESEARCH IN READING AND WRITING IN BILINGUAL EDUCATION AND ENGLISH AS A SECOND LANGUAGE

Andres Rodriguez, Jr.

INTRODUCTION

Literacy is a national goal in education (Commission on Reading, 1985), understandably so, since it is an important skill that enables individuals to function in society. Participants in a society must understand and express concern for those policies or decisions that affect their daily existence and literacy helps citizens achieve these goals.

Proficiency in listening and speaking a language, however, cannot be separated from the process of learning written communication skills in a native or second language (Anderson and Joels, 1986). Communication skills are interdependent, especially in teaching reading or writing to bilingual children.

Limited English proficient (LEP) children must become biliterate if they are to function effectively in schools and society. Biliteracy is important because bilingual children who achieve literacy in the native language first demonstrate a faster transference of skills development in reading and writing a second language (Rivers, 1986).

This chapter examines such research issues as literacy differences in the process of learning in two languages. In particular, how and when to teach literacy skills in native and second language; the question of transfer of reading skills from a native to a second language; the cultural issues of literacy, biliteracy, and illiteracy; teaching and learning strategies affecting literacy acquisition from a native to a second language; and finally, how to achieve literacy in children who have a non-Roman alphabet language.

To examine these issues, researchers in the areas of linguistics, psycholinguistics, cognitive psychology, anthropology, and sociology, among others, have generated various theories

and hypotheses. Two of the most significant
theories are Krashen's (1984) comprehensive
input hypothesis and Cummins' (1981) interdependent language and common underlying
proficiency theories.

Krashen exemplifies the communicative-based
English as a Second Language (ESL) learning and
teaching approaches by emphasizing natural,
informal acquisition of language forms (e.g.,
sentence patterns, phrases, idioms) and language
functions (e.g., greetings, requests, commands)
in a low-anxiety learning environment. Second
language learners focus on comprehensible data
in a natural environment without a need to
formally structure language learning in the
school or community (Krashen and Terrel, 1983).

Cummins postulates that the more proficient
students are in their native language, the
higher the proficiency they can attain in a
second language. The interdependence of learning two language systems is evident in the
acquisition of vocabulary and concepts first
learned in a native language and then easily
transferred to a second language. Thus, native
language proficiency underlies development of
similar proficiency in a second language.

Speaking proficiency has been linked to
reading achievement in bilingual children. Past
research has emphasized these two language
communication skills (Carrasquillo and Segan,
1984; Ovando and Collier, 1985; Hakuta and
Gould, 1987). Moreover, research support has
been cited for positive transfer of reading
skills from a child's native language to
English, in such classic transfer studies as
those by Modiano, Cohen, Hudelson, Cummins, and
Peal and Lambert (cited by Carrasquillo and
Segan, 1984). Current researchers, however,
take a broader view on issues of literacy in
bilingual children and have integrated perspectives from a combination of past research
studies into a multidisciplinary research framework delineating the "interactive processes"
affecting literacy development in a native and
second language. Based on a "holistic approach"
to teaching and learning in bilingual education
and English as a Second language (ESL) programs,
researchers have begun to examine the relation-

ship of reading to writing in bilingual children (Barnitz, 1985; Rigg and Scott Enright, 1986; Esling and Downing, 1987).

Comprehension based teaching strategies have been underscored in linguistically and culturally different school settings (Anderson and Joels, 1986; Reyhner, 1986). If instruction is to be appropriate to promote literacy or biliteracy in bilingual children, bilingual and ESL teachers need to integrate the four communication skills (listening, speaking, reading, and writing) and to structure content and instructional materials, since positive results are not achieved by discrete, fragmented, and discontinuous skill teaching (Lam, 1986). It is especially important that teachers not isolate teaching of the reading process from writing, listening, or speaking. Thus, instruction which integrates communication skills in the classroom facilitates meaningful learning.

This chapter highlights current research methods and designs: ethnographic, qualitative, and process oriented research; as well as empirical, descriptive studies; all of these converging on the learning and teaching processes in reading and writing in bilingual/ ESL education. Culture and literacy issues are presented first, then research studies are discussed, and finally, conclusions are presented.

The chapter synthesizes current research studies in reading and writing in bilingual education and ESL instruction. The following questions will guide the discussion and interpretation of research findings:

o Should initial literacy be taught in the first language?
o How and when is reading and writing introduced to LEP students? In what language(s)?
o Is there transfer of reading skills from the native language to English?

o What is the best way to introduce
  literacy skills to children who
  speak languages without a written
  tradition or with non-Roman alphabet
  languages?

We hope the information presented in this
chapter will contribute to the development of
appropriate literacy programs for LEP children.
The application of current research findings to
teaching practices can have a positive impact in
improving teaching and learning in the schools.

CULTURE AND BILITERACY

Major research studies have examined the
levels of literacy that are important in
teaching and the role of literacy in schools
and society (Ovando and Collier, 1985; Franklin,
1986; Wells, 1987). Some researchers posit that
acquisition of literacy skills is culturally-
based (McLeod, 1986; Franklin, 1986). Cultures
differ in establishing priorities for the
teaching of reading and writing (Freire, 1985).
It is essential that LEP students participate
effectively in a culture and comprehend and
interpret the goals of such institutions as
schools and government. The development of
biliteracy skills are essential for these
purposes. Freire (1985) maintains that
biliterate individuals have the ability to
interpret the events, institutions, and power
structures that determine their existence; they
can read the world first before the word.
Wells (1987) refers to four literacy
levels, all culturally-bound: performative,
functional, informational, and epistemic. The
performative focuses on speech or the written
code for communication, such as answering
questions or writing a home address; the
functional emphasizes interpersonal communication, such as reading a newspaper, or writing a
job application; the informational assumes that
reading and writing are for informational purposes, such as for accessing the accumulated
knowledge which schools transmit; and the
epistemic level relates to literacy as a mode

of communication and provides ways for literate persons to act upon and transform knowledge and experiences that are unavailable to illiterates. The attitudes encouraged by the epistemic level of literacy are those of creativity, exploration, and critical evaluation.

McLeod (1986) applies the concept of "critical literacy and civic courage" to the reading and writing instructional needs of Jamaican, Nigerian, Pakistani, and Asian children in the London public grade schools. Literacy for thinking and social decision-making will empower language minority children, according to McLeod (1986), to view society in an analytical way so as to claim control of society and counteract present educational emphasis on tests, skills, and external controls which are antidemocratic in their effects.

Franklin (1986) argues that literacy instruction is culturally-based. Teachers hold tacit expectations on how literacy skills should be taught, the use of materials and methods, and the organization of classroom literacy events. These expectations determine the literacy success and failure of children. To examine these findings, she presents excerpts of first grade classroom transcripts and teacher interviews in her study of literacy in bilingual classrooms. She concludes that most first grade teachers expect pupils to have metalinguistic knowledge of sounds, letters, and words before the reading and writing of texts takes place. "When Hispanic LEP children had difficulty with these skills, it was their cultural and language background that was blamed, rather than methods, materials or teacher assumptions." (p. 51)

Like Franklin, other researchers conclude that an emphasis on skill instruction at the expense of the reading and writing of texts impedes the natural literacy development process (Barnitz, 1985; Rigg and Scott Enright, 1986; Anderson and Joels, 1986). Moreover, in the case of bilingual children, language differences are not to be construed as language deficits. Limited English proficiency does not mean the child is limited in the capacity to develop language and thinking skills. For this reason, biliteracy instruction is important for the bilingual child's involvement in a variety of purposes and a variety of settings. Children's bilingual literacy can be studied and measured as communication skills in listening, speaking, reading, and writing for school purposes; that is, for placement, promotion, and grouping. But reading and writing in bilingual education and English as a second language instruction will be the focus of this chapter.

Four dependent and universal language functions are interrelated to the process of reading and writing in a native and second language: the social or pragmatic, semantic, syntactic, and orthographic/graphophonic.

First, the pragmatic function concerns students' self-perceptions within a social and cultural context. Second, the semantic dimension considers the content of printed material, as well as the learner's background knowledge which interacts with literacy tasks. Third, in order to read and write in a second language, some mastery of the grammar of a second language --its functions, structure, and syntactic knowledge-- is required. Finally, familiarity with the written language is necessary before reading or writing skills are learned. That is, knowledge of the orthographic (writing) and the graphophonic (sound-symbol) systems.

Current research studies emphasize the learning of reading and writing as interactive processes. A conceptual framework derived from Goodman and Goodman's (1977) psycholinguistic research has been applied to the reading process. Learning to read reinforces the writing process and vice versa. The universal meaning-making processes of reading and writing are necessary in school learning tasks and for participation in social activities (Ambert and Melendez, 1985; Barnitz, 1985). In the process of composing a written text or in the act of reading a text, the student's background knowledge --linguistic and cultural-- interacts with meaning-making processes. To elicit meaning from textual information presented, there is a sharing of purpose, intention (content), and audience between the student and the author who interact within a social setting.

As the student derives meaning from printed text, there is an interplay between his or her mind and body functions; such as visual, perceptual, linguistic, neurological, memory, affective; with the text's structure and content --its schemata. The levels of printed language which cue meaning are the graphophonic (sound-symbol), the syntactic (grammar and word order), and the semantic (vocabulary and lexicon). For reading comprehension to occur, the reader's private meaning integrates with the author's public meaning (Rigg and Scott Enright, 1986). The reader's interest, motivation, self-concept, and attitudes, as well as teacher expectations, significantly affect student biliteracy outcomes (Rigg and Scott Enright, 1986).

As in the reading process, writing (the creation of an original work or piece) is a psycholinguistic, personal, social, and culturally-based, meaning-making process (Rigg and Scott Enright, 1986; Fuentes, 1987). In light of this perspective, writing as an interactive process is not a classroom dictation or form-filling task, an information report exercise, or any other classroom copying exercise (Connor and Kaplan, 1987). Teachers must focus on the purpose, the intention (content and topics), the audience, or who is responding to the written work, and the final sharing and editing of student products. Responsive teaching focuses on student interests, abilities, and concerns (Rigg and Scott Enright, 1986; Urzua, 1986; Fuentes, 1987).

Writing is a productive, expressive activity which allows the learner to create different types of texts for different purposes. It is expressive of students' personal ideas and should elicit responses from others. Writing is the creation of literary texts in various forms and genres. Informational writing summarizes, describes, records observations of phenomena, and answers questions about content and material (Rigg and Scott Enright, 1986).

In discussing writing purposes and constraints, Hillocks (1987) delineates the interaction between the writer's discourse knowledge and processes (i.e., text schemata and strategies employed for particular writing tasks) with the composer's content knowledge and processes (i.e., strategies for recalling, collecting, and transforming data). In this context, generating written products regarding purpose, knowledge, content, and form is a recursive process ending in the editing or revision stage. For second language composers, writing is a culturally variable event in terms of the audience and the content (topics). Teaching and learning strategies derive from a "holistic approach" for biliteracy instruction (Reyhner, 1986; Rigg and Scott Enright, 1986; Rivers, 1986). Such an approach values the bilingual child's background knowledge and strengths in developing discovery and inquiry learning modes. Thus, teaching is reactive rather than structured instruction. Holistic teaching integrates multilevels of communication skills --listening, speaking, reading, and writing-- simultaneously in the learning process. The whole, rather than its parts, is important (MacGowan, 1985).

From a holistic teaching approach, reading and writing are related processes. Reading can generate writing and writing generates reading. It should be noted that an approach derives from a theoretical perspective, whereas a method or technique is a practical application based on approach. Holistic teaching approaches utilize the four communication skills in every learning situation. Students learn not only through formal instruction, but through the avenues of discovery and inquiry. Learners, furthermore, are surrounded by meaningful language contexts in which they can initiate and respond in the discovery and inquiry process and creatively seek to learn in a reactive, spontaneous manner, rather than in passive, structured learning settings. The holistic teaching methods and strategies most recognized in recent research for bilingual children developing literacy skills in two languages are: the language experience approach, dialogue journal writing, the conference-centered approach, and ethnographic teaching methods. These teaching approaches focus on the communicative functions of bilingual development.

The language experience approach develops native and ESL literacy. Typically, students describe their own knowledge and experiences as the teacher records them in writing. The story is then read aloud to students while pointing to the words. Students read the story aloud, in group or individual exercises. Students then receive the typed or printed story to practice sight words and study new vocabulary. In ESL classes, students say what they know, but learn added vocabulary and reading skills in the process. Initial literacy in ESL is built faster for LEP students with this approach than by using basal or phonics programs. Students exhibit more control and interest in a learning situation where the language experience approach is employed.

Dialogue journal writing is a written conversation between a teacher and student or between students themselves. Daily entries into a personal writing book are made; and the teacher or a peer comments, praises, adds information, responds with remarks or requests, and so forth. ESL teachers, in particular, may have an opportunity to teach new vocabulary, punctuation, spelling, language complexity, rhetorical development with a focus on content and what is important to the LEP child. Positive interaction is developed between a child and teacher and between peers in a writing class.

In conference-centered writing the students are authors and editors of their own texts. Communication and content development are more important than rhetoric or mechanics of writing as in the dialogue journal writing approach. Interaction among writers is central to this writing method focusing on the student's topics and ideas, not on structure or rules for writing. Student's writing pieces are developed through discovery and inquiry, perhaps guided by a peer or teacher. No time limits are set for the student-author as in the dialogue journal writing approach. In a conference with peers or teachers, the student's work is read. An exchange of ideas and comments follows the reading. Publication of students' written pieces culminates the conference-centered approach to writing.

Ethnographic techniques in writing draw on the cultural and social context of the school and the community. Writing is centered on the similarities and differences in communication among groups in a community or peers in the school setting. The uses of language forms and functions (i.e., requests, greetings, commands, inquiries, etc.) are naturally built into the writing process, especially in ESL classrooms where other communication skills are incorporated. Ethnographic techniques for developing written pieces may derive from interviews with community leaders, taping of a particular social event in a community or school, or by visiting a place or person and retelling the event in a written form.

Dialogue-journal, language experience, conference-centered, and ethnographic writing techniques are popular reading and writing approaches in ESL and bilingual classrooms. LEP children derive both social and academic gains from instruction focused on their immediate, personal needs to communicate in the native and second languages, the sharing of their personal experiences and ideas with an audience (the teacher, a peer, or a group), and reading and writing materials integrated with the content and structure of their background knowledge (Rigg and Scott Enright, 1986; Rivers, 1986).

Children who are learning to read and write in a native and a second language must bring to the process not only background knowledge of the multilevel cue system in a language, but also a multifaceted array of personal variables that impact on literacy as a meaning-making activity (Ellinger, 1985). Emotional readiness; motivation; attitude toward reading and writing; neurological, perceptual, and physiological abilities (such as, eye and motor coordination); multiple cognitive abilities (factual or critical creative thinking abilities, for example); expectations; and a positive self-

concept are some of these variables. Research
has emphasized schema theory as the process by
which students' background variables interact
with the social and cultural context (Ovando and
Collier, 1985; Hakuta, 1986; Rigg and Scott
Enright, 1986). These variables, in turn,
interact with the task demands brought upon the
learner by the text. Some of the textual
demands are structure and content (text
schemata); syntactic, semantic, and graphophonic
demands; and what researchers have referred to
as metalinguistic, metacognitive or paralinguistic knowledge contained in written text,
but which must be read into or between the
printed lines by a proficient reader (Barnitz,
1985; Brown-Azarowitz, 1987). Metacognitive
knowledge causes bilingual readers to comprehend
by using rhythm patterns of the language (Brown-
Azarowitz, 1987), selecting the appropriate
reading strategies depending on the reading
purpose, and monitoring their understanding of
the material (Stone and Kinger, 1985; Brown and
Santos, 1987).

Parents, educators, and researchers have
certain expectations and make important
decisions about bilingual children's linguistic
abilities. Research informs us to examine both
the reading process and the reader's product
(Kalaja, 1986; Urzua, 1986).

Based on linguistic cues, the reader must
generate hypotheses about the content of printed
text in order to employ such strategies as
predicting, sampling, confirming, correcting,
and altering (Barnitz, 1985). Strategies for
beginning readers in a second language will
differ from those used by advanced readers.
Language differences and levels of language
proficiency are found to affect reading
comprehension strategies and reading ability in
the second language learner. Cazden (cited in
Rigg and Scott Enright, 1986) warns researchers
against reducing complex concepts of language
and learning. She suggests responding to
children's cultural differences and encouraging
constant communication among children and
adults.

Whether a bilingual reader learns to
process information in two different languages,
considering linguistic and cognitive constraints
and organization strategies employed (i.e.,
chunking, rehearsing, skimming, etc.), is a
matter of mastering a set of related tasks and
components. McLeod and McLaughlin (1987) argue
that second language readers achieve comprehension of text, a higher level goal, by having
mastered, not necessarily in a hierarchical way,
a set of selected activities for a set of
related learning subtasks. On a time-sharing
basis, each subtask is learned by attending
first to the graphic features of print,
selecting meaningful words in a sentence unit,
and constructing the total meaning of a text.
The reader is then free; once having mastered
lower-level skills, such as sound-symbol
relationship, word attack skills, and syntactic
and lexical frequency; to focus on higher level
comprehension subtasks, such as identifying main
ideas or inferring meaning from a given context.

McLeod and McLaughlin (1987) note that the
mastery of cognitive tasks entails two types of
operations. One requires large amounts of
processing capacity and time. The other occurs
quickly and takes little processing energy (p.
110). The two types of operations are referred
to as "controlled" and "automatic." Short and
long-term memory hold mastered cognitive tasks/
information. Restructuring of memory knowledge
occurs when "controlled" or active thinking
processes act to invest renewed capacity on a
task or simultaneous tasks that require equal
amounts of time. Automatic learned tasks, on
the other hand, have been routinized and
long-term memory, or mental structures that
store information on a long-term basis similar
to a mind-map, quickly enable learners to
process information familiar to them in an
automatic way.

In this view of information processing,
learning involves the transfer of information to
long-term memory storage and is regulated by
controlled processes. That is, the learner
first employs controlled processes before
automatic processes develop. McLeod and
McLaughlin (1987) note that second language

learners "restructure" their memory knowledge in processing a new language by devising new memory structures for interpreting new information and for reorganizing information already learned in a native language. Hence, beginning a second language will focus on phonological information in a text on a controlled process basis, whereas more advanced bilingual readers will utilize contextual information on a cognitive automatic basis. Thus, successful bilingual readers automate the mechanical processes in reading and utilize controlled processing to draw meaning from content.

McLeod and McLaughlin (1987) conclude that various aspects of second language learning have an emergent or salient quality. Learners, at times, will modify their organizational knowledge structures in memory. Once they master the content, the meaningful structures in a second language (i.e., semantic, lexical [vocabulary], syntactic [word order], and so forth) are restructured by using language in meaningful social contexts. This is a third type of learning. Some learning will occur continuously by accretion, as is true of "automatic" learning strategies which at some point were formed from "controlled" learning strategies, another type of learning. But restructuring occurs in a discontinuous fashion, and since it is cited as a third type of learning, future research should examine it in relation to young bilingual children who are becoming biliterate. Restructuring of a learner's knowledge seems to occur on the level of reading comprehension. Thus, aside from the linguistic and cognitive tasks related to reading, a description is needed to categorize the intuitive meaning-making event or insight that will reveal a sudden comprehension on the part of the bilingual reader.

Barnitz's (1985) research studies support the notion that it is not necessary to be orally proficient in a second language before attempting to teach reading or writing skills. Reading, a receptive process, may develop faster than the ability to speak, a productive process, especially among older students who may be hesitant to speak for a variety of reasons.

READING IN BILINGUAL AND ESL EDUCATION

A number of research issues in reading in bilingual education and ESL instruction have been raised with regard to such variables as student, text, and culture. The interaction and integration of these variables help the LEP reader to fully comprehend the text. The following section documents research studies concerned with the needs of bilingual and English as a second language readers from different ethnic groups. In the context of pupil background knowledge, written text variables, and social and cultural aspects related to the literacy process; teaching and learning theories and practical considerations for instructional strategies will be discussed, as follows:

o To what extent do orthographic similarities and differences affect learning to read a first and second language?

o Should initial literacy be taught in the first or second language?

o Does a transfer of reading skills take place from a first to a second language?

o What are the comprehension-based teaching and learning strategies in reading in a second language?

o What is the difference between reading in bilingual education and reading in ESL programs?

o How can teachers help facilitate LEP students' literacy growth?

The changing demographic patterns in the United States reflect an increasing language minority student population attending public schools (Anderson and Joels, 1986). Literacy and proficiency in reading and writing a native language and English as a second language vary across language groups and diverse ethnic student populations within a group. For example, cultural and linguistic differences exist among Hispanics; such as Cubans, Dominicans, Mexicans, and Puerto Ricans.

Different groups of Asians; such as Chinese, Vietnamese, and Japanese; are also hetero-geneous. In addition, the visual discourse text form may differ across languages. For example, Japanese, Chinese, Arabic, and Hebrew, among others, require different levels of processing skills and strategies for the second language reader of English.

The following review of recent research studies discusses the educational needs of South Pacific/Asian children, Native American children, Greek children, and Spanish-speaking children.

South Pacific/Asian Children

Children who are immigrants or refugees from Asia and the South Pacific and who have literacy skills in their native languages, can generally transfer literacy skills in reading from the native language to English (Chang and Chiung-Sally, 1987). Research findings support Cummins' (1981) theoretical concept known as the "additive effects" of bilingualism. That is, children can learn a second language while maintaining the native language, as is the case of many Chinese, Vietnamese, Japanese, and Korean youngsters (Chang and Chiung-Sally, 1987).

Native language literacy skills enable pupils to add a second language by employing the same underlying literacy processes of the first language to the second language. However, illiterate children from the South Pacific region find literacy instruction in English as a second language frustrating and confusing. Illiteracy is compounded by limited oral proficiency in English and a lack of knowledge of the Roman alphabet. Thus, levels of native language literacy impact on children's literacy development in the second language.

For example, the Hmong do not have a written language tradition. Only recently have the Hmong adopted a written form which origi-nates from the Lao script rather than the Thai script (modern Romanized form). It is a logo-graphic system based on syllabic units; each scripted character is associated with one or

more meanings.   As in Chinese   script, a logo-
graphic character represents   a   word,   not   a
sound.
       Studies by   Chang   and   Chiung-Sally (1987)
indicate that Hmong children, literate in the
Lao   script,   can   transfer   literacy   skills to
English as a second language with less difficulty than illiterates.   Also, it was found that
literacy in   any of the   languages --Hmong, Lao,
or Thai--   had a   major   positive   effect   on
students'   ESL   performance   (Chang   and Chiung-
Sally, 1987).   The ability to read in the native
language   helped   the   children   learn   a second
language.
       However, Chang and Chiung-Sally (1987) note
that   to   introduce   native   literacy   skills to
Hmong refugees now living in   the United States;
considering   that   they   mostly   come   from   a
printless,   oral   culture;   may not be   the best
approach.   Culturally,   the Hmong people do not
place a high   priority   on literacy development;
therefore,   to   teach   literacy   in   the   native
language may be   a   waste   of   time   and energy
(Chang and Chiung-Sally (1987).   The researchers
further argue that   Hmong children   may   need to
learn   English literacy first   at the functional
level.   A   phonetic   approach   may   help   these
pupils make   the   connection   between   sound and
letter relationships.   Although a written system
has been recently developed for the Hmong, it is
still not   part   of   formal   school   instruction.
Nevertheless, Hmong children who are literate in
the first language, develop literacy in a second
language more effectively.
       Since   Chinese   orthography   is   not alpha-
betic,   a different structure, such as the Roman
alphabet,   imposes   different   demands   on   the
learner   (Chang   and   Chiung-Sally,   1987).   A
Chinese literate child must master between 3,500
and 7,000 monosyllabic characters, primarily by
memorizing each character.   These symbols can be
read   and understood by people   who speak different   dialects.   The   learner   must   deal   with
tonemic   (sound)   discrimination   in   acquiring
Chinese literacy.
       Chang and Chiung-Sally (1987) conclude that
when   speakers   of   languages   using   non-Roman
alphabets   attempt to   handle   new   visual forms,

unfamiliar structures, and strange vocabulary,
the different view of reality that these persons
perceive in English print may prevent them from
making the proper connection when learning to
read and write in English (p. 6). Specific
reading skills in a language such as Chinese
differ from English and require different
speech-print mapping rules. Yet once a person
is literate in a given language, second language
literacy is facilitated (Chang and Chiung-Sally,
1987).

Sakash (1987) distinguishes between pre-
literate students who come from cultures in
which literacy is rare or non-existent,
illiterates, who come from cultures in which
literacy is common, and semi-literates who are
not able to read or write beyond elementary
levels. Teachers and administrators may find
this breakdown useful in planning for
instruction.

Illiterate students constitute two types of
groups based on their background characteristics
(Sakash, 1987). The first type is either born
in the United States or an early immigrant who
has attended elementary schools in the United
States and has failed to develop literacy skills
to function in academic school subjects. The
students in this group are mostly Hispanic. The
second group is primarily found at the junior
high school level. Usually they are proficient
in English and vary in the degree of oral
proficiency in the native language. Students in
the second group are of Vietnamese or Laotian
origin, or come from Jamaica or other Caribbean
islands where English-based dialects are spoken.

Sakash (1987) reports that although
research shows that teaching native literacy
skills first affects positive transfer skills to
reading a second language, time factors and
academic constraints, materials and staffing,
especially at secondary school levels, override
the potential benefits of biliteracy instruction.

In a research study of four Southeast Asian
children, Rigg and Scott Enright (1986) employ a
miscue analysis method which examines the oral
reading errors on the semantic, syntactic, and
graphophonic levels. Miscues are errors in oral

reading performance. The refugee students
studied by Rigg and Scott Enright were attending
intermediate grades of a public school in a
midwestern city of the United States. Their
oral reading performance in ESL narrative texts
was analyzed. Reader profiles were developed
for each subject based on the Reading Miscue
Inventory (Goodman and Burke, 1972). Measures
of graphic similarity, grammatical strength, no
loss of comprehension, retell, and miscues per
hundred words (MPHW) yielded a full reader's
profile. Moreover, readability levels of
materials were examined converging on a discourse analysis of the written text. Discourse
analysis focuses on how an author employs
sentence structure, grammar, vocabulary, idioms,
and usage; and how the author's choice of
language affects a reader's ability to understand the text. The focus of miscue analysis
is not on quantity of errors, but on quality.
The following ratings were used: partially
acceptable error (P), not acceptable (N), or
acceptable (Y). The profile indicates strategies employed by the reader, such as sampling,
predicting, confirming, correcting, and so on,
to make meaning of the text.

Rigg and Scott Enright (1986) found that
when ESL children are reading for teacher
evaluation purposes, not for their own enjoyment
in a relaxed manner, they tend to overcorrect
and read carefully, thus giving the higher
graphic similarity measures in the bilingual
reader profiles. They attend to print rather
than read for meaning. Since the meaning of a
text is not in the print, it is in the head of
the readers, and such meaning is determined by
who does the reading, the authors concluded that
there is no such thing as grade level
readability and reading ability. Yet, the
public refuses to change its views on reading
due to "cultural inertia" or simplicity (Rigg
and Scott Enright, 1986, p. 77).

Finally, from analysis of the text's
structure, Rigg and Scott Enright (1986) show
how content organization and schemata make
demands on the reader's background knowledge.
Discourse analysis of a written text to determine its purposes --narrative, expository,

argumentative, descriptive-- and its task demands, will help clarify the structure and content of reading instruction for second language learners. In comprehension-based reading instruction, therefore, teachers and curriculum specialists in bilingual education and ESL programs are to consider the content and text structure --its schemata-- and discourse differences across languages in reading comprehension. ESL readers will expect discourse to be patterned according to the conventions and constraints in their native culture (Barnitz, 1985). For example, English discourse written forms are represented in a linear structure although there is a hierarchical structure to communicate a message to the reader. The story grammar in English narrative prose, in particular, is hierarchically represented in the reader's mind-set, or code, in such categories as setting, sequentially organized events, and structure episodes (Barnitz, 1985). In addition, "cohesion" devices, or signal cue words, that act as connectives in a text, such as prepositional conjunctions and reference words, are key words that facilitate reading comprehension in English print. For the Asian (and also for the Native American) student, literate in the native language, thought patterns are circular and narrative prose styles may, therefore, focus on a different story grammar (Barnitz, 1985).

The relevant issue of concern to educators is whether the differences in the structure of the text will affect the comprehension of ESL readers from different cultures. Teaching strategies must be aimed accordingly to promote the bilingual child's awareness of discourse text patterns and semantic, lexical features in English as a Second Language instruction.

The use of vernacular languages in South Pacific islands presents interesting issues for biliteracy research studies (Moore, 1987). In islands, such as the Cook Islands, Fiji Islands, and 328 others, English is taught as a second language with a locally developed system employing songs, music, dialogues, reading and writing instruction, and story books. Vernacular languages are Maori, Fijian, Hindi, Urdu, Chinese, Zotuman, and others. Cultural and religious groups operate schools. Research surveys indicate that many children are not able to read in their native language and, not surprisingly, have problems reading in English. Developing orthographic systems for some of these vernacular languages is a popular research activity. Moore (1987) concludes that the quality of books for instructional literacy will determine further development of orthographies for distinct South Pacific cultures.

Native American Children

Rehyner (1986) has compiled descriptive research on the approaches and methods to teach culture, reading, ESL, and content areas to Native American students. In light of the Tribal Language Policies, native language instruction is emphasized. There are 206 spoken Indian languages in the United States. Developing a simplified orthographic system will be suitable for teaching literacy in the native language. Tribal leaders play key roles. They speak the native language fluently and have fully experienced the Indian culture. Literate Native American children may have a role in teaching the elders reading and writing skills in the new orthographic system. A cooperative social environment is appropriate to the culture, although not traditionally practiced in learning in the schools.

Reading in an ESL setting for Native American children needs to stress the power of words and organic reading, since words must have an intense meaning for the Indian child. Words must be part of his or her being (Reyhner, 1986, p. 25). ESL instruction, of course, differs from bilingual education methodology and programs for Native American children. Although learning and teaching strategies overlap in teaching second language reading and language arts, Reyhner (1986) suggests a variety of ESL teaching approaches. For example, silent observation techniques are based on children's learning styles and strategies and place an emphasis on a subjective, artistic view of the world interpreted through drawing and other visual and spatial skills. These approaches are important in teaching the Native American child. Instruction that emphasizes the mainstream American education model which values objective, scientific approaches to reality are not effective when teaching the Native American student (Reyhner, 1986, p. 128).

Greek Children

Tchaconas (1985) studied the oral reading strategies in Greek and English of twelve second grade bilingual children and identified their cognitive learning styles as either field dependent or field independent. The field dependent (global perceptual style) group differed in its oral reading performance from the field independent (analytical perceptual style) group. The field independent group predicted more, employed more syntactic and semantic cues in the text, and their retell scores reflected higher comprehension than the field dependent group. The author concluded that when Greek bilingual children show a decline in literacy skills when learning to read in English as their second language, maintenance bilingual programs are useful to teach native reading skills that can transfer to the second language.

Cognitive learning styles of Greek bilingual children were studied by Tchaconas and Spiridakis (1986) in New York City. In this descriptive research study the authors explored what differences, if any, exist in the oral reading strategies used by subjects while reading in English as compared with their oral reading strategies while reading in Greek. Attention was given to any differences in the oral reading strategies for field dependent Greek bilingual children as opposed to field independent Greek bilingual children while reading in both English and Greek. Cognitive styles focused on the student's way of perceiving, attending to, and analyzing text, and remembering and recalling specific text and data. Bilingual Greek children were considered field dependent, if they employed a global

perceptual approach to learning. They were
considered field independent, if they used an
analytical perceptual style to learning.

In this study Tchaconas and Spiridakis
(1986) randomly selected twelve second grade
public school Greek bilingual pupils who had
been in bilingual programs since kindergarten.
To determine level of proficiency, the Language
Dominance Language Proficiency Test was
administered in both English and Greek. Other
test measures and student data were examined,
such as the bilingual children's performance on
the California Achievement Test.

Oral readings from a Greek basal text were
recorded and retelling scores were noted for
each child. Probe questions were asked to help
the children recall information in Greek. The
same procedures and methods were repeated in the
English language. The Reading Miscue Inventory,
developed by Goodman and Burke (1972) was used
for providing general guidelines in determining
the inclusion or exclusion of miscues or oral
reading errors of pupils.

Comprehension proficiency was determined
according to the patterns of responses obtained
from each of the categories of correction,
semantic acceptability, and meaning change.
Finally, the Children's Embedded Figures Test
assisted in identifying the Greek bilingual
children as either field dependent or field
independent in cognitive learning style. A
summary of results shows ten categories of coded
data analyses for children's reading comprehension abilities in both Greek and English in
terms of the linguistic cues; and graphophonic,
syntactic, semantic, and students' corrections
strategies.

Findings indicated that Greek bilingual
children utilized similar reading strategies in
both languages (i.e., sampling, predicting,
testing, confirming, correcting, etc.), but the
extent to which they were used by the subjects
varied. This conclusion argues for common
methodologies across languages while teaching
reading.

The field independent Greek children
processed printed materials in both English and
Greek more successfully than their field

dependent counterparts. This finding points to
the teacher's need to develop the less
frequently used strategies of field dependent
bilingual children, such as predicting and
testing. Infrequent use of specific strategies
impedes comprehension-based, whole language
learning in children with a field dependent
cognitive learning style. Bicognitive flexibility can be developed by teaching children in
alternative modes, and not just in their
preferred learning modality. The study concludes that there is one reading process. It would
make sense to teach bilingual children in their
stronger language, the native language, at the
time they enter school and transfer their
reading skills and strategies to the second
language later.

Spanish-speaking Children

Although reading is not a universally
learned phenomenon across cultures, research
reveals the universal aspects of the reading
process (Ambert and Melendez, 1985; Barnitz,
1985; Rigg and Scott Enright, 1986). Biliteracy
is independent of the languages in which the
bilingual child learns to read. For native
Spanish-speaking literate students, the similarities in the discourse printed languages in
Spanish and English in both form (grammar, vocabulary, orthographies, mechanics) and function
(demands, questions, commands, requests, decla-
rations) facilitate rapid transference of
reading skills from the native to the second
language (Cohen, 1987). The following research
discussion examines the complex cognitive
processes, from different theoretical viewpoints, of Hispanic youngsters learning to read
in Spanish and English as their second language
and will conclude with general and specific
implications for teachers.

Padron (1985) utilized the cognitive
reading strategies of her bilingual students in
Spanish and English to improve English reading
comprehension. Her purpose was to investigate
whether the cognitive strategies bilingual
students used during the reading process

differed by grade, gender, or ability level in reading and to what extent instruction enhanced reading comprehension in English as a second language.

Cognitive strategies were identified by interview form and categorized by number and type, such as recalling, summarizing, remembering, locating information, analyzing, generalizing, interpreting or concluding, and evaluating by use of contextual clues.

Padron's method employed randomly selected control groups with a pre/posttest design. Ninety-two Hispanic bilingual students in Texas, ages eight to twelve, were stratified by ability levels to form four groups (two control, two experimental). Experimental group number one was taught English reading by using the reciprocal teaching approach. Teachers asked students to answer and form their own questions on the content of the reading task and to predict the meaning of the assignments. Experimental group number two was instructed on how to locate information in reading tasks. Control group number one was instructed to read stories independently and answer comprehension questions. Control group number two did not receive any additional instruction. Students participated in the experiment for periods of thirty minutes, twice a week, for one month.

Experimental and control findings showed that bilingual children used similar reading comprehension strategies as those used by monolingual students. She identified thirteen strategies employed by bilingual experimental groups, such as text sampling, predicting, confirming, rejecting, correcting, altering, making inferences, interpreting, inserting information, deleting, adding, and omitting. Differences between genders were inconclusive. Students in the higher grades who were higher achievers used a greater number of strategies and higher level cognitive strategies. Finally, once students were proficient readers in their native language, instruction in cognitive strategies in English as a second language did not improve their comprehension. Reading instruction, then, must be differentiated for bilingual students by using appropriate teaching

strategies. Moreover, learning styles of
bilingual students and proficiency in the native
language significantly affect learners' reading
achievement in English (Padron, 1985).

In studying Spanish-speaking readers who
experience difficulty in learning to read,
Rivera Viera (1986) supports the case-study
approach. Like Rigg and Scott Enright (1987),
Rivera Viera employed a miscue-analysis profile
for a Puerto Rican, middle-class, seven-year old
boy, who had serious reversal problems in
decoding in his native Spanish. The subject
received remedial reading instruction for one
hour twice a week during one academic year. The
language experience approach was used in
teaching and the researcher found this method
particularly appropriate to the boy's strengths
because he enjoyed storytelling. Cloze
exercises were used to teach word attack skills
and comprehension. Rivera Viera concluded that
the subject's problems originated from ineffec-
tual use of native language reading strategies.
ESL and bilingual teachers may gain substantial
information on a bilingual child's linguistic
strengths employing a comprehensive assessment
in a case study format.

Question-asking and reading comprehension
have been related to reading ability and
question-asking ability in bilingual Spanish/
English students (Henry, 1985; Hewlett-Gomez,
1985; Monteiro, 1986). Question-asking research
models and studies are comprehension based in
teaching second language learners. Pre-reading
adjunct questions affect students selective
attention and selective rehearsal strategies for
important materials and cause the reader to
activate relevant background knowledge schemata
which can help encode and organize new
information (Monteiro, 1986).

Hewlett-Gomez (1985) completed 24 classroom
observations and collected tape recorded
discourse from the classrooms of four bilingual
teachers over a six-week period. Five bilingual
students from each classroom, grades two
through five, verbally interacted with the
bilingual teachers during second language
instruction in reading. Types of questions and
responses elicited by both teachers and students

were coded. Findings revealed that teachers
asked more lower level cognitive questions than
bilingual students. It was also found that
teachers talked too much. Students initiated
more questions in their second language when
teachers talked less. Students mimicked teacher
questioning patterns such as question-response
and evaluation response. Hewlett-Gomez (1985)
concluded that teacher talking and questioning
patterns affect positive achievement in second
language reading comprehension. Teacher talk
and questions and use of other response forms
can, therefore, create an environment that
stimulates students' curiosity, fostering motivation and enabling expansion of language.

In an effort to identify the characteristics of effective bilingual and ESL literacy
programs for bilingual learners, Soler-Galiano
and Prince (1987) conducted a longitudinal
research study, from 1983 to 1985. They
analyzed bilingual reading and writing instruction in three elementary public schools in
Connecticut. The purpose of the study was to
identify and describe the administrative,
curricular, and instructional practices which
contribute to program success and biliteracy
achievement in Spanish-speaking children.
Eleven first and second grade Spanish/English
bilingual classrooms were visited twice a month.
Classroom observation techniques, teacher
interviews, student and staff interviews, examination of curricular materials, and collected
student writing samples provided qualitative
measures linked to student test scores.

Successful program characteristics reported
included strong academic curriculum in bilingual
instruction, well-defined instructional plans to
teach reading and writing, strong administrative
support, strong support for native language
instruction as a bridge to learning English, and
integration into and acceptance of the school's
mainstream culture.

Comparable bilingual student performance
measures in English and Spanish, writing
samples, and standardized reading achievement
results in Spanish and English were correlated
to program and curricular characteristics. In
linking process information to bilingual student

literacy outcomes, evaluations in bilingual education can begin to employ such a model to meaningfully improve literacy instruction and program designs for second language learners (Hakuta, 1986; Soler-Galiano and Prince, 1987). Results of this study indicate that reading instruction reinforces writing skills acquisition and writing skills reinforce reading.

READING STRATEGIES AND INSTRUCTIONAL PROGRAMS

Monteiro (1986) studied students who were already English proficient. According to Monteiro, student generated questions compel the reader to actively process information referred to as an "active processing hypothesis." Also, students' awareness of their cognitive processes and products improves reading comprehension known as the "metacognitive hypothesis." In addition, question asking tasks activate prior knowledge, referred to as schema theory. Therefore, enhancing students' questioning abilities enhances reading comprehension. Types of questioning used by teachers in bilingual/ESL literacy programs merit future research attention.

Feldman (1987) argued that areas of content knowledge are shared across cultures. She presented three case studies of successful reading comprehension based programs developed by school districts to meet the needs of culturally-diverse student populations. The Structured Teaching in the Areas of Reading and Writing (STAR) was implemented in School District 4 of New York City, grades three through nine. STAR was developed with the assistance of researchers and university consultants.

Another study described by Feldman (1987) focused on the reading problems of poor Hawaiian primary students who spoke Hawaiian English. The Kamehameha Early Education Program (KEEP) was developed by consulting university instructors and anthropologists. Writing instruction was integrated into the teaching of reading skills as in the STAR program. In this approach,

teachers employed   narrative events familiar to
the children, such as the Hawaiian "talk story"
(p. 32).

In   another   attempt   to   improve   the
achievement of poor readers, the Instructional
Program in Reading and Language Arts (IPIRLA)
was implemented in Montgomery County, Maryland,
where many children are of limited English
proficiency.

Feldman (1987) concluded that there is a
need for basing reading instruction for any
student, in particular second language learners,
on current theory and research.   District and
building administrators should support such
efforts, and consultant experts from research
institutions can make contributions in the areas
of theory and program development, implementation, and evaluation.

TRANSFERENCE OF READING SKILLS

Current research continues to support the
theory that the bilingual learner transfers
native literacy skills in reading to a second
language in an interactive, reciprocal process
(Barnitz, 1985; Garcia and Padilla, 1985; Cohen,
1987).   Although past studies reflected
linguistic interference in transferring reading
skills from a first to a second language (Segan,
1984), current investigations raise the issues
of the nature of orthographic differences
between a first and second language and how
these influence the transfer of literacy from
one language to another (Barnitz, 1985;
Centurion, 1986; Chang and Chiung-Sally, 1987;
Sakash, 1987).

At present other topics in the transfer of
reading skills in bilingual education focus on
"metacognitive" strategies for reading (Brown-
Azarowitz, 1987), such as the use of rhythmical
patterns in silent and oral reading by second
language learners in relation to reading
comprehension. The English language structures
(nouns, pronouns, punctuation marks, connectives, verbs, adverbs, adjectives, and
prepositions) that affect reading comprehension
for second language learners are also being

addressed, considering whether or not these language structures appear in the literate student's native language.

Additional current concerns deal with levels of literacy and biliteracy, the special circumstances of students who are literate in a native language with a non-Roman alphabet, students who come from a language background with no written tradition, and the language proficiency skills that will support literacy learning in a second language (Chang and Chiung-Sally, 1987; Sakash, 1987).

Anderson and Joels (1986) among others, point to the lexical or vocabulary differences across languages and how these affect reading comprehension, in particular, when transferring lexical meanings and concepts from a first to a second language. The "vocabulary-concept knowledge" construct developed by Cummins (1981) interrelated the context of the written word, the schemata (text structure and content), and the child's language proficiency in reading comprehension. For example, the English word _dormitory_ is different in meaning from the Spanish and Italian word _dormitorio_. It is important, thus, in analyzing the transfer of reading skills phenomenon to consider first and second language lexical differences, such as the use of figurative language, metaphors, idioms, similes, and affective meanings in words which impact reading comprehension (Garcia and Padilla, 1985; Dubin, et al., 1986).

Cohen (1987) developed two transferability models in teaching reading to Spanish-speaking children in the United States. Factors such as student placement in a bilingual education program, English as a second language instruction, types of instructional materials, and strategies employed; affect the transferability process. These factors, in turn, relate to philosophical and practical considerations in a school and culture. Some important factors are the teacher's view of teaching literacy to bilingual children and program alternatives, such as individualized native language reading instruction coupled with reinforcement of comparable skills taught in the native language in the ESL class.

The Transferring Individual Skills (TIS) model from Spanish to English on a skill-by-skill basis as they are acquired in English, focuses on a fragmented, skill dependent process, whereas the preferred Transferring Organized Clusters (TOC) model promotes the transference of similar skills clustered, by degree of difficulty and format, at the comprehension level (Cohen, 1987, p. 11). Remembering sequence, re-arranging for correct sequence, and cause-effect relationships comprise a cluster (Cohen, 1987).

Cohen (1987) distinguishes between reading as a language process and language as a communication process. The bilingual teacher working on transferability must understand reading as a visual and cognitive task; as thinking; and as personal, emotional, and social communication (p. 13). If there are reading transferability problems, bilingual and ESL teachers who have knowledge of reading as a psycholinguistic and interactive process can determine whether these problems are language related or based on reading circumstances. ESL reading instruction of LEP pupils should be compatible with native language instruction in reading, if transfer of reading skills is to enhance the process of students' reading comprehension.

To conclude the discussion on reading research in bilingual education and ESL instruction, three major areas point to general and specific teaching implications in terms of strategies or approaches. First, educators must possess linguistic knowledge and cultural sensitivity to the LEP child's home language and community. Second, understanding of cognitive processes related to learning reading and writing in bilingual education and ESL instruction helps meet the needs of LEP pupils. Third, the content of a curriculum for LEP children must be relevant and interesting.

The process of teaching reading in English to LEP students is similar to teaching reading in the native language. Thus, teachers must first look at the language area, that is, the goals and objectives for promoting biliteracy in bilingual children, the teaching strategies and teacher input. Teacher talk, questioning

techniques, teaching methods, and curricular
materials should be examined in terms of aiming
reading instruction for effective comprehension.
It is important to relate linguistic knowledge
to other major categories of teacher and student
knowledge. Cultural, pragmatic, functional, and
the basic interpersonal communications skills
(BICS) posited by Cummins (1981) are all
important. Language discourse text forms and
purposes; narrative, expository, and descriptive; should also be analyzed. Teaching
approaches can then be employed to set a balance
between similar literacy goals in bilingual and
ESL classes. In bilingual education reading
programs, however, research suggests compatible
teaching reading approaches in both the native
and second languages (Tchaconas, 1985; Dubin,
et al., 1986; Cohen, 1987).

In the cognitive area, teachers should
examine the pupils' different levels of thinking
and interaction (peer, child, adult, etc.) in
acquiring literacy skills in a second language.
Thematic teaching approaches with student
hands-on activities (sequencing stories in
pictures and written exercises, for example) can
promote comprehension thinking skills and active
participation in a natural setting which is
affectively-based. Low-anxiety learning tasks
promote bicognitive flexibility as suggested in
the research (Tchaconas and Spiridakis, 1986).

Finally, the third area deals with content
in the curriculum. Bilingual education teachers
aim to teach content in two languages, whereas
ESL teachers teach language and literacy skills
in the second language. School academic language proficiency, referred to as Cognitive
Academic Language Proficiency (CALP) by Cummins
(1981), distinguishes between a bilingual
learner's language proficiencies in a first or
second language. Integrating curriculum content
for teaching reading and writing skills in a
second language, in addition to listening and
speaking communication skills, emphasizes a
whole-language approach in the development of
reading and writing materials for the bilingual
child. In this case teachers do not select the
learning content, rather, content is based on
what the students know, and teaching materials

promote and expand upon the student's knowledge.
Thus, reading programs for bilingual children
should balance the need for language development
in a first and second language and content
development in curriculum for promoting
biliterate reading achievement.

WRITING RESEARCH AND BILINGUAL CHILDREN

In the past teachers and researchers have
assumed that a LEP child must first be orally
proficient in English before reading and writing
can be taught (Hudelson, 1984). Current research, however, supports the teaching of
writing skills simultaneously with speaking,
listening, and reading in a second language
(Barnitz, 1985; Rigg and Scott Enright, 1986).
LEP children should not be perceived as limited
in expressing their needs, interests, and ideas
in written form in a second language.

As in learning the reading process in a
second language, the classroom and social
context, as well as teacher expectations,
interact with the student's composing behavior.
The writing process is learned across two
languages, not acquired (Conner and Kaplan,
1987). The following research issues have
pointed out linguistic and cultural differences
affecting writing development of LEP children:
how are reading and writing integrated for
teaching the LEP child; what appropriate
teaching strategies affect bilingual children's
composing behaviors; can students transfer
writing skills from one language system to
another; and finally, how can bilingual/ESL
teachers evaluate LEP children's writing.

Research supports the universality of
learning the writing process, although it is not
a universally distributed school phenomenon
(Conner and Kaplan, 1987). Both reading and
writing require cognitive planning and problem
solving behaviors. The writer's content
knowledge and composing processes subsume his or
her learning strategies for recalling, collecting, and transforming data; and a structure or
written schemata (written discourse knowledge
and processes). This entails selecting a topic,

purpose, and audience for specific written forms (narrative, descriptive, or expository) (Hillocks, 1987). Thus, the writer will employ a different lexicon depending on the purposes and constraints of the writing event.

Lately, dialogue journal, conference centered, and consumer skills writing approaches have been popular with ESL and bilingual teachers working with LEP students (Ovando and Collier, 1985; Edelsky, 1986; Raines, 1986). Research findings illustrate the benefits of such approaches to promote bi-literacy in limited English-speaking children (Center for Education and Research, 1986; Peyton, 1986).

Smolen (1987) is presently conducting writing research in Akron, Ohio, on the dialogue journal writing method in bilingual education and ESL programs. Initial findings of her study showed that reading and writing reinforce each other and the two processes can be developed simultaneously in LEP children. Journal entry, a form of a written daily diary about some event or events, may have a distinct audience and differs in purposes from dialogue journal writing which is a written conversation between co-participants (teacher-student or student-peers) and is another form of daily language communication.

The teacher asks questions, makes comments, or expands on the students' writing without correcting (Smolen, 1987). The response is to the written meaning rather than form. The instructional benefits of dialogue journal writing are that (a) language is used in a context the LEP student understands; (b) the absence of set guidelines free students to write without constraints on topics of interest to them; (c) reading and writing processes are interrelated; (d) motivation is high; and (e) interaction takes place between teacher and student in a low-anxiety situation.

Smolen (1987) studied the writing samples of eighteen elementary and secondary students in ESL classrooms. Teachers were given a brief explanation of dialogue journal writing and were instructed not to correct student writings. The teaching method was not presented. Smolen then

focused on the teacher comments and questions on
students' writing samples. The following
teacher response categories were found in
student dialogue journal pieces: praise,
comments, critical comments, restrictive type
questions (yes/no, either/or), "what" questions
(asking for specific kinds of information),
open-ended questions (i.e., what did you do on
the weekend?), and directive questions (i.e.,
tell me about the baseball game). Frequencies
were reported for each of the teacher response
categories and results showed that the majority
of teacher responses were comments in contrast
to the few directive, open-ended, extended types
of questions which expand upon pupils language
writing skills.

Monteiro (1986) also reported that teachers
use less demanding types of questions in reading
and writing. The implications of these studies
is that teachers must adjust types of questioning and response strategies to the proficiency
levels of LEP pupils in their native and second
languages and need to ask more questions on
higher cognitive levels of instruction.

Another study of LEP student's dialogue
writing samples focused on a topic to elaborate
information in written discourse form (Smolen,
1987). Samples were examined from first, sixth,
seventh, and twelfth grade LEP students. The
topic was important to the individual writer
since it was not directly shared with readers;
and to effectively write on a topic, the writer
must elaborate information in a detailed manner.
Smolen is now examining teachers' topic initiat-
ing and questions to students' writing pieces.
The study is near completion and findings will
be reported soon. However, preliminary research
results of Smolen's study, as well as other
research findings, indicated that dialogue
journal writing is an interactive process
that promotes teacher-pupil communication and
pupil independence to elaborate, in writing,
on personally relevant student topics (Ovando
and Collier, 1985; Fuentes, 1987).

How pupils perceive writing tasks is
related to their independence in communicating
to a reader and strategies for composing an
original work (Rigg and Enright, 1986). Halsall

(1986) examined bilingual children's composing behaviors during classroom writing and their perceptions of writing. Bilingual students were observed from kindergarten to fifth grade, for 145 hours, using ethnographic methods. Halsall conducted formal and informal student interviews. Findings revealed twelve composing behaviors used by bilingual students: reading back, invented spellings, copying, body language, prewriting, concealing writing, play, confirmation questions, talking while writing, asking questions, making statements about writing, and taking breaks. In particular, it was noted that bilinguals talked while they wrote in order to make the transition to writing. They used Spanish phrases to get started writing. They read back, confirmed questions, and concealed writing more than any of the other composing behaviors. It is suggested that teachers serve as models in oral and verbal behaviors, encourage LEP children's expressions in talk and writing tasks based on their important agendas, learn from them, and accept their individual composing behaviors.

To change Mexican-American students' perception of writing tasks as "impossible," Hayes (1985) studied LEP fifth graders who were children of farm laborers. After teachers read to the children in the ESL class, opportunities to read and write focused on topics, such as love letters, family, biographies of others, and so on. Results showed that children's low self-concept in academic learning and their proficiency levels in English significantly improved by the end of the school year.

Miller (1987) studied what LEP students write and what is most important to them, such as the family, friendship, or daily events, and correlated these to their positive self-esteem. A class of bilingual third graders in Boston was observed during 45 minute daily periods of writing instruction. Two periods emphasized dialogue journal writing and three periods focused on story writing. Students decided on their own topics, received feedback from peers and wrote daily. Results showed that LEP children assumed responsibility for writing in

the second or native language during writing
time independent of teacher direction or a given
structure for composing.

Hudelson (1986) performed a case study
analysis of four Asian children's writing.
Cham, Sonkla, Khamla, and Vuong were
attending intermediate schools. Sonkla, Cham,
and Vuong spoke Khmer, whereas Khamla spoke Lao.
Several writing samples examined for each
student indicated that: (a) ESL writing
instruction can be provided to LEP students
before they master the mechanics and grammar of
English structures; (b) learners create different kinds of texts for different purposes;
(c) LEP children learn to revise and edit their
own writing in English; (d) the classroom
context and teacher impact on a child's
development of writing; and (e) individual
linguistic and cultural differences affect
writing development in LEP children. Finally,
Hudelson (1986) offers the following suggestions
for classroom teachers: (a) provide daily time
for LEP students to write; (b) employ a holistic
approach to teaching writing; (c) allow children
to contribute their own personal or narrative
expression to given informational-expository
writing assignments; (d) ESL children vary in
the rates at which they grow as English writers
and this must be taken into consideration; (e)
expose ESL learners to a variety of classroom
writing assignments; and (f) give ESL students
time for unassigned writing, for writing what
they choose to write. To evaluate ESL
children's writing, teachers should examine many
pieces of writing, not just one; consider the
context in which writing takes place before
evaluating a LEP student's writing; and examine
teacher expectations and assumptions about
school writing.

According to Urzua (1986), writing helps
LEP students to better understand the self and
the world. The composing, editing, and revising
processes will determine the pupil's strategies
in composing a piece (Urzua, 1986). Studying
the same children as Hudelson (Cham, Khamla,
Vuong, and Sonkla), Urzua conducted an
ethnographic analysis of the children's writing
samples and related them to the school and home

contexts through teacher and family interviews. As a result of her study, Urzua urges other researchers and teachers to make certain they gather data from a number of different sources before making decisions about a student's linguistic abilities. Teachers should look at both the process and product of learning and recognize that children function differently during linguistic learning tasks. Learning should be evaluated with consideration to other influential factors and teachers should keep informed about children's human development and growth (Urzua, 1986).

In evaluating LEP children's writing behaviors, Samway (1987) employed a case study approach with Pedro, a thirteen-year-old sixth grader from Puerto Rico, who experienced academic difficulties in New York City. Like Urzua's (1986) conclusion, Samway states that education must examine LEP children's writing processes in terms of a best performance model rather than a deficit model.

Gonzalez and Grubb (1985) propose the model <u>Composing Writing Prompts</u> as a process by which students learn to make decisions about writing: topic, audience, level of content, intent, type of writing, organization, and viewpoint. Practical teaching strategies are provided along with a description of each component. Various samples of student writing in Spanish and English were examined by the authors for purposes of training teachers on how to adjust their writing assignments and on which levels to assign composing tasks.

The research on writing in bilingual education and ESL learning suggests the following implications for teachers:

o Writing in a second language, like other communication skills, is learned through interaction with others (peers, teachers) and with the content, purpose, and structure of the task.
o It is important for the LEP child to express his/her personality in the writing process and for others to accept it.

o Dialogue journal writing approaches facilitate
  language expansion in the native language
  and ESL.   It is aimed for communication and
  is a meaning-making activity.
o Writing can be integrated with the process of
  teaching reading in the native and second
  languages and reading can be incorporated into
  the teaching of writing.
o Cooperative learning environments tap the
  learning styles of LEP children. Restructuring the classroom setting and mode of
  instruction will promote cooperativeness.
o As in the case of Native American children
  learning from tribal elders, value is placed
  on human resources to participate in promoting
  literacy skills in LEP children. Parents,
  peers, and the community can provide role
  models.
o LEP children need time to develop as writers
  of English.
o A comparative study of rhetorical conventions
  across cultures is of pedagogical value in
  bilingual and ESL programs.

     Finally, LEP children should feel comfor-
table in composing writing assignments; evaluation must examine various samples of students'
writings before any conclusions can be drawn;
and writing is a recursive activity, students
review, revise, and edit what they write.
Although purposes and constraints in the writing
process may differ across cultures and
languages, the topic's purpose, audience, and
content knowledge may be universal in writing
school assignments. Teaching strategies may
need to focus on writing processes embedded in
the context of the LEP child's composing
behaviors.

          SUMMARY AND CONCLUSIONS

     The effectiveness of classroom instruction
for LEP children, especially in reading and
writing, will be enhanced by the teacher's
understanding of the differences which exist
(cultural, lexical, in discourse forms) between
the student's native and second languages. Such

differences require development of multilite-
racies on the part of LEP students; and this
will affect the acquisition of biliteracy
skills. Yet language proficiency in a native
language facilitates rapid literacy in a second
language. Native language literacy facilitates
transference of reading and writing skills to a
second language. Nevertheless, transference and
biliteracy may not be possible for LEP children
who are illiterate in their native language and
more difficult for children whose first language
system has a non-Roman alphabet. For the
latter, contrastive analysis teaching strategies
in oral language structures may aid in
transferring oral proficiencies in a native
language to learning literacy skills in a second
language (Barnitz, 1985).

A holistic approach interrelated to the
teaching of the four communication skills may
help to meet LEP students' special educational
needs. Not only are reading and writing
proficiencies dependent upon language proficiency in a first language, but cognitive
development in the native language also
facilitates academic and linguistic proficiency
in the second language. These proficiencies
underlie and affect literacy teaching skills and
content. There is a need to develop first the
functional, communicative dimension of biliteracy in bilingual children in order to
promote academic achievement in other school
areas. Moreover, teachers influence the degree
of expressiveness in the LEP child, thus
instruction should be affectively-based.

In addition to basing reading and writing
instruction for LEP students on a comprehension-
based interactive teaching approach, teachers
need to show bilingual students how reading and
writing interrelate in areas such as
spelling, punctuation, syntax, lexicon, and
orthography; and reinforce each other in both
of the child's languages as meaning-making
communication modes. The value of any approach
depends upon the teacher's creativity and
ability to adapt materials or methods for
teaching LEP children. Qualitative and case
study research methods, moreover, respect the

individuality and differences of LEP students by
considering the process rather than the program
product.

Future   research in biliteracy development
in   bilingual   students   should   tie together
reading and writing methodologies and show how
each affects the other in the learning process
of   LEP   students   and   how   cross-cultural
differences in   orthography, rhetorical, and
discourse language factors influence the LEP
child's development and transfer of literacy
skills to a second language. Further research is
needed   to   assess   the   impact   of teacher
questioning abilities on reading comprehension
in   bilingual   students   acquiring biliteracy
skills.

The aim of this chapter was to synthesize
current literacy research in bilingual education
and ESL instruction. Reading and writing as
interactive processes were emphasized as
language dependent modes of communication. Such
context variables as the nature of the
orthographic system, culture, and the learners'
proficiency in the native and second languages
were shown to affect literacy acquisition and
transference of skills from the native language
to English. Different ethnic groups in the
process of reading and writing acquisition, in
the native language and in ESL, were studied.
Suggestions were made for teaching the universal
reading and writing process across different
languages and cultures; although the purpose,
context, and structure of the language system
known to a bilingual learner may differ and
affect reading comprehension or the composing
behaviors in writing tasks. Comprehension-
based, holistic teaching approaches and
methods were stressed for promoting biliteracy
in second language learners.

ACKNOWLEDGEMENTS

The author is especially indebted to the
Office of Bilingual Education staff of the City
of New York Board of Education.   In particular,
Dr. Frances Segan, who gave much of her time to
proofread and suggest ways to organize the

chapter; Ms. Carmen Gloria Burgos, Bilingual Librarian, who provided up-dated sources in the research literature; and for typing of the manuscript and continuous assistance, many thanks to Ms. Elba O. Melendez and Ms. Carmen N. Rodriguez, Bilingual Secretaries. Many thanks also to the New York City Multifunctional Resource Center (MRC) staff, above all, Ms. Carmen Mercado, for guidance in communicating with other MRC's in the nation and for conducting one of the ERIC searches. Finally, much appreciation is owed for the abundance of materials received from other MRC's (Title VII) across the United States and Hawaii, Service Areas 1, 2, 5, 7, 14, and 15.

REFERENCES

Ambert, A.N. and Melendez, S.E. **Bilingual Education: A Sourcebook.** New York: Teachers College Press, 1985.

Anderson, B. and Joels, R.W. **Teaching Reading to Students with Limited English Proficiencies.** Springfield, Ill: Charles C. Thomas, 1986.

Barnitz, J.G. Reading Development of Non-Native Speakers of English: Research and Instruction. Monograph of the Center for Applied Linguistics. Washington, D.C.: ERIC Clearinghouse. ED No. 256182, 1985.

Brown, D.L. and Santos, S.L. "Promoting Literacy in the Classroom." In Rodriguez, R. (Ed.) **Teaching Reading to Minority Language Students.** Rosslyn, Va: National Clearinghouse for Bilingual Education, 1987.

Brown-Azarowitz, M. "Oral Interpretation: A Metacognitive Strategy for Reading." In Rodriguez, R. (Ed.) **Teaching Reading to Minority Language Students.** Rosslyn, Va: National Clearinghouse for Bilingual Education, 1987.

Carrasquillo, A. and Segan, P. (Eds.) **The Teaching of Reading in Spanish to Bilingual Students.** New York: Ediciones Puerto Rico de Autores Nuevos, 1984.

Center for Education and Research. "Interactive writing: Making writing meaningful for language minority students." **NABE News**, 1, 19-21, 1986.

Centurion, C.E. The Use of the Informal Reading Inventory to Evaluate Oral Reading, Reading Comprehension, and Language Interference/Transfer in English as a Second Language Students. Unpublished doctoral disserta-

tion, Texas A & I University, 1986.
(Available from UMI, Ann Arbor, MI, Order
No. DA8527088.

Chang, W.L. and Chiung-Sally, C. English
Literacy for Persons of Languages with
Non-Roman Alphabets. Paper presented at
the Title VII Directors Information
Gathering Meeting, Arlington, Va., June,
1987.

Cohen, B. Issues Related to Transferring
Reading Skills from Spanish to English.
Paper presented at the Annual Conference,
National Association for Bilingual
Education, Denver, Colo., April, 1987.

Commission on Reading. **Becoming a Nation of
Readers.** Washington, D.C.: National
Institute of Education, 1985.

Conner, U. and Kaplan, R.B. **Writing Across
Languages: Analysis of L2 Text.** Reading,
Mass.: Addison Wesley, 1987.

Cummins, J. "The Role of Primary Language
Development in Promoting Educational
Success for Language Minority Students."
In **Schooling and Language Minority
Students: A Theoretical Framework.** Los
Angeles, Calif.: California State
Department of Education, Evaluation,
Dissemination, and Assessment Center,
California State University, 1981.

Dubin, F.; Eshey, D.E.; and Grabe, W. (Eds.)
**Teaching Second Language Reading for
Academic Purposes.** Reading, Mass.:
Addison Wesley, 1986.

Edelsky, C. **Writing in a Bilingual Program.**
Norwood, N.J.: Ablex Publishing, 1986.

Ellinger, R.J. An Analysis of Reading Strategies Used by a High and Low Proficiency
Group of Students Learning English as a

Second Language. Unpublished doctoral dissertation, Oklahoma State University, 1985.

Esling, J. and Downing, J. "What do ESL students need to learn about reading?" **TESL Canada Journal**, 1, 55-68, 1987.

Feldman, D. "Research based reading instruction for LEP students." **The Journal of the New York State Association for Bilingual Education**, 2, 2, 25-39, 1987.

Franklin, E.A. "Literacy instruction for LES children." **Language Arts**, 63, 1, 51-60, 1986.

Freire, P. "Reading the world and reading the word." **Language Arts**, 62, 1, 15-22, 1985.

Fuentes, J. "From theory to practice: Writing as process with bilingual children." **NABE News**, 10, 3, 9-16, 1987.

Garcia, E.E. and Padilla, R.V. "Effects of Language Transfer on Bilingual Proficiency." In Garcia, E.E. and Padilla, R.V. (Eds.) **Advances in Bilingual Education Research**, Tucson: University of Arizona Press, 1985.

Gonzales, P.C. and Grubb, M.C. "Composing Writing Prompts." **Writings in Reading and Writing and Language Arts**, Ginn Occasional Papers, No. 19. Columbus, Ohio: Ginn and Company, 1985.

Goodman, Y.M. and Burke, C.L. **Reading Miscue Inventory Manual: Procedure for Diagnosis and Evaluation.** New York: Macmillan, 1972.

Goodman, K.S. and Goodman, Y.M. "Learning about psycholinguistic processes by analyzing oral reading." **Harvard Educational Review**, 47, 3, 317-333, 1977.

Hakuta, K. **Mirror of Language: The Debate on Bilingualism.** New York: Basic Books, 1986.

Hakuta, K. and Gould, L.J. "Synthesis of research in bilingual education." **Educational Leadership,** 44, 6, 38-45, 1987.

Halsall, S.W. An Ethnographic Account of the Composing Behaviors of Five Young Bilingual Children. Paper presented at the Annual Meeting, American Educational Research Association, San Francisco, Calif., April, 1986.

Hayes, C.W. To Read You Must Write: Children in Language Acquisition. Paper presented at the International Conference on Second/Foreign Language Acquisition by Children: Theoretical Aspects and Practical Applications, Oklahoma, March, 1985.

Henry, R. "Reader-generated questions: A tool for improving reading comprehension." **NABE News,** 8, 3, 4-9, 1985.

Hewlett-Gomez, M.R. Bilingual Teacher's Questions and Responses and Their Influence on Bilingual Students Responses during Instruction in English Reading. Unpublished doctoral dissertation, The University of Texas at Austin, 1985.

Hillocks, Jr., G. "Synthesis of research on teaching writing." **Educational Leadership,** 44, 8, 71-82, 1987.

Hudelson, S. "ESL Children's Writing: What We've Learned; What We're Learning." In Rigg, P. and Scott Enright, D. (Eds.) **Children and ESL: Integrating Perspectives.** Washington, D.C.: Teachers of English to Speakers of Other Languages, 1986.

Kalaja, P. "Reading in English as a second language: Some recent research." **Watesol Working Papers**, No. 3, 1986.

Krashen, S.D. **Writing: Research, Theory, and Applications.** Elmsford, N.Y.: Pergamon Press, 1984.

Krashen, S.D. and Terrel, T.D. **The Natural Approach: Language Acquisition in the Classroom.** Hayward, Calif.: Alemany, 1983.

Lam, A.S. Vocabulary and Other Considerations in Reading Comprehension: Implications Across the Curriculum. Paper presented at the RELC Regional Seminar on Language Across the Curriculum, Singapore, October, 1986.

MacGowan, A. "Holistic teaching and learning methods. Why they work so well and how to use them in your classes." **Connections: A Journal of Adult Literacy.** Boston: Roxbury Community Literacy Resource Institute, 1985.

McEvedy, R. "Some social, cultural, and linguistic issues in teaching reading to children who speak English as a second language." **Australian Journal of Reading,** 9, 3, 139-152, 1987.

McInnes, M.M. A Preliminary Report on an Investigation Using a Piagetian Model to Teach Reading to Spanish-Speaking Secondary Students. Paper presented at the Annual International Bilingual/Bicultural Education Conference, Chicago, April, 1986.

McLeod, A. "Critical literacy: Taking control of our own lives." **Language Arts,** 63, 1, 37-49, 1986.

McLeod, A. and McLaughlin, B. "Restructuring of automaticity? Reading in a second language." **Language Learning,** 36, 2, 109-123, 1987.

Miller, C.H. "Ready, set, write! A teacher taps the talent of bilingual third graders." **Equity and Choice**, 3, 2, 3-9, 1987.

Monteiro, R.P. Question Asking and Reading Comprehension: The Relationship between Reading Ability and Question-Asking Ability. Paper presented at the Annual Conference, American Educational Research Association, San Francisco, April, 1986.

Moore, B. Summary of Vernacular School Material Development and Literacy Issues in the South Pacific. Paper presented at the Title VII Directors Information Gathering Meeting, Arlington, Va., June, 1987.

Ovando, C.J. and Collier, P. **Bilingual and ESL Classrooms: Teaching in Multicultural Contexts.** New York: McGraw Hill, 1985.

Padron, Y. N. Utilizing Cognitive Reading Strategies to Improve English Reading Comprehension of Spanish-Speaking Bilingual Students. Unpublished doctoral dissertation, University of Houston, 1985.

Peyton, J.R. "Literacy through written interaction." **Passage**, 2, 1, 24-29, 1986.

Raines, A. Teaching Writing: What We Know and What We Do. Paper presented at the Annual Meeting, Teachers of English to Speakers of Other Languages, Anaheim, Calif., March 1986.

Reyhner, J. (Ed.) **Teaching the Indian Child: A Bilingual/Multicultural Approach.** Billinger: Eastern Montana College, 1986.

Rigg, P. and Scott Enright, D. (Eds.) **Children and ESL: Integrating Perspectives.** Washington, D.C.: Teachers of English as a Second Language, 1986.

Rivera Viera, D. "Remediating reading problems in a Hispanic learning disabled child from a psycholinguistic perspective." Journal of Reading, Writing, and Learning Disabilities International, 2, 1, 85-97, 1986.

Rivers, J. Whole Language in the Elementary Classroom. Paper presented at the Annual Meeting of the Teachers of English to Speakers of Other Languages, Annaheim, Calif., March, 1986.

Sakash, R. English Literacy for Non-Literate Secondary LEP Students. Paper presented at the Title VII Directors Information Gathering Meeting, Arlington, Va., June, 1987.

Samway, R. "Formal evaluation of children's writing. An incomplete story." Language Arts, 64, 3, 289-298, 1987.

Segan, P. "Teorias sobre la adquisicion y la transferencia de destrezas de lectura." In Carrasquillo, A.L. and Segan, P. (Eds.). Teaching of Reading in Spanish to Bilingual Students. New York: Ediciones Puerto Rico de Autores Nuevos, 1984.

Smolen, L. Teacher's Strategies and the Development of Students' Writing in Dialogue Journals. Unpublished monograph, April, 1987.

Soler-Galiano, A. and Prince, C.D. Reading and Writing Instruction in Three Bilingual Education Programs in Connecticut. Hartford, CT: Connecticut State Department of Education, Office of Research and Evaluation, 1987.

Stone, R.J. and Kinger, C.R. Effects of English/Spanish Language Pattern Differences and ESL Learners Comprehension of English Text. Paper presented at the

Annual Meeting of the National Reading
Conference, San Diego, Calif., December,
1985.

Tchaconas, T.N. Oral Reading Strategies in
Greek and English of Second Grade Bilingual
Children and Their Relationship to Field
Dependence and Field Independence.
Unpublished doctoral dissertation, Columbia
University, Teachers College, New York,
1985.

Tchaconas, T.N. and Spiridakis, J.N. "Reading
and cognitive styles of Greek bilingual
children." The Journal of the New York
State Association for Bilingual Education,
2, 1, 21-31, 1986.

Urzua, C. "A Children's Story." In Rigg, P.
and Scott Enright, D. (Eds.). Children and
ESL: Integrating Perspectives. Washington, D.C.: Teachers of English to Speakers
of Other Languages, 1986.

Wells, G. "Apprenticeship in literacy." Inter-
change, 18, 12, 109-123, 1987.

ANNOTATED BIBLIOGRAPHY

Assink, E.M.H. "Algorithms in spelling instruction: The orthography of Dutch verbs." **Journal of Educational Psychology,** 79, 3, 228-235, 1987.

Describes a large-scale field experiment aimed at improving spelling instruction in Dutch schools using a newly developed algorithm method.

Brophy, H.S.C. and Khong, N. **An Activity Book: The Fox and the Eagle. K-3 Reading, In English and Hmong.** Sacramento, Calif.: Voqui and Associates, 1985.

Hmong folktales written in English and Hmong. Narrative style provides continuity of story topic by use of pictures and summary sentences. Follow-up student activities focus on drawing and writing.

Bruder, M.N. and Henderson, R.T. **Beginning Reading in English as a Second Language.** Washington, D.C.: Center for Applied Linguistics, 1986.

Discusses theories and problems in reading in English as a Second Language. Describes methods to assess components of reading skills and offers practical suggestions for classroom reading instruction.

Cambourne, B. "Process writing and non-English speaking background children." **Austalian Journal of Reading,** 9, 3, 126-138, 1986.

Explores the consequences of not developing competence in oral forms of the second language, which, according to this author, is the intermediate step in the recommended sequence of bilingual literacy development.

Center for Language Education and Research. "Interactive writing: Making writing meaningful for language minority students." **NABE News,** 10, 1, 19-21, 1986.

Describes interactive writing methods, specifically dialogue journals, to improve language minority students' writing abilities.

Edelsky, C. **Writing in a Bilingual Program: Habia Una Vez.** Norwood, N.J.: Ablex, 1986.

Examines writing of children enrolled in a bilingual program in the Southwest that emphasized writing in the first language until literacy was well established and which attempted to offer an integrated curriculum. As a result, research findings indicate that children's spelling in both Spanish and English, their written code switches, segmentation, beginnings and endings of pieces, quality of the content of what they wrote, the relationship of first and second language writing, the role of the teacher in children's writing dispel many of the common misunderstandings about native language instruction for LEP children.

Fischer-Kohn, E. Teaching Cloze Reading for ESL/EFL: Uses and Abuses. Paper presented at the Annual Meeting of Teachers of English to Speakers of Other Languages, Anaheim, CA, March, 1986.

Describes cloze-reading techniques and detailed oral analysis of brief texts which are used to teach EFL reading in the People's Republic of China. Compares this approach with the ESL methods used in the United States which emphasize global comprehension.

Frost, R.; Katz, L.; and Bentin, S. "Strategies for visual word recognition and orthographical depth: A multilingual comparison." **Journal of Experimental Psychology**, 13, 1, 104-115, 1987.

Examines naming performance in Hebrew,
English and Serbo-Croatian to investigate
the psychological concept of orthographical
depth and its influence on visual word
recognition.

Goldman, S.R. "Transfer of knowledge between
    languages." **Focus Newsletter**, National
    Clearinghouse for Bilingual Education, 19,
    8-9, 1985.

A study that supports the transference of
reading skills from a native to a second
language in elementary school, grades K-6.
Participants were monolingual and bilingual
(English/Spanish) students attending a
bilingual program and receiving ESL
instruction; bilingual students transferred
to an English-only regular classroom; and
monolingual native English speakers learning Spanish as a second language.
Narrative reading comprehension on tasks
and follow-up oral testing of children on
recall and reading analyses skills
performed by children showed positive
transfer of knowledge and linguistic skills
in both monolingual and bilingual
children in two languages. Specific
teaching strategies aimed for young and
older children are discussed in terms of
questioning techniques and narrative
discourse reading instruction.

Goldman, S.R. and Trueba, H.T. (Eds.) **Becoming
    Literate in English as a Second Language.**
    Norwood, N.J.: Ablex, 1987.

Brings together recent empirical research
relevant to the educational experiences of
language minority students in the United
States. Discusses general issues in
literacy, its development, and adult
literacy training; discourse skills of
minority language students; and classroom
and school level interaction patterns.
Deals with the performance of children for
whom English is a second language.

Kirk, B.V. Listening Enhances Reading Comprehension for LEP Students. Paper presented at the International Bilingual Bicultural Education Conference of the National Association for Bilingual Education, March, 1987.

Discusses specific techniques to teach listening skills to LEP students aimed at increasing reading comprehension.

Lehman-Irl, D. "Early reading as a means of reinforcing and enriching the home language of a bilingual child." The Bilingual Family Newsletter, 3, 2, 5-6, 1986.

Describes case studies of bilingual preschool children who learned to read in their two languages.

McInnes, M.M. A Preliminary Report on an Investigation Using a Piagetian Model to Teach Reading to Spanish-Speaking Secondary Students. Paper presented at the Annual International Bilingual Bicultural Education Conference of the National Association for Bilingual Education, Chicago, Illinois, April, 1986.

Describes a study which focuses on content area (horizontal) reading instruction of 63 high school Spanish dominant LEP students randomly assigned to two experimental groups and two control groups. The experimental group students received instruction on how to infer main ideas from reading in English and Spanish using Piagetian classification techniques. The control students were taught in English only how to infer ideas from reading without the classification schemes. Significant gains were shown for all pupils in inference reading skills achievement, but bilingually instructed pupils showed higher gains than monolingual students. Recommendations for future studies using

Piagetian classification tasks in bilingual education has pedagogical and cross-cultural value, according to the author.

Miller, C.H. "Ready, set, write!: A teacher taps the talents of bilingual third graders." Equity and Choice, 3, 2, 3-8, 1987.

Discusses the writing process of a class of bilingual third graders learning English as a second language.

Mohan, B.A. and Au-Leung, Y. "Academic writing and Chinese students: Transfer and developmental factors." TESOL Quarterly, 19, 3, 515-534, 1985.

Discusses problems in native language interference and potential transfer learning problems in Chinese students writing English as a second language. Chinese student writing samples collected in Hong Kong and British Canada focused on three areas: contrastive analysis between Chinese and English language discourse forms, error analysis, and transfer of skills in writing (i.e., organization of content, discourse forms, etc.) from the first to the second language. Developmentally, English as a second language Chinese learners need time and exposure to culturally different discourse written patterns, but research supports transfer of writing skills from Chinese to English as a second language when based on the discourse content and form narrative, rather than at the sentence level.

Moll, L.C., Diaz, E.; Estrada, E; and Lopes, L.M. "Making Contexts: The Social Construction of Reading Lessons in Two Languages." In Saravia Shore, M. and Arvizu, S. (Eds.) Communicative and Cross Cultural Competencies: Ethnographies of Educational Programs for Language Minority Students in Community Contexts (in press).

An ethnographic study of reading instruction in a combined second and third grade
bilingual maintenance program in San Diego.
Children received reading instruction in
Spanish, their native language, and English
as a second language. The children were
sufficiently proficient in English to
participate in this dual language system.
The reading classes were videotaped.
After detailed observation of the two
reading classes, the authors noted that in
the Spanish reading lessons sophisticated,
high-level reading skills had been
developed, whereas the English reading
lessons emphasized decoding (which the
children could already do) and accurate
pronunciation. An interesting finding was
that the Spanish and English teachers were
not aware of what was occurring in the
other's classroom. This disparity in
instructional organization made the
children competent readers in Spanish, but
inadequate in English. The authors
conclude that transfer of the children's
highly developed reading skills from the
native language to English was hindered by
inconsistent teaching methods in the two
classrooms.

Oster, J. **From Reading to Writing: A Rhetoric
Reader.** Boston, MA: Little, Brown and
Company, 1987.

Presents models for teaching ESL writing to
advanced non-native English speakers at the
secondary school level. Discourse forms
and style are examined in terms of writing
purposes and constraints for second
language learners. Specific teaching
strategies and exercises are suggested.

Raines, A. Teaching Writing: What We Know and
What We Do. Paper presented at the Annual
Meeting of Teachers of English to Speakers
of Other Languages, Anaheim, Calif., March,
1986.

Describes recent research which sheds light on writing instruction in English as a second language. Focuses on contrastive rhetoric (the interference of first language rhetoric experienced by the second language learner), patterns of development in English scientific texts that cause problems for second language readers, the contrastive use of other text features, and error patterns. Reviews 10 recent writing textbooks which were found to continue with the traditional emphasis on prescribed form. According to the author this indicates that current theory about writing instruction has not been fully translated into theory of the acquisition of writing ability and instructional materials that attend to concerns about product in the context of a process approach to writing.

Saunders, G. "Teaching children to read at home: A look at some of the literature." **The Bilingual Family Newsletter**, 3, 2, 3-4, 1986.

Addresses parents who are bringing their children up bilingually and discusses methods they can use to teach reading to their children in two languages. Suggests further readings.

Thomas, M.H. and Dieter, J.N. "The positive effects of writing practice on integration of foreign words in memory." **Journal of Educational Psychology**, 79, 3, 249-253, 1987.

Investigated the effect of copying foreign language vocabulary words and/or pronouncing them aloud while attempting to learn their English counterparts. In Experiment 1, writing practice enhanced written recall of the foreign words in response to their English equivalents. Recall of the foreign words in the oral modality was not influenced by these variables. In Experiment 2, when recall of English words was measured, neither variable was found to have a significant effect. In Experiment 3, written free recall of foreign language words was found to be enhanced by writing practice, whereas associative recall, as measured by a matching test, was not reliably influenced by this variable. Results of the study support the view that copying foreign language words assists in the formation of memory codes for their written forms.

Urzua, C. "'You stopped too soon': Second language children composing and revising." TESOL Quarterly, 21, 2, 279-303, 1987.

Discusses a six-month observational study of four Southeast Asian children as they wrote and revised texts in English, their second language. The author reports that an analysis of transcripts of peer response sessions, weekly compositions, and twice-weekly dialogue journals shows important cognitive, social, and linguistic skills. By writing and revising with trusted peers, the children developed three areas of writing skill: (a) a sense of audience; (b) a sense of voice; and (c) a sense of power in language.

Williams, V. "Second phase learners: An analysis of some issues, expectations, and strategies." Australian Journal of Reading, 9, 3, 167-179, 1986.

Discusses terminology of first and second phase learners, focusing on the disadvantages experienced by the latter. Examines teacher expectations, possible areas of difficulty for students, parental involvement, teacher sensitization, pedagogical aims of a course for these students, and bilingual factors as assets.

Chapter 3

CURRENT LEGAL ISSUES IN BILINGUAL EDUCATION

Jay Heubert

INTRODUCTION

In the recent past there have been many legal developments affecting bilingual education and other services for limited-English-proficient (LEP) students in public schools.

This chapter surveys these recent developments, focusing primarily on provisions of federal law. In Part A, it discusses the equal protection clause of the Fourteenth Amendment, and the extent to which school desegregation litigation is a vehicle for obtaining educational services for LEP students. In Part B, it discusses the declining scope of protection available to LEP students under Title VI of the Civil Rights Act of 1964 (Title VI) with respect to bilingual education, ability grouping and teacher testing. In Part C, it discusses obligations of state education officials under the Equal Educational Opportunities Act (the EEOA), and a recent decision that may expand the range of remedies available under the EEOA. Part D of this chapter discusses the current status of the Bilingual Education Act, which is now up for re-authorization, and the extent to which federal funds for bilingual education must actually be used for instructional approaches that use native language instruction. Finally, Part E of this chapter discusses briefly whether the equal protection clause or other provisions of federal law provide a basis for challenging state "official English" laws.

Overall, this chapter concludes that, recent attacks on native language instruction notwithstanding, federal law remains an important source of rights for LEP students.

A. THE EQUAL PROTECTION CLAUSE

The equal protection clause of the Fourteenth Amendment to the United States Constitution provides that no state shall "deny to any person within its jurisdiction the equal protection of the laws". Courts have held that the failure of public school officials to provide bilingual education to LEP children is not, in itself, a violation of the equal protection clause (1). For reasons discussed in sections B and C of this chapter, federal civil rights statutes --Title VI of the Civil Rights Act of 1964 and especially the Equal Educational Opportunities Act-- often provide better protection to LEP students than does the equal protection clause. Nonetheless, there are several ways, discussed below, in which the equal protection clause may figure in the debate over bilingual education and improved educational opportunities for LEP children.

1. School Desegregation Litigation

One of these ways is through school desegregation litigation. Intentional segregation of public school students on the basis of national origin is a violation of the equal protection clause (2). Moreover, once deliberate segregation has been demonstrated, school officials are under an obligation to eliminate the vestiges of that segregation --continuing patterns of segregation among students and staff as well as the continuing educational deficits of minority students-- "root and branch" (3). This "affirmative duty" to eliminate the vestiges of segregation means, among other things, that public school officials may not implement even racially neutral policies if doing so will "preserve the effects" of prior illegal segregation (4).

Where there exists proof of recent unconstitutional segregation, courts have ordered desegregation of Hispanic and Anglo students and have approved bilingual education programs, taught by certified bilingual teachers, as an appropriate remedy for continuing educational vestiges of prior segregation (5).

This remains the law, and the equal protection clause still affords litigants a basis for challenging both intentional segregation and its educational consequences. In August of 1987, for example, attorneys from Multicultural Education Training and Advocacy filed a federal lawsuit against the school committee of Lowell, Massachusetts, seeking both to reduce the isolation of Hispanic, Cambodian and Laotian students in public schools there and to improve bilingual education programs for such students. This lawsuit appears to be based, in part, on the equal protection clause (6).

Where the findings of intentional segregation are more remote in time, however, courts are increasingly reluctant to find continuing constitutional violations based on either continuing patterns of segregation or continuing educational deficits among Hispanic students.

This important trend is illustrated by two recent court decisions. One, Castaneda v. Pickard (Castaneda II), (7) involved the Raymondville, Texas Independent School District (RISD). In 1972, a federal court declared that the RISD had intentionally segregated Hispanic and Anglo students. In 1983, Hispanic students challenged as unremedied vestiges of prior segregation (a) the continuing racial identifiability of a school that remained 97.9 percent Hispanic in a district that was 23 percent Anglo; and (b) an ability grouping scheme which produced a high degree of racial identifiability in the district's classrooms. Without much discussion, the court rejected both these claims. Contrary to the requirements of earlier Supreme Court decisions, the Castaneda II court did not even place on the RISD the burden of demonstrating that the patterns in question were not causally related to earlier deliberate segregation.

The Court of Appeals for the Fifth Circuit reached a similar result in United States v. LULAC (8). In LULAC, Hispanics challenged a rule requiring students at public colleges in Texas to pass a standardized test before entering undergraduate teacher training programs. In preliminary trials, 66 percent of

Hispanics and 77 percent of blacks, compared with only 27 percent of Anglos, failed the test. One ground for the challenge was that high failure rates for minority students would drastically reduce the number of minority teachers, in violation of a 1971 desegregation order requiring Texas to "obliterate all remaining vestiges of the former[ly segregated] system ... and ... to achieve racially integrated schools, including fully integrated facilities and staff". The Court of Appeals rejected this challenge. It held, in effect, that the 1971 order imposed no special duty on Texas to avoid a drastic reduction in minority teachers in 1986.

Castaneda II, LULAC and other decisions like it (9) suggest that there will be fewer and fewer situations in which findings of unconstitutional segregation --at least those made in the early 1970s, when most desegregation cases were filed-- will provide grounds in 1987 and beyond for challenging racially identifiable schools, student assignment patterns that produce racially identifiable classrooms or tests that threaten to decimate the ranks of minority teachers. If federal courts are less inclined to attribute present educational problems to past illegal segregation, there will be fewer instances in which judges see a need for educational remedies, such as bilingual education for LEP students, as part of court-ordered desegregation.

On the other hand, the last year has seen some noteworthy voluntary efforts to combine desegregation with improved educational services for LEP children. In February of 1987, for example, the school committee of Fall River, Massachusetts voluntarily adopted a plan, believed to be the first in the nation, to desegregate its students on the basis of language rather than race. The purpose of the plan was to reduce the concentration of language-minority students --chiefly LEP students of Portuguese background-- in schools considered less desirable. Under the plan, which uses a strategy called "controlled choice", language-minority students may enroll at any school in the district rather than being

limited to their neighborhood schools. The
district will also begin parent education
programs and improve schools that have, until
now, been serving mostly language-minority
students (10). This appears to be a promising
development for LEP children.

2. Other Equal Protection Issues

Outside the realm of school desegregation
litigation, court decisions, some quite recent,
suggest several other ways in which the equal
protection clause of the Fourteenth Amendment
may figure in the debate over bilingual education and improved educational opportunities for
LEP children. First, in <u>Olagues v. Russoniello</u>
(11), a 1986 decision, the Court of Appeals
for the Ninth Circuit declared unconstitutional
a governmental action that singled out and
disadvantaged LEP persons. Second, earlier
Supreme Court decisions have held that
governmental action violates the equal
protection clause if (a) it is motivated, at
least in part, by an intent to discriminate
(12), (b) it alters the political process so as
to hinder efforts by minority groups to protect
and advance their interests, (13) and/or (2) it
is arbitrary and capricious.
     Laws, rules and policies that burden LEP
students may be unconstitutional in one or more
of these ways. These issues are discussed more
fully in the section below on "official
English".

B. TITLE VI OF THE CIVIL RIGHTS ACT OF 1964

1. Overview

Title VI of the Civil Rights Act of 1964
was the basis of the Supreme Court's famous
decision in <u>Lau v. Nichols</u> (14), which greatly
increased public awareness of and concern for
the educational needs of LEP students. It was
also the legal authority for the "Lau
Guidelines", used for years to assess the
adequacy of public school programs for LEP

students.   As recent court decisions demonstrate, however, Title VI is no longer as
important a factor as other provisions of
federal law --notably the Equal Educational
Opportunities Act, discussed in Section C
below-- in efforts to improve educational
services for LEP students. The discussion below
surveys recent developments under Title VI. It
also points out that a new administration in
Washington, D.C. could greatly enhance the
importance of Title VI by promulgating new
regulations that define broadly the rights of
LEP students under Title VI.
    The text of Title VI of the Civil Rights
Act of 1964 is as follows:

> No   person in the United States
> shall, on the ground of race, color,
> or national origin, be excluded from
> participation in, be denied the
> benefits of, or be subjected to
> discrimination under any program or
> activity receiving Federal financial
> assistance (15).

    The Supreme Court's 1974 decision in
Lau established several important principles.
One was that a violation of Title VI could be
established without proof that the defendant had
acted with intent to discriminate; for Title VI
purposes, the Supreme Court ruled, it was
sufficient to demonstrate that the challenged
policy or action had a discriminatory --i.e.,
disproportionate-- adverse effect. In this
respect, the requirements of Title VI are easier
for a plaintiff to satisfy than those of the
equal protection clause. Second, the Court
ruled that LEP children were, in fact, denied
equal educational opportunity when school
officials took no steps whatever to help those
children participate meaningfully in the public
school program (16).

2. The Evolving Legal Standard

    The Supreme Court expressly declined to
prescribe a remedy for the type of unequal
opportunity present in Lau (17), but the U.S.

Department of Health, Education and Welfare (now
the Department of Education) adopted guidelines
(18) to use in assessing the adequacy of
educational services for LEP students. These
guidelines prescribed a transitional bilingual-
bicultural education for LEPs (19). In 1980,
having negotiated some 360 "Lau" plans to remedy
past discrimination, the Department of Education
proposed formal regulations that would have
required bilingual instruction in any public
school enrolling 20 or more LEP children with
the same native language (20).

These activities were all based on the
Department of Education's authority to monitor
compliance with Title VI. Several developments,
however, undermined efforts to use Title VI as a
vehicle for obtaining educational services for
LEP students.

First, in 1978 the Supreme Court called
into question the "effect" standard it had
approved in Lau, and upon which federal
regulations were based (21). This issue was only
resolved in 1983, when the Supreme Court, in a
case known as Guardians, narrowly upheld the
validity of Title VI regulations based on an
effect standard (22). In the intervening five
years, however, many lower courts ruled against
LEP students whose Title VI claims did not
include allegations of intentional discrimination (23).

Second, the Department of Education's
proposed regulations on bilingual education,
which had generated considerable opposition even
while President Carter remained in office, were
withdrawn soon after the Reagan administration
arrived in Washington, D.C. Thereafter, the
pace of the government's Title VI enforcement
efforts slowed considerably.

Third, a 1984 Supreme Court decision
greatly narrowed the scope of Title VI and two
other federal civil rights statutes. In Grove
City College v. Bell (24), the high court ruled
that the antidiscrimination provisions of Title
VI apply only to the actual programs or
activities that receive federal funds. Thus,
Title VI continues to protect LEP students who
receive services through Chapter 1, the
Bilingual Education Act or other federally

funded programs, but no longer protects LEP
students who do not receive services purchased
with federal funds (25). As a result of
Grove City, those who enforce Title VI are
spending more time deciding which exact "program
or activity" is receiving federal funds and less
time actually fighting discrimination (26).

For all these reasons, Title VI has
become less important to those who seek to
address the educational needs of LEP students.

3. Recent Legal Developments

Though the trend is not irreversible,
recent legal developments tend to confirm the
declining importance of Title VI.

First, and perhaps most significant, there
has been no recent court decision in which
courts have relied on Title VI in ordering
educational services for LEP students. In
Castaneda v. Pickard (Castaneda II) (27) a 1986
decision, the court upheld under Title VI an
ability grouping plan that resulted in the
isolation of LEP students. The court apparently
assumed that Title VI, like the equal protection
clause, embodies an "intent" standard. In view
of the Supreme Court's 1983 ruling in Guardians
(described above), upholding an "effect"
standard under Title VI regulations, the court
in Castaneda II apparently erred in failing to
consider whether the ability grouping plan at
issue had the effect of discriminating (28).
In two 1987 decisions, both involving suits
brought by LEP students, courts recognized an
effect standard under Title VI but focused
primarily on the relief available to LEP
children under the Equal Educational Opportunities Act. These decisions, Gomez v.
Illinois State Board of Education (29) and
Teresa P. v. Berkeley Unified School District
(30), are discussed in section C below.

Second, in cases not brought by LEP
students, courts have interpreted Title VI
narrowly with respect to such issues as ability
grouping, placement of minority children in
classes for the mentally handicapped, and
teacher testing. For example, in Georgia State
Conference of NAACPs v. State of Georgia (31),

the court ruled that there was no Title VI
violation where disproportionately high numbers
of black children were placed in low-track
classes and classes for the mentally
handicapped. The court recognized that Title VI
has an effect standard, but ruled that the
placement schemes at issue were justified
--notwithstanding their discriminatory effect--
by "educational necessity". This finding of
"educational necessity" was based primarily on
the fact that many other school districts
classify students in the same ways (32).

In United States v. LULAC (33), a teacher
testing case described in section A above, the
court reached a similar result. The court
recognized that Title VI has an effect standard.
It also noted that the test --one to screen
students wishing to enter undergraduate teacher
training programs-- had a highly disproportionate adverse impact on Hispanics and blacks.
The court did not, however, place on the
defendants the burden of justifying use of the
test as the sole criterion for selecting teacher
trainees (34). This case is still pending.
Like Castaneda II and Georgia Conference of
NAACPs, however, it suggests that Title VI
offers only limited protection to LEP students
and other minority group plaintiffs.

That said, the decline of Title VI may not
be irreversible. First, Congress is now
considering legislation that would effectively
overrule Grove City and extend coverage of Title
VI to all activities of a federal fund
recipient. While action is not imminent (35),
the proposed "Civil Rights Restoration Act" has
broad support in Congress. Such action would
not, however, alter the results in Castaneda II,
Georgia Conference of NAACPs or LULAC.

A second development, which could greatly
expand the rights of LEP students under Title
VI, would be the adoption of new Title VI
regulations specifically addressing the
educational needs of LEP students. After
Guardians, courts would probably uphold
regulations that made clearer the requirements
of Title VI with respect to (1) services school
districts should provide to LEP students and (2)
legal standards courts should use in reviewing

testing mechanisms that disproportionately burden LEP students or minority students generally. It is unlikely that the Department of Education would promulgate such regulations in the present political climate. If the climate changes, however, Title VI could acquire new significance for LEP students. For the present, LEP students must rely principally upon the Equal Educational Opportunities Act, which is discussed in the section that follows.

C. THE EQUAL EDUCATIONAL OPPORTUNITIES ACT

1. Overview

At present, the federal law that protects most extensively the educational interests of LEP children is the Equal Educational Opportunities Act (EEOA). The pertinent language of the EEOA is as follows:

> No State shall deny equal educational opportunity to an individual on account of his or her race, color, sex, or national origin by ....
> (f) the failure by an educational agency to take appropriate steps to overcome language barriers that impede equal participation by its students in its instructional programs (36).

The EEOA was enacted primarily with the purpose of minimizing busing as a remedy in school desegregation cases. Not surprisingly, therefore, Congress said little or nothing about what it intended to accomplish for LEP children through the EEOA. Judicial interpretations of the EEOA, however --including important decisions in 1987-- have made it an important source of federal rights for LEP children in public schools.

This importance is due to several factors. First, the EEOA's coverage is fairly broad. Unlike Title VI, discussed in the preceding section, the EEOA's coverage is not limited to programs or activities that receive federal financial assistance.

As discussed more fully below, all activities of state and local education officials are subject to the EEOA. Second, violations of the EEOA can be demonstrated more easily than can violations of other federal civil rights provisions. Unlike the equal protection clause, also discussed above, violations of the EEOA can be established without proof that LEP students have been the victims of intentional discrimination on the part of school officials. The "intent" requirement, often a significant obstacle to plaintiffs in civil rights actions, is simply not an issue under the EEOA. Finally, the ultimate measure of compliance with the EEOA --whether educational programs are actually enabling LEP students to overcome their language barriers-- is an educational outcome standard that affords broader protection than many other civil rights provisions.

2. The Evolving Legal Standard

The actual legal standard for EEOA cases, first established in such earlier cases as <u>Castaneda v. Pickard (Castaneda I)</u> (37) and <u>Keyes v. Denver School District No. 1</u> (38), has recently been reaffirmed --and in some respects extended-- by the Court of Appeals for the Seventh Circuit in <u>Gomez</u> (39). These decisions are discussed below. Each part of the legal standard for EEOA cases is discussed separately.

a. Is the theory acceptable?

Under the three-part test, the first inquiry concerns the <u>theory</u> upon which the educational program for LEP children is based. "The court's responsibility in this regard is to ascertain whether a school system is pursuing a program [of instruction for LEPs] informed by an educational theory recognized as sound [or at least legitimate] by experts in the field" (40). This inquiry is a narrow one; courts have shown great deference to educators on theoretical matters. As the <u>Gomez</u> court put it, "[o]ur function is not to resolve disputes among competing bodies of expert educational opinion.

So long as the chosen theory is sound, we must
defer to the judgment of the educational
agencies in adopting that theory, even though
other theories may also seem appropriate" (41).
    In Gomez, a 1987 case, school officials had
no trouble satisfying this requirement. Given
the sharp and continuing disputes among scholars
about appropriate instructional strategies for
LEP students, it is unlikely, at least for the
foreseeable future, that LEP students will
succeed in invalidating on theoretical grounds
whatever instructional approach(es) --immersion,
ESL, transitional bilingual education, or bilingual-bicultural maintenance-- a school district
uses to serve LEP students.

    b. Are the programs used reasonably calcu-
    lated to implement the educational theory
    effectively?

    The second inquiry courts make under the
EEOA is "whether the programs actually used ....
are reasonably calculated to implement
effectively the educational theory adopted
....." (42). The issue here is often one of
resources: Can school officials put their theory
into practice with the resources they have made
available? On this question --unlike that of
what theory is most sound-- courts have been
less reluctant to find violations of the EEOA.
    Two early cases are instructive in this
regard. In Castaneda I, the Court of Appeals
for the Fifth Circuit found two respects in
which there was inadequate implementation of
programs for LEP children, in violation of the
EEOA. One deficiency was that many "bilingual"
teachers were not actually bilingual; the court
ruled that the school district, in violation of
the EEOA, had made inadequate efforts "to
overcome the language barriers confronting
teachers assigned to the bilingual program"
(43). The second deficiency was that LEP children receiving bilingual instruction were being
tested and evaluated using English- language
standardized tests. The court ruled that the
district, having adopted a bilingual approach

to serving LEP children, was obliged under   the
EEOA to   use Spanish-language   achievement tests
to assess the progress of LEP children (44).

Similarly, in <u>Keyes</u>, a district court found
the   following   implementation   problems   with
Denver's programs for LEP students: inadequate
bilingual   skills   on   the   part   of "bilingual"
teachers,   seniority   rules   that   prevented
bilingual teachers from being assigned to teach
LEP   students,   inadequate   training   of ESL
teachers, failure to provide all LEP students
with   instruction   tailored   to   their   special
needs, insufficient time (40 minutes per day)
spent by LEP students in ESL classes, and
failure to measure adequately the impact of
programs   for LEP students (45).   In both
<u>Castaneda I</u> and <u>Keyes</u>, the defendant school
districts were ordered to modify their programs
for LEP students to address these inadequacies
(46).   Other   districts   in   which   such
inadequacies exist are also vulnerable to suit
under the EEOA.

The   1987   decision in <u>Gomez</u> clarifies and
expands   in   important   ways   the   duty   of
educational   officials to   implement effectively
whatever   educational theory   they   are using as
the basis for services to LEP students.

In <u>Gomez</u>, the court asked what obligation
the EEOA imposes on state --as opposed to
local-- educational agencies for the implementation of programs designed to provide LEP
children with an equal educational opportunity
(47).   This is a significant question.   The
likelihood of obtaining adequate services for
LEP children is almost certainly greater if
state   departments   of   education   enforce
provisions of the EEOA, rather than leaving to
private   litigators   the   responsibility   for
seeking enforcement.   Similarly, the task for
LEP advocates is simplified somewhat, if
statewide   improvements   in   service   for   LEP
children can be obtained through a single
lawsuit against state and local educational
officials rather than through multiple suits
against different school districts.

The _Gomez_ court ruled that the obligation to take "appropriate action" to overcome language barriers is one that falls on state as well as local educational agencies: "[The EEOA] requires that state, as well as local, agencies ensure that the needs of LEP children are met" (48).

The _Gomez_ court also undertook to define, at least in broad terms, what would constitute "appropriate action" on the part of state officials. First, noting that "appropriate action" must mean "something more than 'no action'", the court indicated that state agencies "cannot, in the guise of deferring to local conditions, completely delegate in practice their obligations under the EEOA" (49). Further, while declining to define precisely the duties of state education officials under the EEOA, the court indicated that state officials --at least where they have authority under state law to supervise local school districts-- must establish and enforce "minimums for the implementation of language remediation programs" (50). The Court of Appeals, remanding the case, ordered the district court to determine whether state regulations governing programs for LEP students --and state enforcement of those regulations-- satisfy the state's duty to implement effectively whatever educational theory they have adopted as the basis for serving LEP students. For reasons noted above, these are promising developments for LEP students and their advocates, in Illinois and elsewhere.

c. Are language barriers actually being overcome?

The third inquiry under the EEOA is whether a program --even one based on an accepted theory and adequately implemented-- is actually succeeding at reducing language barriers for LEP students. As the _Gomez_ court put it, "[j]udicial deference to the school system is unwarranted if over a certain period the system has failed to make substantial progress in correcting the language deficiencies of its students" (51). This is a

remarkable standard. In no other federal
civil rights provision is compliance ultimately
dependent upon the achievement of satisfactory
educational outcomes by those the provision
protects.

That said, there has been no reported
decision in which a court has even gotten to the
third part of the test, in which satisfactory
achievement by LEP students is the measure of
compliance with the EEOA. In Castaneda I, Keyes
and Gomez, problems at stage two --whether
school officials were implementing their theory
adequately-- made it unnecessary for courts to
reach stage three. It is premature, therefore,
to speculate on what may happen if and when a
court actually reaches this step in considering
claims under the EEOA. At the same time, for
reasons discussed more fully in sections below,
the third part of the EEOA standard may figure
in challenges to legal provisions declaring
English the official language of a state.

3. Other Developments Under the EEOA

Law under the EEOA has developed in several
other important ways not already discussed
above.

First, the Gomez court ruled that the
Eleventh Amendment to the United States
Constitution does not bar suits against states
under the EEOA. This ruling was based on the
assumption (1) that Congress has authority under
the Fourteenth Amendment to abrogate Eleventh
Amendment immunity if it expresses a clear
intent to do so; and (2) that Congress, which
refers in the EEOA itself to what "no State"
shall do, must have intended to subject states
to suit under the EEOA (52). This is an
important ruling. Had the court ruled otherwise,
it could not have held, as it did, that the EEOA
"requires that state, as well as local agencies
ensure that the needs of LEP children are
met"(53).

Second, the decision in Teresa P. seems to
expand in an important way the remedies
available to LEP children who demonstrate
violations of the EEOA. In Castaneda I, Keyes
and Gomez, where courts found violations of the

EEOA they ordered public school officials to improve in-school services for LEP students. In Teresa P., however, the court went further, stating that "students seeking relief for inadequate or inappropriate language programs that deny them equal educational opportunity may seek essential corrective relief [such as] reimbursement for private tutoring in academic subjects" (54). This is quite significant. Where EEOA violations cause continuing educational problems for LEP children, those children may now be able to obtain private remedial services, at the expense of the offending educational agency, to address those problems. Teresa P. thus provides public school officials with an additional --financial-- incentive to operate effective programs for LEP children. It is also the first judicial declaration that the EEOA may give rise to remedies for individual students rather than merely programmatic improvements; this too is noteworthy (55).

For all these reasons, the EEOA is almost certainly the federal law that protects most extensively the educational interests of LEP children. Its importance, moreover, is increasing as a result of the legal developments described above.

D. THE BILINGUAL EDUCATION ACT

1. Background

Title VII of the Elementary and Secondary Education Act, a federal statute also known as "The Bilingual Education Act", is less a civil rights law than a vehicle for providing federal funds to programs designed to address the unique educational needs of LEP students.

Since Title VII's original enactment in 1968, there have been vigorous debates over two central issues. The first is funding. Funding grew from $7.5 million in school year 1969-70 to $167 million in 1980-81. Then, even as the estimated number of eligible LEP children was rising sharply (56), funding declined to $133 million in 1986-87.

The second conflict has been over the extent to which Title VII funds should be earmarked for programs emphasizing native-language instruction. Despite its names the original Bilingual Education Act did not require bilingual education. Since 1974, however, when Congress reauthorized Title VII, the law has required programs receiving federal grants to include instruction in the LEP children's native language and culture. Title VII was last reauthorized in 1984. At that time, despite the Reagan administration's strong opposition to Title VII's emphasis on native-language instruction, the new law said that no more than 4 percent of Title VII funds could be used for programs not using native language instruction (57). Moreover, the new law prohibited the United States Department of Education "from redefining transitional bilingual education, which mandates native-language instruction 'to the extent necessary for LEP students to achieve grade promotion and graduation standards'" (58).

In response to this Congressional action, Education Secretary Bennett, who took office in 1985, notified school districts across the country that they were free --even if he was not-- to reinterpret what is meant by "transitional bilingual education." He also wrote to some 500 school districts that had written agreements with the Department of Education to provide bilingual services to LEP students. Bennett offered to renegotiate these agreements. Only 15 of these districts responded, some only to say they hoped to expand programs involving native-language instruction (59).

2. Current status

In 1987 the Bilingual Education Act is once again up for reauthorization. On May 22, 1987, the House of Representatives, by a vote of 401 to 1, passed HR-5, the omnibus "School Improvement Act of 1987," which includes a new Title VII. Under this House measure, funding for native-language instruction and for English-only instructional approaches would remain the same as under the 1984 bill, apart

from adjustments for inflation.   If funding did
increase, however, the bill would direct 70 to
75 percent of the new funding to English-only
instructional approaches --"special alternative
instructional programs," or "SAIPs," in the
jargon of the bill-- with only 25 to 30 percent
going to programs emphasizing bilingual methods
of instruction.   Hispanic members of the House
Education and Labor Committee objected strongly
to this modification (60).

The   Senate has not yet taken up the
reauthorization of Title VII, and is unlikely to
do so before the 100th Congress, which convenes
in 1988.   On May 20, 1987, however, the Senate
Labor and Human Resources Committee reported out
S. 1238, which, if enacted into law, would amend
Title VII.   The Senate bill would do less than
HR-5 to ensure that future federal funding for
bilingual programs is not reduced.   It would
also put pressure on school districts to move
children through bilingual programs more quickly
than at present;   a LEP student could remain in
a bilingual program longer than three years only
if the school evaluated the student and found
that failure to master English continues to
impede the student's academic progress (61). In
no event could Title VII funds be spent on a
student who has spent more than five years in a
class where there is native language
instruction.   Bill S. 1238 is now before the
full Senate.

Neither HR-5 nor S. 1238 is yet law, but
both seem to reflect an emerging consensus on
two points.   One is the desire to maintain
present federal funding levels for programs that
involve native-language instruction.   This is
encouraging in one sense;   opponents of
native-language instruction have failed in their
concerted effort to eliminate federal funding
for bilingual programs.   It is also
discouraging, however; there seems to be little
likelihood of restoring to the Title VII budget
what has been cut since 1980-81 or of securing
federal funding adequate to serve the rapidly
increasing numbers of eligible LEP children.

A second trend, evident in HR-5 and, to a
lesser extent, in S. 1238, is to increase
federal funds to English-only programs for LEP

students. This is encouraging in one sense. As
things now stand, funding for English-only
approaches will be increased only if overall
federal expenditures under Title VII exceed
present levels. For this reason, advocates of
English only instruction, including the Reagan
administration,   may   become   advocates   of
increased appropriations for Title VII.   It is
at least possible, therefore, that the upshot
will be greater federal resources available to
address the educational needs of LEP students.
On   the   other   hand,   Congress's   apparent
willingness to fund English-only alternatives
may   help fuel   attacks   on native-language
instruction.

      For these reasons, the controversies that
have   surrounded Title VII since its inception
--over funding levels and over the extent to
which Title VII funds should be earmarked for
programs   emphasizing   native-language instruc-
tion-- remain live issues today.

      E. FEDERAL LIMITS ON "OFFICIAL ENGLISH"

      1. Overview

      In   recent   years,   there   have   been
efforts in at least 37 states --and successful
efforts in at least twelve-- to enact provisions
declaring English "the official language" (62).
Of the twelve, some states have enacted official
English provisions through legislation, some by
amending their state constitutions, and some
through voter referendum.

      While these provisions vary from state to
state, there appear to be certain questions
common to all.   First, proponents of the
measures seem to share a concern that recent
immigrants, aided by government programs for LEP
persons,   are   not   learning   English   and
assimilating into the American mainstream
quickly enough.   Second, many opponents of the
measures share the belief that official English
provisions are motivated by animosity toward
national-origin minorities, and fear that

enactment of such provisions will lead to curtailment of bilingual services for LEP persons.

In most, if not all, of the states in question, it is still too early to determine what legal and practical effects these new provisions will have (63). It is not premature, however, to ask whether an official English provision that did require school districts to eliminate native-language instruction for LEP students would violate federal law (64).

That is the question considered below. The discussion that follows will consider first whether an official English provision requiring curtailment of bilingual services to LEP students would violate federal statutes: Title VI, the EEOA and/or the Bilingual Education Act. Next it considers briefly the legal questions that official English provisions raise under the equal protection clause (65).

2. Federal Statutes

Title VI, the EEOA and the Bilingual Education Act all offer possible --though not strong-- grounds for challenging official English provisions that bar native-language instruction.

As noted in Part B above, the Supreme Court ruled in _Lau_ that school districts are not required under Title VI to furnish LEP students with bilingual education. It appears, therefore, that Title VI does not at present constitute an obstacle to implementation of official English provisions that limit or prohibit native-language instruction. At the same time, however, the _Guardians_ decision recognizes the authority of the federal government to adopt regulations that go beyond Title VI itself in advancing the objectives of Title VI. For this reason, properly promulgated Title VI regulations that required bilingual education for some or all LEP students --or required that native language instruction be one option available to local educators-- would almost certainly be valid. Once enacted, such regulations would render invalid any provision of state law to the contrary, at least in programs or activities receiving federal financial assistance (66).

The EEOA could also furnish a basis for challenging state official English provisions. As noted in Part C above, courts have fashioned a three-part test in considering claims under the EEOA. Under the first part of this test -- whether services for LEP students are based on an acceptable theory-- courts are unlikely to question the judgment of educators. Therefore, if educators indicate a preference for instructional methods that do not entail native-language instruction, it is unlikely that courts will question it. If, however, local or state education officials --notwithstanding an official English provision to the contrary -- expressed an educational preference for native language instruction, it is possible that courts would respect that educational judgment and require bilingual education as a matter of federal law. Similarly, if the federal government adopted regulations under the EEOA --either requiring bilingual education or requiring that educators decide what instruc-tional strategy would be most appropriate-- a state official English provision to the contrary would be invalid. Finally, the third part of the test under the EEOA asks whether programs for LEP children are actually working. As noted in Part C, no court has yet decided an EEOA case on this ground. If over time, however, a state's immersion or other English-only techniques did not enable LEP students to overcome their language barriers, a court, as a matter of federal law under the EEOA, might order the state or a school district to provide native-language instruction to LEP students.

The Bilingual Education Act (Title VII) does not appear to prevent a state or school district from relying exclusively on English-only instruction for LEP students. In its present form, Title VII expresses a preference for bilingual education, stating that only four percent of Title VII funds may be used in programs that do not use native language instruction (67). For this reason, a state or

district that relied exclusively on English-only
approaches in serving LEP students would be
ineligible for most Title VII funds. There is no
apparent reason, however, why states and
districts prepared to forgo Title VII funds
could not rely exclusively on English-only
instruction.

3. The Equal Protection Clause

As noted in Part A above, the equal
protection clause of the Fourteenth Amendment
provides several grounds on which to challenge
official English provisions that bar native-
language instruction. Since a recent Harvard
Law Review article (68) considers these issues
in some detail, the discussion here will be
brief.

One basis for challenging official English
provisions under the equal protection clause is
furnished by a 1986 decision of the United
States Court of Appeals for the Ninth Circuit,
which includes California. _Olagues v._
Russoniello (69) was brought by organizations
promoting the voting rights of Chinese Americans
and Hispanic Americans in the San Francisco
area. These organizations challenged an
investigation of alleged vote fraud, initiated
by the local United States Attorney shortly
before a deadline for voter registration, that
focused solely on foreign-born voters who had
requested bilingual ballots. The Court of
Appeals, by a vote of six to five, ruled that
the investigation had violated the equal
protection clause. In so doing, the court
stopped short of saying that any governmental
action that burdens only LEP persons would be
unconstitutional (70). The court did, however,
liken the investigation in _Olagues_ --which
singled out foreign-born, recently-registered,
LEP voters-- to plainly unconstitutional
governmental actions, such as those that
single out members of racial or national-origin
minority groups for special, discriminatory
treatment. Since LEP students share many of
the characteristics of the plaintiffs in
Olagues, the decision is one that could also

apply where LEP students challenge official
English provisions that bar native language
instruction (71).

Official English provisions are also
subject to challenge under the equal protection
clause on the grounds that they are motivated,
at least in part, by a desire to harm LEP
persons or the national-origin minority groups
to which they belong (72). Such intent is not
easy to prove, however; the disproportionate
impact of official English provisions on LEP
persons would not, by itself, be enough (73).
Second, even if LEP advocates could show that
leading proponents of official English
provisions were motivated by racial animus,
which would not be easy in most situations, it
would be even harder to establish that members
of a legislature or, in the case of an official
English provision adopted by referendum, the
voting public at large had acted based on an
intent to discriminate. Thus, while it may be
possible under specific circumstances to furnish
adequate evidence of such invidious intent (74),
it is unlikely that many courts will strike down
official English provisions as intentionally
discriminatory.

Official English provisions are subject to
challenge under the equal protection clause on a
third ground: that they "distort governmental
processes in such a way as to place special
burdens on the ability of minority groups to
achieve beneficial legislation" (75). Thus,
"[i]f a court finds that a state's
official-English declaration is designed to
impair the ability of language minorities to
pursue their interests in the political process,
it too should invalidate the declaration insofar
as it 'seriously curtail[s] the operation of
those political processes ordinarily to be
relied upon to protect minorities'" (76).
Official English provisions adopted through
referendum are subject to challenge on a related
but distinct ground. The referendum process
itself may sometimes be suspect, especially
where the referendum concerns a matter of
special interest to members of minority groups.
It is potentially suspect because it circumvents
the procedures --including those that protect
minority interests-- by which governmental

decisions are customarily made and may thereby make it easier for majorities to take advantage of minorities (77). For this reason, official English provisions adopted by referendum could be challenged successfully if its LEP advocates could show that the purpose of the referendum was to distort the political process to the detriment of LEP students.

Official English provisions can be also challenged under the equal protection clause, at least in theory, on the ground that such provisions are not rationally related to the attainment of a legitimate governmental objective. This is not an approach likely to succeed. The stated objective of official English provisions --to help LEPs learn English and enter the mainstream more quickly-- is plainly a legitimate one. And while proponents of bilingual education regard English-only instructional methods as unwise, even unhealthy, it would be difficult to persuade a court that such approaches were wholly without rational basis. An equal protection challenge on this ground would, therefore, be unlikely to succeed.

In sum, there are several grounds, some more promising than others, on which official English provisions are subject to challenge under the equal protection clause of the Fourteenth Amendment.

CONCLUSION

The conclusion of this legal update is that provisions of federal law --the equal protection clause, Title VI, the Equal Educational Opportunities Act and the Bilingual Education Act-- continue to protect in important ways the educational interests of LEP students. Each of these provisions is evolving, moreover, in ways that already affect LEP students in important ways. As a result of recent court decisions, the Equal Educational Opportunities Act is now the provision of federal law that best protects the educational interests of LEP students. Title VI, once the key provision of federal law for LEP students, has become less important, but this may change if the Civil

Rights Restoration Act were enacted and the
Department of Education promulgated new Title VI
regulations covering services for LEP students.
Finally, each of these provisions of federal
law may provide some basis for challenging
state official English provisions that serve to
curtail bilingual education for LEP children.

NOTES

1. In <u>Guadalupe Org., Inc. v. Tempe Elementary School District No. 3</u>, 587 F.2d 1022, 1024 (9th Cir. 1978), the Court of Appeals for the Ninth Circuit ruled "that the Constitution neither requires nor prohibits ... bilingual and bicultural education."

2. <u>See Keyes v. Denver School District No. 1</u> 413 U.S. 189, 195-198 (1973).

3. <u>See Green v. New Kent County School Board</u>, 391 U.S. 430 (1968) and <u>Milliken v. Bradley</u> <u>("Milliken II")</u>, 433 U.S. 267 (1977).

4. <u>See McNeal v. Tate County School District</u>, 508 F. 2d 1017, 1020-1021 (5th Cir. 1975) and <u>Debra P. v. Turlington</u>, 644 F. 2d 347 (5th Cir. 1981).

5. <u>See Keyes v. Denver School District No. 1</u>, 575 F. Supp. 1503, 1520 (D. Colo. 1983).

6. <u>See</u>, e.g., Britton, "Minority parents file class action suit against city over desegregation proposal." <u>The Sun</u>, August 7, 1987.

7. 781 F.2d 456 (5th Cir. 1986).

8. No 85-2579, Slip Op. (5th Cir. July 1, 1986) (clarification of Part VIII filed September 2, 1986).

9. <u>See</u>, e.g., <u>Georgia Conference of NAACPs v. State of Georgia</u>, 775 F. 2d 1403 (11th Cir. 1985).

10. Snider, "Massachusetts District Backs Plan to Integrate Its Students on Basis of Language, Not Race." <u>Education Week</u>, February 11, 1987, pp. 1 and 15.

11. 797 F.2d 1511 (9th Cir. 1986) (<u>en banc</u>).

12. See e.g., <u>Washington v. Davis</u>, 426 U.S. 229 (1976) and <u>Personnel Administrator of Massachusetts v. Feeney</u>, 442 U.S. 256 (1979).

13. See e.g., <u>Washington v. Seattle School District No. 1</u>, 458 U.S. 457 (1982) and <u>Hunter v. Erickson</u>, 393 U.S. 385 (1969).

14. 414 U.S. 563 (1974).

15. 42 U.S.C. sections 2000 d to 2000d-6.

16. <u>Lau v. Nichols</u>, note 13 <u>supra</u>, 414 U.S. at 568.

17. As the Court put it, "[t]eaching English to the students of Chinese ancestry who do not speak the [English] language is one choice. Giving instruction to this group in Chinese is another. There may be others...." <u>Id.</u>

18. These guidelines were never adopted formally, and hence did not carry the force of law.

19. See Sacken, "A Choice for the People to Make: The Necessity of Legislative Reform of Arizona's Bilingual Education Policy." 26 <u>Ariz. L. Rev.</u> 81, 84-85 (1984).

20. See Crawford, "Bilingual Policy Has Taken Shape Along Two Distinct Federal Tracks." <u>Education Week</u>, April 1, 1987, pp. 21-25.

21. See e.g., <u>Regents of the University of California v. Bakke</u>, 438 U.S. 265 (1977).

22. The decision in question is <u>Guardians Ass'n of New York City v. Civil Service</u>, 103 S. Ct. 3221 (1983). In <u>Guardians</u>, the Supreme Court held, by a vote of five to four, that Title VI <u>itself</u>, like the equal protection clause, requires proof of discriminatory intent. The Court also held, however, by the same vote, that Title VI <u>regulations</u> -- which are based on an <u>effect</u> standard -- are also valid. This unusual and important decision permits

federal agencies with Title VI enforcement authority to go beyond the statute itself in advancing the objectives of Title VI.

23. See e.g., Castaneda v. Pickard, 648 F.2d 989 (5th Cir. 1981).

24. 104 S. Ct. 1211 (1984).

25. Grove City is in marked contrast to Lau itself. In Lau, the Supreme Court assumed that all activities of a federal fund recipient were subject to Title VI: "[Title VI] bans discrimination in ... any program or activity receiving Federal financial assistance. The school district involved in this litigation receives large amounts of federal financial assistance."

26. For an analysis of Grove City's impact, see ACLU and NAACP Legal Defense and Educational Fund, Justice Denied: The loss of Civil Rights after the Grove City College Decision (March 1986).

27. Castaneda v. Pickard, 648 F.2d 456 (5th Cir. 1986).

28. Id. at 462-463.

29. 811 F.2d 1030 (7th Cir. 1987).

30. No. C-87-2396 DLJ, Memorandum Decision and Order (N.D. Cal. September 8, 1987).

31. 775 F.2d 1403 (11th Cir. 1985).

32. Id. at 1417-1418. The court was correct to insist that defendants justify their actions as educationally necessary. What is remarkable is that the court was so easily persuaded that ability grouping is, in fact, an educational necessity. In any event, this decision appears to foreclose most challenges to ability grouping schemes that have racially disproportionate impact.

33. No. 85-2579, Slip Op. (5th Cir. July 1, 1986) (clarification of Part VIII filed September 2, 1986).

34. Id. at 7013-7014. Instead, the court ruled that liability under Title VI hinged almost entirely on whether the test was valid. The court did not ask, as it might have, whether the test was educationally necessary, or whether there existed other screening mechanisms that have less disproportionate impact.

35. On September 8, 1987, the New York Times reported that there would be no action on such proposals before Congress reconvenes in 1988.

36. The EEOA is codified at 20 U.S.C. sections 1703 et seq.

37. Castaneda v. Pickard, note 23 supra, 648 F.2d 989.

38. Keyes v. Denver School District No. 1, note 5 supra, 575F. Supp.1503.

39. Gomez v. Illinois State Board of Education, note 29 supra, 811 F.2d 1030.

40. Id. at 1041.

41. Id.

42. Id. at 1041-1042 (emphasis added).

43. Castaneda v. Pickard, note 23 supra 648 F. 2d at 993.

44. Id.

45. Keyes v. Denver School District No. 1, note 5 supra, 576 F. Supp at 1517-1519.

46. In Castaneda II, note 27 supra, 781 F.2d at 470-471, the Court of Appeals for the Fifth Circuit upheld a district court's finding that problems identified in Castaneda

I had been addressed adequately where 16 of
27 newly hired teachers were native speakers
of Spanish and where, consistent with state
law, the school district provided five
in-service training sessions to newly hired
teachers.

47. _Gomez v. Illinois State Board of Education,_
note 49 _supra_, 811 F.2d at 1042.

48. _Id._ at 1043.

49. _Id._

50. _Id._ The court made clear, however, that the
EEOA does not give state officials the right
to sue local officials in federal court for
violations of the EEOA. _Id. See also Board of
Education of the City of Peoria v. Illinois
State Board of Education,_ 810 F.2d 717 (7th
Cir. 1987).

51. _Id._ at 1042.

52. _Id._ at 1035–1037.

53. _Id._ at 1043.

54. _Teresa P. v. Berkeley Unified School
District,_ note 30 _supra,_ Memorandum Decision
and Order at 21 (dictum) (emphasis added).

55. I am grateful to Roger Rice for his
thoughts on the significance of _Teresa P._

56. In 1986, about 180,000 LEP children
were served through projects funded under
Title VII, even though estimates of eligible
children range from 1.2 to 5.3 million.

57. _See_ generally Crawford, "Bilingual
Education: Language, Learning and Politics."
Education Week, April 1, 1987, pp. 21–25.

58. Hertling, "Flexibility Stressed in New
Rules for Bilingual Classes." _Education Week_,
November 27, 1985, pp. 1, 16.

59. Crawford, note 56 _supra_, at 25.

60. _See_ Lyons, "The View from Washington." _NABE News_, June 1987, pp. 5 and 10.

61. _Id._

62. Crawford, "Thirty-Seven States Consider 'English Only' Bills, with Mixed Results." _Education Week_, June 17, 1987, pp. 1 and 14.

63. Some provisions may permit or require lawsuits that could lead to reduction of bilingual services. Others may permit or encourage state legislatures to enact new laws curtailing such services. Still others may be interpreted by state courts to have purely symbolic importance.

64. Under the Supremacy Clause of the U.S. Constitution, any such conflict would have to be resolved in favor of federal law.

65. It is beyond the scope of this chapter to treat this important issue in great detail. Fortunately, a recent note in the Harvard Law Review provides thoughtful discussion on this very issue. _See_ Note, "'Official English': Federal Limits on Efforts to Curtail Bilingual Services in the States," 100 _Harv. L. Rev._ 1345-1362 (April 1987).

66. If Congress does enact a law making the nondiscrimination provisions of Title VI applicable to all activities of a federal-fund recipient, any new Title VI regulations would cover all programs carried out by a school district receiving federal funds.

67. This formula, moreover, is likely to remain the same once Title VII is reauthorized, unless the total appropriation for Title is increased.

68. See footnote 67 above.

69. <u>Olaques v. Russoniello</u>, note 11 <u>supra</u>, 797 F.2d 1511.

70. The <u>Olaques</u> court based its ruling on the fact that the voters in question were not only LEP but also foreign born and recently registered. In fact, the court distinguished <u>Olaques</u> from other decisions holding that the constitution does not prohibit classifications based on English proficiency.

71. On the other hand, advocates of official English would attempt to distinguish the two situations. No one could argue in <u>Olaques</u> that the plaintiffs there were being singled out for a <u>benefit</u>. Advocates of official English, however, argue that curtailment of bilingual services -- which plainly affects LEP persons most directly -- will benefit LEP persons, by increasing the incentive to learn English promptly.

72. A governmental action violates the equal protection clause if it is motivated, at least in part, by a desire to harm those burdened by the action. <u>See, e.g., Washington v. Davis</u>, note 12 <u>supra</u>, 426 U.S. 229 (1976) and <u>Personnel Administrator of Massachusetts v. Feeney</u>, 442 U.S. 256.

73. In fact, proponents of official English would assert that official English provisions, by providing new incentives to master English quickly, disproportionately help rather than hurt LEP persons. Any court that accepted this argument would be unlikely to find the requisite intent to harm.

74. The Supreme Court has listed some of the types of evidence that might be used to demonstrate intentional discrimination. The list includes actions or patterns explainable only by an intent to discriminate, the historical background of the challenged decision, irregularities in the process by which a decision was reached, actions that contradict policies generally endorsed by the decisionmaker, and direct statements of

decisionmaker. See <u>Village of Arlington Heights v. Metropolitan Housing Development Corp.</u>, 429 U.S. 252 (1977).

75. <u>Washington v. Seattle School District No. 1</u>, note 13 <u>supra</u>, 458 U.S. 457, 467.

76. "Official English," note 66, <u>supra</u>., 100 <u>Harv. L. Rev.</u> at 1362, quoting <u>Washington v. Seattle School District</u>, note 75, <u>supra</u> at 486.

77. <u>Id.</u> at 1361.

REFERENCES

American Civil Liberties Union and NAACP Legal Defense and Educational Fund. **Justice Denied: The Loss of Civil Rights after the Grove City College Decision.** New York: American Civil Liberties Union, 1986.

Baker, K. and de Kanter, A. "Assessing the legal profession's contribution to the education of bilingual students." **La Raza Law Journal,** 1, 3, 295-329, 1986.

Board of Education of the City of Peoria v. Illinois State Board of Education, 810 F. 2d 717 (7th Cir. 1987).

Britton, C. "Minority parents file class action suit against city over desegregation proposal." **The Sun,** August 7, 1987.

Cardenas, J. "The role of native-language instruction in bilingual education." **Phi Delta Kappan,** 359-363, January 1986.

Castaneda v. Pickard (Castaneda I), 648 F.2d 989 (5th Cir. 1981).

Castaneda v. Pickard (Castaneda II), 781 F.2d 456 (5th Cir. 1986).

Crawford, J. "Thirty-seven states consider 'English Only' bills, with mixed results." **Education Week,** 1 and 14, June 17, 1987.

Crawford, J. "Bilingual policy has taken shape along two distinct federal tracks." **Education Week,** 21-25, April 1, 1987.

Crawford, J. "Bilingual education: Language, learning and politics." **Education Week,** 21-25, April 1, 1987.

Cummins, J. "Empowering minority students: A framework for intervention." **Harvard Education Review,** 56, 1, 18-35, 1986.

Debra P. v. Turlington, 644 F.2d 347 (5th Cir. 1981).

Featherstone, H. et al., "When children speak little English: How effective is bilingual education?" **Harvard Education Letter**, 2, 6, 1-4, 1986.

Georgia State Conference of NAACPs v. State of Georgia, 775 F.2d 1403 (11th Cir. 1985).

Gomez v. Illinois State Board of Education, 811 F.2d 1030 (7th Cir. 1987).

Grove City College v. Bell, 104 S. Ct. 1211 (1984).

Green v. New Kent County School Board, 391 U.S. 430 (1968).

Guadalupe Org., Inc. v. Tempe Elementary School District No. 3, 587 F.2d 1022 (9th Cir. 1978).

Guardians Ass'n of New York City v. Civil Service, 103 S. Ct. 3221 (1983).

Hertling, J. "Flexibility stressed in new rules for bilingual classes." **Education Week**, 1 and 16, November 27, 1985.

Hunter v. Erickson, 393 U.S. 385 (1969).

Keyes v. Denver School District No. 1, 575 F. Supp. 1503 (D. Colo. 1983).

Keyes v. Denver School District No. 1, 413 U.S. 189 (1973).

Lau v. Nichols, 414 U.S. 563 (1974).

Lexion, V.L. "Language minority voting rights and the English language amendment." **Hastings Law Quarterly**, 14, 657, 1987.

Lyons, J. "The view from Washington." **NABE News**, 5 and 10, June 1987.

McNeal v. Tate County School District, 508 F.2d 1017 (5th Cir. 1975).

Milliken v. Bradley, 433 U.S. 267 (1977).

Moran, R. "Bilingual education as a status conflict." California Law Review, 75, 361, 1987.

Note, "'Official English': Federal limits on efforts to curtail bilingual services in the States." Harvard Law Review, 100, 1345-1362, 1987.

Olagues v. Russoniello, 797 F.2d 1511 (9th Cir. 1986) (en banc).

Personnel Administrator of Massachusetts v. Feeney, 442 U.S. 256 (1979).

Regents of the University of California v. Bakke, 438 U.S. 265 (1977).

Roos, P. "Implementation of the Federal Bilingual Education Mandate: The Keyes Case as a Paradigm." La Raza Law Journal, 1, 3, 257-276, 1986.

Rossell,C. and Ross, M. "The Social Science Evidence on Bilingual Education." Journal of Law and Education, 15, 4, 385-419, 1986.

Sacken, M. "A Choice for the People to Make: The Necessity of Legislative Reform of Arizona's Bilingual Education Policy." Arizona Law Review, 26, 81, 1984.

Snider, W. "Massachusetts District Backs Plan to Integrate Its Students on Basis of Language, Not Race." Education Week, 1 and 15, February 11, 1987.

Teresa P. v. Berkeley Unified School District, No. C-87-2396 DLJ, Memorandum Decision and Order (N.D. Cal. September 8, 1987).

United States v. LULAC, No. 85-2579, Slip Op.
    (5th Cir. July 1, 1986) (clarification on
    Part VIII filed September 2, 1986).

Village of Arlington Heights v. Metropolitan
    Housing Development
    Corp., 429 U.S. 252 (1977).

Washington v. Davis, 426 U.S. 229 (1976).

Washington v. Seattle School District No. 1 458
    U.S. 457 (1982).

ANNOTATED BIBLIOGRAPHY

Baker, K. and de Kanter, A. "Assessing the Legal Profession's Contribution to the Education of Bilingual Students." La Raza Law Journal, 1, 3, 295-329, 1986.

The authors assess the impact of federal legislation, regulation and litigation upon education of LEP children. They also challenge the educational assumptions on which legal support for transitional bilingual education rests and offer an agenda for lawyers and educators seeking to improve education for LEP children.

Cummins, J. "Empowering Minority Students: A Framework for Intervention." Harvard Education Review, 56, 1, 18-35, 1986.

Focusing primarily on programs for LEP students, the author argues that the achievement of minority students improves when schools acknowledge and attempt to alter existing power relationships between dominant and subdominant communities. He supports his thesis with examples and suggests specific ways in which educators can help alter such power relationships.

Featherstone, H.; et al. "When Children Speak Little English: How Effective is Bilingual Education?" Harvard Education Letter, 2, 6, 1-4, 1986.

The authors summarize concisely research from the United States and elsewhere on instructional strategies that are effective with LEP children. They conclude that the best research supports approaches using native language instruction, particularly with students who are young, non-literate and/or members of politically subdominant groups.

Lexion, V. "Language Minority Voting Rights and the English Language Amendment." Hastings Law Quarterly, 14, 657-681, 1987.

The author provides a history of "English-only" movements in the United States. She also explores whether and how the voting rights of LEP persons would be affected by adoption of a federal constitutional amendment declaring English the official national language.

Moran, R. "Bilingual Education as a Status Conflict." **California Law Review,** 75, 361, 1987.

The author provides a sociological explanation for current disagreements over bilingual education. She sees conflicting cultures, customs and values as the principal sources of such disagreements.

Note, "'Official English': Federal Limits on Efforts to Curtail Bilingual Services in the States." **Harvard Law Review,** 100, 1345-1362, 1987.

This article discusses the history of official English movements in the United States. It also considers whether and how state official-English provisions that curtail native language instruction may violate the equal protection clause of the Fourteenth Amendment.

Roos, P. "Implementation of the Federal Bilingual Education Mandate: The Keyes Case as a Paradigm." **La Raza Law Journal,** 1, 3, 257-276, 1986.

The author describes the Keyes case, an important federal-court decision that interprets the Equal Educational Opportunities Act and approves educational measures, including bilingual education, as remedies for illegal school segregation based on national origin. He also describes the specific educational remedies on which the parties eventually agreed, and offers advice on conducting productive negotiations with public-school officials.

Rossell, C. and Ross, M. "The Social Science Evidence on Bilingual Education." **Journal of Law and Education**, 15, 4, 385-419, 1986.

The authors describe the role of social-science evidence in the development of federal policy --legislative, administrative and judicial-- on education of LEP children. They also provide a meta-analysis of research on the effectiveness of different instructional strategies used with LEP children, and endorse structured immersion over transitional bilingual education.

Sacken, M. "A Choice for the People to Make: The Necessity of Legislative Reform of Arizona's Bilingual Education Policy." **Arizona Law Review**, 26, 81, 1984.

The author analyzes the legal status of educational programs for LEP students, focusing on Title VI of the Civil Rights Act of 1964, the Equal Educational Act and the Bilingual Education Act. He also describes ways in which Arizona state law conflicts with federal laws protecting LEP students, and offers specific proposals for changing state law accordingly.

Chapter 4

LANGUAGE ACQUISITION AND BILINGUALISM IN EARLY CHILDHOOD: CURRENT RESEARCH FINDINGS

Yvonne De Gaetano

INTRODUCTION

The most recent research demographic analyses for the United States indicate that non-English-speaking populations are growing and will continue to grow (Education Week, 1986; Hodgkinson, 1985). From 12 to 25 percent of the populations of the major cities in the Northeast and as high as 40 percent of the populations of the West Coast are dominant in a language other than English (Yawkey, 1986). There is, in addition, the forecast of an accompanying increase in the percentage of women in the labor force. According to the 1984-1985 United States Bureau of the Census, women with children under the age of fifteen are increasingly joining the work force (Education Week, 1987). These two trends hold many implications for child care and the concommitant early education needs of children of non-English-speaking backgrounds.

Inextricably tied to early childhood education or child care for the non-English-speaking child are issues of language. Many questions continue to be posed. How can we provide linguistically different children with an environment that will enable them to continue to develop their home language so that learning new concepts will not be interrupted as they are exposed more and more to a second language? Under what conditions and how should second language acquisition occur in young children? Indeed, should we introduce a second language at an early age?

In the late sixties and throughout the seventies, the public and private conscience was more aware of and sympathetic to the needs of non-English-speaking children. Notably, in 1975 the Agency for Children, Youth and Families initiated the Head Start Strategy for Spanish-Speaking Children. It supported and emphasized curriculum development, staff training, resource networks, and research for early childhood bilingual education (Arenas, 1978). Although the results of those efforts were documented as positive, the reduction in federal funds for bilingual early childhood has unfortunately resulted in fewer research efforts. Yet, immigration trends indicate that non-English-speaking populations will continue to grow, so the need for more research in the area of dual language development in the early childhood years is greater than ever.

This chapter focuses on national and international bilingual early childhood research issues in the literature during the year 1986-1987. Specifically, the first part will focus on language and language-related research reported in the available literature for the current year. The second section will focus on the programmatic issues related to early childhood education. The chapter will conclude with a discussion and recommendations for future research.

LANGUAGE AND LANGUAGE-RELATED ISSUES

The issues prominent in the research efforts for the current year have revolved around the linguistic characteristics of bilingual young children. In the following section, the research reviewed will include: a study of the private self-regulatory speech of young children; two studies on the dual language acquisition process in submersion environments; language competence and turn allocation; adult-student interactive language use in the classroom; the influence of parental use of interlanguage on their children; metalinguistic awareness in young monolingual and bilingual children; and cultural and language test revision procedures.

Young children use private speech (self-regulatory verbalizations) as a helping strategy for solving cognitive tasks. One previous research study (Amodeo, 1977) conducted on bilingual children concluded that bilingualism negatively affects the use of private speech. Diaz (1986) identified flaws in the methodology of that study and conducted his own research to determine the relation between bilingualism and the private speech of young children. He studied three- to four-year-old bilingual preschoolers who exhibited varying degrees of bilingualism. Language dominance was measured with the Peabody Picture Vocabulary Test (Dunn and Dunn, 1981) and the Bilingual Syntax Measure (Hernandez-Chavez, Burt, and Dulay; 1976). He assessed the children's language for dominance in either English or Spanish and classified them as proficient bilingual, partial bilingual, and limited bilingual. The children were video and audiotaped while performing three types of tasks previously rated for degree of difficulty: (1) making puzzles; (2) classification; and (3) sequencing tasks.

Diaz examined the children's private speech under the categories of task-related and task-irrelevant speech. Results of the study demonstrate that bilingual preschoolers use private regulatory speech in the same way as do monolingual preschoolers; that is, the more difficult the task, the greater the production of private speech. As with monolingual children, task-related speech production is greater than non-task-related speech. Confirming his previous work on the positive relationship between bilingualism and cognition, Diaz found that the proficient bilingual children produced more efficient self-regulatory private speech with a consequent higher level of performance on cognitive tasks.

A case study of a three-year-old's use of two languages, English and Irish, done by Owens (1986) focused on context and content of language. The supportive role of the parent in learning the second language is emphasized in this study. The bilingual preschool teacher used the second language almost exclusively, while the parent (also the researcher) reinforced Irish during meals and storytelling.

Owens reports that for the first year, the child spent most of the time listening and comprehending the basic structures of the second language, although she repeated songs and rhymes and a few phrases learned at school. During the second year of the child's preschool experience she began using Irish more extensively. Owens recorded the child as much as possible during this period and commented that there was a concentration on the content rather than on the form of the language in the recorded interactions with the child. She concludes that the acquisition of Irish did not negatively affect the child's development and use of English.

The notion that the acquisition of a second language is not detrimental to the development of a first language is generally accepted (Cummins, 1982; Garcia, 1983). The best time at which to introduce a second language, however, is still being investigated. Madrid and Torres (1986) conducted a study on negation training (how to formulate negative sentences) with four-year-old children which suggests that training in the second language may inhibit first language production when young children are not yet proficient in their first language. Children who spoke English as the first language (L1) and Spanish as the second language (L2) were studied. Three groups of four-year-old children from bilingual homes were randomly assigned to: (a) English and Spanish (L1 and L2) negation training; (b) Spanish (L2)-only negation training; and (c) a control group. In each of the groups there were four English-proficient monolingual speakers and four non-proficient English monolingual speakers. Each language negation training consisted of eight sessions. The control group received no training. The results of the training demonstrated that the children who were proficient in English obtained 100 percent correct responses in the second language and maintained 100 percent responses in English when trained in L1 and L2 simultaneously and L2 negation only. The non-proficient English speakers trained in L1 and L2 as well as L2 only, did not receive 100 percent responses in either English or Spanish, although those children trained in L1 and L2 showed an increase in the mean score in both languages. The non-proficient English-speakers trained independently in L2 demonstrated an improvement score in Spanish and a decline in English.

Although there was no control for the developmental levels of the children in the study, research of this type indicates that attention needs to be paid to the level of proficiency of the first language and to its continued development as a second language is introduced.

Verhoeven and Boeschoten (1986) studied the levels of first language proficiency in a submersion environment. Specifically, the Turkish spoken by two groups of Turkish children (aged 4.4 and 6.4 years) living in the Netherlands was compared with two comparable groups of children (aged 5.4 and 6.4 years) living in Turkey. The younger groups of children were tested a minimum of twice a year and the older groups were tested three times a year. There was a one year interval between testing sessions.

Three types of first language development in a language submersion environment are possible: (1) language delay: an initial delay in first language development with an eventual catching up in language proficiency; (2) language stagnation: an initial delay with a constant remaining lag in the first language; and (3) attrition: an initial delay in first language development with its eventual loss. Results of the study indicate that after a four year period, the first language of a group of children in a language submersion situation becomes stagnated. When first language instruction was introduced to the children at age seven, there was a corresponding increase in first language competence. The level of competence, however, never reached that of the children in the first language environment because of the limited occasions of first language use in a submersion situation.

In her study on the language competence and turn allocation (cues that elicit conversational turn taking) of three- and four-year-old Spanish-dominant bilingual children, Volk (in press) describes clearly how the young children she studied function in two languages. Through ethnographic methods, that is, detailed observations of the environment and context in which language occurs, she monitored four children in an early childhood educational setting for a period of one year. The purpose of the study was to determine the form and function of the language used in relation to the child's speech partner. It focused on how young children, who were dominant in their home language and in the process of becoming bilingual, use two languages in context. The study explored specifically how young children employ turn allocators to elicit speech responses from children who had the same or different language dominance. Language dominance was determined after classroom observations, parent and teacher interviews, and the audio and videotaping of the children.

In order to analyze the children's conversations, Volk divided the classroom into categories occurring during free play, lunch, and clean up times. Some of the free play situations were: organizing for dramatic play; dramatic play; toy/book language exchange; and table/floor play. After analysis of the children's conversations, the turn allocators were identified. Volk found that for 90 percent of the time the four children studied used language appropriate to their speech partner's language dominance. Notably, the children distinguished between English monolingual children and English-dominant bilingual children.

Overall results of the study underscore the linguistic competence of four-year-old bilingual children in using speech creatively to elicit responses from peers of different language dominance profiles. Significantly, comparison with monolingual children indicates that bilingual children demonstrated greater sensitivity to the language dominance of others by consistently using the language allocators appropriate to the individual partner or to the language dominance of the majority of the group.

Garcia (1987) studied turn taking of a different nature, as well as the instructional conversations occurring in the bilingual kindergarten classrooms of three Phoenix schools. He audio and videotaped classroom teachers and volunteer parent aides for a twelve-week period. During this period he analyzed adult-student interactions during skill building and story telling. He modified and used the Mehan model of analysis, which characterizes teacher-student interactions as a sequence that includes: (a) teacher topic initiation; (b) student response; and (c) teacher evaluation. Specifically, Garcia was interested in determining if parents' instructional interactions with kindergarten children was different from the teacher interaction reported in the literature and from the particular teachers in the classrooms in which they were aides. After analyzing the teaching styles of both teacher and parent aides, he found some differences. The teacher interactions involved initiations geared to produce child responses that were of the product (fact) and process (opinion) type. The teacher responses were either repetitions of the student responses or positive evaluative comments. During storytelling time the language used more frequently was English, whereas during skill development time, it was generally Spanish.

Analysis of the parents' teaching style showed differences between the sequence of interactions during skill development and story time. During skill development, informatives (providing facts) and directives (ordering) were dominant in the parents' initiations. Because these types of statements do not demand responses, child participation was not encouraged. The storytelling parent initiations, however, did encourage responses, albeit of the product type (e.g., "The boy's shirt was blue"). Like the teachers, the parent responses were of the repetition and evaluation kind (e.g., "Very good"). The parents used Spanish during storytelling and both English and Spanish equally during skill building. An interesting finding of the study indicated that when children tended to change the topic of the lesson, the parents demonstrated flexibility in allowing the children to follow their own interests, whereas the teachers brought the children back to the topic at hand.

In sum, teachers of the bilingual kindergarten children in the study demonstrated the teaching interactional style reported in the

literature.   Although   parents   had   some
interactional   characteristics   similar   to
teachers,   they   tended to dominate   the lessons
and   elicit   less   student   participation.   They
were,   nevertheless,   more flexible than teachers
in   permitting   student   topic   changes   during
lessons.   Garcia suggests that   the parents may
be   demonstrating a culturally   related style of
interaction.   The   style,   characterized   by
initial adult domination   over   students, is one
that later allows student   interests to prevail.
Garcia goes on to imply that teachers' inability
or lack of flexibility in allowing student topic
shift   may   be   problemmatic   for linguistically
different children.

Parents'   language was also the   focus of a
study conducted in Australia on the English used
in   homes of   non-native-English   speakers (Rado
and   Foster,   1986).   Acknowledging that   the
children   from   non-native-English-speaking
backgrounds   consistently   obtain   lower   test
scores   than   do   native   English   speakers, the
authors concur with other   researchers that lack
of English proficiency holds these children back
from performing   better   academically.   Based on
previous   investigations,   findings suggest that
regardless of   the length of time   in Australia,
foreign-born   working and   middle-class families
speak   a form   of   English interlanguage   in the
home.   (Interlanguage is the speech used by the
second   language   learner   during   the   language
acquisition process.)   Rado and Foster examined
the   English   spoken   in   the   homes   of   three
different   linguistic   groups   --Italian, Greek,
and   Macedonian--   under   the   premise   that
interlanguage is more difficult to   process from
the   receiver's   perspective than   is a standard
conventional   language   form.   The   researchers
were   also   interested   in   investigating   the
possible influence interlanguage may have on the
English language used by the children.

Two   groups   of   parents   of   primary-aged
children were   used   for the   study.   One group
consisted of   native-English   speakers   (ES) and
the   other group of   non-native English speakers
(NES).   Through   interviews,   Rado   and   Foster
obtained   language   clauses   and   analyzed   the
nature   and frequency   of   errors   made   by both

groups. Predictably, they found more errors per
clause in the NES group than in the ES group.
They concluded that children of parents who
speak an interlanguage form of English have a
more difficult task in processing what they hear
than they would have in processing a regularized
form of English. The question remains as to how
this more difficult language processing task
influences the English used by the children and
how it is manifested in their language.

     In two related studies, Bialystok (1986)
examined the language processing and linguistic
control of bilingual and monolingual young
children. Using the same design and methods in
both studies, she focused on the metalinguistic
awareness of groups of children aged five, seven
and nine. She conducted the first study in two
urban schools with working-class, largely
immigrant, populations. Approximately one half
of the 119 children who took part in the study
were bilingual, representing diverse linguistic
groups. The other half were monolingual English
speakers. All the children were fluent speakers
of English according to their teachers. The
second study took place in a suburban,
middle-class school. One half of the 128
participating children were bilingual
native-English speakers, aged seven and nine,
who were participating in a French immersion
program. The other half were native English
speakers, aged five, seven and nine, who were
receiving regular English-only schooling.

     Bialystok tested each group of children in
English on three separate tasks: digit span,
judgments, and sentence corrections. The digit
span task was to obtain a quick gauge of
intelligence measure. The judgment tasks
consisted of judging four types of sentences
according to whether they were: (1) grammatical
and meaningful (GM); (2) ungrammatical and
meaningful (gM); (3) ungrammatical and
non-meaningful (gm); and (4) grammatical and
non-meaningful (Gm). The correction tasks
consisted of adjusting sentences for grammar and
meaning. After a few practice sessions, the
children used puppets to perform the different
tasks for the actual testing. A summary of the
findings suggests that in the first study, age

was a determining factor in tasks involving linguistic knowledge. Bilingualism was the significant factor involving control of linguistic processing. In the correction task, grammatical knowledge was positively related to age and meaning control showed a positive relation to bilingualism.

In the second study, the monolingual children performed better than the bilingual children in tasks involving ungrammatical sentences, whereas the bilingual children did better in tasks involving incongruent meaning. Bialystok suggests that monolingual and bilingual children may approach tasks with different strategies based on the development of different skills. Monolingual children seem to be attuned to grammaticality and bilingual children to a higher developed sense of meaning. Two important conclusions of this study are that metalinguistic ability (conscious awareness and knowledge of language construction and use) appears to be present at an earlier age than was previously thought and that children of different language experiences may be developing different metalinguistic skills at different rates of development.

An important concern of researchers and practitioners is whether we can truly assess language proficiency through formal testing measures. In test-oriented societies such as ours, the prevailing attitude is that we must use what has been developed until "something better comes along." The reality in the United States is that many youngsters arrive without school documents and there is often a lack of personnel and appropriate tests to assess linguistically different children's development for placement purposes. These reasons underscore the pressing need to adapt existing tests for cultural and linguistic relevance.

Khammash (1986) describes the methods and procedures used to adapt the Peabody Picture Vocabulary Test-Revised (PPVT-R) (Dunn and Dunn, 1981) into a linguistically and culturally relevant placement test for modern Arabic speaking five- to nine-year-old children. Rather than simply translating the PPVT-R, Khammash outlines the care taken to translate, change the test into Arabic format, and select pictures of objects which are culturally appropriate symbols (e.g., a lute instead of a guitar). The test was validated and standardized in Jordan. The Arab student population included in the standardization represented diverse dialect and socioeconomic groups as well as equal representation of gender. Although the revision and refinement of the test were reported to be time consuming and costly, it is a generalizable procedure for ensuring linguistic and cultural validity for the development of test for other groups.

PROGRAM AND PROGRAM-RELATED ISSUES

The focus of the following studies and reports is on the content of classroom teaching and programs, as well as issues regarding programs for young ethnolinguistically different children. In much of the work reviewed, the importance of the teacher's role is once again underscored, for it is how teachers conduct their classrooms and implement programs that most affect students and their learning. One may conclude that it is ultimately the environment fostered by teachers that encourages or inhibits children's behaviors and attitudes toward learning.

For a study on the writing behaviors of young bilingual children, Halsall (1986) selected five first through third graders who were in the process of becoming bilingual and who participated in English as a Second Language (ESL) classrooms for a minimum of two hours a day. The children were Hispanics who had at least one parent attending college on a full-time basis.

Through ethnographic methods, twelve behaviors were identified during children's writing. Some of these were reading back, invented spelling, talking while writing, and copying. Although many of the composing behaviors had been observed previously in monolingual children, there were some behavioral patterns specific to bilingual children. These were: reading back, concealing writing, and confirming questions. Additionally, as the children were writing in English, they used Spanish as a starting strategy.

The classroom environment and teacher practice played a significant role in the children's attitude toward writing. As the teacher encouraged children's interactions and language use, the children's writing moved from a teacher centered to a more child centered focus and the children became more productive writers. The children in the study were active language users because they were allowed many opportunities for language interactions.

There are many attempts to seek out and employ particular methods that will improve learning. In one such attempt, teachers used Suggestopedia to determine whether the teaching of English as a Second Language (ESL) would measurably improve over conventional teaching methods (Ramirez, 1986). Suggestopedia is a method of teaching designed to increase learning through a series of breathing, relaxation, suggestion, and concentration exercises.

Ninety Spanish-dominant third grade students of lower socioeconomic background from a rural Texas community were subjects of the study. The children were randomly divided into three groups. They were taught new English vocabulary using: (a) Suggestopedia; (b) Suggestopedia minus imagery (key words); and (c) conventional methods. All the children in the study were administered a pretest and they were then taught the same content, for the same amount of time, during a four-day-period with each of the three approaches. After the four days, posttests were administered. The results showed higher scores for the children taught through the two Suggestopedia methods. There were no significant differences between Suggestopedia and Suggestopedia minus imagery. Ramirez advocates the use of Suggestopedia, particularly for children of low socioeconomic status, but acknowledges the difficulties in implementing the method in large public schools where lack of space and consistent staff training would impede proper implementation.

In an attempt to provide citywide staff training to a large number of teachers, the New York City Board of Education (1986) planned and implemented a series of staff development activities for early childhood bilingual teachers. The evaluation report describes the program and highlights program outcomes and recommendations. The staff development program was designed for bilingual and ESL teachers of early childhood who had four years or less of teaching experience in the field. The goal of the program was to provide state of the art training in four related areas: (1) bilingual curricula and instructional methodologies; (2) the teaching of reading; (3) second language instruction through content areas; and (4) skills and strategies for instructing limited English-proficient (LEP) students. A specialist in the field presented in each area in one of four sessions. The 430 teachers selected for the staff development program then attended any of the approximately 10-14 concurrent workshops. Evaluations of the program were conducted through surveys, evaluation forms, on-site observations, and formal and informal interviews of participants and the program director.

Results of the evaluation indicate that the goal of the program was achieved. Participants rated the program highly on overall organization and on the quality of the presentations and workshops. Recommendations for future staff development revealed that the participants felt the need for more and longer training time for bilingual teachers, particularly those with less experience. A significant recommendation was the need to gauge whether or not the transfer of training into the classroom had occurred as a result of the staff development activity.

There are many approaches designed and utilized for the instruction of young linguistically different children with the intent of improving their later school achievement. Promoting Intellectual Adaptation Given Experiential Transformation, or Project P.I.A.G.E.T. (Yawkey, 1986), is one example. The goals of the program are to develop English language competence, maintain the Spanish language proficiency of Hispanic kindergarten students, and foster strong home school relations with the Hispanic families involved in the program.

Based on the work of Piaget, the program is described as one that has strong foundations in the diagnosis of individual developmental levels, experiential and active learning. At the same time, the program developers have enumerated 38 instructional objectives for mastery at the kindergarten level in language and cognition. The program has two main strands: (1) the Classroom/Center Component; and (2) the Home Component. Staff development is provided for teachers and aides in the implementation of the project.

The Classroom/Center Component emphasizes active learning and the cognitive development of bilingual children. An important feature of the project is the low teacher-student ratio in the classroom --one adult to eight children. In addition, all teachers and aides are bilingual. As program participants, parents enroll in the Home Component. An assigned aide goes to the homes to instruct parents on how to work with their children in learning tasks to reinforce what has been introduced at school. The home instruction is highly organized around a five-part cycle that includes such items as the parents' reporting on activity with the child during the previous week, instruction by the aide on new concepts and materials, and demonstrations or modeling. Home instruction takes place once a week for the duration of the school year.

Project evaluation procedures have been extensive. Participating children and control groups receive seven batteries of tests during the pretest and posttest periods. The parents take five batteries of pre and posttests. Results of the tests indicate that children participating in the program obtain higher developmental levels scores when compared to non-participating children. One may, nevertheless, question evaluation procedures involving such extensive testing of young children.

In contrast to the extensive test-based
evaluation processes of Project P.I.A.G.E.T.,
the evaluation of the Multilingual Preschool
Program reported little quantifiable data. The
evaluation report of the Title VII funded
program of the Sacramento City Unified School
District (Fox, Lew, and Talbert; 1986) provides
a summary of a five-year preschool program. The
goal of the project was to provide multilingual
education to preschool limited English
proficient children and their families.
Essentially, the program was an enrichment
supplement to the children's regular English
language preschool program. The project staff
consisted of a bilingual resource teacher and
three bilingual aides (Spanish-English,
Chinese-English, and Vietnamese-English).
During the last two years of the program, a
Hmong-speaking and a Laotian-speaking aide
joined the staff. Staff visited each
participating preschool center once a week to
instruct the children in their native language.
They distributed learning materials reflecting
the cultures of children in the programs. The
parental component of the program consisted of
home visitations by the bilingual aides to
instruct the parents on how to participate in
classroom activities and to help children's
learning in the home. The teachers of
participating centers also had in-service
training in the program.

        The program evaluation examined the
students' classroom and developmental progress
using classroom observations and the Thorpe
Developmental Inventory (TDI) (Thorpe, 1973).
The program itself was evaluated through surveys
administered to teachers and parents. Most
teachers and parents were favorable towards the
program, especially when they saw gains in the
children's development. The evaluation design
and the data collection showed some weaknesses.
The TDI test was discontinued because of
questions regarding its cultural relevance and
lack of standardization with the groups
participating in the program.

        Programs emphasizing strong parental
involvement in the classroom and in the home are
sorely needed throughout the schooling of

ethnolinguistically different students. Good evaluation designs and procedures that indicate outcomes, but do not overtax children, cannot be overemphasized.

Other reports discuss the evaluation of curriculum for early childhood bilingual populations. The North Carolina Standard Course of Study and the accompanying Teacher Handbook (North Carolina State Department of Public Instruction, 1986) explicitly outline the philosophy, content, and implementation of a curriculum that is competency based, emphasizes student responsibility to self and others, and stresses self fulfillment through an interrelated global approach to learning. An important aspect of the global perspective includes the study of a second language for all students. In kindergarten through grade three, listening, speaking, and culture are the foci of second language acquisition. Goals and objectives are specified for each skill area and examples are provided in competency goal areas.

The Texas Education Agency (1986) has clearly described its programs for prekindergarten children of limited English proficiency. The focus of the program is to present developmentally appropriate teaching strategies, learning activities and materials for non-English speaking preschoolers. It provides and outlines, for bilingual and monolingual teachers alike, helpful rules for implementing the program, as well as practical teaching strategies. Notably, the program strongly advocates continued development of the child's home language in the educational setting.

El Arco Iris (Texas Education Agency, 1986), a televised program for Spanish-speaking four-year old children and their parents, is an alternative to conventional preschool programs. The program prepares preschoolers for formal schooling, emphasizes the development of Spanish and English, and fosters parental involvement in the schooling and learning process through televised viewing.

After seeing a videotape, children and parents receive instruction separately from individual aides. One reinforces the children's lessons; the other instructs parents on how to extend and further reinforce children's lessons at home. Each videotape has three related activities: the lesson, storytelling, and home activity. The developers of the program point out that, contrary to most television instructional programs, El Arco Iris activities and lessons are designed to produce active responses by the children.

The program evaluation demonstrated that students with more than twelve hours of instruction have significantly improved in reading readiness skills both in Spanish and English as measured by the Comprehensive Preschool Inventory. Scores on the National Curve Equivalency also demonstrate that children instructed through El Arco Iris had higher reading scores in the first and second grades when compared with other students in the schools and district.

Recent research on effective strategies for teaching linguistically different children (Tikunoff, 1983; Wong Fillmore, et al., 1985), have documented ethnolinguistic differences in learning and interactional styles. These studies have led to more research with a similar focus. Garcia's (1986) work on identifying the characteristics of effective teachers of Mexican-American children is one of these. Garcia videotaped and recorded a first grade teacher who consistently had been nominated as an effective teacher by other teachers, administrators, and parents. Additionally, for more than two years, her classes produced academically achieving children.

After using an adapted version of Mehan's model for interactional analysis (analysis of how persons relate conversationally), Garcia found an interactional style somewhat different from that reported in the literature. In the class of the teacher under study, there was greater child topic control and higher student-student interaction, than reported in the classrooms of monolingual teachers. The teacher, however, tended to elicit choice responses from children. The teacher promoted very few higher level thinking skills since there were few process (opinions and interpretations) and even fewer metaprocess (reflective) elicitations. There were, consequently, few opportunities for language extensions and higher order thinking.

In a later and similar study on the analysis of interactional styles of academically successful kindergarten, first, third and fifth grade classrooms, Garcia (1987) again did not find teachers eliciting higher level thinking responses in the lower grades. In the fifth grade, however, more product (24 percent) and process (26 percent) elicitations were evident. Interestingly, Garcia noted that teacher-student and student-student interactions were predominantly in Spanish in kindergarten, Spanish and English by the third grade and by the fifth grade, English only.

The preschool program of the Carpinteria School District is one of the few programs in which Spanish is the only language of instruction (Cummins, 1986). Before the program began, young children who had participated in preschool bilingual programs were found to be below the readiness level of monolingual English-speaking children. In an attempt to raise the readiness level of the children to that of their English-speaking peers, the Carpinteria preschool program was developed using Spanish exclusively with monolingual Spanish or Spanish dominant children. Families of participating children were of low socioeconomic and educational levels. The families participated on a voluntary basis.

One of the most important features of the program is how language is used. Not only is language central to every activity, but its use is encouraged in ways that promote problem solving skills and higher level thinking in the children. Parents also play an essential role in the program. They are encouraged to take part in and reinforce school learning at home.

After one year, the readiness levels of the program children were compared to Spanish-speaking children who had attended bilingual preschools and to groups of English-speaking children. The scores obtained were 21.6 for program children compared to 14.6 and 23.2 respectively. Results of the readiness levels

for the following program year were 23.3 for the
Spanish-only children, 16.0 for children in
bilingual programs, and 23.4 for
English-speaking children. One of the dramatic
results of the Carpinteria program was the high
scores attained by the children on the Bilingual
Syntax Measure in both Spanish and English upon
entry into the kindergarten. These results
strongly suggest that a good foundation in the
home language provides a positive transfer to
the second language.

DISCUSSION AND RECOMMENDATIONS

At the beginning of this chapter, questions
were posed regarding dual language issues for
the non-English speaking young child. Some of
these questions were addressed in the literature
that emerged in the field of bilingual early
childhood during 1986-1987. Fundamentally, the
research on language dealt with two broad areas:
developing language proficiency and degrees of
language competence. The literature on programs
and programmatic issues essentially regarded
program and curriculum descriptions and
evaluations. Within these broad areas, themes
emerged that cut across each category. For
example, the research conducted by Rado and
Foster (1986) and by Owens (1986) direct
attention to the vital role parents exert on
children's language acquisition.

Owen's description of what she as a parent
did to reinforce and support her three-year-old
in the acquisition of the second language,
seemed crucial to the child's linguistic
development. Perhaps most important of all was
the positive attitude and the manner in which
the parent integrated language reinforcement in
every day activities. Additionally, the
development of the child's language learning
process was clearly described in the
ethnographic study. Rado and Foster's study
suggests that the interlanguage spoken by
non-native English speaking families may be more
difficult for children to process than is
conventional English. There is no indication,

however, of exactly how interlanguage has
influenced the English spoken by the children of
these families.

Madrid and Torres (1986) studied issues of
language proficiency. There are important
implications in the study, particularly for the
teaching of children considered non-proficient
in their home language. The research implies
that continued teaching in the home language of
young children while introducing a second
language is beneficial to the continued
development of both languages. When non-
proficient children were taught in the second
language only, gains were evident in that
language at the expense of the first language.
Verhoeven and Boeschoten's research (1986) also
is concerned with dual language proficiency in a
situation similar to that found in the United
States and other countries where large numbers
of linguistically different populations reside.
Research of this nature, which indicates that
the first language of a group stagnates in a
submersion environment, can facilitate planning
for the continued teaching and learning of the
language. The loss of a language at an early
age, or indeed at any age, is unpardonable.

The research of Bialystok (1986), Diaz
(1986), and Volk (in press) all underscore
linguistic strengths of very young bilingual
children. Bialystok's research suggests that
the bilingual child's linguistic skills are
developed in different ways and at different
rates from those of monolingual children. This
knowledge can provide clues about teaching young
bilingual students. Researchers and
practitioners need to work closely to discover
how this information can be utilized in the
classroom to enhance learning.

Diaz demonstrated that young proficient
bilingual children do indeed use self regulatory
private speech for performing cognitive tasks.
Practitioners and researchers might think of
ways to teach this natural helping strategy to
partial and limited bilingual students. The
research conducted by Volk, which highlights the
linguistic sensitivity of three and four-year
olds also underscores the competencies and
strengths of preschool children. Working from

children's strengths is the hallmark of good
early childhood education and the knowledge
gained from the research cited informs our
practice.

The programs reported in the literature had
certain characteristics in common. All were
developed or implemented to improve the outcomes
of schooling for young linguistically different
children. Ramirez (1986) found positive results
in children's learning with the use of
Suggestopedia. The New York Board of Education
staff development program for early childhood
bilingual teachers achieved its goal of
providing the latest theory and practice in the
field. Programs such as Project P.I.A.G.E.T.,
the Multilingual Preschool Program, and El Arco
Iris combine early childhood learning approaches
with strong parental components important
throughout the entire schooling process.
Perhaps the most compelling results for
children's schooling were obtained by the
Carpinteria School District preschool program
with their use of Spanish exclusively.

Garcia's (1986 and 1987) work is an
important contribution to further our
understanding of effective teaching and
interactions in the classroom. This research
brings awareness of the importance of culturally
relevant interactions combined with interactive
language strategies that promote and enhance
higher thinking skills.

There can be no doubt that more language
related research needs to be conducted in the
field of early childhood. Recent research has
demonstrated the value of teaching children in
the native language (Cummins, 1984 and 1986;
Hakuta, 1986; McLaughlin, 1985). Nevertheless,
more systematic research needs to be conducted
to determine just how the use of the native
language is beneficial to the cognitive
development of children (Garcia, 1987).
Research suggests that how English is used in
the classroom has been found to be more
significant for English language acquisition
than the amount of English used (Wong Fillmore,
et al., 1985). Similarly, how first language
only or both first and second languages are used
in the classroom for maximum learning results,

also need careful study. Many different research questions are still to be answered regarding the most favorable context for developing proficient bilingualism. Diaz (1986) urges further research on the immediate cognitive effects of learning a second language in early childhood. Also, longitudinal studies must be conducted to determine the long range effects of preschool programs that emphasize multiculturalism and bilingualism. Finally, the exclusive development of the home language for certain groups of children in the preschool years should be explored further.

We are in a period in the history of the United States when large waves of immigrant populations are entering the country. Other countries are also experiencing similar immigrations. The children of immigrants and the children born in the countries to which their parents immigrated, need special attention. It is not only humane, but politically and economically expedient, to prepare the young children of these groups for success in the schooling process. The educational setting in the early childhood years lays the foundation for what will happen in the later school years. Also, what happens to the home language and culture young children bring with them undoubtedly affects the way they will interact with the new language and culture they encounter. There is still a great deal that we do not know about first and second language acquisition and its relation to self concept, cognition, and learning in the early childhood years. It is time for researchers and practitioners to come together to ask more questions and seek answers.

In the preparation of this chapter the author gratefully acknowledges Joe McGill for his patience and fine editing skills and Nancy Dew for her sharp insights, encouragement and generosity.

REFERENCES

Amodeo, L. The Functional Significance of Private Speech During Problem-Solving in Monolingual and Bilingual Two-to-Five Year Old Preschoolers. Unpublished doctoral dissertation, University of California, Los Angeles, 1977.

Arenas, S. "Bilingual/bicultural programs for preschool children." **Children Today**, 43-48, 1978.

Bialystok, E. "Factors in the growth of linguistic awareness." **Child Development**, 57, 2, 1986.

Brownsville Consolidated Independent School District. **El Arco Iris: A Bilingual Prekindergarten Instructional Television Program**, Texas Education Agency, 1986.

Cummins, J. "Linguistic interdependence and the educational development of bilingual children." **Review of Educational Research**, 49, 222-251, 1979.

Cummins, J. "Empowering minority students: A framework for intervention." **Harvard Educational Review**, 56, 1, 18-36, 1986.

Diaz, R.M. The Self Regulatory Functions of Bilingual Private Speech. (Final Report, Grant No. R03MH39396) Washington, D.C.: Department of Health and Human Services, Public Health Service, National Institute of Mental Health, 1986.

Dunn, L.M. and Dunn, L.M. **Peabody Picture Vocabulary Test-Revised.** Circle Pines, Minn.: American Guidance Service, 1981.

Education Week. "Census bureau finds working mothers increasingly dependent on child care." **Education Week**, p. 8, May, 1987.

Education Week. "Today's numbers, tomorrow's nation." **Education Week**, p. 14, May, 1986.

Fox, F.; Lew, M; Talbert, J.; and Watts, E.C. The Multilingual Preschool Parent Participation Project of the Sacramento City Unified School District, Summary of Evaluation Report. Paper presented at the Annual Meeting of the American Educational Research Association, San Francisco, California, 1986.

Garcia, E. **Bilingualism in Early Childhood.** Albuquerque: University of New Mexico Press, 1983.

Garcia, E. "Bilingual development and the education of bilingual children during early childhood." **American Journal of Education**, 95, 1, 96-121, 1986.

Garcia, E. Use of L1 and L2 During Instructional Discourse in Effective Hispanic Classrooms. Working Paper No. 3. Effective Schooling for Hispanics Grant. Inter-University Program for Latino Research and Social Science Research Council, 1987.

Garcia, E. Bilingual Development and the Kindergarten Child. Paper presented at the Annual Meeting of the American Educational Research Association, Washington, D.C., 1987.

Hakuta, K. **Mirror of Language: The Debate on Bilingualism.** New York: Basic Books, 1986.

Halsall, W.W. An Ethnographic Account of the Composing Behaviors of Five Young Bilingual Children. Paper presented at the Annual Meeting of the American Educational Research Association, San Francisco, California, 1986.

Hernandez-Chavez, E.; Burt, M.; and Dulay, H. **The Bilingual Syntax Measure.** New York: The Psychological Corporation, 1976.

Hodgkinson, H.L. All One System: Demographics of Education: Kindergarten through Graduate School. Washington, D.C.: Institute for Educational Leadership, 1985.

Khammash, S.B. A Pictorial Test Assessing Aural-Vocabulary of Arabic-Speaking Children at Kindergarten and Early Primary Levels. Paper presented at the Annual Meeting of the American Educational Research Association, San Francisco, California, 1986.

Madrid, D. and Torres, I. "An experiential approach to language training in second language acquisition: Focus on negation." Journal of Applied Behavior Analysis, 19, 2, 203-208, 1986.

McLaughlin, B. Second Language Acquisition in Childhood: Volume 2. School Age Children. Hillsdale, New York: Erlbaum, 1985.

New York City Board of Education. The New York City Staff Development Program for Bilingual Early Childhood Teachers 1984-1985 OEA Evaluation Report, 1986.

North Carolina State Department of Public Instruction. North Carolina Standard Course of Study, Raleigh: Division of Instructional Services, 1986.

Owens, M. Eithne: A Study of Second Language Development. Paper No. 15. Center for Language and Communication Studies. Dublin, Ireland, 1986.

Rado, M. and Foster, L. The Language Environment of Children with a Non-English Speaking Background. Paper presented at the Ethnicity and Multiculturalism National Research Conference, Melbourne, Australia, 1986.

Ramirez, S.Z. "The effects of Suggestopedia in teaching English vocabulary to Spanish-dominant Chicano third graders." Elementary School Journal, 86, 3, 325-333, 1986.

Texas Education Agency. A Guide for Prekindergarten Education. Austin: Texas Education Agency, 1986.

Thorpe, H.S. Thorpe Developmental Inventory. Davis, Calif.: T.D.I. Consultants, Inc., 1973.

Tikunoff, W.J. and Vazquez, J. A. "Components of Effective Instruction for LEP Students." In Tikunoff, W.J. (Ed.) Teaching in Successful Bilingual Instructional Settings. San Francisco: Far West Laboratory for Educational Research and Development, 1983.

United States Department of Commerce, Bureau of the Census. Current Population Reports. Population Characteristics. Series No. 404. Washington, D.C.: Government Printing Office, 1985.

Verhoeven, L. and Boeschoten, H.E. "First language acquisition in a second language submersion environment." Applied Psycholinguistics, 7, 241-256, 1986.

Volk, D. "Communication Competence in a Bilingual Early Childhood Classroom." In Saravia Shore, M. and Arvizu, S. (Eds.) Communicative and Cross Cultural Competencies: Ethnographies of Educational Programs for Language Minority Students in Community Contexts. (In press)

Wong Fillmore, L.; McLaughlin, B.; Ammon, P.; and Ammon, M.S. Learning English Through Bilingual Instruction. Final Report to the National Institute of Education. Berkley: The University of California, 1985.

Yawkey, T. Overview of Project P.I.A.G.E.T. for
    School District Adoption and Replication.
    Technical Paper   200.   The Pennsylvania
    State University, 1986.

ANNOTATED BIBLIOGRAPHY

Ada, A.F. and Olave, M.P. **Hagamos caminos.** Reading, Mass.: Addison-Wesley, 1986.

A reading series developed for Spanish-speaking elementary school children. Geared toward enabling children to develop a strong foundation in the home language. The Teacher's Edition contains a suggested sequence to foster critical thinking skills and creativity in language and thinking. The style and language used in the series in appropriate to the many Hispanic groups residing in the United States. Includes stories and folk tales of interest to children from the first through the fourth grades.

Arnberg, L. **Raising Children Bilingually: The Preschool Years.** Avon, England: Multilingual Matters, 1987.

Intended for parents who desire to raise their children bilinguallly, the book introduces the reader to the theory and research in language acquisition and bilingualism. Provides language strategies and practical suggestions for promoting and supporting bilingualism.

Cox, B.; McCauley, J.; and Ramirez, M. III. **Nuevas fronteras.** New York: Pergamon Press, 1980.

A pre-academic subject-oriented curriculum which promotes cultural democracy based on respect for differences. Conscious use of cognitive styles and specific learning behaviors of children are utilized to develop bicognitive flexibility. Story books are included in the curriculum materials as well as record-keeping forms for the teacher.

Escobedo, T.H. (Ed.) **Early Childhood Bilingual Education: A Hispanic Perspective.** New York: Teachers College Press, 1983.

Three broad areas: language, culture and
classroom teaching strategies are presented
in a series of articles focusing on the
bilingual Hispanic young child.   Based on
original research,   reviews of existing
literature and on field experience, the
articles provide a well-rounded picture of
available knowledge in the field of early
childhood bilingualism.

Evans,   M.   "Linguistic accommodation in a
bilingual family: One perspective on the
language acquisition of a bilingual child
being raised in a monolingual community."
**Journal of Multilingual and Multicultural
Development**, 8, 3, 231-235, 1987.

Presents a report on one longitudinal
aspect of the language acquisition process
of a Welsh/English bilingual child raised
in England. The father is L1 Welsh, but
the mother learned Welsh in order to speak
it to her son.   Identifies the areas in
which parental accommodation takes place,
that is, the father accommodated both the
mother's and child's linguistic errors in
Welsh.   The data collected was part of a
longitudinal study of the child's language
from 1-6-1/2 years.

Fantini,   A.E.   **Language   Acquisition   of   a
Bilingual   Child: A   Sociolinguistic
Perspective.**   San   Diego, Calif.:   College
Hill Press, 1985.

A sociolinguistic case study of a young
child's acquisition of Spanish and English.
The study follows the child's language
acquisition process from birth to age ten
through data collected in audio taping and
diary notations.   Emphasizes the role of
socialization in language acquisition.

Garcia, E. **Early Childhood Bilingualism.** Albuquerque: University of New Mexico Press,
1983.

Presents all facts of early childhood bilingualism including bilingual education in the early school years. Terms used in the literature on bilingualism are clearly defined. Describes several studies that provide examples of such phenomena as language switching, language transfer, and mother-child discourse in early childhood.

Garcia, E. "Bilingual development and the education of bilingual children during early childhood." **American Journal of Education**, 95, 1, 96-121, 1986.

Considers linguistic, cognitive, and social attributes of children and schooling contexts in the early education experience of language minority children.

Harding, E. and Riley, P. **The Bilingual Family: A Handbook for Parents.** New York: Cambridge University Press, 1987.

Written by professional applied linguists who are also parents of bilingual children, this book addresses the question: "Should we raise our children to be bilingual?" The book is divided into three parts: (1) a survey of language learning and the nature of bilingualism, and factors to consider when deciding whether or not to raise a child bilingually; (2) case studies of bilingual families; and (3) an alphabetical reference on the most frequently asked questions about bilingualism.

Holley, C. "ESL in early childhood education." **International Quarterly**, 5, 3, 27-33, 1987.

Describes a bilingual pre-kindergarten program at the American School in Madrid. Discusses the development milestones of language acquisition and the characteristics of children learning English as a second language.

Levy, A.K. "Increasing preschool effectiveness: Enhancing the language abilities of 3- and 4-year-old children through planned sociodramatic play." **Early Childhood Research Quarterly**, 1, 2, 133-140, 1986.

Describes a study that supports the idea that participation in sociodramatic play builds language competence of young children and that play is a vital part of a good preschool program. Implications for preschool LEP children can be drawn from the article.

McLaughlin, B. **Second Language Acquisition in Childhood: Volume 1. Preschool Children.** Hillsdale, N.J.: Erlbaum, 1984.

A comprehensive overview of contemporary theories of second language acquisition. Commonly held beliefs about second language acquisition in young children are questioned based on the most current research. Among the topics included are comparisons of adult and young children's second language acquisition, simultaneous and successive acquisition of two languages and results of bilingualism in early childhood. Questions are posed for future research.

Multilingual Matters. **Every Child's Language. An In-Service Pack for Primary Teachers.** Avon, England: Multilingual Matters, 1985.

A language training pack prepared for British teachers, but of interest to linguists, students of language and teacher trainers because of the parallels between the situations and language issues found in both the United States and England. Book 1 addresses such topics as the diversity of English dialects (an accompanying cassette provides interesting language examples), the bilingual child, and experiences in reading and writing. Book 2 contains case studies illustrating topics presented in Book 1. Book 3 provides resources and materials available to teachers.

Ramsey, P. **Teaching and Learning in a Diverse World.** New York: Teachers College Press, 1987.

An indepth theoretical and practical treatment of the concept of multiculturalism for preschool children. The book is organized and written to enable teachers and administrators to better understand the rationale underlying multiculturalism for preschool children. Each chapter presents a topic focused around fostering positive attitudes toward differences in young children, followed by practical classroom activities for the implementation of a multicultural approach to early childhood education.

Reyhner, J. **Teaching the Indian Child: A Bilingual/Multicultural Approach.** Billings: Eastern Montana College, 1986.

Provides the background and rationale for teaching in ways sensitive to the culture of Indian students. Emphasizes the need for a culturally relevant curriculum. Presents many helpful and practical teaching ideas. Among the topics included are the history of Indian education in the United States, self concept, teaching strategies and the use of microcomputers for the Indian students. Also discusses the role of parents as children's first teachers and how parents and teachers can work together for an effective education.

Schneider, B.; Doret, H.; and Brown, H. **Sharing a Song.** Reading, Mass.: Addison-Wesley, 1987.

A music centered approach to teaching and enriching English language skills. Provides ideas for the integration of art, creative writing and reading into music lessons. An emphasis on multiculturalism is evident in the content, rhythm, and music of the activities presented. Includes a Teacher's Guide, Activity Book, and cassettes.

Williams, L. and De Gaetano, Y. **ALERTA: A Bilingual Multicultural Approach to Teaching Young Children.** Reading, Mass: Addison-Wesley, 1985.

A comprehensive approach to bilingual multicultural learning, this process oriented curriculum model for preschoolers emphasizes the utilization of a diversity of cultures and languages in the content and classroom environment of a preschool setting. The inclusion of parents and staff as a team is underscored at every level of implementation. The manual contains the theory and practice underlying the model, training of teachers and parents, and samples of classroom activities that promote bilingualism and multiculturalism.

Zamora, G.R. and Barrera, M.B. **Nuevo Amanecer.** Chicago: National Textbook Company, 1985.

A curriculum model that utilizes an eclectic approach to teaching young children. Enables teachers to follow a classroom management system and incorporates bilingual, multicultural strategies. First and second language activities are based on the concepts, motor skills, and behaviors to be promoted. Materials included are a Teacher Reference Book, Master Sheet Book for record keeping, Circle Time Activity Book, and Learning Center Idea Book.

Chapter 5

ADVOCACY AND EMPOWERMENT: POLICY AND PROGRAM DESIGN FOR STUDENTS OF LOW INCIDENCE LANGUAGE GROUPS

Judy Kwiat

INTRODUCTION

A pattern of school failure among minority students has been documented by educational research in the last twenty years. The school dropout rate among Mexican-American and mainland Puerto Rican students is between forty and fifty percent (Valadez, 1986; Jusenius & Duarte, 1982). The dropout rate for white and black students is fourteen and twenty-five percent, respectively. This pattern of school failure is also reflected in special education programs. In Texas, Spanish-speaking students are overrepresented by a factor of 300 percent in categorical programs designed for students who have been labelled "learning disabled" (Ortiz and Yates, 1983).

The dropout rate for native American students is twice the national average in public and federal schools and even approaches 100 percent in some school districts. Achievement levels of Indian children are two to three years below those of white students, and the Indian child falls progressively further behind the longer the student remains in school (Gilliland, 1986).

Koh (1987) suggests another kind of failure that characterizes Asian-American students. She believes that the increased dropout rate of Asian high school students, the growing number of incidents of unlawful behavior and crimes reported in the mass media, and the increasing number of cases with serious emotional disturbances referred to Asian mental health agencies all suggest that Asian-American adolescents are in a high risk state despite apparent academic success which is solely based on high test scores. Koh states that bilingual and multicultural education has long neglected the affective development of students due to its emphasis on cognitive learning. She calls for studies that assess the psychological cost of being a language minority student within a school system that makes Asian-American students victims of their own academic success.

Current research indicates that the pattern of school failure of minority students has remained basically unchanged in spite of costly educational reforms aimed at reversing this pattern (Gonzalez and Grubb, 1987; Cummins, 1986; Cazden, 1984). Jim Cummins (1986) suggests that a major reason attempts at educational reform have been unsuccessful is that the social, cultural and political relationships between teachers and minority students, and between schools and minority communities, have remained unchanged. Cummins argues that in order to reverse the pattern of widespread minority group educational failure, it will be necessary for educators and policy-makers to redefine their roles within the classroom, the community and society so that educational programs begin to empower minority students rather than disable them.

The purpose of this chapter is to examine the relationship among low incidence minority language groups, their position within a larger social order, and school programs which have been successful in reversing patterns of school failure among these groups.

HISTORICAL OVERVIEW

In the United States, the education of language minority students has been shrouded with controversy and misunderstanding. In the early history of our country, newly arrived peoples demanded native language instruction for their children and struggled for the preservation of their linguistic and cultural traditions. By the late 1600's, eighteen different languages were spoken by European immigrants including English, German, Dutch, French, Swedish and Polish (Castellanos, 1983). Native American tribal languages numbered in the hundreds. Diversity of language was the rule rather than the exception even though this policy was not embraced by the empowered social classes of the times.

In 1753, Benjamin Franklin tried in vain to persuade German speakers in Pennsylvania to allow their children to be taught in English. A short time later, during the war between England and the colonies, opinions about language swung the other way and anti-English sentiments ran high. There was even an attempt to establish German as the national language in place of English. After the American Revolution, as part of a unifying movement, English was more accepted as the unofficial national language. Native language instruction still prevailed, however, wherever linguistically and culturally different peoples maintained political and financial power. In the 1800's German-English schools were common in Baltimore, Cincinnati, Cleveland, Indianapolis, Milwaukee, and St. Louis. In Louisiana, schools were operating in both French and English, and in the Territory of New Mexico, Spanish-English schools were fully authorized. It was generally thought by educators that specialized schooling for the children of language minority groups was not only fair but necessary. William Harris, once a St. Louis superintendent of schools and later a United States Commissioner of Education, wrote: "National memories and aspirations; family traditions, customs, and habits; moral and religious observances cannot be suddenly removed or changed without weakening the personality," (Crawford, 1987).

By the late 1800's, however, spurred by growing nationalism and isolationism, sentiments turned against anything that was foreign. The immigrants of the late 19th Century arrived in poverty and often remained powerless. They obtained access to the American way of life through their second and third generation offspring. The majority of these immigrants achieved low levels of literacy in English even though many "Americanization" programs were established to meet their needs. They learned enough English to survive in the factory jobs born of the industrial revolution. During the early 1900's, fear and hatred for all that was foreign became ingrained in American life. The words of President Theodore Roosevelt mirrored the thoughts of most Americans: "There is no room in this country for hyphenated Americanism...Any man who comes here...must adopt the language which is now the native tongue of our people, no matter what the several strains in our blood may be. It would not be merely a misfortune, but a crime to perpetuate differences of language in this country," (Crawford, 1987).

World Wars I and II further cemented xenophobia into the crossroads of American life and established an unwritten policy toward future immigrant groups. A policy which strongly suggests that they leave behind their cultural traditions, customs and languages and that they replace them with all that is American. A policy which places most linguistically and culturally different people in a disadvantaged position within the larger social order and within the educational environment.

Language Policy Decisions

Formal programs for limited English proficient students were first revived in the early 1960's in Florida. Much of the revival was due to the political and financial power of Cuban refugees from educated and professional backgrounds who fled Cuba after the revolution in 1959. Dade County school district officials established programs in the Coral Way Elementary School in English as a Second Language as well as Spanish for Spanish speakers. The district also offered a two-way bilingual program to both English and Spanish speaking children. The goal of this program was to foster bilingualism in both languages for all the students. In English reading, both the English speaking students and the Spanish speaking students performed as well as or better than their peers in monolingual English classes. The Spanish speaking students achieved at comparable levels in Spanish reading. These programs, for the most part, were deemed a success, and the feasibility of programs for language minority students, especially programs which included native language instruction, was established (Hakuta, 1986). Since the 1960's federal and state governments have enacted laws, provided funding and set policy for programs for language minority students.

Unfortunately formal government intervention has changed the focus of bilingual instruction from developing fluency in two languages to a compensatory remedial program designed to help students overcome the "language handicap" of not speaking English (Crawford, 1987). In 1968, President Lyndon B. Johnson signed the Bilingual Education Act or Title VII of the Elementary and Secondary Education Act. Even though the title suggested instruction in two languages, the original Bilingual Education Act did not require bilingual instruction. Instead the law focused on helping students who were poor and educationally disadvantaged because of the inability to speak English. There was, however, a remarkable amount of support across the country for programs aimed at helping limited English proficient students. Massachusetts was the first state to pass a bilingual education law in 1971. Within ten years a total of 30 states had similar statutes; nine of these required native language instruction and 21 provided financial aid to local school districts under specified circumstances. Along with the growth in the number of programs for limited English proficient (LEP) students, came a significant increase in the number of studies devoted to evaluating these programs. The quality of a portion of this research, however, remains questionable.

THE ROLE OF RESEARCH

Hakuta and Snow (1986) have identified two strains of research in the field of language minority education: evaluation research and basic research. Evaluation research typically compares bilingual education to alternative programs for limited English proficient (LEP) students that usually include some forms of submersion education with an English as a second language (ESL) pull-out program. Evaluation research has dominated the debate on the effectiveness of bilingual education programs. Critics of bilingual education use the questionable conclusions from evaluation research to support their claims that bilingual programs are no more effective in promoting the development of English language skills than other alternative programs. A major critic of bilingual education, Secretary of Education William J. Bennett, used the findings from two such studies (Danoff, et al, 1977, 1978; and Baker and de Kanter, 1981) as the basis for this criticism. He contends that, "the research shows that other methods of instruction are often equally as effective as transitional bilingual education." The methods used in evaluation research to measure the effectiveness of bilingual education programs have been criticized by several researchers and governmental agencies (McLaughlin, 1985; Willig, 1985; and United States General Accounting Office, 1987).

Basic research, which focuses on the linguistic and psychological development of bilingual children, has played a less prominent role in the debate over effective programs for LEP children (Hakuta and Snow, 1986; Hakuta and Gould, 1987). The goals of basic research involve understanding how children learn a second language, how the first and second languages interact, how language relates to thought and how rates of acquisition differ according to cognitive abilities as well as learning styles. Those who do basic research are psychologists, linguists, anthropologists, and sociologists. Hakuta and Snow (1986) state that the findings from basic research have not received sufficient consideration by educators and policy makers. They also point to the "severe technical and conceptual problems with the evaluation studies that have been carried out." They conclude that "these problems are so severe that relying on the results of these studies to guide policy making could be dangerous." Hakuta and Snow contend that using information from basic research is preferable to using findings from evaluation research. They believe that information produced by basic research should be instrumental in enacting policy decisions.

Another form of research, which can be referred to as naturalistic, descriptive research, has also not received sufficient consideration by educators and policymakers. This research, which is based on a humanistic philosophy, is qualitative and narrative in nature. The aim of this type of research is to describe programs and program effectiveness in terms of measurable improvement in the affective characteristics of students such as self-concept and attitudes towards school, parents, learning, the community, and society. Those who do naturalistic research are teachers, program coordinators and other educators who work directly with students. Often program effectiveness in descriptive studies is not defined solely by scores on commercially developed norm-referenced tests, but is also defined by growth in student self-esteem, the length of time students remain in school, and how successfully students function in mainstream classes and later in their communities. Behavioristic, quantitative researchers have a difficult time admitting the relevance of studies of this type because of the subjective nature of the findings. Naturalistic studies, however, provide invaluable information about effective programs in terms of approaches, methods and techniques.

EFFECTIVE PROGRAMS FOR STUDENTS FROM LOW INCIDENCE LANGUAGE GROUPS

The METS Program

The Multidisciplinary Educational Training and Support Program (METS) in the Montgomery Public Schools, Montgomery County, Maryland, is a program designed for limited English proficient (LEP) students who have experienced little school success (Schabb and LaNeve, 1987). There are 93,000 students in the Montgomery Public Schools; 10,000 are international students from 100 countries who speak 60 different languages. There are 150 schools in the district, 135 of which contain programs for language minority students. The number of students in a program varies from 265 in one school to one student in another school.

Students in the METS program are generally from low socio-economic status, often dysfunctional, families. There are also many unaccompanied minors. The majority of these students have not made adequate social and emotional adjustments to the academic environment and many have had very little prior schooling. There were approximately 4,600 LEP students in the school district in 1987; there were 2,100 LEP students in 1979 in the same district. The population has not only changed in number, but also in prior academic experience. In 1979 most of the LEP students were international students who were literate in their native language; now the majority of the students are from immigrant and refugee groups who often lack basic literacy skills in any language. Even with this lack of prior academic experience, very few have been found to be learning disabled. It is the opinion of the program's director, Maria Malagon Schaub, and the staff, that most of the students have simply not had enough of the kinds of experiences that are needed if the students are to enjoy academic success.

The goals of the METS program define what Schaub and the staff consider to be academic success: the students will acquire proficiency in English in the areas of listening, speaking, reading, and writing along with academic skills in the content areas; the students will appreciate the long-term benefits of education and will remain in school until graduation; and the students will understand and adjust to the school environment and to the community. There are two METS programs in elementary schools which serve students in grades three through six. In the junior intermediate and middle schools (JIM) there are five METS programs which serve students in grades six through nine.

Enrollment in a METS program is limited to two years. After leaving the METS program, however students still receive support services through ESOL (English to Speakers of Other Languages) classes.

There are three major components to the METS program: the instructional program which includes literacy development, mathematics and social sciences; the counseling program which includes both students and their families; and the parent program. METS classes at the elementary level are self-contained and are limited to a maximum of fifteen students who are grouped according to their native language. Each class has one ESOL teacher and one bilingual instructional assistant. All of the ESOL teachers are elementary teachers or teachers with background knowledge in special education.

The METS program at the JIM level is a half day self-contained program which is limited to a maximum of fifteen students who are grouped by language for classes in reading, social studies, and math. These students also receive two additional ESOL classes and two mainstream departmental classes in either home economics, physical education, art or industrial arts.

Each student is assessed prior to placement in the program and the equivalent of an individual educational program is designed for the student. The assessment instruments are locally developed instruments. In math, students are assessed using a set of criterion-reference tests which were developed to match the district's math curriculum, An Instructional System in Mathematics. To assess listening, speaking, reading and writing in English, the students are given another locally constructed instrument called the <u>Minimum English Competency (MEC) Test</u>. Information about native language proficiency is gathered informally by the bilingual instructional assistants.

The reading program for all METS students is based on the language experience approach to reading and is supplemented with other readers. The reading program is also tied to the social studies program. There is no social studies textbook. The curriculum is based on field trips and experiences which focus on four areas: Myself, My Home, My Community, and the United States.

The Math program is based on an adapted version of the district's math curriculum and focuses on the use of principles of mathematics in the students' everyday lives and in the environment.

The counseling component and the services to parents are closely related to the instructional program. The METS counselor provides counseling for students on a variety of topics which are tied to the instructional program: school rules and regulations, getting a job and keeping it, manners and customs, child abuse and self-protection, sex education and cultural differences. A survival handbook has been developed by the METS staff which is also used by a specialist who works directly with the parents. The parent program was developed to improve parental participation in the educational process of their children, to foster community involvement and to help parents adjust to their new environment.

Montgomery County school officials believe that the students in the METS program are accomplishing the stated objectives of the program: increased proficiency in English, higher achievement in the content areas, greater appreciation of the benefits of long-term education, and better adjustment in the school and community environments. An attitude questionnaire administered orally to students also indicates that students perceive a sense of accomplishment in these areas.

The strengths of the METS program are that the program planners have established realistic goals for educating at-risk LEP students. These goals are not just academically oriented, but also encourage the development of the whole child. The curriculum focuses on empowering students and extends outside of the school into the community and into the homes of these children.

The weaknesses in the program would appear to be caused by reality constraints. Because there are so many different languages represented in the program, it has been difficult to find qualified teachers to teach in the native languages. Appropriate native language instruction has been proved to be more effective, in the long run, than instruction in English. A second major weakness is that the students normally are expected to spend only two years in the program. Research has also shown that students benefit greatly from programs of longer duration (Troike, 1986).

The San Mateo Adult School

The San Mateo Adult School, in conjunction with the San Mateo Union High School District in San Mateo, California, provides specialized services to approximately 2,000 language minority students from various language groups (Roddy, 1987).

The school district offers Competency Based Adult Education (CBAE) programs designed to serve the needs of high school drop-outs and young adults. Many of the teachers in the ESL program use a curriculum which is largely based on the pedagogy of Paulo Freire. This curriculum is flexible, constantly changing and is generated by the students themselves. Each instructor is asked to develop a needs assessment for the purpose of gathering information about students.

Such assessments often include topics, such as reasons for studying English, opinions about what skills are to be learned, and preferences for trips and experiences. Students are also assessed using the Competency Adult School Assessment System (CASAS) Survey Achievement

Test which provides information on academic
achievement for program and instructional
planning. Instructors also follow Freirean
principles in gathering information about the
students by making frequent interactional
observations based on every day experiences in
the lives of the students. Students are
presented with topics related to aspects of
their lives, and they are guided to organize,
analyze, synthesize, and evaluate those topics.
Throughout this process, the instructors are
carefully observing and using new information to
generate curricular experiences and activities.
In addition to the student generated portion of
the curriculum, instructors also teach from a
list of prescribed competencies which include
literacy skills, grammatical skills, life
skills, and critical thinking skills. The
emphasis, however, is that the students will
develop within themselves the ability to achieve
personal goals at their own pace without having
to sit through instruction of material already
mastered. Students come to see education as
real, specific, and attainable. The focus,
therefore, is on empowering students with more
sensitive perceptions of their own realities.
The teachers use questioning and dialogue
techniques which are based on a problem or a
central concern for the group. The teacher
participates as an equal co-learner, by asking
referential questions --questions for which the
teacher does not know the answer. In this way,
the teachers help students both discover and
change problem situations as a group. The
focus, then, of the lessons is a collective
approach to problem solving through critical
thinking which is based on free expression and
communication.

Since the curriculum is largely student
generated, the instructional component varies
with each group. Certain experiences, however,
characterize much of the classroom activities:
cooperative learning groups; interactional
two-way tasks; dialogue journals between
students and instructors; student writing
projects, such as newsletters, letters to

government officials, and student produced
culture capsules; interactional sessions with
guest speakers; and oral reports.

ESL teachers in this program, who base
their teaching on the pedagogy of Paulo Freire,
perceive the program to be successful (Roddy,
1987). Many students earn high school diplomas,
some go on to junior colleges or vocational
training, and most are able to find employment
and stay employed. The most significant measure
of success for program participants, however, is
the increased motivation, self-respect and
self-confidence of the students. Students who
complete the program indicate on student
attitude surveys that they have more confidence
in their own abilities to function in their
environments, to take greater risks in terms of
seeking more challenging employment
opportunities, and to go on to institutions of
higher education.

Urbana School District No. 116

The Urbana School District in Urbana,
Illinois, is a K through 12 district with six
elementary schools and one combined junior and
senior high school. Each year for the last
three years the district has served between 180
and 190 LEP students from 28 different language
groups, including Korean, Vietnamese, Lao,
Cambodian, Japanese, Chinese, Arabic,
Indonesian, French, Portuguese, Spanish, and
others (Fritz, 1987).

The two groups with the largest numbers of
students are Korean and Vietnamese. The Martin
Luther King Elementary School is a magnet school
for all of the LEP students (grades K-6) in the
district. Within the district are hundreds of
families of foreign students who are attending
the University of Illinois at Champaign-Urbana
and many families of recent immigrants and
refugees.

Mary Fritz, the district's bilingual
coordinator, directs both the elementary and the
high school programs. In the King Elementary
School, the program provides sheltered
instruction through native language tutors and a
content-based ESL program. Students are first

screened for oral language proficiency and are then assessed in English and the native language in reading and math using locally developed informal measures. In addition, the staff gathers information about each child, such as length of schooling in country of origin, prior academic achievement, educational level of the parents, literacy level of the parents, socioeconomic status of the family, languages spoken in the home, and any other information which would help in designing a program for the student.

Instruction for LEP students in the King School is provided by bilingual teachers, bilingual aides, cooperative mainstream teachers, and peer tutors. There are bilingual teachers for seven language groups: Spanish, Portuguese, Korean, Japanese, French, Chinese and Vietnamese. There are bilingual tutors for 15 languages: Korean, Japanese, Chinese, Malay, Indonesian, Vietnamese, Farsi, Arabic, Hebrew, Spanish, French, German, Portuguese, Urdu, and Pakistani. All of the teachers and the majority of the aides were teachers in their own countries and are also mothers and fathers of children in the school district.

The content-based ESL program is a half-day whole language approach which integrates the language arts with social studies and science. All classrooms focus on relating knowledge about the world to the students' own lives. The teachers facilitate the process by which the students acquire knowledge about science and social studies through demonstrations, experiments, role playing, and other interactional activities which can be transformed into language experience narratives, stories, and reports. All classrooms are literate environments filled with printed material which include the children's own work as well as teacher made and commercially developed materials. Native language instruction is also provided by either a teacher or an aide and depends on the needs of the child. For the other half of the day the students are in a regular classroom where they receive instruction in math and participate with their classmates in classes such as art, physical education, music, library, and science. Much of the instruction in math is done in the native language by bilingual aides who work with cooperating teachers.

The combined junior and senior high school program is departmentalized for ESL, social studies and science. For these students, native language instruction is provided by either an aide or a teacher in Spanish, Portuguese, Korean, Japanese, French, Chinese, and Vietnamese. All students take six subject area classes. For LEP students, three out of the six classes provide them with sheltered instruction based on adapting activities and materials in such a way that students experience gains in achievement as a result of students' improved perception of their self-concept. Many of these classes employ team teaching techniques. The goals of the program are accomplished through a curriculum based on promoting cooperation and interaction among students and students and among students and teachers. The curriculum also includes teacher made materials and commercial materials both in English and the various native languages.

Another component of the program, which Fritz and her staff consider to be of utmost importance, is the parent training component. Parents and staff members participated in several training sessions in which parents were coached in techniques for working with their children at home. Parents were guided to become better involved in the children's education and to participate in the evaluation of the effectiveness of the program.

In 1986 the program was formally evaluated using several measures in oral language proficiency, reading, and academic achievement.

English Language Proficiency

Evidence was gathered from pre and posttests using the <u>Functional Language Assessment</u> (FLA), developed by the Chicago Board of Education. Local norms for the FLA have been developed for Urbana over a period of several years. This is a test of aural-oral language which includes the following: oral directions, repetition of sentences, and free speech in response to questions by the interviewer. The

The final item is the generation of a question by the subject. The perfect score of 75 is almost always attained by native speakers. Table 1 describes the gains of the subjects in oral English as measured by the FLA.

Table 1

Mean Gain of LEP Students in Oral English as Measured by the Functional Language Assessment

Grade	Mean Entry Score	Mean Exit Score	Mean Months in Program	Mean Gain per Month	Number of Students
First	.05	54.7	10.1*	5.4	16
Second	17.7	62.0	12.5*	4.2	17
Third	12.2	61.8	8.3	4.2	13
Fourth	9.8	60.0	7.7	6.5	18
Fifth	10.6	50.4	9.3*	4.3	10
Sixth	16.0	60.7	9.7*	4.6	7

Interpretation: A comparison of the exit scores and the months in the program indicates that the most rapid acquisition of oral skills by LEP students develops early.

* Some students who entered in August had spent the previous year in another district which had a pullout ESL program. In order to calculate gain in terms of months, it seemed more useful to include this time of study. Since there were only a few of these students, the data should not be much affected, especially since the students made less progress than the others in the group.

Reading

The Urbana Reading Test includes a wide-range of skills and was developed by the staff at the King School. It was administered to program participants at the time of entrance in the program and again in April 1987. Norms for King School were established and are given in Table 2.

Table 2

Mean Gain of LEP Students in Reading as Measured by Urbana Reading Test

Grade	Mean Entry Score	Mean Exit Score	Mean Months in Program	Mean Gain per Month	Norm	Number of Students
First	.8	23.1	6.0	3.7	43	19
Second	19.3	44.3	6.9	3.6	55	18
Third	13.5	53.7	6.4	6.4	62	14
Fourth	19.9	52.8	4.9	6.7	68	16
Fifth	36.1	63.6	6.3	4.4	75	8
Sixth	40.0	69.7	7.2	4.1	83	6

Interpretation: The gain per month for English proficient speakers as measured by the same test is less than 1; it is clear that the gap between English speakers and the LEP program participants was greatly reduced. The reading composite scores of program participants who were deemed able to attempt the Comprehensive Test of Basic Skills (CTBS) is further evidence of achievement in English language skills. In only three cases had students been able to attempt the CTBS the previous year. These were second grade students, and their reading composite percentile scores were 2, 4, and 7. All others were unable to do the sample items in the test or were in the first grade. (Urbana does not administer the CTBS to students under

second grade level).   The mean percentile ranks
for the composite reading scores on the CTBS are
given in Table 3.

Table 3

Mean Percentile Ranks for Reading Composite Scores for CTBS

Grade	Mean Percentile Rank	Months in English Medium School	Number of Students
2	30.7	10.8	15
3	18.3	9.5	11
4	21.6	13.0	9
5	20.5	11.7	6
6	27.8	11.2	7

Interpretation: The gain in percentile rank is
substantial.   Students who were able to attempt
the CTBS had been in an English speaking school
for more   than   one academic year.   There is a
small but not consistent trend toward the higher
percentile ranks being associated with length of
time in a school where English is the medium of
instruction.   It was hypothesized that it takes
longer to reach national norms as one moves from
lower   to   higher   grades since   the language
demands are greater at higher grade levels.

Academic Achievement

In March 1986 the California Test of Basic
Skills (CTBS) was administered to all students
from a non-English background who had been
screened as LEP and who had been present in the
program for at least five months. Since this
was a pretest, students were required to attempt
the test regardless of their level of English.

Table 4

Mean Percentile Ranks of LEP Students on CTBS,
Spring 1986

Reading	Math Computation	Science	Social Studies
2	23	7	6

The extremely low mean percentiles on all but math computation reflect the fact that all LEP students were tested regardless of their reading ability in English.

The CTBS was administered again in March 1987 to LEP students who had been in the program for at least five months. Preliminary results of the third grade LEP students and all of the fourth grade LEP students are recorded in Table 5.

Table 5

Mean Percentile Scores of LEP Students on CTBS,
Spring 1987
(Incomplete Results Based on 3rd and 4rd Grades)

Reading	Math Computation	Science	Social Studies
29	68	48	40

Interpretation

Although the posttest scores represent only a part of the total group, there is reason to believe that the pattern will be consistent for all the LEP classes. It is interesting that the scores of children completing five months to eight months in the program exceed those of children thought to be no longer LEP because they had been in the English medium program for at least a year and a half.

These scores on English proficiency tests and the CTBS indicate an important reduction of the gap in academic achievement between LEP and English proficient students in the district. Administrators, teachers, parents, and students

have also indicated through informal measures
that they perceive the program to be effective
in helping students to be successful in
mainstream classes.

The Chinle Navajo Parent-Child Reading Program

Native American children have historically
been high risk students who do not succeed in
most traditional academic settings (Gilliland,
1986). Recently, with the increase in the
number of programs that provide instruction in
the native language due to a 1978 change in
Title VII legislation, a brighter outlook can be
predicted. Native language instruction was not
provided to indigenous language groups in the
United States for several reasons. For the most
part, many of these languages were dying out as
fewer and fewer Indians mastered their native
tongue. English was the dominant language in
most families even though these same family
members were considered to be limited English
proficient. Indian languages had no status
within the mainstream culture and many Native
Americans did not hold their own language in
high esteem (Crawford, 1987). The widespread
academic failure of Indian children is one of
the most dramatic examples of how people who
have virtually no power are victimized by a
traditional educational system that disables
them rather than empowers them.

The reading program at the Chinle Primary
School in Chinle, Arizona, is an example of how
restoring the status of a native language
directly affects the self-esteem of a people and
that in turn empowers them to achieve
academically (Murphy, et al., 1986). The
children in the program are kindergarteners and
first graders. They receive instruction through
a Chapter I, ESL and language arts program. The
children are read aloud to every day in English
and in Navajo. Each child has a chance to read
alone, and to share a story with a friend, a
group of friends, or the teacher. The
children's stories are read over and over again.
They write their own stories using invented
spelling, or they dictate language experience

stories to the teacher.   They act   out favorite
tales, and they draw pictures about the stories.
Students are also encouraged to think about what
would have happened if a boy had not   adopted a
motherless lamb,   or why the   giant threatened a
whole town   for some bread and honey. Through
these activities they are guided to ask serious
questions   about life,   and to speculate   on the
consequences of   human actions and   the motives
which fuel those actions.   They are encouraged
and guided to explore the mysteries of life and
to experience themes   that   run throughout good
literature.   The   children   take books   home
daily.   The youngsters each share the books with
parents or brothers and sisters and other family
members,   then   they   return the   books and take
home others.
     The   children   in   the   program   exhibit an
excitement for the stories they share, and their
parents are beginning to see the benefits of the
shared storytelling time.   Many of the children
at the pre-reading stage are not reading   in the
sense that   they can   pick up any book   and tell
what the words are.   These children are   in the
crucial state of reading; they are learning that
print   has meaning and that   stories   make sense
and follow logical steps.   Most importantly, the
children see   reading as   pleasurable and as
something that   enhances   their   lives.   Because
they share the books at home,   they are able to
see reading as   something that   fits   into the
lives they lead outside of the classroom.
     The goals of the program   are both academic
and humanistic.   Teachers want the   children to
enjoy   the books and the   narratives   which they
listen to and which they share   with others.   It
is also hoped that parents will gain a   sense of
pride through participating in   their children's
reading lessons.   Parents are assured that even
if   they themselves are not   literate, they can
help their children succeed in school.   Prior to
the start of the program,   parents had expressed
that they   felt   powerless because they   did not
know   what books contained.   These same parents
were rich   sources of   oral   histories, legends,
and   parables in Navajo.   The   program helped
families understand that reading books   could be
just as pleasurable as telling stories, and that

parents and children can share and contribute to what is being learned in school. It is hoped that empowering parents and children with a sense of control over their own learning will eventually lead to higher levels of academic achievement and greater success in leading happy and productive lives.

SUMMARY OF CHARACTERISTICS OF EFFECTIVE PROGRAMS FOR LOW INCIDENCE LEP STUDENTS

An overview of the literature indicates that it is the overwhelming opinion of experts in the field of language minority education that appropriate native language instruction is more beneficial to limited English proficient students than instruction only in English (Genesee, 1987; Hakuta and Gould, 1987; Cummins, 1986; Duran, 1986; Hakuta and Snow, 1986; Hakuta, 1986; Reyhner, 1986; Troike, 1986; Ulibarri, 1986; Krashen, 1985; Ovando and Collier, 1985; Willig, 1985; and Wong Fillmore, et al, 1985).

Even though the research evidence is quite conclusive, most schools (over 51 percent) which have bilingual programs and alternative programs do not use the students native language and an even higher percentage do not employ teachers who speak the students' native language (Development Associates, 1984). It is the belief of many researchers that this, in part, may explain why many programs are not as effective as they might be (Troike, 1986). An effective program is defined as one which reduces or eliminates inequalities of achievement between mainstream native English speaking students and language minority students as measured in English and in the native language in all areas of the curriculum including language arts, mathematics, science, and social studies.

Ineffective programs are products of the mismatch between the differing characteristics of the students and the curriculum of the program. Curriculum planners often do not take into consideration the cognitive, social and cultural differences of LEP students when they develop a curriculum for the student. The most

common practice is to plan the curriculum, order
the books to be used, outline the activities and
experiences, and then hope that the students
will benefit from what has been pre-determined.
Ineffective programs are those that fail to
adequately assess students and adapt curriculum.

Effective programs for LEP students have
been evaluated across the United States,
including programs serving low incidence
language groups. Many of these programs share
characteristics from which program planners and
policymakers can gain insights in program
designs. The following is a summary of
characteristics of effective instruction for LEP
students. (For additional discussions see
Valadez, 1986; California Assembly Office of
Research, 1985; Wong Fillmore, et al., 1985.)

1. Instruction is guided by a carefully
planned curriculum based on a complete
assessment of each child. It sets goals and
objectives for language minority children which
match their diverse characteristics, needs, and
interests.

2. There are high expectations for student
learning and high regards for students'
abilities. There are high expectations and high
standards for all children, regardless of ethnic
background.

3. Students are carefully oriented to
lessons. Teachers help students get ready to
learn, to keep objectives in mind, and to
maintain focus. Teachers assess what the
students already know, and help relate the new
lesson to previous knowledge and previous
lessons.

4. Instruction is clear and focused.
Teaching is presented with the sole purpose of
helping the student to learn. There are
explanations of what is going to be done, and
the teacher goes over the steps of the lesson
which will enable the student to integrate and
internalize the new knowledge. Finally, the
teacher reviews what was done and provides for
reinforcement. In reading, skills are taught to
facilitate the reading process, not to learn
reading skills. The prime objective of
instruction in reading is to create a literate

environment which fosters a love for reading.
Homework is used for practice, not for learning
and figuring out how to do something for the
first time.

5. The learning process is monitored
closely. Monitoring is conducted in both a
formal and informal manner. Students are held
accountable for their academic work. Assessment
is frequent and feedback is immediate.
Monitoring is also used to assess how well
something was taught so that the teacher becomes
a researcher in the classroom.

6. When students do not understand, they
are re-taught using alternative methods. If a
slower pace is required, the material to be
covered is adapted and the curriculum is
adjusted.

7. Class time is used for learning.
Minimum time is taken for settling down to work
and other classroom disruptions.

8. There are smooth, efficient predictable
classroom routines which students can easily
learn. Students are expected to monitor their
own learning. Materials and supplies are
readily available and there is a system for the
management of these materials.

9. Instructional groups are formed to fit
instructional needs. When introducing new
concepts and skills, whole group instruction,
actively led by the teacher, is preferable, if
all the children understand the language of the
teacher. Smaller groups are formed as needed to
ensure that all students learn thoroughly and
for practice. Teachers review and adjust groups
often, moving students when achievement levels
change. For some instruction, mixing
achievement groups is desirable. Children
should not always be placed in homogeneous
achievement groups. Mixed groups provide
opportunities for language development. Each
lesson has oral activities so that the students
can develop language which is related to
particular topics. The teacher facilitates
extended responses rather than single-word
responses by expanding student responses through
rephrasing.

10.   Standards for   classroom behavior are
explicit and consistent.   Rules, procedures and
consequences   are well articulated   early in the
school year   or   semester.   Equitable discipline
is applied to all students.   Disciplinary action
focuses   on   the behavior   or   event not   on the
person.
11.   Personal interaction   between teacher
and   students   is   positive.   Teachers   pay
attention   to   the   students   as   human   beings,
keeping in mind that the students   need to learn
more   than   the subject   matter.   Teachers know
that the classroom is a place where children are
developing attitudes about   themselves and about
the environment in which they live.
12.   Parents are considered as partners in
the instructional program.   Parents are provided
with various options for   getting   involved with
the education of   their   children.   There   is a
positive relationship between home and school.

Another major contributor to the success or
failure of a program for   LEP   students concerns
the attitudes of   the people   in the educational
community towards the   students, their language,
and   their   culture.   If the   cultural   and
linguistic background of the students are viewed
as a handicap, and if educational personnel feel
prejudiced against these   students   and superior
to them,   then the minority student   will indeed
be in a disadvantaged   position.   A disadvantage
not owing to the student's   language or culture,
but to the inequities   of   an educational system
and to the greater social order which molded the
system.

CONCLUSION

School programs which have   been successful
in   reversing patterns   of   school failure among
students   of   low   incidence language   minority
groups are those that are based on   a philosophy
which advocates empowering students   rather than
disabling them.   Every   educator   and   parent
involved   in   the   process   of   facilitating the
growth   of   every child must   become an advocate
for that child.   Teachers must not think of LEP
students   as   handicapped   and   in   need   of

remediation. Because the non-English speaking
child has not succeeded in the traditional
curriculum, many educators immediately blame the
student and attempt to diagnose, remediate, and
cure the student's problem. Why not diagnose,
remediate, and cure the curriculum --the whole
educational environment of the child? If the
traditional curriculum has not worked, change
it. And it does not appear that adapting the
curriculum to include minimal amounts of native
language tutoring and ESL instructions benefits
students in the long run. What does benefit
students is a long term program (from three to
five to seven years in duration) that includes
intensive instruction in the native language and
in English aimed at developing not only a strong
cognitive, linguistic, and academic background,
but also purposeful experiences that develop
respect for the human dignity of others and for
oneself.
     The primary goal of a program for low
incidence language groups, as well as for all
LEP students, should be to arrange the
environment so that students, teachers, and
parents can grow and develop together through a
process which liberates each to develop to his
or her full potential. Parents who are not
empowered cannot empower their children.
Teachers who are not empowered cannot empower
their students. Children who are not empowered
cannot become full participants in their
communities and in the greater social order.
And how would a program of this type facilitate
the personal growth of each individual?
     Teachers would have to abandon traditional
models of instruction that have not been
effective and would need to become active
advocates of those models which best match the
characteristics of the students they are
teaching. They would need to experiment with
carefully planned lessons to accommodate the
goals of the program and the needs of the
students and to analyze and evaluate those
lessons. Teachers would need to observe and
coach each other and in this process would need
the support --both emotional and technical-- of
other educators and administrators who are
themselves advocates for changing the system.

Researchers would need to focus on basic research questions which involve understanding how children learn a second language, how first and second languages interact, how language relates to thought and how rates of acquisition differ according to cognitive abilities as well as learning styles. Educators would also need to be researchers in the classroom in order to refine and analyze programs aimed at developing within the students themselves improved self-concept and improved attitudes toward school, the community, and society. Above all, educators, parents, and students would need to work to abandon prejudices and negative attitudes which undermine the educational process of minority students.

REFERENCES

Baker, K.A. and de Kanter, A.A. **Effectiveness of Bilingual Education: A Review of the Literature.** Washington, D.C.: Office of Planning, Budget, and Evaluation, United States Department of Education, 1981.

California Assembly Office of Research. **Bilingual Education: Learning English in California.** Sacramento, Calif.: Joint Publications Office, 1986.

Castellanos, D. **The Best of Two Worlds: Bilingual/Bicultural Education in the U.S.** Trenton: New Jersey State Department of Education, 1983.

Cazden, C. Effective Instructional Practices in Bilingual Education. Research review prepared for the National Institute of Education. Harvard University, 1984.

Crawford, J. "Bilingual education: Language, learning, and politics." **Education Week,** 19-50, April 1, 1987.

Cummins, J. "Empowering minority students: A framework for intervention." <u>Harvard Educational Review</u>, 56, 18-36, 1986.

Danoff, M. N.; Coles, G.J.; McLaughlin, D.H.; and Reynolds, D.J. **Evaluation of the Impact of ESEA Title VII Spanish/English Bilingual Education Programs.** Palo Alto, Calif.: American Institute for Research, 1977, 1978.

Development Associates. **Descriptive Study Phase: The National Longitudinal Evaluation of the Effectiveness of Services for Language-Minority Limited English Proficient Students.** Final report submitted to Office of Planning, Budget and Evaluation. Washington, D.C.: United States Department of Education, 1984.

Duran, R.P. Academic Achievement of Language
    Minority Children. (Document No. 1/4. Ed.
    8/1: Serial No. 99-R). One of nine papers
    presented to the Committee on Education and
    Labor, House of Respresentatives, 99th
    Congress, 2nd Session. Washington, D.C.:
    United States Government Printing Office,
    June 1986.

Fritz, M. Getting from Here to There: A
    Statewide Perspective on Transitioning LEP
    Students to the Mainstream Program. Paper
    presented at the Illinois TESOL/BE
    Conference, Champaign, Illinois, February,
    1987.

Genesee, F. **Learning Through Two Languages:
    Studies of Immersion and Bilingual Educa-
    tion.** New York: Newbury House, 1987.

Gilliland, H. "The Need for an Adapted Curricu-
    lum." In Reyhner, J. (Ed.) **Teaching the
    Indian Child.** Billings: Eastern Montana
    College, 1986.

Gonzales, P.C. and Grubb, M.H. Effective
    Language Arts Program: Chapter I and
    Migrant Education. Unpublished manuscript,
    1987.

Hakuta, K. **Mirror of Language: The Debate on
    Bilingualism.** New York: Basic Books,
    1986.

Hakuta, K. and Gould, L.C. "Synthesis of re-
    search on bilingual education." **Educa-
    tional Leadership,** 44, 38-45, 1987.

Hakuta, K. and Snow, C. "The role of research
    in policy decisions about bilingual
    education." <u>NABE News</u>, 18-21, 1986.

Jusenius, C. and Duarte, V.L. **Hispanics and
    Jobs: Barriers to Progress.** Washington,
    D.C.: National Commission for Employment
    Policy, 1982.

Koh, T.H. Preventive Mental Health Services for Asian-American Adolescent Students. Paper presented at the annual Illinois State Bilingual Conference, Lincolnwood, Ill., 1987.

Krashen, S.D. **Inquiries and Insights.** Hayward, Calif.: Alemany Press, 1985.

McLaughlin, B. **Second Language Acquisition in Childhood: Volume 2: School–Age Children.** Hillsdale, N.J.: Lawrence Erlbaum Associates, 1985.

Murphy, B.; Gray, A.; and Viola, M. Navajo Parent/Child Reading Program. Paper presented at the Annual TESOL Conference, Anaheim, Calif., March 1986.

Ortiz, A.A. and Yates, J.R. "Incidence of exceptionality among Hispanics: Implications for manpower planning." **NABE Journal,** 7-41-54, 1983.

Ovando, C.J. and Collier, V.P. **Bilingual and ESL Classrooms: Teaching in Multicultural Contexts.** New York: McGraw Hill, 1985.

Reyhner, J. **Teaching the Indian Child.** Billings: Eastern Montana College, 1986.

Roddy, M. Adapting the Pedagogy of Paulo Freire for at Risk Adults. Paper presented at the symposium: A Dialogue with Paulo Freire: Literacy and Participatory Education, University of California, Irving, Calif., July 1987.

Schabb, M.M. and LaNeve, M.Y. Children with Limited Previous Schooling: Meeting Their Needs. Paper presented at the Annual TESOL Conference, Miami, Fla., April 1987.

Troike, R.C. Improving Conditions for Success in Bilingual Education Programs. (Document No. 1/4. Ed. 8/1: Serial No. 99-R.) One of nine papers presented to the Committee on Education and Labor, House of Representatives, 99th Congress, 2nd Session. Washington, D.C.: United States Government Printing Office, June 1986.

Ulibarri, D.M. Issues in Estimates of the Number of Limited English Proficient Students. (Document No. 1/4. Ed. 8/1: Serial No. 99-R.) One of nine papers presented to the Committee on Education and Labor, House of Representatives, 99th Congress, 2nd Session. Washington, D.C.: United States Government Printing Office, June 1986.

United States General Accounting Office. **Bilingual Education: A New Look at the Research Evidence.** (Document No. GAO-PEND-87-12 BR). Washington, D.C.: United States Printing Office, 1987.

Valadez, C.M. Effective Teachers for Language Minority Students. (Document No. 1/4. Ed. 8/1: Serial No. 99-R.) One of nine papers presented to the Committee on Education and Labor, House of Representatives, 99th Congress, 2nd Session. Washington, D.C.: United States Government Printing Office, June 1986.

Willig, A.C. "A meta-analysis of selected studies on the effectiveness of bilingual education." **Review of Educational Research,** 55, 269-317, 1985.

Wong Fillmore, L.; Ammon, P.; McLaughlin, B.; and Ammon, M.S. **Learning English through Bilingual Instruction: Executive Summary and Conclusions.** (NIE-400-80-0030) Washington, D.C.: United States Department of Education, 1985.

ANNOTATED BIBLIOGRAPHY

Committee on Education and Labor, House of
Representatives 99th Congress, 2nd Session.
**Compendium of Papers on the Topic of
Bilingual Education** (Document No. 1/4, Ed.
8/1: Serial No. 99-R). Washington, D.C.:
United States Government Printing Office,
June 1986.

Report submitted to the Committee on
Education and Labor which contains nine
scholarly articles from experts in the
field of language minority education: R.C.
Troike, J.E. Alatis, K. Hakuta and C. Snow,
R.F. Macian, D.M. Ulibarri, R.P. Duran,
C.M. Valadez, P. Barron, and A.H.
Leibowitz. Article titles include:
Improving Conditions for Success in
Bilingual Education Programs;. The Role of
ESL in Bilingual Education; The Role of
Research in Policy Decisions about
Bilingual Education; Teacher Preparation
for Bilingual Eduction; Issues in
Estimates of the Number of LEP Students;
Academic Achievement of Language Minority
Students; Parental Involvement in Bilingual
Education; and Educational Policy and
Political Acceptance: The Imposition of
English as the Language of Instruction in
American Schools. Many of the articles
point to the situation of low incidence
language groups.

Crawford, J. "Bilingual education: Language
learning and politics." **Education Week,**
19-50, April 1987.

Discusses bilingual education and language
minority education in general from three
perspectives: an historical perspective, a
research perspective and the perspective of
programs and problems, including the issue
of low incidence language groups. The
author is the Washington editor of
Education Week and provides a fresh

perspective on current issues: politics, legislative decisions and research implications.

Cummins, J. "Empowering minority students: A framework for intervention." **Harvard Educational Review**, 56, 18-36, 1986.

Presents a theoretical framework for analyzing minority students' school failure and the relative lack of success of previous attempts at educational reform such as compensatory education and bilingual education. The author suggests that these attempts have been unsuccessful because they have not altered significantly the relationships between educators and minority students and between schools and minority communities. Compares the performance of Burakumin students in Japan and in the United States and describes a British program for multiethnic students in which children read to their parents at home on a regular basis.

Genesee, F. **Learning Through Two Languages: Studies of Immersion and Bilingual Education.** New York: Newbury House, 1987.

Provides a comprehensive overview of second language immersion programs in Canada and the United States. Also focuses on bilingual education programs in the United States. This readable text presents a complete review of programs for language minority education by integrating actual program data, research findings, theoretical discussions, and educational implications.

Government Accounting Office. **Bilingual Education: Information on Limited English Proficient Students.** (Document No. GAO/HRD, 87-85 BR.) Washington, D.C.: United States Printing Office, April 1987.

Provides information concerning LEP
students who are supported by federal funds
appropriated under the Bilingual Education
Act (Title VII of the amended Elementary
and Secondary Education Act of 1965).

Hakuta, K. **Mirror of Language: The Debate on
Bilingualism.** New York: Basic Books,
1986.

Provides an in-depth discussion of major
issues facing educators of language
minority students: historical overview,
political and legal issues, bilingualism,
language acquisition, the relationship
between first and second language
acquisition, considerations of native
language instruction and the role of
research.

Hakuta, K. and Gould, L.J. "Synthesis of
research on bilingual education." **Educational Leadership,** 38-45, 1987.

Outlines substantial research which
supports teaching language minority
children in their native language and which
suggests that bilingualism is a cognitive
asset.

Ovando, C.J. and Collier, V.P. **Bilingual and
ESL Classrooms: Teaching in Multicultural
Contexts.** New York: McGraw-Hill, 1985.

Combines theory with practice in each
chapter to clarify concepts involving the
components of language and culture which
shape the instructional processes in
bilingual and ESL classrooms. Also
provides insights for discussions of
politics, federal regulations and resources, assessment issues, and school/
community relations.

Reyhner, J. (Ed.) **Teaching the Indian Child.**
Billings: Eastern Montana College, 1986.

Designed to aid teachers with ideas about resources and methods especially appropriate for Indian students. Nineteen chapters provide a thorough coverage of the issues facing educators of Native American students.

Trueba, H.T. (Ed.) **Success or Failure: Learning and the Language Minority Student.** New York: Newbury House, 1987.

Discusses the issues of underachievement, educational equity, and acquisition of knowledge by language minority students. This collection of ten chapters is based on ethnographic methods and anthropological perspectives. The original research papers describe the basic steps that students from diverse linguistic and cultural backgrounds must follow to function in academic settings.

Wong Fillmore, L. and Valadez, C. "Teaching Bilingual Learners." In Wittrock, M. (Ed.) **Handbook of Research on Teaching.** New York: Macmillan, 1986.

Discusses instructional issues relating to the education of LEP students and reviews the research dealing with these students.

Chapter 6

TRENDS IN BILINGUAL SPECIAL EDUCATION: THE DOUBLE BIND

Alba N. Ambert

One of the most compelling issues in bilingual special education today continues to be the inappropriate placement of linguistic minority children in special classes. Because of limitations in English language performance, a disproportionate number of linguistic minority children are still placed in classes for the mentally retarded, the emotionally disturbed, and increasingly, the learning disabled. The current status of the problem will be discussed in this chapter. Since instances of true learning problems exist in linguistic minority populations, as in the population as a whole, a discussion of current research findings in limited English proficient children with learning problems will also be covered.

REFERRAL AND ASSESSMENT PROCEDURES

Current studies in bilingual special education focus on the special education process itself. Inappropriate referrals, discriminatory assessment, and overrepresentation of linguistic minorities in special education classes still hold the attention of researchers and practitioners in the field. Despite decades of denouncing discriminatory practices and the procedural safeguards of Public Law 94-142, bilingual researchers today are documenting the placement of linguistic minority children in special classes based on biased assessment techniques. A lack of understanding on the part of teachers, educational psychologists, and school administrators of the second language acquisition process appears to negatively affect the evaluation process The only major shift brought about by more stringent assessment regulations and mounting criticisms of discriminatory evaluation and placement practices seems to be the underrepresentation of language minorities in classes for the mentally retarded and their overrepresentation in classes for the learning disabled and speech and language impaired.

In 1971 Mercer published the results of an important study which showed that Mexican-American children were overrepresented in classes for the mentally retarded. She concluded that the bias inherent in assessment instruments as well as misinformed teachers, school psychologists, and other school personnel about the learning process in ethnic minority children contributed to the inappropriate placement of these students in special classes.

Over a decade later, Cummins (1984) conducted a study of the assessment process for language minorities, including an analysis of teacher referral forms and psychological evaluations, and arrived at a similar conclusion. Cummins examined referrals and assessments of 428 language minority children in Canada. The children were from Italian, Portuguese, and South American backgrounds. He analyzed the reasons for referral and found that the children were referred mainly because of poor school progress, special learning difficulties, and language problems. Many teachers wanted to know whether a child's academic problem was due to English language deficits or to specific learning disabilities. They also requested IQ testing for a determination of "real learning ability" in the children referred. Apparently teachers were not aware that in language minority children intelligence testing will not reveal a child's "true learning ability" nor will it determine, because of the limitations of the tests, whether a child's problem is due to English language limitations or true learning disabilities. This brings us to the issue of test validity. The children were evaluated by English-speaking psychologists using the WISC-R or the WPPSI for younger children. Cummins analyzed the validity of WISC-R subtests for language minority children and found that the majority of the Verbal IQ subtests focus on student's knowledge of the English language and North American culture instead of verbal cognitive and academic ability. The verbal

subtests were found to be biased against limited
English proficient children. The most biased of
the verbal subtests, according to Cummins, was
the Information subtest because it reflects
previous learning experiences of middle-class
native English-speakers. The least biased were
the Arithmetic and Digit Span subtests. Yet,
the Information subtest was administered to the
language minority children on almost all
occasions while the Digit Span and Arithmetic
subtests were frequently omitted.

The most disturbing fact to emerge from
Cummins' analysis of the referral forms and
assessment reports was the almost absolute lack
of knowledge on behalf of teachers and school
psychologists about the second language
acquisition process in language minority
children. In many of the referrals and reports,
no mention is made of the children's language
background and children were frequently
considered proficient in English although they
had been in Canada for less than two years.
Teachers and school psychologists apparently
confused the ability to use the English language
in the limited context of social face-to-face
interaction with academic language proficiency.
If children had acquired the necessary English
language skills to respond to questions, follow
directions, and so forth, yet experienced
academic difficulties (as is the usual situation
for children acquiring a second language),
teachers questioned whether the academic
difficulties were due to a learning problem
rather than a limitation in English language
skills. As Cummins states (1984):

> "It is clear that among the students in
> the present study acquisition of fluent
> English speaking and listening skills
> does not necessarily imply commensurate
> development of English conceptual or
> academic proficiency." (p.35)

Another disturbing finding of this study,
documented by other studies of this nature
(Ortiz and Maldonado-Colon 1986; Maldonado-
Colon, 1986) is the similarities between the
linguistic functioning and other behaviors of

limited English proficient students and the learning disabled. Not only are syntax, articulation, and vocabulary errors common in both populations, but behaviors such as distractibility and short attention span are also experienced by the two groups. In the case of the limited English proficient child, linguistic errors are normal in the process of acquiring a second language and inappropriate behaviors are common when children cannot follow what goes on in the classroom. Cummins also found similar discrepancies between verbal and performance IQ scores in the limited English proficient children as are found in learning disabled learners. Second language errors, inappropriate behaviors, and verbal and performance IQ discrepancies should not be construed as evidence of learning disabilities in language minority populations.

Based on an analysis of the data, Cummins suggests that it is appropriate to assess children's cognitive and academic abilities in the native language, if they have been in the host country less than two years. Caution should be exercised after two years. A possible regression in native language abilities may occur because of lack of exposure to more complex concepts in the first language. Nevertheless, he says that greater confidence results from the assessment of language minority children in their stronger language by professionals fluent in the children's language and familiar with dialectical differences that may exist.

Other researchers have found similar problems. Ortiz and Yates (1983) documented an overrepresentation of 300% of Hispanic students in the learning disabilities category. Dew (1984) analyzed data in one hundred school districts which appeared to discriminate in the placement of limited English proficient (LEP) students. She concluded that sixteen districts had placed 100 percent of their LEP students in special education classes. Furthermore, over forty districts had placed between 50 and 100 percent of their LEP students in special education. In a study of the effects of student characteristics in the placement of Hispanic students in classes for the learning disabled (Garcia, 1984), it was found that placement of Hispanic students in programs for the learning disabled and speech handicapped were often related to the acquisition of English as a second language. Referring teachers seemed unable to distinguish true language disorders from the developmental process of acquiring English as a second language.

Maldonado-Colon (1986) conducted a study of randomly selected special education students' program folders in a district with a school population of approximately 75 percent Hispanic. Results of the study revealed an important pattern (pp. 71-73).

1. Special education referrals were heavily influenced by deviant English language production and poor academic performance.

2. Children's language dominance was determined by the weakest of evidence, such as teacher's statement to the effect that "the child is Spanish dominant" or "the parent says the child speaks English at home."

3. English language proficiency was assessed by performance on standard English measures developed for native English-speakers.

4. Most students were tested in English regardless of native language background.

5. Spanish tests were used infrequently.

6. The testing procedure for language minority children was not modified.

7. Results of language proficiency tests administered up to two years before was frequently used.

8. Results of assessments were interpreted the same for Hispanics as for English-speakers. This resulted in labelling them language delayed and making them eligible for special education placement.

9. Special education placement was heavily influenced by teacher referral and test performance in English.

According to the author, results of this study of referral, assessment, and placement procedures indicate that limited English proficient children are still exposed to biased assessment and placement due to the inability of teachers and school psychologists to understand the process of second language acquisition and the linguistic variables that affect a child's performance on academic tasks.

Based on a number studies on the inappropriate referral of language minority children for special education evaluation and placement, Ortiz and Maldonado-Colon (1986) argue that many of the behaviors teachers associated with learning problems are characteristic of children who are in the process of second language acquisition. It appears that much confusion exists in the distinction between limited English proficiency and language and learning disabilities. An important and critical factor such as English language proficiency is often misjudged. Teachers and school psychologists are unaware of the linguistic characteristics of children acquiring a second language, they have unrealistic expectations about the rate of acquisition which varies from child to child, and little understanding of what constitutes language proficiency. Therefore, they consider a child proficient when mastery of surface conversational skills is achieved although skills in more cognitively demanding tasks may be lacking. Since language minority students achieve peer-appropriate conversational skills in about two years, yet require an average of five to seven years to achieve grade norms in academic skills in the second language, it is imperative that school personnel understand the distinctions between proficiency in academic areas and surface conversational skills (Cummins, 1984). Until this distinction is understood, language minority children will continue to be referred for special education assessment, be subjected to biased assessment processes, and inappropriately placed in special classes solely because of their limitations in English language proficiency.

An encouraging finding among recent studies (Collier, 1986; Walsh and Carballo, 1986) is that limited English proficient children participating in bilingual education programs are less likely to be referred for special education services than limited English proficient children in mainstream programs. One can conclude from these studies that the familiarity of bilingual teachers and other bilingual personnel with the second language acquisition process, as well as their ability to spot true learning problems in the native language, account for the lower percentage of referrals.

Valero Figueira (1986) provides an overview of the treatment of language minority students in special education and concludes that not only are language minority students with no learning problems overrepresented in special education classes, but limited English proficient children who are in need of special services remain underserved; this includes a lack of appropriate services for language minority gifted children. Although legal support exists for the provision of special services to children of limited English speaking ability who have true learning problems, the needs of these children are not being met.

TRUE LEARNING PROBLEMS AND BILINGUALISM

Few research studies have focused on exceptional bilingual children. That is, children who experience true learning problems not associated with limitations in English, and who are living and learning in bilingual settings. These children's learning problems are evident in the native language. An important concern of educators is whether children who are already burdened with a learning problem, such as learning disabilities or mental retardation, can or should be exposed to two languages. Do the same tenets that apply to normally developing limited English proficient children, apply to the exceptional child? In other words, is the language acquisition process the same? Does the potential to learn two languages exist? Should they be instructed in the native language or English, if a choice of language is to be made? How can these children be assessed appropriately?

Several studies have looked into the appropriate assessment of limited English proficient children with language disorders. Linares-Orama (1977) studied the applicability of diagnostic measures for the evaluation of syntax in preschool Spanish-speaking youngsters to determine deviancy. The study compared the performance of normal and language disordered three-year-old Puerto Rican children living in Puerto Rico. They were tested to determine whether the mean length of utterance (MLU) and Lee's Developmental Sentence Scoring Procedure (1974) adapted for Spanish by Toronto (1976) were sensitive to the linguistic differences of Puerto Rican children within the three-year range. The results were positive.

Two groups of twenty-five Spanish-speaking children between the ages of six and eight were studied by Wyszewianski-Langdon (1983) in Boston. One group was developing normally, the second group was composed of language disordered youngsters. A series of tests was administered to the children, in Spanish and English, in the areas of articulation of words, articulation in connected speech, auditory discrimination, sentence comprehension, sentence repetition, and sentence expression. After an analysis of test results and comparisons between groups, the author concludes that the language disordered group made more errors in both Spanish and English than the control group.

Merino (1983) compared and contrasted the language development of normal and language disordered Spanish-speaking children of limited English proficiency. A battery of tests was administered to fifty monolingual Spanish-speakers in Mexico to establish baseline data. The same battery was then administered to a group of twenty-two language disordered Spanish-speaking children in the United States. It was found that the language disordered group presented difficulties in oral production skills, but not in comprehension. Since comprehension was tested by asking the child to select one of two pictures, the results for the comprehension part of the test were less dependable, according to the author. Merino concludes that significant differences in

performance exist between language disordered
and non-language disordered children on the
tests.

Pragmatic criteria were compared with
traditional surface structure criteria in the
diagnosis of language disorders in bilingual
children in a study performed by Damico, et al.
(1983). Spontaneous language samples were
obtained from ten Spanish/English bilingual
children between six and eight years of age who
had been referred for special education
evaluation. The language samples were examined
for normalcy following structural and pragmatic
criteria. According to the authors, results of
the study indicate that the two sets of criteria
identified different subgroups as language
impaired and that the pragmatic criteria were
more effective in predicting school achievement
over a seven-month period.

Sixty (60) Mexican American children
between the ages of seven and ten were subjects
of a study to develop and validate an assessment
procedure for the identification of language
disorders in bilingual children (De Leon, 1986).
The children were tested using an assessment
procedure that incorporated a multidimensional
approach. Results of the study indicate that
the Toronto Test of Receptive Vocabulary in
Spanish proved to be the only statistically
significant measure predicting classroom
language.

These studies provide valuable information
on the applicability of diagnostic measures
adapted or developed for Spanish-speakers
with language disorders and on the importance
of utilizing pragmatic criteria with
traditional structural criteria in
assessing language disordered children.
Nevertheless, the question of what constitutes
a true language disorder in children of limited
English proficiency remains.

To shed some light on this question,
Ambert (1986) conducted a study to identify
the characteristics of Spanish-speaking
children living in the United States who have
true language disorders and who are of limited
English proficiency. The study focused
on the specific characteristics of these

children's receptive and expressive language in Spanish. The influence of English on their linguistic development was considered as well as dialectical differences in the Spanish spoken by the children involved in the study. A group of thirty Spanish-speaking Puerto Rican children, who were both limited in English proficiency and language disordered, were selected for the study. The children were between the ages of five and twelve and were identified as language disordered by qualified bilingual speech and language pathologists, fluent in Spanish and familiar with the regional variety of Spanish spoken by the children. The analysis of the children's language was global, including structural analysis (phonology, morphology, syntax, and semantics) and pragmatic (analysis of meaningful verbal and nonverbal interaction). Results of the study indicated that the children included in this study deviated from the language of Spanish-speaking children acquiring language normally. The children presented specific structural difficulties as well as pragmatic problems. Although the children were living in a bilingual setting, the impact of English on their language development was minimal.

Now, what does the research tell us about the acquisition of a second language in children with learning problems?

In a study of 19,000 South African students from Afrikaans and English backgrounds, E.G. Malherbe (cited in Cummins, 1984) found that children with below-average IQ levels placed in bilingual programs were performing just as well in their native language as equivalent IQ children in monolingual schools and almost twice as well in their second language as children in higher intelligence groups.

The most influential study done to date on learning disabilities and bilingualism was performed by Bruck (1978) with language disordered English-speaking children attending a French immersion program in Canada. The purpose of the study was to determine whether the language disordered English-speaking children should continue in French immersion programs or be transferred to an all-English program. Four groups of English-speaking children were selected in kindergarten and followed on a yearly basis until the third grade. The four groups consisted of:

FP: Children with language disabilities who were placed in French immersion programs (French problems).
EP: Children with language disabilities in English programs (English problems).
FC: Children with normal language development who were placed in French immersion programs (French control).
EC: Children with normal language development in English programs (English control).

The progress of these children from kindergarten through the third grade was followed in the areas of first and second language skills, cognitive development, and school achievement. All the children were of normal intelligence as evidenced by the Wechsler Preschool Primary Test of Intelligence and were screened for language disorders. After selection the children were given a battery of tests each year to assess their English and French language skills, academic achievement in English, and cognitive functioning. Results of the study indicate that by the third grade the FP children performed as well as or better than the EP children on all tests given. Their participation in the French immersion program, according to the researcher, did not appear to have been detrimental to their English cognitive or linguistic development. Furthermore, they learned to read and spell in English. In math, the FP children performed similarly to the EP children. The scores on the French tests indicate that in terms of aural comprehension the FP children were acquiring proficiency in French, although the FP group had more difficulty expressing themselves than the FC group. Based on the results of this study,

Bruck recommends that language disabled children remain in the French immersion program with appropriate remedial help.

Cummins (1984) cites a case study of a learning disabled English-speaking child attending a Chinese-English bilingual program and receiving Chinese as a second language instruction. It was found that the child had difficulty with all classes except Chinese and learning a second language enhanced his self-image.

The positive effects of bilingualism on children's metalinguistic awareness (knowledge of language which includes adopting different speech styles for different contexts, awareness of the sounds, meanings, and grammar of the language) has been documented (McLaughlin, 1984). In a study of monolingual and bilingual mildly retarded children, Rueda (1983) found that the bilingual subjects had developed a greater awareness of some metalinguistic aspects of language. Nevertheless, on Piagetian measures of cognitive development, no differences between the monolingual and bilingual children were found.

In an ethnographic study of a mildly handicapped special education classroom (Flores, Rueda and Porter; 1986), bilingual and trilingual students were exposed to holistically-based writing experiences to develop their literacy skills more effectively. Holistic writing experiences are based on the assumptions that traditional approaches to literacy development are ineffective with children with learning problems. Traditional approaches emphasize a "skills" model in which children progress from sound recognition to letter-sound correspondence to word recognition skills followed by reading simple sentences and vocabulary controlled stories. Writing is also learned in a sequential step-by-step order. Correct spelling and grammatical usage is deemed essential in this model and all reading and writing must be error-free. Holistic approaches to literacy development, on the other hand, emphasize the social and functional aspects of reading and writing. The principal assumption of this approach is that

"language and literacy (either in L1 or
in L2) are best learned when presented
in authentic situations reflecting real
needs, purposes and functions."
(Flores, Rueda and Porter; 1986; p.
152)

In the Flores et al., study, the
researchers were interested in developing higher
order literacy skills, that is, creative
communication of meaning. When students were
exposed to written drill sheets which focused on
grammatically correct discrete subskills, they
experienced substantial problems. Once the
teacher shifted to interactive journal writing
in which an authentic exchange occurred between
teacher and student and the writing focused on
creative communication (disregarding "correct"
writing conventions), students became more
creative communicators. The researchers
analyzed the bilingual special education
students' journal entries during one year and
concluded that without a change from a skills
oriented literacy approach to a holistic one,
the students would have acquired only minimal
literacy skills.

The crucial question of transfer of skills
between languages addressed in the first chapter
of this book is also relevant for children with
learning problems. Special education
practitioners have expressed the
intuitively-based opinion that children with
serious learning problems will have difficulty
transferring skills from one language to
another. Bilingual special education teachers,
though, routinely witness the phenomenon of
skill transfer in language minority children
with learning problems. In an attempt to
understand the process of transfer of skills in
bilingual children with learning problems,
Ambert (1979) did a study to test the
hypothesis that learning disabled children
taught concepts in their native language will
transfer the knowledge into English without
formal instruction in English. The only
prerequisite is that the child be exposed to the
second language informally (English-speaking

peers, TV, games, music, etc.). The investigator worked with a twelve-year-old Puerto Rican child who had serious language impairments and other learning disabilities. He exhibited language deficits in his native language and in English. He was pretested for knowledge of basic concepts and results of the testing indicated that he did not know the concepts <u>on top of</u>, <u>between</u>, <u>different</u>, and <u>after</u> in Spanish or English.

A language intervention program was developed in Spanish, his stronger language. After the child had successfully mastered the concepts in Spanish, he was tested in English to determine whether he had transferred his knowledge of the concepts learned from Spanish to English. Test results indicated that he did effect the transfer. Without formal instruction of the concepts in English, the child scored correctly on all the items he learned in Spanish when tested for the concepts in English.

CONCLUSION

Current research results clearly reveal the overrepresentation of language minority children in special classes. Placement of these children is determined, in most cases, by their limitations in English language proficiency and not by true learning problems and is due, to a great extent, to the inability of teachers and evaluation specialists to understand the differences between the natural process of second language acquisition and specific learning and language disabilities. Furthermore, researchers who have focused on the overrepresentation issue, have uncovered the striking similarities in test performance, classroom behaviors, and English language performance between children in the process of acquiring a second language and children with true learning and language deficits. These similarities can only heighten the problem. On the other hand, limited English proficient children participating in bilingual education programs are less likely to be referred for special education services. It seems clear from

an analysis of the research that language
minority students continue to be penalized for
not living up to the expectations of teachers
and evaluation personnel in their second
language development. Instead of analyzing
their own limitations, school personnel insist
on placing the burden on those least able to
bear it.

Research findings have also concluded that
limited English proficient children with true
learning problems often do not receive the
services they require. In addition, children
from language minority backgrounds are woefully
underrepresented in classes for the gifted and
talented. Legislation and case law have affirmed
LEP children's rights to special educational
services in their dominant language, as well as
instruction in English as a second language.
School districts are responsible for the
provision of an appropriate education to LEP
students with special educational needs.
Bilingual special education programs, with
qualified bilingual personnel, fulfill the need
to provide LEP exceptional children with
remediation of their special educational needs
in a language they can understand while they
acquire the English language skills needed to
survive in this society. The research findings
on bilingualism and special education indicate
that bilingual children with learning problems
can transfer skills from one language to another
and have a greater metalinguistic awareness than
monolingual children with learning problems.
These special abilities of bilingual handicapped
children need to be taken into consideration in
developing appropriate programs for this
population. In addition, as the Rueda, et
al. (1986) study indicates, bilingual
handicapped children can achieve important
literacy skills when innovative techniques are
used which emphasize the children's strengths
and not their weaknesses.

RESEARCH NEEDS FOR THE FUTURE

As Willig (1986) says, "...one of the most
critical issues in the education of
language-minority children is the determination

of language dominance, or relative language proficiency." Because language minority children's placement in special classes continues to be determined by their second language proficiency, instead of true abilities or disabilities, measures of language proficiency assessment are essential to gauge LEP children's true linguistic functioning and to assist practitioners in selecting appropriate testing techniques, both in the native language and in English. Native language testing is not always appropriate. As Cummins (1984) suggests, after two years of English instruction a child will experience native language loss or fail to develop academic language abilities in the native language. This will affect his or her performance on native language tests. It appears that research directed at developing appropriate assessment techniques for LEP children at different levels of both native language and second language proficiency is needed.

More empirical studies are needed to establish the differences between second language learners and children with true learning and language disorders.

We also need to know more about the learning process in bilingual children with special educational needs. More evidence is warranted on the transfer of skills between languages and whether it occurs in bilingual children with different types of disabilities. We also need more information on the process of second language acquisition in children with learning problems. Does the process follow the same stages as in children who have no learning problems?

More research evidence is needed on the advisability of providing instruction to LEP handicapped children in the native language while they acquire a second language.

Detailed analysis of culturally-determined behaviors manifested by language minority children and considered inappropriate in the schools is also necessary.

REFERENCES

Ambert, A.N. Language Disorders and Bilingual-
    ism. Unpublished Monograph, Harvard
    University Graduate School of Education,
    1979.

Ambert, A.N. "Identifying Language Disorders in
    Spanish-Speakers." In Willig, A.C. and
    Greenberg, H.F. (Eds.) **Bilingualism and
    Learning Disabilities: Policy and Practice
    for Teachers and Administrators.** New York:
    American Library Publishing, 1986.

Bruck, M. "The suitability of early French
    immersion programs for the language-
    disabled child." **Canadian Journal of
    Education,** 3, 51-72, 1978.

Collier, C. The Referral of Hispanic Children
    to Special Education: A Comparison of
    Acculturation and Education Characteristics
    of Referred and Nonreferred Culturally and
    Linguistically Different Children. Paper
    presented at the Annual Meeting of the
    National Association for Bilingual Educa-
    tion, Chicago, Illinois, April, 1986.

Cummins, J. **Bilingualism and Special Education:
    Issues in Assessment and Pedagogy.** Avon,
    England: Multilingual Matters, 1984.

Damico, J.S.; Oller, J.W.; and Storey, M.E.
    "The diagnosis of language disorders in
    bilingual children: Surface-oriented and
    pragmatic criteria." **Journal of Speech and
    Hearing Disorders,** 46, 385-394, 1973.

De Leon, J. An Investigation into the Develop-
    ment and Validation of an Assessment Proce-
    dure for Identifying Language Disorders in
    Spanish/English Bilingual Children. Unpub-
    lished doctoral dissertation, New Mexico
    State University, 1986.

Dew, N. "The Exceptional Bilingual Child:
Demography." In Chinn, P.C. (Ed.) **Education
of Culturally and Linguistically Different
Exceptional Children.** Reston, Va.: Council
for Exceptional Children, 1984.

Flores, B.; Rueda, R.; and Porter, B. "Examining
Assumptions and Instructional Practices
Related to the Acquisition of Literacy
with Bilingual Special Education Students."
In Willig, A.C. and Greenberg, H.F.
**Bilingualism and Learning Disabilities:
Policy and Practice for Teachers and
Administrators.** New York: American
Library Publishing Co., 1986.

Garcia, S.B. Effects of Student Characteristics,
School Programs and Organization on
Decision-making for the Placement of
Hispanic Students in Classes for the
Learning Disabled. Unpublished doctoral
dissertation, The University of Texas at
Austin, 1984.

Lee, L. **Developmental Sentence Analysis.**
Evanston, Ill.: Northwestern University
Press, 1974.

Linares-Orama, N. "Evaluation of syntax in
three-year-old Spanish-speaking Puerto
Rican children." **Journal of Speech and
Hearing Research,** 20, 350-357, 1977.

Maldonado-Colon, E. "Assessment: Considerations
upon Interpreting Data of Linguistically/
Culturally Different Students Referred
for Disabilities or Disorders." In Willig,
A.C. and Greenberg, H.F. (Eds.)
**Bilingualism and Learning Disabilities:
Policy and Practice for Teachers and
Administrators.** New York: American
Library Publishing Co., 1986.

McLaughlin, B. **Second Language Acquisiton in
Childhood: Volume 1. Preschool Children.**
Hillsdale, N.J.: Lawrence Erlbaum, 1984.

Mercer, J.R. "Institutionalized Anglocentrism: Labeling Mental Retardates in Ten Schools." In Race, Change, and Urban Society, P. Orleans and W. Rusell, Jr. (Eds.), Urban Affairs Annual Review, Vol. V. Los Angeles: Sage Publications, 1971.

Merino, B.J. "Language development in normal and language handicapped Spanish-speaking children." Hispanic Journal of Behavioral Sciences, 5, 379-400, 1983.

Ortiz, A.A. and Maldonado-Colon, E. "Reducing Inappropriate Referrals of Language Minority Students in Special Education." In Willig, A.C. and Greenberg, H.F. (Eds.) Bilingualism and Learning Disabilities: Policy and Practice for Teachers and Administrators. New York: American Library Publishing Co., 1986.

Ortiz, A.A. and Yates, J.R. "Incidence of exceptionality among Hispanics: Implications for manpower planning." NABE Journal, 7, 41-54, 1983.

Rueda, R. "Metalinguistic awareness in monolingual and bilingual mildly retarded children." NABE Journal, 8, 55-68, 1983.

Toronto, A. "Developmental assessment of Spanish grammar." Journal of Speech and Hearing Disorders, 41, 150-171, 1976.

Valero Figueira, E. "Preliminary overview of the treatment of language minority students in special education." NABE News, IX, 4 and 5, 3-10.

Walsh, C.E. and Carballo, E.B. Transitional Bilingual Education in Massachusetts: A Preliminary Study of its Effectiveness. Bridgewater, Mass.: Bridgewater State College, 1986.

Willig, A.C. "Special Education and the Culturally and Linguistically Different Child: An Overview of Issues and

Challenges." In Willig, A.C. and Greenberg,
H.F.   (Eds.)   **Bilingualism and Learning
Disabilities: Policy   and   Practice   for
Teachers and Administrators.** New York:
American Library Publishing, 1986.

Wyszewianski-Langdon, H. "Assessment and intervention   strategies   for   the   bilingual
language disordered student." **Exceptional
Children,** 50, 37-46, 1983.

ANNOTATED BIBLIOGRAPHY

Ambert, A.N. "Identifying language disorders in
    Spanish-speakers." Journal of Reading,
    Writing, and Learning Disabilities Interna-
    tional, 2, 1, 21-41, 1986.

    A study to identify the characteristics of
    Spanish-speaking children living in the
    United States who have true language
    disorders and who are of limited English
    proficiency. The author studied a group of
    thirty Spanish-speaking Puerto Rican
    children who were both LEP and language
    disordered. An analysis of the children's
    receptive, expressive and pragmatic lan-
    guage was done. A taxonomy of the
    characteristics of Spanish-speaking lan-
    guage disordered children is given.

Arrigo, R. Chinatown Meets the Barrio: Innova-
    tions in Cross-Cultural Special Education
    Teacher Preparation. Paper presented at
    the Ethnic and Multicultural Concerns
    Symposia, National Association for Bilin-
    gual Education, Dallas, Texas, November,
    1986.

    Describes a teacher training program
    designed for Hispanics and Asians in New
    York.

Benavides, A. and Valero-Figueira, E. Pre-
    Referral Screening for Language Minority
    Students. Paper presented at the Ethnic
    and Multicultural Concerns Symposia,
    National Association for Bilingual
    Education, Dallas, Texas, November, 1986.

    Describes two screening instruments that
    can be used to determine whether language
    minority students should be referred for
    special education or be considered for
    additional ESL/bilingual instruction.

Carrasquillo, A. "The parent factor: Teaching
    language skills to limited English
    proficient learning disabled students."

Journal of Reading, Writing, and Learning
Disabilities International, 2, 1, 57-71,
1986.

According to the author, special education
is based on the premise that all students
have the right to and should receive an
adequate, meaningful education. Meeting
the cognitive and linguistic needs of
learning disabled limited English proficient (LEP) students is the school's and
parents' responsibility. Caution should be
taken not to confuse language differences
with language disorders. If LEP students,
through appropriate testing, are placed in
classes for learning disabled students,
the instructional staff should use parents
as reinforcers of instructional language
development. Instructional activities are
described so parents can help the school
develop creative and meaningful language
activities.

Chen, S. Identifying and Serving Handicapped
Children Among Asian Populations. Paper
presented at the Ethnic and Multicultural
Concerns Symposia, National Association for
Bilingual Education, Dallas, Texas,
November, 1986.

Offered recommendations for working with
Asian populations, including specific
suggestions for gathering case study
information, dealing with cultural identify
and severe emotional trauma issues,
awareness of culturally-determined behaviors, identifying medical needs, among
others.

Chinn, P.C. and Hughes, S. "Representation of
minority students in special education
classes." Remedial and Special Education,
8, 4, 41-46, 1987.

Examines representation of minorities in
special education classes since 1978.
Analyzes the most recent Office of Civil
Rights Surveys of elementary and secondary

schools   on   student   enrollment   and
placement.   Data from the surveys indicate
a   decline   of   overrepresentation   in some
areas   such   as   Hispanics   in   classes for
educable mentally retarded students,   but a
continued   overrepresentation   of blacks in
classes   for   educable   mentally   retarded,
trainable mentally retarded,   and seriously
emotionally   disturbed   students.   Underrepresentation in classes for the gifted   and
talented   continues   to   be   a   problem,
according   to   the   surveys,   for   blacks,
Hispanics, and American Indians.

Collier,   C.   The Referral of Hispanic Children
    to   Special   Education: A   Comparison   of
    Acculturation and Education Characteristics
    of Referred and   Nonreferred Culturally and
    Linguistically   Different   Children.   Paper
    presented   at   the   Annual   Meeting   of the
    National   Association   for Bilingual Educa-
    tion, Chicago, Illinois, April 1-5, 1986.

    A study of   the characteristics of Hispanic
    elementary   school   children   in   bilingual
    education   programs.   Attempted to identify
    those   education   and acculturation charac-
    teristics which distinguished   children who
    had   been   referred   to   special   education
    from   nonreferred   children.   The   sample
    consisted of 95 Hispanic children, of whom
    51   had never been referred and 44 had been
    referred to   special   education.   Of those
    referred,   only   17   had   been   placed   in
    special   education   programs.   Contrary to
    expectations,   the   results   indicated   no
    significant differences   between groups for
    any   educational   characteristic   except
    degree of teacher   concern, but achievement
    was   found   to   be   related   to   years   of
    bilingual   instruction,   language profi-
    ciency,   minority   enrollment,   and overall
    acculturation   level.   In   addition, there
    was   a meaningful   effect   size between the
    achievement   of   non-referred   and   that of
    placed children.   Placed children tended to
    be the   most   acculturated   and   more often
    came   from   schools   with   low   minority

enrollment. Those referred but not placed were the least acculturated and had the lowest achievement in all content areas. The findings imply that culturally and linguistically different children are disproportionately referred for special education, possibly as a function of minority enrollment and availability of alternative programs and that the psychodynamics of acculturation must be considered in the identification and instruction of culturally and linguistically different children with special needs.

Cummins, J. "Psychological assessment of minority students: Out of context, out of focus, out of control?" **Journal of Reading, Writing, and Learning Disabilities International,** 2, 1, 9-19, 1986.

Analyzes the psychological/educational assessment process of language minority students and argues that many so-called learning disabilities identified may be pedagogically-induced and that psychologists are ignoring the academic and identity problems of minority students.

De Leon, J. An Investigation into the Development and Validation of an Assessment Procedure for Identifying Language Disorders in Spanish/English Bilingual Children. Unpublished doctoral dissertation, New Mexico State University, 1986.

Developed and validated an assessment procedure for the identification of language disorders in bilingual children incorporating a multidimensional approach.

Dew, N. An Introduction to Feuerstein's Theory or Structural Cognitive Modifiability for Bilingual Special Education. Paper presented at the Ethnic and Multicultural Concerns Symposia, National Association for Bilingual Education, Dallas, Texas, November, 1986.

Discussed use of the Learning Potential
Assessment Device and Instrumental
Enrichment developed by Feuerstein and the
importance of these methods in serving the
culturally and linguistically diverse
exceptional student in the United States.
Compared the concepts of Feuerstein's
theory with current educational practices
in assessment, including the active
approach of Feuerstein with the passive
acceptance approach traditionally used in
this country. Discussed the implications
of using this model with bilingual special
education students.

Fafard, M.; Hanlon, R.E.; and Bryson, E.A. Jose
P. v. Ambach: "Progress toward
compliance." Exceptional Children, 52, 4,
313-322, 1986.

An update on the status of a class action
suit filed on behalf of handicapped
children who had been deprived of a free
appropriate education in New York and which
had implications for culturally and
linguistically diverse children.

Fischer, S. and Strum, I. Procedure for
Establishing a Cut-off Score for Determin-
ing Limited English Proficiency among
Severely and Profoundly Handicapped
Students. Paper presented at the Annual
Meeting of the American Educational
Research Association, San Francisco,
California, April, 1986.

A five-item rating scale was developed for
the New York City schools to determine
eligibility for English as a Second
Language instruction in Category C
exceptional students exempted from testing.
The test was piloted with 163 students
including severely, trainable, and
profoundly mentally retarded and autistic
children. Results of the study indicated
that in most cases the form discriminated
well between verbal nonverbal students

because of the difficulty in assessing language proficiency. It was recommended that the form be modified for autistic and severely and profoundly mentally handicapped populations.

Flores, B.; Rueda, R.; and Porter, B. "Examining Assumptions and Instructional Practices Related to the Acquisition of Literacy with Bilingual Special Education Students." In Willig, A.C. and Greenberg, H.F. (Eds.) **Bilingualism and Learning Disabilities: Policy and Practice for Teachers and Administrators.** New York: American Library Publishing Co., 1986.

Describes a traditional approach to literacy education and proposes a new approach based on theoretical and research advances which stress holistic literacy in real situations. An example of interactive journal writing between a teacher and a mildly handicapped trilingual child is described.

Fort Hamilton High School Project SPEED. **Special Education to Eliminate Dropouts.** Evaluation Report, New York City Board of Education, 1986.

Project SPEED provides instruction in English as a second language (ESL) and native language arts in addition to bilingual instruction in mathematics, social studies, computer skills, and typing to 490 students of limited English proficiency in grades 9 through 12. All program students were born outside the United States and their native languages included Spanish, Arabic, Chinese, Vietnamese, and Khmer. Over 59 percent of the students were overage for their grade. To achieve a major goal of dropout prevention, instruction stressed development of English language skills. Evaluation of student achievement data indicates that students met program objectives in English reading, mathematics, business/vocational courses and attendance. Objectives were not met for English language achievement.

Gajar, A.H. "Foreign language learning disabilities: The identification of predictive and diagnostic variables." **Journal of Learning Disabilities**, 20, 6, 327-330, 1987.

Presents a method for identifying predictors of success in learning a foreign language at the university level and compares the performance of students identified as learning disabled on these predictors. The scores of regular students enrolled in introductory foreign language classes on the Modern Language Aptitude Test were compared with their foreign language course performance. Two subtests predicted a relationship to learning a foreign language. University learning disabled students exhibited significantly lower performance on all five of the Modern Language Aptitude subtests. The results of this study suggest that the information provided by the Modern Language Aptitude Test is potentially valuable to the diagnostic process.

Garcia, S.B. and Yates, J.R. "Policy Issues Associated with Serving Bilingual Exceptional Children." In Willig, A.C. and Greenberg, H.F. (Eds.) **Bilingualism and Learning Disabilities: Policy and Practice for Teachers and Administrators.** New York: American Library Publishing Co., 1986.

Describes a study which focused on district policies and practices in the identification and placement of 111 Hispanic and non-Hispanic students in programs for the learning disabled in an urban school district in Texas. Student characteristics were compared by ethnicity, as well as variables such as membership of students' referral and placement committees, assessment practices, and the nature of services recommended. Information was also obtained on the educational background, training and experience of 131 school personnel involved in the referral, assessment and placement process. Results of the study indicate that the most frequent reasons for referral for all students were problems in reading and language. Hispanic students were more likely to be referred for culturally determined behaviors and low English proficiency appeared to affect the test performance of Hispanic students who scored lower than non-Hispanics on all subtests of the WISC-R Verbal Scale. Hispanics performed as well as non-Hispanic students on the Performance Scale. Only Hispanic students identified as learning disabled were referred for speech therapy. Non-Hispanics usually received counseling or other secondary service.

Green, D.W. "Control activation and resource: A framework and a model for the control of speech in bilinguals." **Brain and Language**, 27, 2, 210-223, 1986.

The author says that impaired language performance in bilingual aphasics results not from impairment in the language system itself, but in the means for controlling intact language systems. Speech production is seen to be similar to regulation of other skilled actions, so that selection of a particular word would involve regulation of a single underlying variable of amount of activation. Further, regulation involves use of a means of increasing or decreasing activation of some internal component. A model of both normal and impaired bilingual language function is developed based on these considerations. The model predicts that in cases where there is no speech, linguistic activity may still exist, but proper control over the intact systems has been lost.

Hedley, C.N. "What's new in software: Computer programs for bilingualism." **Journal of Reading, Writing, and Learning Disabilities International**, 2, 1, 101-106, 1986.

Reviews software appropriate for the development of English language skills of bilingual special learners.

Holtzman, Jr.,W.H. "Issues in the Implementation of Master's Level Training Programs for Bilingual Special Education." In Willig, A.C. and Greenberg, H.F. (Eds.) **Bilingualism and Learning Disabilities: Policy and Practice for Teachers and Administrators.** New York: American Publishing Co., 1986.

Describes characteristics of appropriate training programs for bilingual special education teachers.

Jackson, S. Use of Pragmatic Criteria in Assessing the Language Skills of Hispanic Students. Paper presented at the Ethnic and Multicultural Concerns Symposia, National Association for Bilingual Education, Dallas, Texas, November, 1986.

Describes language assessment procedures used in the assessment of LEP learning disabled and speech handicapped children.

Kief, E. and Correa, V. Bilingual Special Education Needs of Visually Impaired Learners. Paper presented at the Ethnic and Multicultural Concerns Symposia, National Association for Bilingual Education, Dallas, Texas, November, 1986.

Discussed methods of assessing bilingual visually impaired students and their learning characteristics. Also discussed computer assisted instruction programs for the visually impaired which include ESL programs and appropriate teaching techniques for this population.

Maldonado-Colon, E. "Assessment: Interpreting data of linguistically/culturally different students referred for disabilities or disorders." Journal of Reading, Writing, and Learning Disabilities International. 2, 1, 73-83, 1986.

An exploratory descriptive study of randomly selected students' special education program folders in a district whose school population was approximately 75% Hispanic. Analysis of the data revealed that the linguistic character-istics of bilingual and LEP students were evaluated with the same instruments utilized with native speakers of English. Also, their errors were interpreted as stringently as errors of native speakers of the English language without taking into account the characteristics of children acquiring a second language. As a result, the children were erroneously classified as disordered.

Marchesi, A. El desarrollo cognitivo y linguistico de los ninos sordos. Madrid: Alianza Editorial, 1987.

Reviews basic premises in cognitive, linguistic and reading skills development in children and analyzes specific strategies used by deaf children to develop these three areas. The author discusses appropriate instructional strategies to help deaf children learn more effectively.

McLean, M. and Mendez, A. Working with Hispanic Parents of Deaf Children. Paper presented at the Ethnic and Multicultural Concerns Symposia, National Association for Bilin-gual Education, Dallas, Texas, November, 1986.

Describes program developed in San Antonio, Texas, to teach American sign language to Spanish-speaking parents.

Narang, H.L. **An Annotated Bibliography of Articles on the Teaching of Reading to Children with Special Needs.** ED Document 274951, 1986.

Includes citations with brief annotations on such aspects as spelling, cloze procedure, language acquisition and remedial reading instruction. The annotations are divided into the following sections: general, English as a Second Language (ESL), bilingual children, gifted children, reluctant readers and remedial/disabled readers.

Office for Civil Rights, **Elementary and Secondary Civil Rights Survey,** District Summary, Volumes 1 and 2, Washington, D.C., June, 1986.

This survey was conducted to obtain data on the characteristics of public school students in the 50 states and the District of Columbia. The 3,510 school districts that participated were statistically sampled from approximately 16,000 U.S. school districts. The report includes data on individual racial/ethnic categories, children in need of bilingual education (language assistance programs), gifted/talented, educable mentally retarded, trainable mentally retarded, speech impaired, seriously emotionally disturbed, specific learning disability, as well as LEP students identified as in need of language assistance programs, but not enrolled in such programs.

Ortiz, A. and Maldonado-Colon, E. "Recognizing learning disabilities in bilingual children: How to lessen inappropriate referrals of language minority students to special education." **Journal of Reading, Writing, and Learning Disabilities International,** 2, 1, 43-56, 1986.

Examines reasons for over-referral of language minority students for learning disabilities placement, including misinterpretation of problem behaviors stemming from linguistic or cultural differences. Stresses the importance of documenting prior interventions to distinguish differences from handicapping conditions.

Orum. L.S. **Education of Hispanics: Status and Implications.** Washington, D.C.: National Council of La Raza, 1986.

Provides an overview of the educational status of Hispanics and notes the implications of the data. It includes sections on each of the following: the history of Hispanics in the United States; demographics; school enrollment; educational conditions; literacy and educational conditions of Hispanic adults; postsecondary education; and the composition of the teaching force. The final section of implications for education policy makers emphasizes the importance of programs aimed at early school success; adequately trained bilingual special education teachers, as well as teachers for the gifted and talented; combating curricular tracking; tutoring at the high school level and for younger students; dropout recovery programs and prevention programs that begin before high school.

Pellegrini, S. The Bilingual Home Inventory. Paper presented at the Ethnic and Multicultural Concerns Symposia, National Association for Bilingual Education, Dallas, Texas, November, 1986.

Discussed an inventory appropriate for use with severely and multiple handicapped children. The inventory examines the likes and dislikes of the individual, modes of communication, skill levels and learning styles. It also assists the family in establishing projected goals for the individualized educational program. According to the presenter, the Bilingual Home Inventory has resulted in an increase in parental involvement during the special education process.

Plata, M. "Instructional planning for limited English proficient students." **Journal of Instructional Psychology**, 13, 1, 32-39, 1986.

Suggests that methods used in teaching limited English proficient mentally disabled students must integrate special education and bilingual education instructional strategies. An instructional management and lesson plan model is proposed, components of the model are described, and advantages of the model for teachers of limited English proficient disabled populations are reviewed.

Ragosta, M. and Nelson, C. **TOEFL and Hearing Impaired Students: A Feasibility Study.** New York: New York University, 1986.

The Test of English as a Foreign Language (TOEFL) was administered to 26 hearing impaired college students in order to test the assumption that the English-language deficiencies of hearing impaired students are similar to those of foreign students. Results of the study indicated that the TOEFL appeared to have potential for measuring the English language proficiency of deaf students.

Rivera Viera, D. "Remediating reading problems in a Hispanic learning disabled child from a psycholinguistic perspective: A case study." **Journal of Reading, Writing, and Learning Disabilities International**, 2, 1, 85-97, 1986.

Describes a case study of a seven year old Puerto Rican child with learning disabilities. He received remedial reading instruction based on the Reading Miscue

Inventory (RMI)   The RMI was found to be a useful instrument in developing reading strategies, based on a psycholinguistic reading model, for the learning disabled reader.   As a result of the reading program, the subject improved his reading comprehension.

Simich-Dudgeon, C.   "A Multidisciplinary Model to Educate Minority Language Students with Handicapping Conditions." In Willig, A.C. and Greenberg, H.F. (Eds.) **Bilingualism and Learning Disabilities: Policy and Practice for Teachers and Administrators.** Willig, A.C. and Greenberg, H.F. (Eds.) New York: American Library Publishing Co., 1986.

Discusses a pilot program implemented by the Fairfax County Public Schools to service LEP/NEP students with special needs. A multidisciplinary model was developed by an ESL/Special Education resource teacher providing a continuum of ESL services, from consultative to direct instruction based on student variables. The program will result in training of special education and ESL teachers.

Teller, H. and Echeverria Ratleff, J. California Bilingual Special Education Model Sites (1984-1986) Programs and Research. Paper presented at the Ethnic and Multicultural Concerns Symposia, National Association for Bilingual Education, Dallas, Texas, November, 1986.

A description of the model-site programs which are based on the premise that provision of appropriate services to language minority students with special needs can only be accomplished with the cooperation of monolingual English special education teachers, bilingual aides, bilingual program teachers, ESL teachers, English resource teachers for reading and math, and regular English classroom teachers. Discusses types of interventions,

parental contact, a bilingual individualized education program, staffing, and
parent training for the effective provision
of special services.

Valero Figueira, E. "Preliminary overview of
the treatment of language minority students
in special education." **NABE News**, 9, 4 and
5, 3-10, 1986.

Analyzes studies conducted by The
Handicapped Minority Research Institute on
Language Proficiency at The University of
Texas at Austin, the National Research
Council and data collected by Vazquez
Nutall Associates which suggest that
language minority children without learning
problems are placed in special education
programs, whereas limited-English
proficient children with true learning
problems are not receiving the services
they need.

Valero Figueira, E. "Bilingual special
education personnel preparation: An
integrated model." **Teacher Education and
Special Education**, 9, 2, 82-88, 1986.

A description of a bilingual special
education teacher training program at
George Mason University in Virginia. The
program produces special education teachers
conversant in bilingual issues and
bilingual special educators specifically
skilled in second language acquisition,
cultural variance, and related content.

Walsh, C.E. and Carballo, E.B. **Transitional
Bilingual Education in Massachusetts: A
Preliminary Study of Its Effectiveness.**
Bridgewater State College, Massachusetts,
April 1986.

A study of the effectiveness of transitional bilingual education (TBE) programs
for Hispanic students in five Massachusetts
school districts. Analyzed data on
students' personal and educational char-

acteristics. The student sample consisted of 214 students in grades 1 through 12 and included TBE students, mainstream students who had previously been in TBE, and limited English proficient students never enrolled in TBE. A major finding was that although only nine percent of the TBE students had been referred for special education, 12 percent of the mainstream and 26 percent of the non-TBE students had been referred.

Weinrich, B.D., et al. **A Sourcebook of Adolescent Pragmatic Activities: Theory and Intervention for Language Therapy (Grades 7-12 and ESL).** Tucson, Arizona: Communication Skill Builders, 1986.

Contains a series of lesson plans for remediating pragmatic problems in adolescents and students of English as a second language (ESL). Provides an observation checklist for the identification of pragmatic errors and describes the nature and application of pragmatic therapy. Lesson plans are prefaced by a definition and discussion, guidelines for therapy, behavioral characteristics and a goal model showing how the stated goals of a lesson are embedded in the lesson activities.

Willig, A.C. and Greenberg, H.F. **Bilingualism and Learning Disabilities: Policy and Practice for Teachers and Administrators.** New York: American Publishing Co., 1986.

Reprints the articles appearing in the first issue, second volume, 1986, of the **Journal of Reading, Writing, and Learning Disabilities International.** Includes a discussion of issues in psychological assessment, language disorders, referral and placement, parental involvement, remediation of reading disabilities, teacher training models, and school policies.

Wood, F.H.; Johnson, J.L.; and Jenkins, J.R. "The Lora case: Nonbiased referral, assessment, and placement procedures." Exceptional Children, 52, 4, 323-331, 1986.

An update on the Lora v. Board of Education of the City of New York suit which was filed to correct abuses in the identification and placement of Black and Hispanic students in segregated special day schools for emotionally disturbed students.

Yates, J. and Ortiz, A. Characteristics of Learning Disabled, Mentally Retarded and Speech/Language Handicapped Hispanic Students at Initial Evaluation and Re-Evaluation. Paper presented at the Ethnic and Multicultural Concerns Symposia, National Association for Bilingual Education, Dallas, Texas, November, 1986.

Findings of the Handicapped Minority Research Institute on Language Proficiency indicate that LD students' IQ scores are significantly lower at re-evaluation, achievement scores have not changed from placement scores and most students demonstrate increased language performance reflecting greater English proficiency. In spite of lack of progress, all non-dismissed students spent significantly more time in special education after re-evaluation.

Yee, L. Identifying and Serving Handicapped Children among Asian Populations. Paper presented at the Ethnic and Multicultural Concerns Symposia, National Association for Bilingual Education, Dallas, Texas, November, 1986.

Discussed the problems associated with the evaluation of Asian students referred for special education. Offered five practical suggestions to reduce biased assessments.

Chapter 7

LANGUAGE MINORITIES IN AN INTERNATIONAL
CONTEXT: MANY COUNTRIES, ONE THEME

Alba N. Ambert

Thousands of languages are spoken in the
world today. India has over 150 languages,
Africa close to a thousand, the Soviet Union
130. Indians of the Americas speak over a
thousand languages. Bolivia, for example, has
the highest percentage of Indians in the
hemisphere with five indigenous languages
spoken. Countries with predominant speakers of
one language maintain diverse linguistic groups.
Catalan, Galician and Basque are spoken in
Spain; Sardinian and Rhaeto-Romanic in Italy;
Provencal and Breton in France; Sorbian in
Germany; and Frisian in The Netherlands to name
a few. Most countries have language minorities
that were present before the nations were
established. The Welsh in Great Britain, the
Catalonians in Spain, the Francophones in
Canada, many Hispanics in the United States, and
the Native American Indians are only some
examples. Many countries have more than one
official language. Switzerland has four:
German, French, Italian and Romansch; Belgium
has two: Flemish and French; Israel has Hebrew
and Arabic; Canada has two: English and
French; Ireland has English and Irish (Gaelic).
Nigeria, the most populous nation in Africa, has
about 250 languages, and although English is the
official one, Hausa, Yoruba and Fulani are
spoken extensively. India is the most
linguistically diverse country in the world.
Hindi is the official language and English was
established by the Indian constitution of 1965
as the associate official language of the
country. Even Japan, the most linguistically
uniform country, has a population of 500,000
speakers of Korean and a small number of Ainu
speakers (Katzner, 1986).

In addition to native inhabitants of
nations who speak diverse languages, frequent
migrations among countries also account for the
existence of different language groups in a

country. Guestworkers in Sweden and West Germany come from Greece, Italy, Portugal, Spain, Turkey, and Yugoslavia. Great Britain, France and Holland have large numbers of immigrants from former colonial territories. Educational systems throughout the world, therefore, provide services to children who do not speak the national language. In this chapter we will explore the educational treatment of language minorities in this international context. We will also describe immersion programs in Canada (developed for majority-language children) and how these differ from the educational treatment afforded to language minorities in that country.

A GENERAL OVERVIEW

A comparative study was done by Churchill (1986) on the education of linguistic and cultural minorities in the OECD. The Organization for Economic Cooperation and Development is composed of the following countries: Australia, Austria, Belgium, Canada, Denmark, Finland, France, (Federal Republic of) Germany, Greece, Iceland, Ireland, Italy, Japan, Luxembourg, The Netherlands, New Zealand, Norway, Portugal, Spain, Sweden, Switzerland, Turkey, United Kingdom, United States of America, and Yugoslavia. In this important study, Churchill identified three types of language minority student groupings for instructional purposes:

1. submersion into classes with majority language pupils;
2. placement of language minority students in separate groups; and
3. periodic teaching of dispersed small groups by itinerant teachers (Churchill, 1986, p.67).

In the first approach, in which minority students are mixed with majority students, it is assumed that interactions with majority language users will help develop· language skills in minority language students. The approach is also used to avoid the segregation of minority children in separate programs.

The second approach, that is, concentration of language minority students in separate groups, is the norm in many countries, on a short or long term basis. Some form of "pull-out" program appears to be the most convenient way to provide special instruction to linguistically different children.

The last approach, in which itinerant teachers are used periodically, is commonly seen in teaching of indigenous peoples, such as the Aboriginal population of Australia's outstations.

According to Churchill, the principal differences in policy for teaching linguistic minorities in the OECD countries are in the roles given to the teaching of the minority language and of the majority language. The two languages (native and second) are either taught as a subject or used as medium of instruction. The variety of combinations that exist in the use of the two languages is quite broad. A common thread in the educational treatment of language minorities in the countries studied is the requirement by all that minority students acquire the majority language. In the case of Switzerland, the acquisition of a second and/or third national language is required during compulsory schooling.

Two basic structures in second language teaching were identified in the study: sequential and parallel treatments.

Sequential treatments refer to three main approaches: First, submersion in the second language with no instruction in the native language. It is referred to as sequential because second language learning follows the first language. This method usually includes a short period of intensive language instruction in small groups often called "reception classes". In France and Switzerland, they are called "induction classes". The second sequential treatment consists of short-term teaching of certain subjects in the native language and concurrent intensive second language instruction. In some countries this approach is called "short-term preparatory classes". The third sequential approach is long-term teaching of most subjects in the native language and limited instruction in the second language with gradual transfer to an entirely second language teaching environment (Churchill, 1986).

Parallel or concurrent second language instructional treatment also includes three approaches: First, additional or remedial language instruction is provided to students who are studying courses in the second language. Almost all countries in this study provide this type of instruction to language minority students once they are placed in majority language programs. The second approach is referred to as a gradual transfer program and it involves using the two languages for certain periods of time in the same class. An increase in the proportion of second language instruction time occurs gradually until all instruction is in the second language. Language is taught as a subject and is used as a medium of instruction. The third approach consists of long-term study of the second language as a subject. (Churchill, 1986, pp.70-71.)

Furthermore, the educational systems studied by Churchill varied in the importance given to the native language of minority students. Systems ranged from a strong commitment to native language instruction, by using the home language as medium of instruction for more than two years, to no encouragement of the home language in or out of school.

After analyzing the data on treatment of language minority students in different countries, the author concludes that an evolutionary process has occurred in policy decisions and there is a greater tolerance for linguistic diversity, while not much emphasis is given to monolingual education in the countries studied. The OECD countries have responded to the special needs of linguistic minorities by providing them with special services. Nevertheless, the effectiveness of educational treatment for language minorities is still in question since in most cases, goals set by policymakers have not been achieved. That is, in most instances the educational needs of linguistic minorities remain unmet. The author suggests a number of reasons why this occurs. First of all, no systematic or consistent monitoring of language minority instruction exists within or among countries, making improvement of services difficult. Broader societal considerations also contribute to the situation. Linguistic minorities constitute "disenfranchized" groups and the education of their children is beyond their control. The attitudes of society towards minorities are mirrored in the schools and the educational treatments applied to new linguistic minorities and indigenous peoples, especially, are based on deficit models where language minority students are treated as handicapped. The study also revealed that teachers who work with language minority populations are ill-trained, to the extent that in some districts they do not fulfill even minimal teacher training requirements. In addition, teachers of linguistic minorities receive little or no support from their school districts.

Results of this extensive study on the education of linguistic minorities in the OECD countries point to serious problems in the provision of adequate services to children who do not speak the majority languages. It appears that because of serious deficits in the implementation of programs, the needs of language minority students remain unmet. The role of minorities in a nation and the attitudes shared by the majority population towards minorities, seem to spill into the educational system. The reason why bilingual education programs for English-speakers have proven to be effective in Canada is because the educational treatment is given to majority language children who hold a privileged position in society as a whole.

POLICIES IN SPECIFIC COUNTRIES

To illustrate specific differential treatments accorded to language minority populations, we will analyze bilingual education policies and programs in several countries.

The Soviet Union

The Soviet Union is a multinational and multilingual country. Over 130 languages are spoken and national literatures are written in 78 languages. School textbooks are written in 59 languages, journals published in 46, and radio programs broadcast in 67 languages. The educational treatment prescribed by the Communist Party of the Soviet Union consists of the development of the native languages of the different national groups along with the development of the Russian language. Bilingualism in the National Languages and Russian is, therefore, promoted by official policy (Guboglo, 1986).

In the Soviet Union 59 different languages are used as media of instruction. One of the reasons for the Soviet state's tolerance towards the use of non-Russian languages in education is the concern that if Russian is used exclusively as the language of instruction, many non-Russian speakers would be illiterate. Universal literacy was achieved in the Soviet Union by providing an education in children's native languages. A second reason for native language use is that Soviet educators are convinced of the importance of the native language in learning a second. They maintain that there is a "set," or single language competence, which underlies the two languages of a bilingual person. This broad language competence which crosses over both languages allows for competent learning of a second language once competence in the native language is achieved (McLaughlin, 1986).

Soviet language teaching techniques are uniform and precise. Because of limited time and resources, a mass system of teaching languages has been created in which standard procedures, teaching methods, materials and equipment are used. The theory behind the teaching methodology is that language is a rule-governed behavior. A student must be made aware of linguistic rules and how these are interrelated. Pattern practice is used to bring to students' consciousness the composition of the linguistic structures drilled, although the drills are used for active communication (McLaughlin, 1986).

McLaughlin (1985) describes several approaches to teaching language minority children in the Soviet Union:

Non-Russian, National Language Schools.

In the different republics that constitute the Soviet Union, children are educated in the official language of the republic (such as, Armenian, Azerbaydzhani, Lithuanian, Ukrainian, Uzbek). Russian is taught as a second language from the first grade, but the quality of second language instruction is variable. In some cases, children acquire only a limited ability in Russian. This may be due to the resistance of national groups to learn the Russian language and to the inability to attract qualified teachers of Russian to work in remote areas. However, in some republics it is possible to study in an institution of higher education where instruction is in the national languages (for example, in Armenia, Georgia and the Ukraine).

Minority-Language Schools.

In these schools, instruction is in a language of a non-Russian minority group and not in the national language of the republic. A major problem with these schools, according to McLaughlin, is that children receive language instruction during more than 50 percent of their school time. They must participate in language classes in the majority language of the republic, Russian, and foreign languages, in addition to native-language instruction. Perhaps because of this difficulty, many language-minority parents choose Russian-medium schools and minority-language schools are disappearing (McLaughlin, 1985).

Russian-Medium Schools for Non-Native Speakers.

Because of the linguistic diversity in the Soviet Union, it is not uncommon for children of many different nationalities to attend a school. It is often uneconomical, if not impossible, to educate all children in the native language. Furthermore, many parents are convinced that Russian-medium education offers better opportunities for their children. These are some reasons given for the increase of Russian-medium schools for non-native speakers (McLaughlin, 1985).

Parallel-Medium Instruction.

In this approach, children from different language groups attend the same school. The children receive instruction in their native languages and Russian is used in play and other extracurricular activities. In parallel-medium schools, there is no mixing of languages in instruction since the mixing of two languages for instructional purposes is forbidden in the Soviet Union. According to Soviet educators, children in parallel-medium schools learn more Russian than in national or minority-language schools. Furthermore, the children are not segregated by linguistic group (Guboglo, 1986; McLaughlin, 1986).

Regardless of the medium of instruction, Russian must be taught as a second language in all schools. In some instances, Russian instruction begins in pre-school or kindergarten levels. Eventually, all children are transferred to all-Russian schools, usually at the secondary level, although in some areas, the transfer to all-Russian occurs earlier (McLaughlin, 1985).

Educational practice is closely tied to research in the Soviet Union. In the education of linguistic minorities and the teaching of Russian as a second language, the latest research findings in psycholinguistics is incorporated into educational practice. On the other hand, very little is known about the effects, positive or negative, of programs for language minorities.

The Philippines

The national language of the country is Pilipino (with a p), a variety of Tagalog. However, Tagalog is only one of many indigenous languages. The other major Filipino languages are Cebuano, Ilokano, Hiligaynon, Bicol, Waray, Kapampangan, Pangasian. These languages are spoken by over 85 percent of the population. The rest of the people speak approximately 75 other languages and 300 dialects (Smolicz, 1986).

A major effort has been made to impose Tagalog/Pilipino as the language of instruction in the school system. Bilingual policy in the Philippines requires the use of Pilipino and English as languages of instruction, although many children speak neither of these languages. Because other Filipino languages have been prohibited in the schools, children enter schools where two foreign languages are used as media of instruction. The effects of this policy is that children do not become literate in their mother tongue, and have a weak command of Pilipino and English. It appears, then, that children finish school without being fully literate in any language. In addition, research has shown a steady decline in the knowledge of English among entering university students (Smolicz, 1986).

The detrimental results of the language policy upheld in the Philippines confirms the notion advocated by many researchers (Thonis, 1981; and Cummins, 1986; for example) that language minority children who learn to read and write in their first language before they receive literacy training in the second language will do well in both. Learning to read and write in a language children do not master is, as can be seen in the Philippines case, detrimental to the achievement of literacy skills as well as other learning skills in children from language minority backgrounds.

West Germany

Children from Turkish, Yugoslavian, Italian, Greek, Spanish, Portuguese, and other language backgrounds, attend West German schools. McLaughlin (1985) describes four approaches used by the school systems in West Germany to educate language minority children.

The Integration Model.

Because many foreign "guestworkers" have no intention to return to their native countries, German school systems have attempted to integrate their children into the mainstream as quickly as possible. At first, children were simply placed in all-German classrooms with no special assistance. German educators realized that in this situation language minority children were unable to compete academically with native speakers of the language, and the "Berlin Model" was developed to remedy the problem. In this program, language minority children receive special intensive instruction in German upon entering school and continue to do so until they are fully integrated into the all-German program. In the meantime, instruction in the home language and culture is provided outside the school in supplementary programs carried out by consulates and embassies.

In other integration programs, parallel classes have been established for language minority children to provide intensive German instruction during the first two grades. In another variation of the integration program, school districts offer children half their instruction in segregated classes, and some instruction in the native language, while they are gradually integrated into the all-German program. Because of the strong emphasis on all-German instruction and little, if any, native

language use in the schools, foreign students do
not perform well in German schools that follow
the integration model.

The Segregation Model.

German educators and the guestworker
community became convinced that the integration
approach to the education of language minority
students was not working. In the segregation
model, students without sufficient knowledge of
the German language are placed in classes where
all instruction is in the first language.
German is taught as a second language for up to
eight hours a week. In the fifth grade,
children receive regular subject instruction in
German and they may remain in these schools, if
their parents wish, after they have acquired
mastery of German. Otherwise, they may transfer
to an all-German school.

The Combined Model.

A compromise between the two extremes of
integration and segregation, the combined
approach to the education of language minority
children consists of integrating German and
foreign children in mathematics, music, and art
classes from the first grade. Other subjects
are taught separately to the two groups in the
native languages. As children progress in the
second language, they take more subjects in
German until they are fully incorporated into
the all-German program. (McLaughlin, 1985.)
In an analysis of the German school system,
Skutnabb-Kangas (1981) argues that the stated
goals of programs for language minority children
differ greatly from what really occurs in the
classrooms. Goal implementation is haphazard
and too frequently teachers of German are not
trained in second language teaching. On one
extreme, children are taught very little German
so they cannot integrate effectively into the
all-German program. On the other end of the
spectrum, children are not encouraged to
participate in voluntary native language
instruction. As an example of faulty

implementation, Skutnabb-Kangas cites the case of Kurdish children who receive instruction in Turkish, a language they do not understand.

Sweden

Immigrants from about 130 different countries live in Sweden. Most immigrants are from Finland (45 percent) and other large groups migrate from Denmark, Greece, Norway, Poland, Turkey, West Germany, and Yugoslavia (McLaughlin, 1985).
Three types of programs exist in Sweden for the education of language minority children (Skutnabb-Kangas, 1981 and McLaughlin, 1985):

Parallel Language Approach.

Children take five hours a week of home language instruction on a voluntary basis. The rest of the time instruction is through the Swedish language and with Swedish students. In some instances a preparatory class of intensive Swedish as a second language teaching may precede placement in the all-Swedish program. Some support can be given to language minority children through special classes in which Swedish language instruction or subject matter is taught through Swedish, the native language, or both. This is the most common approach used in educating language minority children.

Composite Approach.

In the first grade children spend about 60 percent of school time in native language instruction. They spend the other 40 percent in classes with Swedish students. In the second grade, home language teaching is reduced to about 40 percent, in the third grade it is about 30 percent. From the fourth to sixth grades, they receive four to five hours of native language instruction a week on a voluntary basis.

Language Shelter Approach.

All instruction is in the native language
until the third grade when oral Swedish lessons
are given twice a week. By the fifth grade,
instruction is half in the native language and
half in Swedish and by the seventh grade all
instruction is in Swedish. Most programs using
the native language as medium of instruction are
in Finnish, but classes also exist in Arabic,
Assyrian, Chinese, English, German, Greek,
Polish, Serbo-Croat, Spanish, and Turkish.
Research done on the educational treatment
of language minority students in Sweden suggests
that native language instruction is important
to successful second language acquisition. Yet
many problems continue to exist in the actual
implementation of programs. One problem faced
in providing appropriate services to language
minorities is the lack of teacher training.
Only 31 percent of native language teachers have
teaching certificates and 28 percent of Swedish
language teachers have no formal teacher
training. Many teachers of Swedish working
with language minority children teach Swedish in
the same way English is taught to Swedish
children. The approach emphasizes grammar and
not oral proficiency. Another problem confron-
ted in educating language minorities is in the
introduction of English as a third language.
English is compulsory in Swedish schools from
the third grade. Most language minority
children begin English instruction at the same
time as Swedish children, while they are still
attempting to learn Swedish. In addition, many
language minority children are placed in
all-Swedish language arts classes where they
must compete with native speakers of the
language. These difficulties in program
implementation have resulted in negative
effects. (McLaughlin, 1985.)

Canada

English and French are the official
languages of Canada; 67 percent of the
population speaks English as a first language

and 27 percent speaks French as a native language. The rest of the population speaks a Canadian Indian, Eskimo, European or Asian language. Although English and French are officially recognized, English dominates the economic and political spheres of the country (McLaughlin, 1985). To illustrate the dominance of English over French in Canadian society, Hakuta (1986) states that in cities with more than 50 percent native English-speakers, most of the French native-speakers become bilingual, whereas in cities where French is the native language of 80 to 90 percent of the population, less than 50 percent of native English-speakers become bilingual. Furthermore, 1981 census figures revealed that 34 percent of French mother tongue Ontarians reported using English as their principal language of communication at home (Mougeon and Heller, 1986).

Approaches to second language teaching vary according to whether the population educated belongs to a language minority or language majority group. In the following sections we will discuss second language acquisition programs for both populations.

Immersion Programs

Canadian immersion programs have received much attention in the past decade as models of second language instructional programs that work. These programs have been developed for English-speaking, that is, language majority students.

Early total immersion programs.

In 1965 a group of English-speaking parents from the St. Lambert suburb of Montreal agreed to enroll their children in an experimental program designed to teach French as a second language through total immersion in the language. The program began at the kindergarten level with native French-speaking teachers. The French-speaking teacher stressed the development of French language skills through storytelling, vocabulary development, songs, and group

projects.   The project goal was for children to
master their second language in a natural
setting without formal instruction in the
language.   The kindergarten was conducted
entirely in French and lasted two hours a day.
Its primary purpose was to give the children
enough knowledge of French to handle the
contents of the first grade curriculum.   In the
first grade and thereafter the children were
exposed to the normal curriculum of the
French-Canadian school system of Montreal. All
material was in French, designed for children
who spoke French as a first language.   The
program of study at each level focused attention
on the development of expected academic skills,
with language purposely incidental: French
language arts were taught as they would have
been taught to a class of French-speaking
children.   In the second grade, English language
arts were introduced, again taught as they were
normally to English-speaking children (Lambert
and Tucker, 1972).   As children progressed
through the primary grades, the use of the
native language in instruction increased to the
extent that in the late primary grades, English
was the medium of instruction for specific
academic subjects.   The ultimate goal of the
program was achievement of the same level of
English literacy skills in project participants
as the English-speaking children educated in
English.   Parents did not want their children
to learn French at the expense of their English
(McLaughlin, 1985).

Some important considerations in analyzing
early total immersion programs are that the
programs were developed for children from the
majority-language population and all participating children were non-speakers of French. The
school personnel involved in the programs
valued and supported the children's native
language and culture.   In addition, they worked
closely with parents in achieving the goals of
the program.   Since children and their parents
came from a majority-language background, their
language and culture were valued by themselves
and society.   Children and their parents valued
the acquisition of a second language.

Early partial immersion.

In this type of immersion program two languages are used as media of instruction in kindergarten or grade two. Both languages are continued and used equally during the elementary grades. In total immersion programs reading begins in the second language first. In early partial immersion programs, on the other hand, children begin to read in English first, and French reading is introduced in the second grade. Program evaluation results indicate that children in early partial immersion programs do not do as well as children in early total immersion programs in French, though they perform equally well in English language skills (McLaughlin, 1985).

Late immersion.

Use of the second language as medium of instruction is delayed in late immersion programs until after first language literacy skills are achieved. English-speaking children begin all-French instruction in the fourth grade. They take an English language arts class as well. In some versions of this model, all-French instruction begins at the end of elementary school or at the beginning of secondary school (seventh and eighth grades in Canada). Students take preparatory second language classes before immersion.

Comparisons.

It has been difficult to compare the effectiveness of late immersion with early immersion programs. Many important differences exist between the two approaches. Children in early immersion programs have been exposed to the second language more than late immersion students. Also, the type of instruction differs between programs. Early immersion programs tend to use more individualized instruction, while late immersion programs tend to be more group-oriented. Although both early partial and late immersion students appear to have more initial difficulties in meeting the program objectives, in the long run the programs seem to be producing good results (McLaughlin, 1985).

Harley (1986) compared the performance of early and late French immersion participants in a specific linguistic task. Harley's study is significant because it introduces the factor of age in the discussion of comparative effectiveness between early and late French immersion programs. The study focused on the acquisition of the French verb system in young children in an early immersion program and adolescents in a late immersion program. One group of twelve six- to seven-year-olds was selected from the first grade of an early total immersion program beginning in kindergarten, and another group of twelve adolescent students was selected from grades nine and ten of a late immersion program beginning in the eighth grade. The students had all had approximately 1,000 hours of classroom exposure to French. Controls consisted of two groups of native French-speaking children attending French schools in Quebec: one group of twelve first grade students and a group of twelve students at the tenth grade level. The study focused on the verb system based on the assumption that it is a critical structure in the acquisition of a second language and likely to cause major problems for learners of any age.

Individual interviews were conducted using an interview schedule with forty questions. The questions required the expression of a variety of verb constructions in specific semantic contexts. A story repetition task was administered to the older, late immersion and French-control, students. The purpose of this task was to assess eventual second language attainment by late immersion students by eliciting some less frequent types of French verb forms which might not appear in the interview task. In addition, all students performed a translation task from French into English of 13 sentences. The purpose of this task was to determine which French verb forms students could comprehend that they did not produce in French.

Results of the study indicate that after 1,000 hours of classroom exposure to French, the late immersion students had acquired greater oral control of the French verb system than the early total immersion students in some, but not all, areas of the verb system. The author concludes that older late immersion students' superior performance in the acquisition of the French verb system may be due to the following factors: frequency of exposure to the verbal structures in structurally focused second language texts; extensive exposure to the written language; greater cognitive maturity and flexibility; and greater motivation to expand vocabulary on account of demanding curriculum content (Harley, 1986, p. 89).

Double immersion programs.

Immersion programs in which children are instructed in two second languages are called double immersion programs. An example of this approach is a program in which English-speaking children are taught in French and Hebrew. There are two versions of the double immersion method. In early double immersion, instruction is through French and Hebrew; English instruction is postponed until the third or fourth grade. In delayed double immersion, instruction through English begins in kindergarten, in conjunction with instruction through French and Hebrew. It is called "delayed" double immersion because French language instruction is less in the early grades than it is in the early double immersion program. Children in double immersion programs perform as well in most areas as children in early immersion programs. Children in the delayed double immersion program perform lower than children in the early total immersion program in French language skills. (McLaughlin, 1985.)

Programs for Linguistic Minorities

Language minority children receive a different type of educational treatment in Canada. They do not participate in the immersion programs developed for majority

language children. They are either placed in an
all-English classroom with some English as a
Second Language (ESL) instruction (the least
effective approach) or they are enrolled in a
heritage-language program.

Heritage-language programs.

With an increase in migration to Canada in
the past two decades, many children enter the
schools with no knowledge of English or French.
The children of foreign workers and refugees;
they speak German, Greek, Hebrew, Hindi,
Italian, Portuguese, Spanish, Ukranian, Vietnamese, and other languages. For these language
minority children the Canadian government
provides heritage-language programs. These
programs are also established for French-
speaking children in areas where French-speakers
are a minority and for native Indians.

In some programs children receive instruction in the native language during 30 minutes a
day. In others, the native language is used for
50 percent of instruction throughout the
elementary grades. Programs for French-speaking
minorities offer instruction through French for
50-80 percent of the school day from
kindergarten to grade twelve. Studies of
heritage-language programs have concluded that
in well-implemented programs, they are effective
in promoting the native language with no
negative effect on English-language development
(McLaughlin, 1985).

CONCLUSIONS

It appears that diverse approaches are used
by different countries to educate their
linguistic minority populations. Educational
policies range from total submersion of the
children in majority-language programs to the
use of the native language as medium of
instruction with the majority-language taught as
a second language. As many researchers have
pointed out, educational policies are more often
determined by sociopolitical considerations
than by pedagogical soundness (McLaughlin, 1985;
Churchill, 1986; Skutnabb-Kangas, 1986). Even

the much-touted Canadian immersion models, which
have had enormous research coverage and resulted
in effective programs, are for the exclusive
participation of language majority children,
whose language and position in Canadian society
enjoy much prestige. Canadian researchers have
warned, in fact, that immersion programs are
not effective, and potentially harmful if
applied to linguistic minorities.

Most researchers agree that for the
language minority child, instruction in the
native language with gradual introduction of the
second language, appears to be the best
approach. An important factor to consider,
though, consists of proper program implementation. Studies consistently point to the
discrepancies between the way programs are
described "in the books" and actual implementation. Lack of commitment to minority language
instruction by school personnel, lack of formal
training of teachers working with language
minority children, very little research on the
effects of different educational treatments for
language minorities, are some of the problems
encountered in program implementation. In
addition, the attitudes of society as a whole
towards minority groups and the languages they
speak affect the way minority children are
treated in the schools.

REFERENCES

Churchill, S. The Education of Linguistic and Cultural Minorities in the OECD Countries. Avon, England: Multilingual Matters Ltd., 1986.

Cummins, J. "Empowering minority students: A framework for intervention." Harvard Educational Review, 56, 1, 18-36, 1986.

Guboglo, M. N. "Factors Affecting Bilingualism in National Languages and Russian in a Developed Socialist Society." In Spolsky, B. (Ed.) Language and Education in Multilingual Settings. Avon, England: Multilingual Matters Ltd., 1986.

Hakuta, K. Mirror of Language: The Debate on Bilingualism. New York: Basic Books, Inc., 1986.

Katzner, K. The Languages of the World. London: Routledge & Kegan Paul, 1986.

Lambert, W.E. and Tucker, G.R. Bilingual Education of Children: The St. Lambert Experiment. Rowley, Mass.: Newbury House, 1972.

McLaughlin, B. Second-Language Acquisition in Childhood: Volume 2. School-Age Children. Second Edition. Hillsdale, New Jersey: Lawrence Erlbaum Associates, 1985.

McLaughlin, B. "Multilingual Education: Theory East and West." In Spolsky, B. (Ed.) Language and Education in Multilingual Settings. Avon, England: Multilingual Matters Ltd., 1986.

Mougeon, R. and Heller, M. "The social and historical context of minority French language education in Ontario." Journal of Multilingual and Multicultural Development, 7, 2 & 3, 199-227, 1986.

Skutnabb-Kangas, T. **Bilingualism or Not: The Education of Minorities.** Avon, England: Multilingual Matters Ltd., 1981.

Smolicz, J.J. "National Language Policy in the Philippines." In Spolsky, B. (Ed.) **Language and Education in Multilingual Settings.** Avon, England: Multilingual Matters Ltd., 1986.

Thonis, E.W. "Reading Instruction for Language Minority Students." In **Schooling and Language Minority Students: A Theoretical Framework.** Los Angeles: Evaluation, Dissemination and Assessment Center. California State University, Los Angeles, 1981.

ANNOTATED BIBLIOGRAPHY

Arnau, J. and Boada, H. "Languages and school in Catalonia." Journal of Multilingual and Multicultural Development, 7, 2 & 3, 107-122, 1986.

Discusses research on the development of different models of schooling and the linguistic abilities and qualifications of teachers in Catalonia. Results of a recent school evaluation show that the proficiency of pupils in Catalan and Castillian was determined by environmental and individual factors, that is, the presence of a language in the environment and the contact between Castillian-speakers and Catalan-speakers, more than instructional factors.

Brann, C.M.B. "Triglossia in Nigerian education." Journal of the National Association for Bilingual Education. 10, 2, 169-178, 1986.

Describes the differences among three types of language which exist in Nigerian society: the language of the home, the language of formal instruction, and the language of the community. According to the author, the languages of home, community, and school correspond to affective, conative, and cognitive psychological categories. At the pre-primary level, the affective domain predominates through the use of the home language and the community language is introduced through play. At the primary level, the affective and conative domains predominate. The initial language of instruction, or school language, may be the same as the home language. Literacy must be taught first in the community language and later in the school language (in the Nigerian case, school language is English).

British Council. English Teaching Profile: Kuwait. London: British Council, English Language and Literature Division, May 1986.

A review of the status of English language instruction in Kuwait. Concludes that there is a growing need for English language instruction in Kuwait since the language is of great importance in business, education, science, and technology and as a lingua franca. However, the fear that Arabic may be usurped as the national language may be responsible for a lack of clarity in the formulation of language training needs and objectives.

Churchill, S. **The Education of Linguistic and Cultural Minorities in the OECD Countries.** Avon, England: Multilingual Matters, 1986.

Examines the principles used by policy makers in OECD countries to meet the educational needs of linguistic minorities. It is a synthesis of information gathered in more than 30 national case studies and consultants' reports prepared for an OECD-sponsored study.

Day, E.M. and Shapson, S.M. "Assessment of oral communicative skills in early French immersion programmes." **Journal of Multilingual and Multicultural Development,** 8, 3, 237-260, 1987.

Presents the results of an assessment of the oral communicative skills of third grade early French immersion children in Canada. Results indicated that the immersion children were developing good oral communication skills in their second language. They were not comparable to their Francophone peers on the linguistic aspects of their speech (pronunciation, grammar, vocabulary), or in their fluency. It was found, however, that they were comparable or nearly comparable on more communicative measures (story organization, discussion information, and comprehension).

Diehl, J. "A gypsy intellectual speaks out." **International Herald Tribune**, p. 5, December 1, 1986.

  Describes the functions of the Cultural Association of Gypsies in Hungary. With a grant of $160,000 from the Hungarian government, the organization has created a handful of experimental elementary bilingual education programs for Gypsy children; a high school to train teachers in the Gypsy language, Romany; and a newspaper for Gypsies. According to the author, the chief objective of the group is to strengthen the place of Romany in Hungary, through publications and bilingual education. Several Gypsy-language textbooks have already been published.

Fischer, R. "The bilingual school of the Slovenes in Austria." **Journal of Multilingual and Multicultural Development**, 7, 2 & 3, 187-197, 1986.

  Analyzes bilingual education in Slovene and German. Describes curriculum allocation of languages to subjects and the objectives of bilingual education. Concludes with an analysis of the sociocultural factors which will determine the future of language maintenance for the Slovene minority.

Hansen, S. "Mother-tongue teaching and identity: The case of Finland-Swedes." **Journal of Multilingual and Multicultural Development**, 8, 1 & 2, 75-82, 1987.

  Discusses the features in the development of mother tongue teaching in Finland where compulsory schooling is divided on the basis of language into a Finnish and Swedish educational system.

Harley, B. **Age in Second Language Acquisition.** Avon, England: Multilingual Matters, 1986.

Examined differences in second language
acquisition between young children and
adolescents participating in immersion
programs in Canada. The study focused on
the acquisition of the French verb system.
Results of the study indicate that because
of greater cognitive maturity and
flexibility, older students acquired
greater oral control of the French verb
system than the younger students.

Hess, R.D.; Chih-Mei, C.; and McDevitt, T.M.
"Cultural variations in family beliefs
about children's performance in
mathematics: Comparisons among People's
Republic of China, Chinese-American, and
Caucasian-American families." **Journal of
Educational Psychology**, 79, 2, 179-188,
1987.

Describes a study which examined beliefs
about children's performance in mathematics
through interviews with mothers and their
sixth-grade children in the People's
Republic of China (PRC) and in
Chinese-American and Caucasian-American
groups in the United States. Mothers in
the PRC viewed lack of effort as the major
cause of low performance. The Chinese
Americans also viewed lack of effort as
important, but assigned considerable
responsibility to other sources. The
Caucasian Americans distributed responsibility more evenly across options. PRC
mothers offered partial reinforcement to
children who brought home a good grade;
American mothers, both Chinese and
Caucasian, were likely to offer unqualified
praise.

Ho, K.K. "The paradox of immersion in a second
language." **Journal of the National Association for Bilingual Education**, 10, 1, 51-54,
1986.

Investigated the effects of English
immersion on the academic achievement and
second language acquisition of Chinese

(mother tongue) students in Hong Kong. Seventy-four eighth grade secondary school students were randomly assigned to an experimental class and a control class. English was used as the medium of instruction for the experimental class and Chinese was used for instructional purposes in the control class. Students were studied for five months. Results of the study indicate that although the students immersed in the second language were not hindered in their academic achievement, the immersion program did not improve their second language proficiency.

Hunt, J.A. "Education and bilingualism on the French-Dutch language boundary in Belgium." **Journal of Multilingual and Multicultural Development**, 8, 3, 261-282, 1987.

Surveys the complex linguistic and social situation along the French-Dutch language boundary in Belgium outside the Greater Brussels area. Discussion is based on a series of interviews and a detailed questionnaire used with a selected group of senior secondary school students. Results of the statistical analysis of the data reveal the limited extent of bilingualism in the area.

Jorgensen, J.N. "Minority language speaking students' first and second language vocabulary." **Journal of Multilingual and Multicultural Development**, 8, 1 & 2, 103-109, 1987.

Discusses the approximate range of the technical Danish vocabulary needed by an immigrant student attending the auto-mechanical line of the Copenhagen Technical School.

Katzner, K. **The Languages of the World**. London: Routledge & Kegan Paul, 1986.

Analyzes some 500 different languages. Sample texts and translations are provided for nearly 200 of the languages. Shows major language families of the world with a brief description of each language family. Individual descriptions of the more important languages are given. The final section of the book contains a country-by-country breakdown of languages.

Larner, J.F. "Bilingual education in France, or English as the other language." English Journal, 75, 3, 41-45, 1986.

Describes problems of teaching English to mixed classes of native English speakers and non-native speakers. Discusses problems in vocabulary, spelling, punctuation, grammar, and usage, as well as problems involving the concept of bilingual education and cultural differences in the knowledge and expected roles of students.

Lauren, U. "The linguistic competence of mono- and bi-lingual pupils in Swedish in the Finland-Swedish school." Journal of Multilingual and Multicultural Development, 8, 1 & 2, 83-94, 1987.

Presents results of an investigation where 86 bilingual and 86 monolingual pupils from grades 3, 6, and 9 in the Finland-Swedish comprehensive schools are compared. Free written compositions in Swedish were used to study errors in orthography, morphology, syntax, vocabulary and phraseology. Emphasis was placed on interference. Results of the study revealed significant differences between the two groups in syntax, vocabulary and phraseology, with bilinguals producing significantly more errors. Interference was more evident in vocabulary, though it was also noted in syntax. On the other variables, no significant correlations could be established.

Macdonald, Jr., T. "Shuar children: Bilingual-bicultural education." **Cultural Survival Quarterly**, 10, 4, 18-20, 1986.

Discusses the education of Shuar Indian children in a remote jungle of Ecuador. Instead of a non-Indian teacher assigned by the Ministry of Education, children are taught by teacher's aides who are members of the community. The teacher's aide monitors and interprets the lessons of teachers who broadcast instruction by radio from the headquarters of the Shuar Federation. The radio school provides basic and secondary education in the Shuar language in math, reading, writing, history, traditional music and folk tales.

Matthias, M. and Quisenberry, J.D. " Toward increasing literacy in developing countries." **Childhood Education**, 62, 3, 186-190, 1986.

Discusses the problems encountered by children in developing countries in their attempts to learn to read in relation to their "need" to develop a comprehension for and use of print resources. Suggests the production of a variety of print resources, particularly a culture's folk literature.

Miller, B. "Nurturing gifted children in multi-cultural international schools." **International Schools Journal**, 11, 37-41, 1986.

Discusses results of a survey sent to forty international schools in Europe and the Near East on programs for the gifted and talented. Results of the study indicate that teachers need training in identifying gifted and talented children and in developing special programs for them.

Minaya-Rowe, L. "Sociocultural comparison of bilingual education policies and programmes in three Andean countries and the United

States." Journal of Multilingual and
Multicultural Development. 7, 6, 465-477,
1986.

Presents a model of the sociocultural
circumstances surrounding the development
of language policies and planning and of
bilingual education programs in the United
States, Peru, Bolivia and Ecuador. The
model presents the legal framework of the
Andean and North American language
policies, the historical processes of their
establishment and their implementation.
Implications for long-term results are
discussed.

Mougeon, R. and Heller, M. "The social and
historical context of minority French
language education in Ontario." Journal of
Multilingual and Multicultural Development,
7, 2 & 3, 199-227, 1986.

Discusses the development of the minority
French-speaking population in Ontario and
focuses on the political, economic and
demographic processes affecting minority
French-language education. Concludes that
educational objectives for the French
minority will not be achieved without a
higher level of community and government
support.

Nelde, P.H. "Language contact means language
conflict." Journal of Multilingual and
Multicultural Development, 8, 1 & 2, 33-42,
1987.

Describes language contact and language
conflict as interdependently related
elements applicable both to individuals and
to language communities. Analyzes the
characteristics of language conflict.

Osa, O. "English in Nigeria." English Journal,
75, 3, 38-40, 1986.

Examines the past and present position of English in Nigeria and its possible future directions.

Pauwels, A. "Diglossia, immigrant dialects and language maintenance in Australia: The case of Limburgs and Swabian." **Journal of Multilingual and Multicultural Development**, 7, 1, 13-30, 1986.

Investigates whether speakers of standard German and Dutch maintain their language variety better than speakers of German and Dutch dialects. Also investigates the phenomenon of diglossia in immigrant society and shows that the type of diglossia prevalent in the immigrant's home country significantly affects the language situation in the new environment.

Pedersen, K.M. "German minority children in the Danish border region: Code-switching and interference." **Journal of Multilingual and Multicultural Development**, 8, 1 & 2, 111-120, 1987.

Discusses a longitudinal sociolinguistic research project with children from the German minority of Denmark. Most of the children in the study speak a southern Jutland dialect (a Danish dialect) as a first language. They learn German as a second language in the German kindergarten and in the German school where they are taught in German as if it were their native language. Describes the code-switching and interference which results from this situation. The author concludes that in a minority where two languages serve as media of communication, code-switching and interference are manifestations of linguistic creativity. The children speak two languages and the two codes do not seem to have an inhibitory effect on their narrative skill.

Rowley, A.R. "Minority schools in the South
    Tyrol and in the Austrian Burgenland: A
    comparison of two models." **Journal of
    Multilingual and Multicultural Development**,
    7, 2 & 3, 229-251. 1986.

    Compares the education of two minorities:
    the German minority in the Italian South
    Tyrol, which forms a numerical majority,
    and the Croatian minority in the Austrian
    Burgenland, a small minority confined to
    rural areas.

Singh, R. "Immersion: problems and principles."
    Canadian Modern Language Review, 42, 3,
    559-571, 1986.

    Discusses variables affecting the effect-
    iveness of immersion language programs,
    including sociolinguistic context, atti-
    tudes, the structure of immersion
    grammars, and the learning processes of the
    children.

Sondergaard, B. and Byram, M. " Pedagogical
    problems and symbolic values in the
    language curriculum: The case of the
    German minority in Denmark." **Journal of
    Multilingual and Multicultural Development**,
    7, 2 & 3, 147-167, 1986.

    Describes the constraints and tensions in
    German minority schools where the
    curriculum is a combination of Danish and
    German. German is the language of
    instruction, but pupils must attain a high
    degree of proficiency in Danish. Due to
    the symbolic value of German, pedagogical
    advice for making the German schools more
    bilingual has been partially rejected.

Spolsky, B. (Ed.) **Language and Education in
    Multilingual Settings**. Avon, England:
    Multilingual Matters, 1986.

    Includes chapters written by different
    language specialists on the following
    topics: educational use of the mother

tongue; a typology of languages of instruction in multilingual societies; factors
affecting bilingualism in national
languages and Russian in the Soviet Union;
a comparison of multilingual education
between the Soviet Union and Western
countries; language revival in the schools
of Ireland and New Zealand; Namibian
educational language planning; language
policies in the Philippines; linguistic
consequences of ethnicity and nationalism
in multilingual settings; conflicting
paradigms in minority education research;
and a concluding chapter by Bernard Spolsky
on overcoming language barriers in a
multilingual world.

Thomas, B. "Schools in ethnic minorities:
Wales." **Journal of Multilingual and Multicultural Development**, 7, 2 & 3, 169-186,
1986.

A historical overview of the Welsh
language. Welsh medium education and Welsh
as a Second Language instruction are
analyzed. The author argues for a fully
bilingual society in Wales.

Ureland, S. "Language contact research in
Northern Scandinavia." **Journal of Multilingual and Multicultural Development**, 8, 1
& 2, 43-73, 1987.

Analyzes contact-linguistic research on the
Samis and the Finns of Scandinavia.
Discusses different contact patterns and
the rise of Europe's only pidgin (Russe
Norsk) as a result of language contact
among Norwegians, Russians, Samis, Finnish,
Swedish, combined with an international
trade jargon.

Vila, I. "Bilingual education in the Basque
Country." **Journal of Multilingual and
Multicultural Development**, 7, 2 & 3,
123-145, 1986.

Describes the status of the Basque language
in the educational context of Spain and
France.   Analyzes different models of
bilingual education for Basque-speakers.

Chapter 8

PSYCHOEDUCATIONAL ASSESSMENT OF BILINGUAL
STUDENTS: CURRENT TRENDS AND MAJOR ISSUES

Maria Dolores Alvarez

INTRODUCTION

The last two decades have witnessed increased concern over the sensitive and unbiased assessment of language minority students. Legislative rulings, testing moratoriums, activism of civil rights groups, professional debates, have all been influential in calling attention to, and in propelling change, regarding measures and procedures used in psychological and educational testing. At the same time, the growing numbers of limited English proficient students, together with the availability of publicly-funded Bilingual Education and more recently, of bilingual special education programs, have generated an unprecedented need for assessment instruments and techniques appropriate for this growing population.

This chapter reviews the literature in the general area of educational assessment of bilingual students, emphasizing 1986 and 1987 publications (though in the interest of providing needed background, earlier literature is included). The chapter is divided into two major sections. The first section presents an overview of the types of assessment used with bilingual students. The second section focuses on issues and practices surrounding psycho-educational assessment of bilingual students, by far the most controversial kind of assessment in the current educational scene. Encouraging trends and lingering barriers are summarized. Conspicuously absent is the "list of tests" that usually follows a chapter on assessment (even those write-ups critical of standardized testing!). The emphasis here is on communicating a more global vision of assessment, one that relies on methods, approaches, and on an understanding of issues, learners, and processes rather than on specific instruments.

It should be pointed out at the outset that the assessment of language minority students is not an autonomous field; rather it is embedded in the broader context of assessment in general. Therefore, it profits from its advances and is constrained by its drawbacks. Additionally, the literature suggests a time lag between the emergence of a technique and its application to non-mainstream groups. Thus, criterion-referenced tests were already popular in the early 70's (Gronlund, 1973; Popham, 1971), yet hardly any of the tests created for bilingual students reflect this approach.

MAJOR TYPES OF ASSESSMENT FOR BILINGUAL STUDENTS

Four major approaches to assessing bilingual students can be identified: English Proficiency Testing, Language Proficiency Testing, Language Assessment proper, and Psychoeducational Assessment. While they may impact language minority students in special ways, other kinds of assessment, such as minimum-competency testing, or assessments conducted as part of local, state, and national education monitoring systems, are considered beyond the scope of this chapter.

There is a myriad of measures and techniques used in assessment of language competencies. Standardized tests occupy a prominent role, but other popular methods are interviewing, checklists, rating scales, self-report. Techniques may be close-ended as in tests probing responses to specific questions, or may be characterized by various degrees of open-endedness, such as storytelling, story retelling, structured interviewing. Other techniques are non-intrusive and observational, as in videotaping or recordings of children in regular interaction with peers or at home.

English Proficiency Testing

This approach usually entails an evaluation of general oral communication ability in English and is a method popular in assessing newly-arrived students from low-incidence language groups. In this kind of evaluation, a student's language skills are only explored in the second language, which in the context of the United States, is English. This type of evaluation may or may not include assessment of written language skills; in many cases its scope is restricted to oral language, given the limited writing proficiency of most newly-arrived students.

Language Proficiency Testing

The second approach, language proficiency testing, concerns the general screening for language proficiency that takes place when students are identified for regular or bilingual education. In pedagogical contexts, proficiency testing usually entails an assessment, in two languages, of both oral and written competencies. At the oral level, both comprehension (listening) and production (speaking) are explored. At the written level, both reading (a receptive skill) and writing (an expressive skill) are assessed.

In exploring oral skills, reference is usually made to criteria such as phonology (mastery of the sound system/accent), morphology (vocabulary and word knowledge), syntax (command of grammatical rules), fluency (smoothness of communication), semantics (how much is understood and how meaningful are the responses), and pragmatics (getting one's point across effectively). In exploring written language skills, it is customary to evaluate decoding (word recognition), reading comprehension (literal and inferential), and writing ability (spelling, organization, vocabulary, mechanics, general communication ability).

Some linguists consider phonology, morphology, and syntax to be underlined level structures of language, while semantics and pragmatics are viewed as _deeper_ dimensions. Each one is separate and at the same time interdependent with the other. The iceberg metaphor (see Figure 1) graphically captures these linguistic structures. Above-water are the surface-level dimensions and under-water are the deep level aspects (Shuy, 1978). In many ways, the deeper one goes into this language iceberg, the harder it is to measure and quantify. For instance, the sound system, the very tip of the iceberg, is usually easier to characterize. There are fairly straightforward elicitation procedures that can be used to identify the total inventory of phonemes and allophones in a language. In contrast, analysis and quantification become trickier, and inter-observer agreement less automatic, the further we proceed into the deeper structures of language. Not surprisingly, there are more tests of vocabulary available than there are of semantics or of pragmatics.

Looking at language from a less structural angle, language used in everyday context-embedded conversation is different from language required in more rigorous context-reduced academic tasks (Cummins, 1984). Figure 1 also illustrates this conceptualization of language (Cummins, 1984 and Shuy, 1978). In addition, the figure reflects the receptive and expressive dimensions of language, so important in educational settings (see Figure 1, page 301).

Another important distinction emphasized by students of language is the context-sensitive nature of linguistic dominance. Sociolinguists have emphasized the importance of various sociolinguistic domains such as home, school, church, community. These domains become diagnostically relevant to the degree that a student may be more proficient in one language for one domain and in another language for another. The home/school distinction is important, particularly among young children, as elementary school children tend to be dominant in the language of their home (Alvarez, 1983).

According to Hamayan, Kwiat, and Perlman (1985), current trends in language testing call for holistic, integrative assessment methods since language is no longer viewed as the sum of

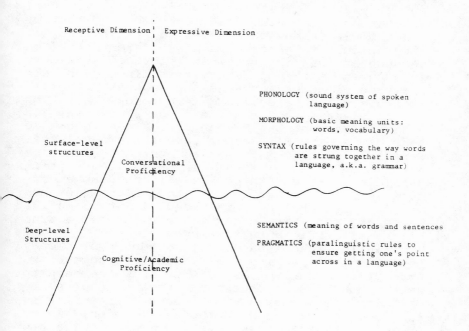

Figure 1. Surface and deep levels of language proficiency
(Adapted from Cummins, 1984). After Alvarez, 1986).

its parts, but as a total entity whose subskills need to be assessed holistically. For the purpose of assessing English language proficiency in bilingual students, they propose a tripartite method consisting of, (a) spontaneous language samples; (b) a test of reading comprehension; and (c) a writing sample. Spontaneous language samples are obtained through an oral interview and through the more structured task of story retelling and are analyzed along the domains of accent, grammar, vocabulary, fluency, and comprehension. The second element, reading comprehension, is assessed through The Boston Cloze Test, a graded test of reading with each seventh word deleted. Finally, writing is assessed through dictation --for students limited in English writing proficiency--, and through a writing sample, for more proficient writers. Equivalent elements would need to be evaluated in the native language too, in order to constitute a true bilingual proficiency assessment.

While school-based language proficiency assessment remains a highly test-based enterprise --due to expediency and the need to screen hundreds of students-- there is pressure building for more spontaneous, free-flowing language elicitation methods (Cazden, 1977; Prutting, 1984). As more and more is learned about language development in general, and about bilingual language development in particular, it is clear that the emphasis is gradually shifting from structural to pragmatic criteria, from an emphasis on phonology and syntax, to an emphasis on pragmatics and communicative competence.

Language Assessment in Special Education

This third type of evaluation refers to more thorough and detailed assessment of children's oral language competencies, as may be needed by speech and language clinicians, or by other diagnosticians seeking more differentiated breakdowns of a child's language. While language proficiency testing may touch upon many areas, speech clinicians are usually interested in exploring the various elements of language in

more depth. For instance, a child's inability
to produce certain sounds may not impair
communication --and may not be considered
relevant in a general screening--, yet this
inability may be a legitimate target for
remediation, provided dialectical and developmental influences have been ruled out.
Experienced clinicians (Prutting, 1984)
recommend that evaluations be conducted in the
two language systems to which children are
exposed.

Speech and language evaluations traditionally have focused on structural criteria,
such as mean length of utterance (MLU),
syntactical and semantic errors, subject-verb
agreements, possessives, plurals, irregular
verb forms, past-tense markings, and the like.
Yet the preeminence of these surface-oriented
criteria based on morphological or syntactic
structure is being challenged. Increasingly,
attention is paid to pragmatic criteria.
Pragmatic criteria include perlocutionary
(e.g., touching, smiling) and illocutionary
(e.g., pointing, showing) acts; topic maintenance, selection, and changes; aspects of
turntaking such as initiation, response,
pauses, feedback to speakers, conciseness,
role-playing, etc.

For some language clinicians (Prutting,
1984) pragmatic criteria are an integral part of
assessing communicative competence. Others
(Simon, 1984) are calling for language
clinicians to be communication specialists
rather than speech correctionists and thus to
emphasize the broader aspects of communication.
In addition, many school districts now require
looking into pragmatic criteria --usually via
checklists-- as part of the speech and language
evaluation of children with suspected language
disorders. Empirical evidence is also
strengthening the viability of pragmatics.
Working with a sample of bilingual children
suspected of learning disorders, Damico, Oller
and Storey (1983) found that pragmatic criteria
(i.e., nonfluencies, revisions, delayed
responses, use of nonspecific vocabulary,
inappropriate responses, poor topic maintenance,
and need for repetition) were more predictive of

linguistic and academic performance than surface-oriented criteria based on morphological or syntactic structure.

Psychoeducational Assessment

By far the most controversial of the four types of evaluation (Cummins, 1986b; Galagan, 1985), psychoeducational assessment is intimately linked with special education. Ideally this type of evaluation entails an analysis of a broad gamut of linguistic, cognitive, perceptual, motor, emotional, social, behavioral, and academic data. Data-gathering procedures may rely on tests, observations, interviews, by one or by several observers. Focus may be limited to the children themselves within the microsystem of the testing situation, or expanded to look, with a macrosystemic perspective, at the children in interaction with the different elements of the environments to which they are exposed at home, within their communities, or within their schools.

Among bilingual children particular attention should be given to language and to its interaction with academic skills such as reading and writing. Language is an important element in a psychoeducational evaluation because it permeates just about every aspect of the curriculum even at the early elementary level (Danwitz, 1976), and shows consistent correlations with reading (Hammill and McNutt, 1981). In the case of children exposed to two languages, there are added reasons for looking at their functioning in both languages: (a) the degree of mastery a student exhibits in the first language correlates with mastery of English at both the oral and the written levels (Cummins, 1984); (b) the degree of intactness in both oral and written language functions in the first language is important in entertaining or ruling out learning disorders in English; and finally, (c) a bilingual/biliterate evaluation more accurately represents the full range of oral and written linguistic competencies of a bilingual/biliterate learner, and this more accurate representation has more chances of resulting in better educational planning and more informed decision-making.

A clinician skilled in the nuances and elements of language is in a better position to determine whether school difficulties of limited English proficient students relate to temporary problems due to limited command of English, to transient adaptation difficulties, or to more serious underlying language and learning disorders. This is a critical question, and occupies centerstage among those concerned with the accurate assessment of children (Gavillan-Torres, 1984).

To insist on the importance of assessment in both languages is not to close one's eyes to the existence of different ways of going about the assessment process. As Table 1 indicates, the level of diagnostic attention paid to the two languages differs depending on who conducts the evaluation. At one end of this continuum is full acknowledgement of the two languages by a clinician who is competent in both. At the other end of the continuum is the practice of overlooking the first language and pretending it does not exist at all. Investigators who have reviewed large numbers of student protocols (Cummins, 1984; Garcia and Yates, 1986; Maldonado-Colon, 1986) report that surprisingly little diagnostic attention is being paid to language in bilingual evaluations.

Table 1

Levels of Diagnostic Attention to Language
in relation to
Person Conducting the Evaluation

Person Conducting Evaluation	Levels of Attention to Language
Bilingual Clinician	Both L1 and L2 are explored
Trained interpreter under supervision of monolingual clinician	L2 explored with L1 component
In-service trained, or otherwise sensitized monolingual clinician	L2 explored with sensitivity to L1 (e.g. efforts made to trace L1 skills through self or parental report, past records or other means).
Linguistically-untrained monolingual clinician	Only L2 explores, with minimal or no effort to trace L1 skills

(After Alvarez, 1986)

Yet local and national efforts reflect a concern for moving toward the top of the continuum, for providing a thorough covering of both languages. Universities have instituted training programs for bilingual school psychologists and for educational diagnosticians to serve various language groups. They have also developed in-service models for training monolingual psychologists in non-biased assessment techniques and in deepening understanding of linguistically and culturally different children. The long-standing practice of working through interpreters has ranged from haphazard improvised translation efforts to more systematic work with educators and other school personnel. In fact, proposed bilingual competencies for special education assessment personnel in California (Ramage, 1986), include not only knowledge of assessment procedures and language development, but also demonstrated skills in working with, and in training, interpreters. It is clear that the variable of language cannot be overlooked when working with bilingual children.

CURRENT TRENDS IN PSYCHOEDUCATIONAL ASSESSMENT: THE BREAKTHROUGHS AND THE BARRIERS

The Breakthroughs

While there is reason for optimism, certain issues linger and appear far from resolution. On the positive side is legislation, increased availability of test and non-test based options, an emphasis on referral prevention and/or pre-referral interventions, a shift from placement to instructional planning, and a general effort towards dissemination of information regarding the testing of language minority groups.

Legislation and Litigation

Public Law 94-142, the Education of All Handicapped Children Act of 1975, and Section 504 of the Rehabilitation Act of 1973 are major legislative efforts mandating, among other things, non-biased assessment, placement in the least restrictive environment, testing in the native language, use of behavioral measures, observation of children in different settings, parental participation/consent, and due process procedures. In addition, landmark court cases such as <u>Jose P. v. Ambach</u> have dealt with issues of timely delivery of services to students and of systematic monitoring of these services (Fafard, Hanlon and Bryson, 1986). Another important case, <u>Lora v. Board of Education of the City of New York</u>, dealt mainly with abuses in the identification and placement procedures of Black and Hispanic students, and resulted in standards and procedures set up to prevent and/or detect further discriminatory practices (Wood, Johnson and Jenkins, 1986).

Alternative   Test   and   Non-Test   Based
Techniques

Perhaps resulting   from   the growing disen-
chantment with norm-referenced testing, there is
increased   availability,   use, and dissemination
of alternative techniques, materials, and procedures.   Some are test-based;   others capitalize
on systematic   observation,   or focused   interviewing.   There   is also an   increased emphasis
on   ecology and on   the study   of   environments.
While it had long been suspected   and documented
(Alvarez,   1983)   that much individual variation
in academic achievement resides in   the learning
environment rather than in   the individual,   the
instrumentation   to   permit a   shift in emphasis
was slow in coming.
     Curriculum-based assessment (CBA):   Used in
the evaluation of   academic skills in   basic and
content   areas,   CBA   focuses   on   a   student's
performance   in   relation   to   local   --not
national--   curricular requirements and demands.
It reflects a direct congruence between testing,
teaching, and progress evaluation, so crucial in
special   education   (Bagnato,   Neisworth   and
Capone,   1986).   CBA   is   also   felt   to fit in
better   than   norm-referenced   testing   with the
increased demands for assessment to   be specific
and useful to educational planning   and not just
to   serve   a   general   placement   function (see
Tucker, 1985).
     Criterion-referenced   tests   (CRT):   CRT's
measure   an   individual's   status   against   some
criterion   or   standard   of   performance,   not
against the performance   of   other   test takers.
Central to CRT is task   analysis --which entails
breaking down concepts into a hierarchy of tasks
and skills,   and the specification of objectives
in behavioral   terms.   A   major contribution of
CRT is   that   the emphasis   is   shifted from the
strengths and   weaknesses of the learner   to the
tasks   in   a   given   hierarchy that   have   been
mastered (including to what degree of accuracy),
or   that   are   yet   to   be   mastered.   Another
advantage   is   its   natural   linkage   with
instruction and curriculum.   Plata (1977; 1984;

1985) has repeatedly promoted use of CRT with
culturally and linguistically different
children.

Observation: Observation is receiving more
and more attention as an alternative non-test
based approach to assessment for exceptional
children in general (Oka and Scholl, 1985; Odom
and Shuster, 1986) and for limited English
proficient students in particular (Esquivel,
1985; Wilen and Sweeting, 1986). Observations
may range from the casual to the systematic;
from participant observation to indirect
observation through video-tapes and recordings.
Observations in different settings (classroom,
lunchroom, recess, home, community), and by
different observers (parents, teachers, diagnosticians) are useful since people are known to
behave differently under different circumstances
and under different levels of structure.
Observations may have a restricted or an
expanded focus, depending on whether the object
of study is the individual child, or the whole
group, as seen in classroom interaction
analyses.

Additionally, observation is felt to have
much potential for language assessment
(Hudelson, 1983) given criticisms regarding the
contrived and decontextualized nature of formal
language testing (cf. Cazden, 1977). It is also
becoming a viable tool in understanding and
analyzing classroom behavior, especially with
the emergence of highly systematic pupil-
observation systems such as the one developed
by Alessi and Kaye (1983). A major disadvantage
with observation techniques concerns the time
required, often incompatible with the demands of
heavy caseloads.

Interviews: Interviews also range from the
casual to the systematic and are considered
useful in work with monolingual (Oka and Scholl,
1985; Odom and Schuster, 1986) and bilingual
(Figler, 1979; Esquivel, 1983; Wilen and
Sweeting, 1986) exceptional students and
families. Interviews may serve the function of
securing previous history and background
information regarding the child (e.g., developmental history, education, medical information,
traumatic experiences); the family (e.g.,

household composition, coping and support systems, stresses, language use patterns, cultural values, degree of acculturation, support for academic pursuits); or current classroom performance. They may also be useful in assessing children's self-perceptions, feelings, coping skills. Relevant interviewees are children, parents, teachers, and other school personnel.

Interviews conducted in the native language are by far the best alternative; trained interpreters are second best; with improvised interpreters being a third choice. In psychiatric settings, use of interpreters may introduce distortions due to defective linguistic/translation skills, or due to the interpreter's own bias towards client or clinician (Malgady, Rogler and Constantino, 1987). In working with Asian populations, Chen (1986) recommends caution in choosing interpreters. For instance, if a school problem needs to be communicated to the family, a distant relative or a friend is better than immediate family to avoid losing face or bringing shame on the family. By the same token, interpreters should feel comfortable in working with a family. Chen also suggests tact in choosing the questions. Phrasing questions in terms of a medical need is more socially acceptable and may be more productive than emphasizing an emotional concern.

Interviews are used in language assessment as a means of eliciting spontaneous language in both the native and the second language. The format may be open-ended or structured and may range from eliciting descriptive statements to tapping pragmatic competencies by asking the person to negotiate different situations taking other people's standpoints. Systems of scoring may be more or less sophisticated, but usually include measures of pronunciation/accent, grammar, vocabulary, fluency, and listening comprehension. Hamayan, Kwiat and Perlman (1985) propose one such system for use in school-based language assessment.

Ecological assessment: Ecological assessment views the individual as part of, and embedded in, the larger context of an environment. Some two decades ago, Bloom (1964) commented that while psychology had always had a place for the environment in its theories, a corresponding emphasis was not noted in its research procedures and techniques of measurement. A result of this state of affairs was the overabundance of tests, inventories, and questionnaires for studying the individual, in contrast to the dearth of instrumentation for studying environments. Bronfenbrenner (1977, 1979) also argued for a shift from the single-setting behavior of the person to broader social-system settings encompassing variables outside the individual. Recent techniques are finally acknowledging the environment and introducing an ecological component into children's evaluations.

Environmental inquiries explore the academic environment, including curriculum, classroom climate, teachers, and teacher/student interactions (Shapiro and Lentz, 1985; Lentz and Shapiro, 1986; Walker, 1986); the home environment (see Oka and Scholl, 1986 for a review); and other more specialized environments such as hospital wards, work settings, etc. Major tools of ecological assessment are focused observation and interviewing.

Test-teach-test paradigms: Major exponents of the test-teach-test paradigm are Feuerstein and colleagues at the Hadassah-Wizo-Canada Research Institute in Jerusalem. Their diagnostic (Feuerstein, Rand, and Hoffman, 1979) and intervention (Feuerstein, Rand, Hoffman, and Miller, 1980) systems, the Learning Potential Assessment Device (LPAD) and Instrumental Enrichment (IE) respectively, attempt to assess a child's capacity to learn rather than provide a measure of what a child knows. Thus, the LPAD aims at tapping the very act of learning and the manners and modalities through which learning is best achieved. Tasks follow a structured progression, but the emphasis is on flexibility rather than on a rigid adherence to test instructions and procedures, as is required in standardized testing. Since processes --rather than products-- are the key issue, examiners assume the active role of teachers rather than the passive role of test administrators. In Feuerstein's own words, examiners are "vibrant, active, and concerned instead of aloof, distant, and neutral." (1979, p. 102). The educational complement of the LPAD is Instrumental Enrichment, a system of cognitive redevelopment addressed to the process of learning itself, and to developing the strategies for learning how to learn.

Because they stemmed precisely from work with migrant, low SES children and adolescents in Israel, Feuerstein's methods appear to be particularly relevant to language minority students in the United States. Their application to bilingual special education is also being explored (Dew, 1986).

Referral Prevention and Pre-Referral Interventions

The importance of referral prevention and pre-referral interventions when dealing with linguistically and culturally different students is often emphasized (Messick, 1984; Garcia and Yates, 1986; Ortiz and Garcia, 1986; Wilen and Sweeting, 1986; Willig, 1986). In fact, Ortiz and Maldonado-Colon (1986) consider that the key to reducing inappropriate special education placements lies in reducing inappropriate referrals. They offer guidelines to help distinguish "deviant" from "normal" behavior among linguistically and culturally different students. Other investigators concerned with the same problem (Benavides and Valero Figueira, 1986) have independently come up with screening instruments to aid in determining whether language minority students should be referred to special education or be considered for further English as a Second Language services.

Another aspect that would be helpful in preventing referrals is dissemination of the best practices for teaching bilingual learners. A good portion of special education referrals are made due to reading failure. Investigators (Franklin, 1986) have found that there are many misconceptions regarding reading instruction even among bilingual teachers. Experienced reading specialists have found that some methods and techniques are more successful than others for teaching limited English proficiency students (Anderson and Joels, 1986).

Emphasis on pre-referral and referral prevention is so crucial because practice shows that once students are referred to special education, strong gravitational forces towards "placement" are set into motion. In analyzing some 400 psychological assessments of minority students, Cummins (1984) found that psychologists were reluctant to admit to parents and teachers that no clear-cut conclusions could be reached from their data. Furthermore, Cummins (1986a) cites a study by Mehan, Hertweck, and Meihls where it is reported that psychologists continued to test children until they "found" the disability that could be invoked to "explain" their academic difficulties. Thus, by the very nature of current referral/assessment practices, diagnosticians appear compelled to come up with a diagnosis that in most cases leads to placement in some category of special education. The referral process itself --most school systems rely on teacher-initiated referrals-- plays an important role (see Galagan, 1985). Furthermore, the high correlations between referral and placement (Ysseldyke, Thurlow, Graden, Wesson, Deno and Algozzine, 1983) speak for themselves.

Shift from Placement to Instructional Planning

There is increased pressure for assessments to be educationally relevant (Zigmond and Miller, 1986). The aim is not to provide a carefully concocted report, a label, or to pinpoint the least restrictive environment. The issue is to provide appropriate intervention strategies that can be incorporated into a meaningful Individualized Educational Plan (IEP). Thus, the growing popularity of systems such as the CBA or the CRT, with clear curricular applications.

Increased Dissemination Efforts

While it is not surprising to find chapters on assessment of language minority students in bilingual special education volumes (cf. Omark and Erickson, 1983; Baca and Cervantes, 1984), it is encouraging to observe the inclusion of chapters on assessment of ethnic language minorities in major current assessment training textbooks (cf. Satler, 1982; Paget and Bracken, 1983), in major professional handbooks (cf. Thomas and Grimes, 1985), and in professional standard guidelines such as the recently revised American Psychological Association's Standards for Educational and Psychological Testing (1985). Researchers who have retrospectively studied protocols of students referred to special education and have perceived the knowledge gap regarding linguistically and culturally different students, emphasize the importance of pre-service and in-service training. Thus, wide-circulation publications appear to be a step in the right direction.

Yet a bleak picture is portrayed by the limited numbers of ethnic minority students currently enrolled in training programs in school psychology (Zins and Halsell, 1986) and in bilingual special education (Holtzman, 1986). An even bleaker picture is portrayed by projected future shortages of minority teachers ("Minority teacher shortage," 1987).

The Barriers

There are many barriers blocking the sensitive assessment of language minority students. Some appear to be so pervasive that they bring into question the viability of test-based assessment and the very nature of the psychoeducational evaluation process itself. We shall focus on the barriers most recently alluded to in the literature.

Biases in Assessment

Biases built into the instruments used in assessing language minority students remain a major source of concern for those preoccupied with the sensitive and accurate interpretation of minority clients' behaviors and needs (Maheady, Algozzine and Ysseldyke, 1984; Lord, 1987; Malgady, Rogler and Constantino, 1987; Rogler, Malgady, Constantino and Blumenthal, 1987). Misconceptions and misinformation about language and bilingualism alluded to a decade ago (Alvarez, 1977), are still a source of misinterpretation and misjudgment (Garcia, 1985; Ambert, 1986; Ortiz, 1986) both prior to and during the assessment process.

One reflection of bias is the continued misdiagnosis and misplacement of language minority students in special education; only the categories and classificatory labels have changed. Spanish-speaking students formerly abounded in classes for the mentally retarded (Mercer, 1971). Today, they are grossly over-represented in programs for the learning disabled and for the speech and language handicapped and underrepresented in every other category including that of gifted (Ortiz and Yates, 1983).

Lack of Change in the Assessment Process

The psychoeducational assessment model itself has been the object of much criticism in recent years (Maheady, Algozzine and Ysseldyke, 1984; Galagan, 1985; Cummins, 1986b). A major offender appears to be the persistence of the "medical model" approach whereby academic failure is primarily viewed as a function of the individual, and the "causes" for failure are sought primarily within the learners. While alternative test- and non-test based techniques have achieved high refinement, and the value of observation, learning environments, and curriculum has been repeatedly emphasized, the fact remains that in practice most special education assessments are test-based and rely largely on analyzing strengths and needs of

children   as   defined   in   norm-referenced
instruments.   Behavior continues to be perceived
as   a   function   of   the   individual,   not   as a
function of   the individual   in interaction with
an environment.

Use of "Standard" Batteries

Often   referred   to   as   the   "cattle-dip"
approach (what is good for one cow   must be good
for all others), the use of "standard" batteries
has been widely criticized and is felt to be one
of   the   most   insidious   current   assessment
practices   (Ysseldyke,   Regan,   Thurlow,   and
Schwartz,   1981).   Essentially,   this   approach
refers   to   the common practice of   applying the
same   battery   of   tests   for   all   students
regardless   of   referral   concerns or questions.
Batsche (1984)   believes   this approach presents
several   risks: It   may   lead   to   "placement"
rather   than   to   intervention   strategies; to a
one-method as opposed to a   multi-method format;
and it may only be fit to address general rather
than specific   concerns.   As an alternative, he
proposes   a   team-based,   referral-oriented,
consultative   approach   to   assessment   and
decision-making that   entails   review   of   all
existing data   on   a student,   consultation with
the   referral   agent   to   formulate   specific
referral   questions   and   determine   the
interventions already attempted,   formulation of
referral questions in specific behavioral terms,
selection of   appropriate assessment procedures,
and integration of background,   observation, and
test-based data.

Questionable Technical Adequacy of Tests

Questionable adequacy of existing tests for
non-mainstream populations is not a new concern;
it has been   repeatedly   addressed for Hispanics
(Malgady,   Rogler   and   Constantino,   1987)   and
other minority groups (Elliott, 1987).   concerns
have   focused   on   the   questionable   practice of
translating instruments (Ford, 1980; Kim, 1980),
or on the practice of "adapting"   them (Malgady,
Rogler and Constantino, 1987).   As a result some
test developers have   come up with   the strategy

of providing separate norms for separate groups, as seen in the recent Spanish adaptation of the Peabody Picture Vocabulary Test (Dunn, Padilla, Lugo and Dunn, 1986), where norms are provided for Puerto Ricans, Mexicans, and a "composite" Latino group. Other developers (cf. Wechsler, 1982) have made available "research editions" of their tests "in the hope that it will encourage the development of norms based on appropriate groups of Spanish-speaking children in the United States" (p. iv), as is the case of the Escala de Inteligencia Wechsler para Ninos-Revisada (EIWN-R). Yet to this date, the publisher has not even corrected the defective answer sheet of EIWN-R, whose front page score-computation section omits one of the major subtests of the scale, and is a source of potential error for unwary examiners.

More troublesome still are current evaluations of technical adequacy in tests specifically developed for use with bilingual populations. Martin and Sikorsky (1986) reviewed 26 such instruments (14 language dominance or proficiency; 4 cognitive; 3 achievement; 4 social/emotional; 1 other). They found that 38 percent of manuals did not report any validity or reliability studies; 46 percent did not report sample size, and among those that did, 35 percent used fewer than 100 participants as their norm-group. Based on their analysis of technical quality, Martin and Sikorsky felt they could only recommend four or five instruments out of the 26.

CONCLUSIONS

The current state of educational assessment for linguistic minority students is a mixture of positive and negative trends and is inextricably bound to the ecology of the larger assessment context within which it functions and to the state-of-the-art knowledge in particular fields. While advances have been made, some shortcomings show insidious persistence. In the case of bilingual children, language continues to be a major source of misunderstanding and mis-interpretation, both on a pre-referral basis and

also within the process of psychoeducational
assessment itself where little diagnostic
attention may be given to language.

The present review would suggest that no
single technique used in isolation is
fool-proof. A combination of test and non-test
based techniques and methods, emphasis on
pre-referral interventions, consultative team
efforts, and more specificity in handling
referrals may all be steps in the right
direction.

Further research efforts concentrating on
the holistic evaluation of language minority
students, in both languages, and to include
listening, speaking, reading and writing would
be most beneficial to practitioners. More
research is needed which provides specific
guidance in avoiding inappropriate referrals of
limited English proficiency children for special
education evaluation. In addition, continued
research into the inherent bias of assessment
instruments is required, even for tests
specifically developed for use with language
minority children.

REFERENCES

Alessi, G.J. and Kaye, J.H. **Behavioral Assessment for School Psychologists.** Kent, Ohio: National Association of School Psychologists, 1983.

Alvarez, M.D. "Practical Considerations in the Psychoeducational Assessment of Minority Students: The Case of Bilingual Hispanics." **Proceedings of a Multi-Cultural Colloquium on Non-Biased Pupil Assessment.** Albany, N.Y.: State Education Department, 1977.

Alvarez, M.D. An Exploratory Study of Person, Home, and School Variables Among High-Risk Bilingual First Graders. Unpublished doctoral dissertation, New York University, 1983.

Alvarez, M.D. Language Assessment of Language Minority Students: A Foundation. Unpublished manuscript, University of Florida, School of Education, Gainesville, 1986.

Ambert, A.N. "Identifying Language Disorders in Spanish Speakers." In Willig, A.C. and Greenberg, H.F. (Eds.) **Bilingualism and Learning Disabilities: Policy and Practice for Teachers and Administrators.** New York: American Library Publishing Company, 1986.

Anderson, B. and Joels, R.W. **Teaching Reading to Students with Limited English Proficiencies.** Springfield, Ill: Charles C. Thomas, 1986.

Baca, L.M. and Cervantes, H.T. **The Bilingual Special Education Interface.** Columbus, Ohio: Charles E. Merrill Publishing Company, 1984.

Bagnato, S.J.; Neisworth, J.T.; and Capone, A. "Curriculum-based assessment for the young exceptional child: Rationale and review." **Topics in Early Childhood Education,** 6, 2, 97-110, 1986.

Batsche, G.M. **Referral-Oriented, Consultative Approach to Assessment/Decision-Making.** Kent, Ohio: National Association of School Psychologists, 1984.

Benavides, A. and Valero Figueira, E. Pre-Referral Screening for Language Minority Students. Paper presented at the Ethnic and Multicultural Concerns Symposia, Dallas, Texas, November, 1986.

Bloom, B.S. **Stability and Change in Human Characteristics.** New York: Wiley and Sons, 1964.

Bronfenbrenner, U. "Toward an experimental ecology of human behavior." **American Psychologist**, 3, 2, 513-531, 1977.

Bronfenbrenner, U. **The Ecology of Human Behavior: Experiments by Nature and Design.** Cambridge, Mass.: Harvard University Press, 1979.

Cazden, C. "Language assessment: Where, what, and how." **Anthropology and Education**, 8, 2, 83-90,1977.

Chen, S. Identifying and Serving Handicapped Children Among Asian Populations. Paper presented at the Ethnic and Multicultural Concerns Symposia, Dallas, Texas, November, 1986.

Cummins, J. **Bilingualism and Special Education: Issues in Assessment and Pedagogy.** San Diego, Calif.: College Hill Press, 1984.

Cummins, J. "Empowering minority students: A framework for intervention." **Harvard Educational Review**, 5, 6, 18-36, 1986a.

Cummins, J. "Psychological Assessment of Minority Students: Out of Context, Out of Focus, Out of Control." In Willig, A.C. and Greenberg, H.F. (Eds.) **Bilingualism and Learning Disabilities: Policy and**

Practice for Teachers and Administrators. New York: American Library Publishing Co., 1986b.

Damico, J.S.; Oller, J.W.; and Storey, M.E. "The diagnosis of language disorders in bilingual children: Surface-oriented and pragmatic criteria." Journal of Speech and Hearing Disorders, 48, 385-394, 1983.

Danwitz, M.W. Identification and Treatment of Language Disorders in Young Children. Paper presented at the meeting of the Orton Society, New York, N.Y., November, 1976.

Dew, N. An Introduction to Feuerstein's Theory or Structural Cognitive Modifiability for Bilingual Special Education. Paper presented at the Ethnic and Multicultural Concerns Symposia, Dallas, Texas, November, 1986.

Dunn, L.M.; Padilla, E.R.; Lugo, D.E.; and Dunn, L.M. Examiner's Manual for the Test de Vocabulario en Imagenes Peabody. Adaptacion Latinoamericana. Circle Pines, Minn.: American Guidance Service, 1986.

Elliott, R. Litigating Intelligence: IQ Tests, Special Education, and Social Science in the Courtroom. Dover, Mass.: Auburn House Publishing Co., 1987.

Esquivel, G. "Best Practices in the Assessment of Limited English Proficient and Bilingual Children." In Thomas, A. and Grimes, J. (Eds.) Best Practices in School Psychology. Kent, Ohio: National Association of School Psychologists, 1985.

Fafard, M.B.; Hanlon, R.E.; and Bryson, E.A. "Jose P. v. Ambach: Progress Toward Compliance." Exceptional Children, 5, 2, 313-322, 1986.

Feuerstein, R.; Rand, Y.; and Hoffman, M. **The Dynamic Assessment of Retarded Performers: The Learning Potential Assessment Device: Theory, Instruments, and Techniques.** Baltimore: University Park Press, 1979.

Feuerstein, R.; Rand, Y.; Hoffman, M.; and Miller, R. **Instrumental Enrichment: An Intervention Program for Cognitive Modifiability.** Baltimore: University Park Press, 1980.

Figler, C.S. A Comparative Study of Puerto Rican Families with and Without Handicapped Children. Unpublished doctoral dissertation, University of Massachusetts at Amherst, 1979.

Ford, B. "Some Considerations in Construction and Administering Language Proficiency Tests." In Rodriguez, V. (Ed.) **Language Proficiency Assessment: What Does That Mean. A Report of the NABE Pre-Conference Workshop.** Los Alamitos, Calif.: National Center for Bilingual Research,1980.

Franklin, E.A. "Literacy instruction for LES children." **Language Arts** 63, 1, 51-60, 1986.

Galagan, J.E. "Psychoeducational testing: Turn out the lights, the party's over." **Exceptional Children.** 52, 288-299, 1985.

Garcia, S.B. "Characteristics of limited English proficient Hispanic students served in programs for the learning disabled: Implications for policy, practice, and research (Part I)." **Bilingual Special Education Newsletter,** 4, 1-6, 1985.

Garcia, S.B. and Yates, J.R. "Policy Issues Associated with Serving Bilingual Exceptional Children." In Willig, A.C. and Greenberg, H.F. (Eds.) **Bilingualism and Learning Disabilities: Policy and Practice for Teachers and Administrators.** New York: American Library Publishing Company, 1986.

Gavillan-Torres, E. "Issues of Assessment of Limited-English-Proficient Students and of the Truly Disabled in the United States." In Miller, N. (Ed.) **Bilingualism and Language Disability: Assessment and Remediation.** San Diego, Calif.: College Hill Press, 1984.

Gonlund, N.E. **Preparing Criterion-Referenced Tests for Classroom Instruction.** New York: Macmillan Company, 1973.

Hamayan, E.V.; Kwiat, J.A.; and Perlman, R. **The Identification and Assessment of Language-Minority Students: A Handbook for Educators.** Arlington Heights, Ill.: Illinois Resource Center, 1985.

Hammill, D. and McNutt, G. **The Correlates of Reading: The Consensus of Thirty Years of Correlational Research.** Austin, Texas: Pro-Ed, 1981.

Holtzman, W.H. "Issues in the Implementation of Master's Level Training Programs for Bilingual Special Education." In Willig, A.C. and Greenberg, H.F. (Eds.) **Bilingualism and Learning Disabilities: Policy and Practice for Teachers and Administrators.** New York: American Library Publishing Co., 1986.

Hudelson, S. Beto at the Sugar Table: Code Switching in a Bilingual Classroom." In Escobedo, T.H. (Ed.) **Early Childhood Bilingual Education: A Hispanic Perspective.** New York: Teachers College Press, 1983.

Kim, K.K. Adaptation of English proficiency instruments for Korean. In Rodriguez, V. (Ed.) **Language Proficiency Assessment: What Does That Mean. A Report of the NABE Pre-Conference Workshop.** Los Alamitos, Calif.: National Center for Bilingual Research, 1980

Lentz, F.E. and Shapiro, E.S. "Functional assessment of the academic environment." **School Psychology Review**, 15, 346-357, 1986.

Lord, R. "Testing and Evaluation in Multicultural Schools." In Reyhner, J. (Ed.) **Teaching the Indian Child**. Billings: Eastern Montana College, 1987.

Maheady, L.; Algozzine, B.; and Ysseldyke, J.E. "Minority overrepresentation in special education: A functional assessment perspective." **Special Services in the Schools**, 1, 2, 5-19, 1984.

Maldonado-Colon, E. "Assessment: Considerations upon Interpreting Data of Linguistically/ Culturally Different Students Referred for Disabilities or Disorders." In Willig, A.C. and Greenberg, H.F. (Eds.) **Bilingualism and Learning Disabilities: Policy and Practice for Teachers and Administrators**. New York: American Library Publishing Co., 1986.

Malgady, R.G.; Rogler, L.H. and Constantino, G. "Ethnocultural and linguistic bias in mental health evaluation of Hispanics." **American Psychologist**, 42, 228-234, 1987.

Martin, M. and Sikorsky, S. Technical Adequacy of Tests for Bilingual Students. Paper presented at the meeting of the National Association of School Psychologists, Hollywood, FL, April, 1986.

Mercer, J. "Institutionalized anglocentrism: Labeling mental retardates in the public schools." **Urban Affairs Annual Review**, 5, 311-338, 1971.

Messick, S. "Placing children in special education: Findings of the National Academy of Sciences Panel." **Educational Researcher**, 13, 13, 3-8, 1984.

Odom, S.L. and Shuster, S.K. "Naturalistic inquiry and the assessment of young handicapped children and their families." **Topics in Early Childhood Education,** 6, 2, 68-82, 1986.

Oka, E. and Scholl, G.T. "Non Test-Based Approaches to Assessment." In School, G.T. (Ed.) **The School Psychologist and the Exceptional Child.** Reston, Va.: Council for Exceptional Children, 1985.

Omark, D.R. and Erickson, J.G. (Eds.)___The **Bilingual Exceptional Child.** San Diego, Calif.: College Hill Press, 1983.

Ortiz, A.A. "Characteristics of limited English proficient Hispanic students served in programs for the learning disabled: Implications for policy and practice (Part II)." **Bilingual Special Education News-letter,** 4, 1-5, 1986.

Ortiz, A.A. and Garcia, S.B. A Pre-Referral Model for Preventing Inappropriate Placements of Hispanic Students in Special Education. Paper presented at the Ethnic and Multicultural Concerns Symposia, Dallas, Texas, November, 1986.

Ortiz, A.A. and Maldonado-Colon, E. "Reducing Inappropriate Referrals of Language Minority Students in Special Education." In Willig, A.C. and Greenberg, H.F. (Eds.) **Bilingualism and Learning Disabilities: Policy and Practice for Teachers and Administrators.** New York: American Library Publishing Co., 1986.

Ortiz, A.A. and Yates, J.R. "Characteristics of limited English proficient students served in programs for the learning disabled: Implications for manpower planning." **Journal of the National Association for Bilingual Education,** 7, 41-54, 1983.

Paget, K.D. and Bracken, B.A. (Eds.) **The Psycho-educational Assessment of Preschool Children.** Orlando, Fla.: Grune & Stratton, 1983.

Plata, M. "Criterion-referenced assessment for individual learning." Social Policy, 8, 2, 52-55, 1977.

Plata, M. **Assessment, Placement, and Programming of Bilingual Exceptional Pupils: A Practical Approach.** Reston, Va.: Council for Exceptional Children, 1984.

Plata, M. "The use of criterion-referenced assessment with bilingual students." Journal of Instructional Psychology, 12, 4, 200-204, 1985.

Popham, W.J. (Ed.) **Criterion-Referenced Measurement.** Englewood Cliffs, N.J.: Educational Technology Publications, 1971.

Prutting, C. "Assessing Communicative Behavior Using a Language Sample." In Omark, D.R. and Erickson, J.G. (Eds.) **The Bilingual Exceptional Child.** San Diego, Calif: College Hill Press, 1984.

Ramage, J.C. Legal Influences on the Assessment Process. Paper presented at the meeting of the National Association of School Psychologists, Hollywood, Fla., April, 1986.

Rogler, L.H.; Malgady, R.G.; Constantino, G.; and Blumenthal, R. "What do culturally sensitive mental health services mean? The case of Hispanics." American Psychologist, 42, 565-570, 1987.

Satler, J.M. **Assessment of Children's Intelligence and Special Abilities.** Boston: Allyn and Bacon, 1982.

Shapiro, E.S. and Lentz, F.E. " Assessing academic behavior: A behavioral approach." **School Psychology Review**, 14, 325-338, 1985.

Shuy, R. "Problems in Assessing Language Ability in Bilingual Education Programs." In Lafontaine, H.; Persky, H.; and Golubchick, L. (Eds.) **Bilingual Education**. Wayne, N.J.: Avery Publishing, 1978.

Simon, C.S. "Functional-pragmatic evaluation of communication skills in school-aged children." **Language, Speech and Hearing Services in Schools**, 15, 83-97, 1984.

Standards for Educational and Psychological Testing. Washington, D.C.: American Psychological Association, 1985.

"The coming minority teacher shortage." **Equity and Choice**, 3, 3, 58, Spring, 1987.

Thomas, A. and Grimes, J. **Best Practices in School Psychology**. Kent, Ohio: National Association of School Psychologists, 1985.

Tucker, J.A. (Ed.) Curriculum-Based Assessment. **Exceptional Children**, 52, 3, Special Issue, 1985.

Walker, H.M. "The assessment for integration into mainstreaming settings (AIMS) assessment system: Rationale, instruments, procedures, and outcomes." **Journal of Clinical Child Psychology**, 15, 55-63, 1986.

Wechsler, D. **Manual para la Escala de Inteligencia Wechsler para Ninos-Revisada**. New York: The Psychological Corp., 1982.

Wilen, D.K. and Sweeting, C.M. "Assessment of limited English proficient Hispanic students." **School Psychology Review**, 15, 59-75, 1986.

Willig, A.C. "Special Education and the Culturally and Linguistically Different Child: An Overview of Issues and Challenges." In Willig, A.C. and Greenberg, H.F. (Eds.) **Bilingualism and Learning Disabilities: Policy and Practice for Teachers and Administrators.** New York: American Library Publishing Co., 1986.

Wood, F.H.; Johnson, J.L. and Jenkins, J.R. "The Lora case: Nonbiased referral, assessment, and placement procedures." **Exceptional Children,** 52, 323-331, 1986.

Ysseldyke, J.; Regan, R.; Thurlow, M.; and Schwartz, S. "Current assessment practices:The 'cattle-dip' approach." **Diagnostique,** 6, 2, 16-27, 1981.

Ysseldyke, J.; Thurlow, M.; Graden, J.; Wesson, C.; Deno, S. and Algozzine, B. "Generalizations from five years of research on assessment and decision making." **Exceptional Educational Quarterly,** 4, 1, 75-93, 1983.

Zigmond, N. and Miller, S.A. "Assessment for instructional planning." **Exceptional Children,** 52, 501-509, 1986.

Zins, J.A. and Halsell, A. "Status of ethnic minority group members in school psychology training programs." **School Psychology Review,** 15, 76-83, 1986.

ANNOTATED BIBLIOGRAPHY

American Psychological Association **Standards for Educational and Psychological Testing.** Washington, D.C.: Author, 1985.

Provides guidelines for evaluating test quality, testing practices, and effects of test use.   Includes standards for testing in diverse settings (schools, clinical situations, counseling, employment). In- cludes a chapter on testing linguistic minorities.

Baca, L.M. and Cervantes, H.T. **The Bilingual Special Education Interface.** Columbus, Ohio: Charles E. Merrill Publishing Co., 1984.

A major textbook in bilingual special education.   Provides information on a wide range of issues and topics relative to bilingual education, special education, and their interface.   Three chapters are devoted to assessment of bilingual children with special needs.

Baetens Beardsmore, H. **Bilingualism: Basic Principles.** Avon, England: Multilingual Matters, 1986.

The chapter on measurement of bilingualism and biculturalism reviews alternative approaches to language assessment and the identification of cultural elements of bilingual behaviors.   Describes assessment research from different countries.

Cummins, J. **Bilingualism and Special Education: Issues in Assessment and Pedagogy.** San Diego, Calif.:   College Hill Press, 1984.

Deals with major themes in assessment of language minority students: referral, bias in testing, learning disabilities, underachievement, language proficiency, bilingualism, special education evalua- tions, and pedagogical perspectives.

Esquivel, G.   "Best Practices in the Assessment
    of Limited English Proficient and Bilingual
    Children."   In Thomas, A. and Grimes, J.
    (Eds.) **Best Practices in School Psychology.**
    Kent, Ohio: National Association of School
    Psychologists, 1985.

    Presents an overview of LEP children's
    needs, the assessment process, legal and
    ethical   issues,   and   alternatives   for
    training. Informal, formal, and preventive
    strategies are suggested.

Hakuta,   K.   **Mirror of Language: The Debate on
    Bilingualism.**   New   York: Basic   Books,
    1986.

    While   not   specifically   addressed   to
    assessment,   the   chapters   dealing   with
    bilingualism and intelligence, and with
    childhood   bilingualism   underscore   the
    impact of social and political forces on
    testing in a poignant way.

Hamayan, E.V.; Kwiat, J.A. and Perlman, R.   **The
    Identification and Assessment of Language-
    Minority   Students: A   Handbook   for
    Educators.** Arlington Heights, IL: Illinois
    Resource Center, 1985.

    Provides specific guidelines regarding the
    identification   of   language-minority stu-
    dents at the   elementary and secondary
    levels.   Offers procedures to establish
    levels of   first- and second-language
    proficiency.

Hyltenstam,   K.   and   Pienemann,   M.   (Eds.)
    **Modelling and Assessing Second Language
    Acquisition.** Avon, England: Multicultural
    Matters, 1985.

    Discusses the various assessment tests and
    their validity from a psycholinguistic
    perspective.   Also analyzes the political

function of assessment and how tests are used and abused in different contexts around the world.

Kitano, M.K. and Chinn, P.C. (Eds.) **Exceptional Asian Children and Youth.** Reston, Va.: Council for Exceptional Children, 1986.

Integrates research to date and offers insight into the special educational problems of Asian students. Includes chapters on demographics, cultural perspectives, assessment, family, gifted, and curriculum modifications.

Lord, R. "Testing and Evaluation in Multicultural Schools." In Reyhner, J. (Ed.) **Teaching the Indian Child.** Billings: Eastern Montana College, 1987.

An overview of testing which includes theories and models; issues in test reliability, validity, and utility; and the situational and environmental constraints of testing. The author offers specific suggestions on strategies to use and to avoid in testing culturally diverse populations.

Mattes, L.J. and Omark, D.R. **Speech and Language Assessment for the Bilingual Handicapped.** San Diego, Calif.: College Hill Press, 1984.

Presents issues, techniques, and guidelines for language assessment of bilingual children. Includes chapter on cultural and environmental influences. Also suggests alternative assessment methods and procedures.

McLaughlin, B. **Second Language Acquisition in Childhood: Volume 2. School-Age Children.** Hillsdale, N.J.: Lawrence Erlbaum Associates, 1985.

The chapter on assessment offers a good overview of the issues involved in language dominance and language proficiency testing.

Miller, N. (Ed.) **Bilingualism and Language Disability: Assessment and Remediation.** San Diego, Calif.: College Hill Press, 1984.

Sourcebook on assessment and remediation of speech and learning difficulties in bilingual students. Several chapters are devoted to assessment of limited English proficient students.

Reynher, J. (Ed.) **Teaching the Indian Child.** Billings: Eastern Montana College, 1987.

Overview of issues related to Indian children and families. A chapter on assessment is included.

Wilen, D.K. and Sweeting, C.M. "Assessment of limited English proficient Hispanic students." **School Psychology Review,** 15, 59-75, 1986.

Addresses psychoeducational assessment of limited English proficient Hispanic students. Discusses caveats and strategies useful in bilingual evaluations, underscoring the importance of exploring oral and academic skills in two languages.

Willig, A.C. and Greenberg, H.F. (Eds.) **Bilingualism and Learning Disabilities: Theory and Practice for Teachers and Administrators.** New York: American Library Publishing Co., 1986.

A compendium of current articles on assessment, the referral process, language, instructional practices, reading, policy issues, and the special educational needs of culturally and linguistically different children.

Chapter 9

SECOND LANGUAGE/BILINGUAL LANGUAGE ARTS: NEW APPROACHES TO INSTRUCTION

Angela Carrasquillo

INTRODUCTION

Language arts classrooms have been affected by developments in instructional issues and research related to second language learning and teaching. Various methodologies for language teaching have been popular at different times. The 80's have been years of "evaluation and analysis" to find better ways to help students acquire the necessary language skills to achieve the social and academic goals of school. The conceptualization of what constitutes a successful language arts classroom is character- ized by a variety of views on learning and a variety of choices for teaching (Bowers, 1986; Morley, 1987). The role of second-language/ bilingual language arts has changed to reflect research and theory dealing with issues such as: integrating language areas in teaching (listening, speaking, reading and writing); integrating language and content instruction; an emphasis on teaching communicative compe- tence; and, specifically in bilingual class- rooms, the re-identification of the role of native language instruction. The purpose of this chapter is to describe how the topic of the language arts classroom has been recently dealt with in the literature and how the issues mentioned have been incorporated into the conceptualization of a successful language instructional setting. Also, a model has been developed integrating the most recent views of what constitutes the linguistic and instructional characteristics of a second language/bilingual language arts classroom.

Most of the recent literature reviewed shows that there is the tendency to focus on learners as active creators in their learning process, not as passive recipients (Canale and Swain, 1981; Chamot, 1983; Krashen, 1981; Morley, 1987; and Savignon, 1983). Emphasis has

been placed on all four language skills:
listening, reading, speaking, and writing rather
than just on oral skills. Linguistic accuracy
has been de-emphasized and communication of
meaning has been encouraged. Students need
language skills that will allow them to deal
with the language used in school for
instructional purposes. Theory and research
tend to suggest that students have the ability
to acquire or develop second language skills
--provided they are given opportunities to hear
and use the new language. Students must be
given opportunities for quantity and quality of
exposure to the target language in the classroom
by influencing the ways in which they learn to
deal with the language. There is a view that
language is often classified by the function it
serves and the notion it expresses rather than
solely by its grammatical structures.

Most of the literature reviewed presents
the view that language is learned through
communication, and students must use the
language to learn it, providing they use their
language for communicative purposes. Proponents
of this movement have attempted to integrate
communicative strategies with the instructional
program, especially in the language arts
classroom.

Another development in language learning
and teaching is using content as a means to
develop language skills and to acquire
knowledge. This movement emphasizes the idea
that instead of teaching language in isolation
from subject matter, teachers should aim to
integrate language development with content
learning. Language is not only a means of
communication, but a medium for learning.

The issue of the role of native language
instruction in bilingual programs took a
prominent place at the beginning of the decade
of the 80's. The federal government has its own
position on what the place of using the native
language as a medium of instruction should be;
and it has influenced many people to question
whether it is advantageous to the student to use
the native language for learning. A summary of

the issues related to native language instruction and its relationship to the language arts classroom is presented below.

INTEGRATION OF LANGUAGE AREAS IN THE LANGUAGE ARTS CLASS

Until recently, in the native and second language arts classrooms the emphasis had been on the development of auditory processing, speaking, reading, and writing as independent skills. But in the past few years, the field has begun to focus on the interactions in which learners engage to develop language, reading, and writing skills. Language acquisition is a process which involves interactions among all language areas. It is now recognized that language cannot be studied in its entirety, as an isolated linguistic corpus, but that it must be seen as an interactional process in the context in which it occurs. This process has been called the "ethnography of speaking" with an emphasis on the situations and uses, the patterns, and functions of speaking and listening.

Language proficiency is balanced between the two receptive processes of listening and reading, and the two productive processes of speaking and writing. Language is a process of thought and production that must be used if it is to be mastered. Only by using language for a variety of real purposes and a variety of real audiences can students develop language competence.

The integration of language arts skills has been an issue for some time (Smith, 1979). One of the great contributions of the cognitive approach to second language teaching was the realization that the emphasis of the audio-lingual order of first listening, then speaking, then reading and writing was not necessarily a natural order. The argument in favor of the integrated approach is that from the beginning, children learn to use language in meaningful contexts as part of an attempt to understand and relate to the world around them. Smith's argument is that children try to make sense out of language they hear used in the environment.

For example, reading is a language-based skill, and children expect that the written word will make sense or carry meaning. Children note relationships between speech and print. The visual images, letters and concepts represent sounds and meanings stored in the child's brain. Dahl (1981) pointed out that several studies have shown that oral language ability correlates with reading achievement scores and that fluency variables in these studies have been shown to be most valuable in predicting reading achievement. However, there is no accumulated evidence to point to a positive relationship between oral language and reading.

The integration of language skills activities include auditory processing, oral language, reading-related activities, and creative writing. Auditory processing, oral language, and writing are discussed in the following section.

AUDITORY PROCESSING AND ORAL LANGUAGE

Research in second language acquisition has focused on what people do with language rather than on the sequential acquisition of the forms of language. Second language teaching emphasizes communication over drill, where the learner's focus is on doing something through the language (Krashen, 1981). Oral language --listening and speaking-- is the primary language process. Learners need to talk and listen in order to learn. Auditory processing is important to most activities in which people interact. It is the process by which spoken language is converted to meaning in the mind. Little about auditory processing methodology is supported by reliable and replicable research findings. Very little is known in terms of what can be done to enhance auditory processing, to identify the skills unique to auditory processing, and to generate successful curriculums and teaching strategies. What we found in the literature are lists of listening skills; and because auditory processing and reading are both receptive processes, much of the commercial material has adopted the skills common to the reading process.

Listening, an aspect of auditory processing, is an important language arts skill. It deals with perceptual information processing on the basis of information in the perceptual storage of short- and long-term memory. Fox (1986) mentioned that listening is especially important for Indian students who need to expand their vocabularies to gain command of words they may want to use in speaking, reading, and writing. A number of common level factors influence listening: mental set, rate of input, distracting associations, knowledge about language, concentration, and attention (Froese and Stanley, 1981). Ramirez and Stronquist (1979) found five teaching behaviors positively associated with language growth in listening comprehension and oral production in ESL: (a) commands with concrete objects; (b) questions with guided responses --asking students to respond to questions based on information previously presented; (c) explanations of concepts/labels to clarify the meaning of new words using synonyms and antonyms; (d) variation of strategies --utilizing a number of teaching behaviors such as modeling, commanding and questioning; and (e) correction of grammatical errors. Teachers should plan lessons that teach children that listening can be a valuable aid in learning about the world (Hansen-Krening, 1979).

Students practice listening all the time, but it is the language arts classroom which provides specific listening activities such as: when students are read to, as they hear other students contribute to language experience stories, and when students share literature. There is a developmental progression in building listening skills. Students need to listen for sensory awareness, for information, and for critical listening. Listening for information becomes a valuable tool for learning when students are trained to gather information from what is heard. It evolves from becoming knowledgeable about the listening act to being able to identify the content being transmitted. Critical listening is listening to differentiate

among facts, opinions, and fiction. Bilingual/
second language students require teachers to
provide a high motivation and interest to
follow a conversation due to the students lack
of opportunities to hear the language or
because these students cannot understand the
message being conveyed to them.

Oral language is fundamental to the
development of other communication skills.
Second language students are like other
school-aged children in the beginning process of
acquiring language, and classroom teachers need
to provide opportunities for students' language
to grow (Dahl, 1981). What kinds of experiences
can be provided for children? Children learn
their language by listening to models in their
environment who are using language in meaningful
ways. Authorities such as Dahl (1981); Canale
and Swain (1981); Hansen-Krening (1979); Krashen
(1981); and Mohan (1986) suggested activities
such as the following:

1. Active interaction of the teacher and
other adults with children: listening to them
and talking to them, letting them express
language freely, letting them feel that their
speech is accepted, giving them freedom to talk,
and allowing them to make errors.

2. Developing a classroom atmosphere that
serves as a model for language growth and
development.

3. Reading literature (both prose and
poetry) to help expand children's language
competency. Children should be encouraged to
respond to literature in creative ways
(discussion, choral reading, storytelling).

4. Establishing interest centers in the
classroom to build skills in both receptive and
expressive language through any curricular area
(science, mathematics, writing, and listening
centers).

Hansen-Krening (1979) indicates that when
teaching basic skills in speaking teachers must
identify the kinds of situations that require
effective speech and the kinds of speaking
skills needed in those situations. The most
common listening situation shown by students is

talking to themselves to express views about a particular topic. Conversation is talking together about something of mutual interest. Conversation often leads to discussion. Perhaps second language learners cannot participate themselves in problem-solving speaking activities, but the same students can role play or demonstrate a particular act that explains the behavior being expressed. For second language learners, teachers must provide many instructional opportunities for: (a) using oral language in many ways and in many different settings; (b) developing vocabulary for different audiences; and (c) expressing ideas even when they are not clearly presented.

Teachers need to provide a rich language environment in the classroom that is closely related to students' interests and that encourages the use of language in a variety of situations. Among the many activities suggested in the literature for the development of listening and oral skills, the following were summarized by Herschenhorn (1979):

1. Relating anecdotes to the class about personal experiences (family, friends, pets, funny incidents).
2. Teaching students how to take or leave a message, make appointments, get information via the telephone, listen to a story.
3. Conducting interviews in which the listener must process and respond to the interviewer.
4. Using short segments of radio/TV news, reports, music, talks to elicit discussion.
5. Reading and discussing short typed conversations.

Franklin (1986) pointed out the relation-ship between good speakers and vocabulary development. This relationship is seen as a reflection of linguistic conceptual development, between a concept and the world which represents that concept. Because of a lack of opportunities, poor readers tend to be prevented from developing rich vocabularies. Franklin also mentions that what children know should be valued and utilized in the classroom. A language-experience approach which emphasizes the production of texts generated by students themselves, using their own language and ideas, is a recommended approach to help students discuss and explore their own world.

CREATIVE COMMUNICATION THROUGH WRITING

Writing is a highly personal activity and students need to express themselves in written form. But writing is the most difficult and abstract form of verbal thinking. Different students react to assigned writing tasks in different ways because of their developmental status, their home/classroom environments and their interests. Students' writing performance is affected not only by what the teacher and students bring to the writing experience, but also by how the experience is expanded and concluded. Creative as well as practical writing need to be functional and require creativity and knowledge of writing skills. It is assumed that the more knowledge, language background, and imagination students have, the better writers they will become. Research indicates that writing, like speaking, is almost always directed toward an audience whose expectations shape the form and content of the message, making interaction an integral element of the process (Franklin, 1986; Burk and Woodward, 1983; and Krashen, 1984). As writers write and re-write, they approximate more closely the intended meaning and the form with which to express meaning. Also, research on writing points out the importance of the role of the teacher in the writing act. The teacher should: (a) be a writer adviser and critic; (b) help students clarify their own thinking; and (c) help the writer communicate the intended meaning to others.

Students like to listen to stories and enjoy creating their own. Experiencing, getting in touch with one's feelings, and having many opportunities to write are necessary ingredients for writing. Students need a rich and varied literacy environment to which they can add their first-hand knowledge and experiences. Good writers are usually good observers of the world around them.

Recent literature on writing has focused on writing as a process. Students are taught to identify and focus on a topic, identify an audience, and write about the topic for that audience. The process involves idea formation, composition, revision, composition, editing, and re-composition. The structure and grammar components evolve through the editing and revision stages. The study of grammatical definitions and rules has been part of language arts instruction. Although the research evidence points to the inefficacy of teaching formal rules of grammar to improve writing, teachers still insist on extensive study of formal grammar to improve students' writing (Kean, 1981; Straw, 1981).

Writing is viewed as the ability to write one's own ideas and present them in a form for others to read. Fuentes (1986) argued that this model can work with bilingual/second language students since their limitations with the oral and written aspects of English will not stop them from producing text since grammar and rules are not the primary purpose of the writing act. Students will be comfortable and competent communicators, developing writing proficiency through interaction among the need to write, the product, and the reader. Although it is important that students demonstrate an oral foundation, it is not at all necessary for beginning learners to achieve complete fluency in the spoken language before moving on to written language.

Emphasis on the teaching of writing has been expanded to focus on a broader view, encompassing the process of: pre-writing activities and producing a composition for publication. Harste, Burke and Woodward (1983) stated that children who are allowed to take risks with language will generate rules for appropriate language use, if they are given numerous opportunities to interact with texts. As students interact with a variety of texts, they gradually refine their understanding and develop lexicon, syntax, print conventions, and

awareness of text forms (Franklin, 1986).
Second language learners need to write to
communicate meaning through: (a) sentences; (b)
paragraphs; (c) compositions; (d) notetaking;
(e) letter writing; (f) reports; (g) outlining;
(h) poetry; (i) short stories, novels, plays;
and (j) journal dialogues. Experiences in using
the many ways to express ideas in writing will
provide students with opportunities to direct
their message to an audience.

COMMUNICATIVE AND LINGUISTIC COMPETENCE

The concept of communicative competence has
been well-received in the field of second
language and bilingual education. There has
been an emphasis and preference for the
communicative approach as an appropriate methodology in language teaching. The term
"communicative competence" implies the acquisition of the system of language when exposed to
it in meaningful contexts (Acuna-Reyes, 1987;
Brunfit, 1982). The communicative competence
movement, which according to several authorities
began in the early 70's, is having a
significant impact in language teaching and
instruction. Proponents such as Bachman and
Palmer (1982); Canale (1981); Canale and Swain
(1981); and Savignon (1983), have been
successful in convincing language teachers of
the methodological benefits of this communicative approach. There is a switch to the
integration of analytical approaches, language
forms, sociocultural dimensions, and nonverbal
communication in the classroom. Language is
seen as a self-contained system and as a medium
of communication.

Linguistic competence research is answering
the question: what have children learned when
they are able to communicate in the language of
the culture? The children have acquired
linguistic competence, that is, the knowledge of
their native language, including the finite
system of rules needed to enable them to
understand and produce an infinite number of
creative sentences. They are also able to use
that native language to form, express, and
communicate thoughts and feelings. Unconscious-

ly acquired rules govern the use of phonology, morphology, and syntax in the child's communication. Second language will use that first language linguistic competence as a foundation to identify new labels to already known concepts and communication skills. Proponents of the communicative approach indicate that language learners can acquire linguistic competence through this method. Children acquiring language learn the functions of language or how language is used in communication in a variety of ways. They learn how to get meaning by mastering the functions of language (instrumental, interactional, personal, informative, and imaginative).

Proponents of this approach further contend that communicative competence goes beyond linguistic competence, that is, mastery of the grammaticality of the language system. Acuna-Reyes (1987) indicated that the most frequently repeated suggestion in the literature on language learning is that for most learners acquisition of a language will take place only to the extent that these learners are exposed to contextually-rich, genuine, and meaningful communication in the language. Bodman (1979) pointed out that the language arts teacher needs to provide opportunities for students to communicate realistically in class, so that students can feel free to take communication initiative and are motivated to do so. Johnson and Morrow (1981) stated that in order to engage in real communication, participants must be able to deal with spontaneous language beyond the grammatical level. They state further that the ability to manipulate the formal features of language in isolation does not necessarily imply the ability to be communicatively competent.

Most of the authorities that recommend the communicative approach agree that this method gives language arts teachers freedom from extensive drilling, repetition, and memorization of non-contextualized grammatical paradigms of syntactical patterns in an attempt to induce rote learning of a language (Klassen, 1981). Students can concentrate on communicative tasks, on the use of language, and not on formal accuracy. According to Johnson and Morrow

(1981), real communication allows speakers to decide not only what they will say, but also how they will say it. The "language act", rather than the sentence, becomes the basic unit for analysis and practice, and requires the inclusion of social acts and human interactions (Klassen, 1981). The language arts classroom makes use of activities that give second language students opportunities to engage in meaningful dialogues using social formulas, interaction activities, community-oriented tasks, role playing real-life interactions, and problem-solving activities. Klassen (1981) pointed out that these activities require an interpersonal responsiveness to social context and an awareness of when, how, and to whom different levels of the language code are appropriate and effective.

Teachers must provide students with the opportunity to engage in unrehearsed communication to allow students to make appropriate content and linguistic choices. Cathcart-Strong's (1986) study to determine the effectiveness of various types of communicative acts (requests for information, calls for attention, and intention statements), found that although the response rate to some types of utterances was predictable, others did not generate the expected feedback. This study further suggested that in developing communicative strategies of language learners, some tasks and play settings need to provide: (a) opportunities to control the conversation; (b) planned activities in which learners will have enough time to interact with speakers of the target language; and (c) opportunities for children to initiate interactions with adults. Brunfit (1982) suggested that the language arts teacher should use approaches to allow learners great flexibility in exercising their own styles and capabilities. In the communicative approach students are exposed to meaningful situations which prompt them to formulate messages that emanate from real experiences (Acuna-Reyes, 1987; Klassen, 1981). Butzman and Dodson (1980) explained that in teaching communicative competence teachers should focus on two types of interactions: medium-oriented and message-orien-

ted. The medium-oriented interaction is communication about the language. The message-oriented
interaction has to do with   students ability to
satisfy   their   immediate   needs   through
communication.
    Social interaction means understanding the
meaning of what is listened to in informal
situations for basic   comprehension. It is
important to point out here that communicative
competence, in social   interactions only, does
not guarantee success   in academic language
tasks. Language learning includes both communicative competence and the appropriate choice of
language for the many social interactions in
which people find themselves. Together, these
two kinds of knowledge can be called communicative competence. One of the most difficult
tasks language teachers have is to present
instructional programs that will help learners
to acquire the cognitive, social, and linguistic
skills needed to use language effectively.

LANGUAGE AS A MEDIUM OF LEARNING

    Language is the major medium of instruction
and learning. A second language is learned by
using it in meaningful contexts. Language is
not taught in isolation. Language is seen as
the medium of learning. Language provides
opportunities for understanding information
which also promotes communication and second
language   acquisition.   The   integration   of
language learning and content learning is
considered an important pursuit in the field of
language research (Chamot, 1983; Curtain, 1986;
and Mohan, 1986). It became popular as a result
of issues posed by Chamot (1983); Cummins (1981,
1983, 1984); Krashen (1982); and Stevick (1985),
among others. Cummins' emphasis is on the
degree of contextual support available for
expressing or comprehending through language and
the degree of cognitive involvement. Krashen,
in his theory of comprehensive input, describes
language   acquisition in which the acquirer
understands input. In other words, language
learning is related to the degree of active
intellectual or cognitive involvement required
by the communication task that the speakers are

engaged in. Krashen (1981, 1982) and Stevick
(1985) pointed out the distinction between
acquisition and learning. Acquisition occurs in
spontaneous language contexts; it is
unconscious, and it leads to conversational
fluency. Learning is conscious knowledge of the
rules of language and is derived from formal
instruction.

Integration of language and content
instruction is intended to develop both second
language skills and academic concepts because it
is a focus on meaning rather than on form.
Linguistic modifications are necessary for
comprehensible input. Instructional language
uses contextual messages to help convey meaning.
Usually in conversational interaction the
subject content is interesting and real to the
student. Several principles are necessary for
this interaction: the specification of the
instructional objectives; vocabulary; language
functions; and language skills requirements.
The language development component is what
distinguishes a content-based second language
approach from the regular subject matter
instruction.

Language arts is the basic subject area in
which to start using content to develop language
skills. A simple science or social studies
topic is a good framework to help students
develop listening and oral skills, grammar, and
reading and writing skills. Mohan (1986) has
developed a theoretical model for integrating
language teaching and content teaching that
includes: (a) an organizational framework of
language and thinking skills which apply across
the curriculum; (b) improvement of communication
of subject matter; (c) strategies for developing
the language skills; and (d) strategies for the
development of thinking skills.

There are cognitive areas that are
emphasized in all the subject areas. In order
to be able to provide this integration there is
a need to use topics, the learners' experiences,
and appropriate cognitive skills. Mohan (1986)
indicated that there is also the need for the
identification of suggested teaching strategies
to develop language skills using content.
Integration of subject content and language has

been successfully used in immersion and sheltered programs (Genesee, 1986). In immersion programs the second language is used as the medium for subject/content instruction and the second language is learned naturally. In describing the Canadian French-English immersion programs, Genesee (1986) concludes that second language learning is incidental to the students' learning about school subjects and their community and that they "pick up" whatever language skills they need to perform the tasks that comprise school life.

Proponents of this approach indicate that the use of the second language as a primary language of academic instruction allows the students to use their natural language learning abilities. In immersion programs there is an emphasis on communication for academic purposes and as a means of promoting second language learning. In reviewing the research literature, Cummins (1979) pointed out that immersion programs for the majority language child result in high levels of functional bilingualism and academic achievement, while for many minority-language children, they lead to inadequate command of both first and second languages, and poor academic achievement. Wong Fillmore and Valadez (1986) state that one advantage of many immersion programs is that students are grouped by proficiency levels and the instruction is geared at one language level and not at several levels as in many bilingual programs in the United States.

Sheltered English is the use of simplified vocabulary and sentence structure to teach school subjects in which students lack enough English language skills to understand the regular curriculum (Parker, 1985; United States General Accounting Office, 1986). Sheltered English uses content in English as a Second Language (ESL) classrooms. Parker (1985) contended that this approach provides an effective strategy for providing minority language students with the kinds of language skills they need for academic activities. He argued that sheltered English promotes acquisition of language skills appropriate to school-related tasks and at the same time it incorporates the linguistic adjustments that are needed by second language learners. Parker suggested that at the beginning, sheltered English be used for courses that have relatively low cognitive demands and lots of contextual support. Such courses might include physical education, art, and mathematics. Use of the second language could be extended subsequently to include more cognitively-demanding, abstract content, such as science and social studies or history.

There is an emerging idea that visualizes a second language arts classroom where an integrative approach of sheltered, immersion or semi-immersion (use of the second language to teach content in the target language on specific days or topics) is proposed. In this approach, academic and second language learning overlap and the emphasis is not on the second language alone. Having to teach curriculum through the second language need not be viewed as impossible or disadvantageous. Rather, content instruction can provide a powerful means through which language learning can be promoted (Genesee, 1986). Language teachers can use subject area content in their language arts classes. The content to be used must be content that the students are familiar with, understand, and are willing to talk about. The best approach is to develop a lesson around a theme or topic in order to make communication simple and clear, and to highlight opportunities for language development and thinking skills. Language teachers need to organize information in such a way that it fits together into a pattern. This organization may include dividing the topic into specific sub-areas with examples, identifying one example with visual resources, establishing relationships, descriptions, and differences to develop thinking skills. Students must participate in small group activities to engage in meaningful tasks in which students and teachers plan a unit around a topic, providing for experiential work, higher level thinking, and systematic language learning (Mohan, 1986). Action situations, such as dialogues in which learners can interact, use of role playing, and scenarios are recommended in this approach.

The language arts classroom requires language and content tasks that vary along a continuum from cognitively demanding to cognitively undemanding, and language varies along a continuum from context embedded (using contextual clues, paralinguistic feedback from other speakers, and situational clues or meaning) to context reduced (relying heavily on linguistic cues alone and involving abstract thinking). Cummins (1981, 1984) and Chamot (1983) indicated that academic tasks are cognitively demanding and usually require language in which contextual clues for meaning are reduced.

NATIVE LANGUAGE ARTS

The use of two languages in classroom instruction is still a defining characteristic of bilingual programs. In bilingual programs both languages are seen as helping students achieve the academic goals of the school and to develop, enrich, and expand language skills. There have been arguments for and against the use of the native language. In the last six to seven years, information pointing to the positive and negative effects of using the native language as medium of instruction has been frequently mentioned in the literature. Dolson (1985) argues that the underlying pedagogical question in the debate on bilingual education is whether or not instruction in and through the mother tongue is an effective and efficient means to promote English language development and academic achievement. Much of the recent literature is characterized by editorial comments, especially those promulgated by the English-only movement, tending to indicate that any study or use of the native language will have negative effects on progress in English (Simoes, 1987). The English-only movement attempts to have English declared the official language of the United States. There is a tremendous unsupported charge that the use of the native language in school inhibits the learning of English by limited English proficient students. Wong Fillmore and Valadez (1986) identify the two separate misconceptions related to native language instruction: "that little or no English is used in these programs, and that limited English proficient students have to put aside their native language if they are to succeed in learning English" (p. 651). There is a belief that knowledge of a native language other than English results in imperfect mastery of English.

The available literature on the effect of native language instruction in English language development (Anderson, 1981; Carrasquillo and Segan, 1984; Cummins, 1981, 1983; Diaz, 1983; Goodman, Goodman and Flores, 1979; Krashen, 1985; Legarreta-Marcaida, 1981) tends to indicate that bilingualism and native language development have beneficial effects on linguistic minority children's educational progress. It is suggested that most limited English proficient (LEP) students need to learn through their native language first and make a gradual transition to the second language. Instruction in the native language enhances and contributes to a higher level of achievement in the second language.

The Bilingual Education Act authorizes programs in the United States schools for LEP students. The law requires that in most projects funded under the Act, the students' native language be used to the extent necessary. The Department of Education has proposed on several occasions to drop the Act's native language requirement. In support of the proposal, Department officials have stated repeatedly that they are relying on research evidence that points to the negative effects of native language usage. The Department interprets this evidence as failing to show superiority of native language methods. In the GAO Report (United States General Accounting Office, 1987), the question was posed, "Does the research and evaluation evidence on the learning of students with limited English proficiency in school subjects other than English support the legal requirement of instruction to the extent necessary in the native language?" The GAO Report found that research evidence supports the current Title VII requirement pertaining to native language instruction. The GAO Report indicated that native language instruction helps LEP students learn English and meet grade promotion and graduation requirements --the ultimate goals of bilingual education. It also found that programs which do not use the LEP students' native language are not likely to be effective in achieving these crucial goals.

Native language instruction is a very controversial issue; it is more political than educational. Still, bilingual education programs are using the native language to teach subjects areas and for global language development. It is argued that the amount and quality of primary language use in the home is positively associated with student readiness for the academic demands of schooling and continued primary language development (Cummins, 1981; Ramirez, 1985). Cummins stated that the stronger language could be used to develop a common underlying proficiency, a metalinguistic awareness that serves as an important background factor for future school learning in any language. Also, he indicated that the home language and culture can serve to contextually embed the school subjects in the initial stages. Lado (1983) indicated that the cornerstone of native language is literacy in that language. He stated that achievement of functional literacy in the native language with a parallel achievement in English will generally mark achievement in English and will produce educated bilinguals. He also mentioned that since literacy in the native language will not be achieved generally without instruction in school, the key to literacy is classroom instruction. Anderson (1981) and Lado (1983) emphasize that the optimal level for literacy instruction in the native language is in preschool or early childhood because when native language literacy begins at these early levels, English literacy will be achieved more easily and rapidly. Therefore, the language that students bring to the classroom continues its development through content and subject area teaching and learning. The other argument is that the transition from the language of the home to the language of the school must be made gradually to avoid educational trauma. The language arts classroom provides the adequate environment for this development of language skills.

How does the native language approach contribute to facilitating the development of English skills? The language arts classroom program can be designated to facilitate the balanced use of the two languages for instructional purposes. Wong Fillmore and Valadez (1986) cite studies conducted with Mexican and Finnish students in which there is an indication that the use of the native language as the medium for early instruction can lay the foundation for later academic achievement in the second language for linguistic minority students (p. 658). Cummins (1981) attributed the greater success in English among bilingual education students to a better foundation in their home language.

The native language approach should include the following strategies:

1.   Learner centered activities rather than teacher directed drilling of correct sentences.
2.   Inclusion of all four areas of language in the lesson to provide a comprehensive approach.
3.   Discovery learning activities that involve learning through experience. Also, the application of problem solving to rule generalizations to give students opportunities to solve situations using their linguistic skills.

All authorities cited agreed that the use of native language instruction makes the task of teaching academic skills more manageable.

THE ESL/BILINGUAL LANGUAGE ARTS CLASSROOM: A MODEL

The language arts classroom model presented here is based on those language characteristics that are desirable in a language classroom. The examples presented represent some of the many activities that can be used in a language arts classroom that emphasizes integration of the language areas, use of language for learning, the use of communicative approaches, and the use of the native language to develop cognitive and communication skills in both languages. This language arts classroom model integrates theories of communicative competence, the language and content, and the native language use approaches.

The language classroom has several functions. It is a medium to learn languages, to use language to learn, to use language to be understood, and for communication purposes. The focus is more on the cognitive processes than on grammatical forms. The objective of the language arts classroom is to develop the competence to function in the real world of the school, the neighborhood, the home, the city, and the country where students interact. This language arts classroom attempts to supply students with grammatical knowledge, fluency, and effective communicative strategies related to their cognitive and linguistic needs.

Organizing the Classroom for Instruction

The way the language arts classroom is organized will have an effect on the quality and quantity of the students' language development. In other words, the classroom organization, the teacher's behaviors, and the manner in which language is presented, will influence the amount and depth of language skills acquisition. The language teacher plays an important role in directing language learning activities in the classroom. The language used by teachers and classmates in instructional communication activities plays an important part in the acquisition of such skills. Learning takes place when the learners try to make sense of what is being said, when they try to relate what they think people are saying to the language they are using. The classroom environment should provide:

1. A natural setting in which the focus is on the activity and not on the language used. This natural setting will make second language students able to concentrate on the message conveyed and not on the form of the language.

2.   Interaction with native speakers. In the second language/bilingual classroom language minority students should be encouraged to meet English-speaking students and engage in meaningful conversations in English with them. In the native language arts classroom, students should have opportunities to speak with other children of other language backgrounds and listen to good adult linguistic models.

3.   Integration of the language arts used by students outside the classroom in order to make the classroom more closely related to students' interests. It will require an evaluation of the language learners' communicative environment outside the classroom to integrate daily language activity tasks to fit students' needs.

4.   Evaluation of the students language needs, goals, interests, deficiencies, and difficulties to develop appropriate instructional plans.

5.   Integration of communicative competence, input, and use of language as a medium for learning. This language environment provides opportunities for students to: (a) formulate their ideas and thoughts; (b) read and discuss textual materials with comprehension; (c) orally participate in classroom discussions; and (d) ask and answer questions.

6.   Use of language instructional materials integrating language skills with content from the school curriculum subject areas, the classroom environment, and the students' own experiences to develop cognitive and linguistic skills.

Any successful program will supply input in the second language through content that is comprehensible, interesting and relevant to the students. The focus of the program should not be grammar "oriented," but for the purpose of transmitting a message. The classroom atmosphere should be one of not forcing learners to speak before they are ready; and it should tolerate errors in early speech (Krashen, 1981). In a natural communication situation, language minority students will acquire English grammatical structures in a predictable order.

Complete mastery of a specific structure is not a prerequisite for the acquisition of later-learned structures, since speech errors are developmental and a natural part of second language acquisition.

Organizing Language for Instruction

The language arts classroom must provide instructional activities for the development of social and cognitive language skills. Cummins (1979) insists that the language classroom develop both the interpersonal and cognitive skills. LEP students at an early stage of second language acquisition might show not only more interpersonal skills (meaning is partly carried by the situation and by experiences), but need to be able to use language for cognitive functions. This has important implications for language arts teachers who should plan classroom instructional activities around the following principles:

1.   The communication skills of listening, speaking, reading, and writing are learned best together. All four language areas are to be included in the lesson. One or two areas should receive more emphasis, depending on grade level and literacy development in the first and second languages.

2.   At the initial stage of second language development, much of the content of instruction should be in the students' own language and based on their own experiences.

3.   Teachers should concentrate on communicative skills and move up as soon as their students reach the cognitive and linguistic levels needed to attach new labels to unknown concepts or ideas. The verbalization of experiences stimulates thought processes, expands understanding of other people's viewpoints, and increases vocabulary.

4.   Oral language activities should be meaningful. Indian, Hispanic, and Chinese students, among others, have a rich source for oral language practice since they come from cultures with strong oral story traditions. Stories and legends, transmitted to the

children by their parents, can be made into
plays and written stories for students to
recite.

5.   Emphasis is to be placed on cognitive
tasks which are transferrable and can be applied
across the curriculum.

6.   Teachers must provide opportunities for
students to expand their oral command of the
second language to include writing and reading
activities as soon as students are literate in
the first language.

7.   Presentation of the written language
should be active to the extent that students
will identify the need to write and to satisfy
the desire to communicate a written message
through a title, a paragraph, a summary, a
report, or a story.

8.   Materials used should provide students
with real communication topics and include
group-oriented projects for a specific goal or
task, problem-solving activities, and information gathering activities.

SUMMARY

Language arts must teach effective
communication.   Communication is based on
knowledge of the meaning behind symbols as well
as the ability to use these symbols clearly and
creatively.   There are several suggested
methodologies presented in this chapter:
integration of the language arts and content
areas; creative communication through writing;
communicative and linguistic competence;
language as a medium of learning; and the use of
the native language as a language arts approach.
All these methodologies are intended to develop
effective communication through language. These
methodologies will be effective as long as they
are in the hands of creative administrators and
teachers who provide an appropriate classroom
atmosphere and use educationally sound classroom
strategies.

RECOMMENDATIONS FOR RESEARCH

The area of language arts is a broad one. It encompasses learning skills and teaching strategies in the areas of listening, speaking, reading, and writing. To be more specific, it deals with grammar, syntax, oral production, and written production. Therefore, the concept of language arts has not been clearly defined in the literature. Researchers have dealt with specific areas, especially oral production, grammar, and syntax. Most of the professional literature on second language/bilingual education offers one or two pages dealing with language arts as a subject. By examining these texts, it is clear that although it is thought of as a very important component of the second language/bilingual classroom, in-depth theory and research on structuring language activities in these classrooms cannot be presented since none exist. The research by Chamot, Cummins, Krashen, Mohan, and Wong Fillmore has made substantial contributions to increasing the literature on classroom language instruction. But more research is needed in this area. Questions that are still researchable are: What are the criteria for a successful language arts classroom? Who is a successful language student? What are the learning and teaching strategies that can be identified as successful for bilingual and second language students? What language strategies work with what students? The area of auditory processing, especially listening, is still researchable. Characteristics of good second language listeners, non-verbal communication strategies second language learners use when they cannot produce the language, and other strategies to develop expressive communication, are in need of further research.

Research in writing in second language or bilingual classrooms is beginning to look at strategies that have been successful in the first language. Additional studies are needed to try out some of these theories with second language and bilingual students.

There is very little research literature on native language arts. The available literature provides theoretical insights into the philosophical and cognitive reasons for using the native language. But there is a great need to identify the cognitive and linguistic advantages of using the native language, especially as it pertains to English performance.

In summary, the topic of the second language/bilingual language arts classroom has many researchable topics. There is much potential for large-scale studies in a number of areas. A challenge is extended to foundations, to non-profit organizations, corporations, and federal and state agencies to collaborate on research projects in the area of second language/bilingual language arts.

REFERENCES

Anderson, T. **A Guide to Family Reading in Two Languages: The Preschool Years.** Rosslyn, Va.: National Clearinghouse for Bilingual Education, 1981.

Acuna-Reyes, R. Perceptions of Inservice Teacher Training Needs of Foreign Language Teachers in the Area of Communicative Competence. Unpublished doctoral dissertation, Fordham University, 1987.

Bachman, L.F. and Palmer, A.S. "The construct validation of some components of communicative proficiency." **TESOL Quarterly,** 16, 4, 449-464, 1982.

Bodman, J.W. "Student-Centered Education: The Gentle Revolution in ESL Teaching." In Bartley, D.E. (Ed.). **The Adult Basic Education, TESOL Handbook.** New York: Collier-MacMillan, 1979.

Bowers, R. "English in the world: Aims and achievements in English language teaching." **TESOL Quarterly,** 20, 393-401, 1986.

Brunfit, C.A. "Methodological Solutions to the Problem of Communicative Teaching." In Himes, M. and Rutherford, W. (Eds.). **On TESOL '81.** Washington, D.C.: Teaching of English to Speakers of Other Languages, 1982.

Brunfit, C.A. and Johnson, K. (Eds.). **The Communicative Approach to Language Teaching.** London: Oxford University Press, 1979.

Butzman, W. and Dodson, C.J. "The teaching of communication: From theory to practice." **IRAL,** 18, 289-309, 1980.

Canale, M. "From Communicative Competence to Communicative Language Pedagogy." In Richards, J.C. and Schmidt, R. (Eds.). **Language and Communication.** London: Longman, 1981.

Canale, M. and Swain, M. "The Role of Grammar in a Communicative Approach to Second Language Teaching and Testing." In Seidner, S. (Ed.). **Issues of Language Assessment: Foundations and Research.** Rosslyn, Va.: National Clearinghouse for Bilingual Education, 1981.

Carrasquillo, A. and Segan, P. **The Teaching of Reading in Spanish to the Bilingual Student. La ensenanza de la lectura en espanol para el estudiante bilingue.** Madrid: Ediciones Alcala, 1984.

Cathcart-Strong, R.R. "Input generation by young second language learners." TESOL **Quarterly,** 20, 3, 15-30, 1986.

Chamot, A. "Toward a functional ESL curriculum in the elementary school." TESOL **Quarterly,** 17, 3, 459-471, 1983.

Cummins, J. **Linguistic Interdependence and the Educational Development of Bilingual Children.** Toronto: Ontario Institute for Studies in Education, 1979.

Cummins, J. "The Role of Primary Language Development in Promoting Educational Success for Language Minority Students." In **Schooling and Language Minority Students: A Theoretical Framework.** Los Angeles, Calif.: Evaluation, Dissemination, and Assessment Center, California State University, 1981.

Cummins, J. Language and Literacy Learning in Bilingual Instruction: Policy Report (ED 245 575). Southwest Educational Development Laboratories, 1983.

Cummins, J. **Bilingualism and Special Education: Issues in Assessment and Pedagogy.** Clevedon, England: Multilingual Matters, 1984.

Curtain, H.A. "Integrating language and content instruction." **ERIC/CLL News,** 9, 1, 10-11, 1986.

Dahl, S. "Oral Language and Its Relationship to Success in Reading." In Froese, V. and Straw, L.S.B. (Eds.). **Research in the Language Arts: Language and Schooling.** Baltimore: University Park Press, 1981.

Diaz, R.M. "Thought and two languages: The impact of bilingualism on cognitive development." **Review of Research in Education,** 10, 23-54, 1983.

Dolson, D.P. "Bilingualism and scholastic performance: The literature revisited." **NABE Journal,** 10, 1, 1-35, 1985.

Early, M.; Thew, C.; and Wakefield, P. **Integrating Language and Content Instruction K-12: An ESL Resource Book.** Victoria, Canada: Publications Service Branch, Ministry of Education, 1986.

Fox, S. "The Whole Language Approach to Language Arts for the Indian Student." In Reyhner, J. (Ed.). **Teaching the Indian Child.** Billings: Eastern Montana College, 1986.

Franklin, E.A. "Literacy instruction for LES children." Language Arts, 3, 1, 51-60, 1986.

Froese, V. and Straw, B.S. (Eds.). **Research in the Language Arts: Language and Schooling.** Baltimore: University Park Press, 1981.

Fuentes, J. "From theory to practice: Writing as a process with bilingual children." **NABE News,** 10, 3, 9-16, 1987.

Garcia, E. and Padilla, R. (Eds.) **Advances in Bilingual Education Research.** Tucson: University of Arizona Press, 1985.

Genesee, F. "The baby and the bathwater or what immersion has to say about bilingual education: Teaching and learning in bilingual education --significant immersion instructional features." **NABE Journal,** 10, 3, 227-254, 1986.

Goodman, K.; Goodman, Y.; and Flores, B. **Reading in the Bilingual Classroom: Literacy and Biliteracy.** Rosslyn, Va: National Clearinghouse for Bilingual Education, 1979.

Hansen-Krening, N. **Competency and Creativity in Language Arts.** Reading, Mass.: Addison-Wesley, 1979.

Harste, J.C.; Burke, C.L. and Woodward, V.A. The Young Child as Writer-Reader, and Informant (NIE G-80-0121, Final Report). Bloomington, Indiana, Reading Department, 1983.

Herschenhorn, S. "Teaching Listening Comprehension Using Live Language." In Celce-Murcia, M. and McIntosh, L. (Eds.). **Teaching English as a Second Language or Foreign Language.** Rowley, Mass.: Newbury House, 1979.

Johnson, K. and Morrow, K. **Communication in the Classroom.** London: Longman, 1981.

Kean, J.M. "Grammar: A Perspective." In Froese, V. and Straw, S.F. (Eds.). **Research in the Language Arts: Language and Schooling.** Baltimore: University Park Press, 1981.

Klassen, B.R. "Communicative Competence and Second Language Learning." In Froese, V. and Straw, S.F. (Eds.) **Research in the Language Arts: Language and Schooling.** Baltimore: University Park Press, 1981.

Krashen, S. **Second Language Acquisition** and **Second Language Learning.** Oxford: Pergamon Press, 1981.

Krashen, S. **Principles and Practices in Second Language.** Oxford, Pergamon Press, 1982.

Krashen, S. **Writing: Research, Theory and Applications.** New York, Alemany Press, 1984.

Krashen, S. **Inquiries and Insight.** New York: Alemany Press, 1985.

Lado, R. "Valuing native language instruction." **NABE News,** 6, 3, 3-5, 1983.

Legarreta-Marcaida, D. "The effects of program models on language acquisition by Spanish-speaking children." **TESOL Quarterly,** 13, 4, 521-534, 1981.

Mohan, B. **Language and Content.** Reading, Mass.: Addison-Wesley, 1986.

Mohan, B. "Language and content learning: Reading common ground." **ERIC/CLL News Bulletin,** 9, 2, 8-9, 1986.

Morley, J. "Current directions in teaching English to speakers of other languages: A state of the art synopsis." **TESOL Newsletter,** 21, 2, 16-20, 1987.

Omagio, A.C. **Teaching Language in Content.** Boston: Heinle & Heinle, 1986.

Parker, D. Sheltered English: Theory to Practice. Paper presented at the NABE Annual Conference, San Francisco, California, 1985.

Ramirez, A. G. **Bilingualism through Schooling: A Cross-Cultural Education for Minority and Majority Students.** Albany, N.Y.: State University of New York Press, 1985.

Ramirez, A.G. and Stronquist, N. P. "ESL methodology and student language learning in bilingual elementary schools." TESOL **Quarterly**, 13, 2, 145-158, 1979.

Richards, J.C. and Theodore, S.R. **Approaches and Methods in Language Teaching: A Description and Analysis.** Cambridge: Cambridge University Press, 1986.

Savignon, S.J. **Communicative Competence: Theory and Classroom Practice, Texts and Contexts in Second Language Learning.** Reading, Mass.: Addison-Wesley, 1983.

Simoes, A. "English Only: Another viewpoint." **SABE Journal**, 3, 1, 7-14, 1987.

Smith, F. "The language arts and the learner's mind." **Language Arts**, 56, 2, 118-125, 1979.

Stevick, E. **Teaching Languages: A Way and Ways.** Rowley, Mass.: Newbury House, 1985.

Straw, S.B. "Analysis Versus Synthesis." In Froese, V. and Straw, S.B. (Eds.). **Research in the Language Arts: Language and Schooling.** Baltimore: University Park Press, 1981.

United States Department of Education, **What Works: Research about Teaching and Learning.** Washington, D.C.: United States Department of Education, 1986.

United States General Accounting Office. **Bilingual Education: A New Look at the Research Evidence.** Washington, D.C.: United States Department of Education, 1987.

Wong Fillmore, L. and Valadez, C. "Teaching bilingual learners." In Wiltrach, M.C. (Ed.) **Handbook of Research on Teaching.** New York: McMillan, 1986.

ANNOTATED BIBLIOGRAPHY

Acuna-Reyes, R. Perceptions of Inservice
    Teaching Training Needs of Foreign
    Language Teachers in the Area of Communi-
    cative Competence. Unpublished doctoral
    dissertation, Fordham University, 1987.

    Identified and compared the perceived
    teacher training needs of elementary and
    high school foreign language teachers in
    the area of communicative competence with
    respect to three components: principles of
    communicative competence; communicative-
    based curriculum content; and communica-
    tive-based methodology. The researcher
    defined communicative competence as the
    ability to send messages to others in terms
    of their goals and needs.

Ada, A.F. "Creative education for bilingual
    teachers." **Harvard Educational Review**, 56,
    4, 386-394, 1986.

    Prescribes a bilingual teacher-training
    process that is based on a critique of the
    current condition of bilingual education
    and the professional concerns of bilingual
    teachers. Suggests a creative approach to
    teacher training.

Allen, V.G. "Developing contexts to support
    second language acquisition." **Language
    Arts**, 63, 1, 61-66, 1986.

    Discusses ways in which the regular
    classroom teacher can design language
    development programs for limited-English-
    speaking children.

Appleberry, M.H. and Rodriguez, E.A. "Literary
    books make the difference in teaching the
    ESL student." **Reading Horizons**, 26, 2,
    112-116, 1986.

    Suggests materials teachers can use to help
    non-English and limited-English-speaking
    students develop their language skills.

Bilingual Education Evaluation Unit. The
  Transition Program for Refugee Children
  1984-1985. New York City: New York City
  Board of Education, Office of Educational
  Assessment, 1986.

  Describes the third year of operation of
  New York City's Transition Program for
  Refugee Children. Student achievement test
  results based on Criterion Referenced
  English Syntax Test (CREST) scores found
  that program participants were generally
  progressing in their knowledge of reading
  and in mathematics at the same rate as the
  national norms and exceeded the city-wide
  criteria of one CREST objective per month
  of instruction.

Cambourne, B. "Process writing and non-English
  speaking background children." **Australian
  Journal of Reading**, 9, 3, 126-138, 1986.

  Explores the consequences of not developing
  competence in oral forms of the second
  language, which is the intermediate step in
  the recommended sequence of bilingual
  literacy development.

Carrasco, R.L.; Acosta, C.T.; and de la
  Torre-Spencer, S. "Language Use, Lesson
  Engagement, and Participation Structures:
  A Microethnographic Analysis of Two
  Language Arts Lessons in a Bilingual
  First-Grade Classroom." In Saravia Shore,
  M. and Arvizu, S. (Eds.) **Communicative and
  Cross Cultural Competencies: Ethnographies
  of Educational Programs for Language
  Minority Students in Community Contexts.**
  In press.

  An ethnographic study of a group of
  Spanish-dominant bilingual first grade
  students. The students were observed and
  videotaped during two small-group language
  arts lessons, both structured around an
  instructional game. One group was led by a
  bilingual, bicultural Chicana teacher; the

other by a monolingual English-speaking teacher. Results of the study indicate that when there were more student interactions and on-task behaviors with the bilingual bicultural teacher than with the monolingual English-speaking teacher.

Carrasquillo, A. and Segan, P. **The Teaching of Reading in Spanish to the Bilingual Student. La ensenanza de la lectura en espanol para el estudiante bilingue.** Madrid: Ediciones Alcala, 1984.

A dual language text on the theory and methodology of teaching reading in Spanish to language minority students. The book presents chapters in English and Spanish. Each chapter is written in only one language, either English or Spanish, at the preference of its author. Includes a series of focusing questions and follow-up activities appropriate for Spanish-speaking students.

Chamot, A.U. **A Synthesis of Current Literature on English as a Second Language: Issues and Educational Policy.** (ED 261 537). Rosslyn, Va.: National Clearinghouse for Bilingual Education, 1985.

A review of the literature on instruction in English as a second language. Looks at four areas of ESL instruction individually and then derives conclusions for these areas. The four areas are: instructional approaches, program organization, student characteristics, and instructional materials.

Chamot, A.U. and O'Malley, J.M. **English as a Second Language: Cognitive Academic Language Learning Approach, An ESL Content Based Curriculum.** Wheaton, Maryland: National Clearinghouse for Bilingual Education, 1986.

An instructional program for LEP students who will participate in mainstream content instruction. The program provides transitional instruction between English as a second language or bilingual education and mainstream instruction through content area instruction in science, mathematics, and social studies. Offers learning strategies derived from a cognitive model of learning.

Cummins, J. **Language and Literacy Learning in Bilingual Instruction: Policy Report** (ED 245 575) Southwest Educational Development Laboratories, 1983.

Describes findings of a study undertaken by the Southwest Educational Laboratory to assess the extent to which the development of cognitive and academic skills in the native language and in English are interrelated.

Dicker, S.J. Abstracting in Writing: A Case Study of Four ESL College Students. Unpublished doctoral dissertation, Columbia University, Teachers College, 1986.

Investigated the abstracting character-istics in writing of four college ESL students and the ways in which they abstracted on other tasks in order to find out whether the characteristics manifested in writing were particular to the medium of writing or were a function of language proficiency.

Doughty, C. and Pica, T. "Information gap" tasks: Do they facilitate second language acquisition?" **TESOL Quarterly**, 20, 2, 305-325, 1986.

Describes a study conducted to determine the effects of task type and participation pattern on language classroom interaction. Results of the study suggest that tasks which require information exchange are crucial to conversational modification of

classroom interaction and that group and
dyad interaction patterns produce more
modification than teacher-fronted situations.

Early, M.; Thew, C.; and Wakefield, P.
**Integrating Language and Content
Instruction K-12: An ESL Resource Book.**
Victoria, Canada: Publications Service
Branch, Ministry of Education, 1986.

Provides a good source for teaching
suggestions to integrate language and
content in the classroom.

Faber, D. "Teaching the rhythms of English: A
new theoretical base." **IRAL,** 24, 3,
205-216, 1986.

Presents reasons why more emphasis should
be placed on the mastery of the rhythmic
features of the target language in foreign
language teaching. Includes an account of
an important recent theoretical contribution to the description of the principles
underlying English speech rhythm.

Fox, S. "The Whole Language Approach to
Language Arts for the Indian Student." In
Reyhner, J. (Ed.) **Teaching the Indian
Child.** Billings: Eastern Montana
College, 1986.

Presents a rationale to use an integrative
language arts approach called "whole
language". Presents several activities to
be used in a combined approach.

Freeman, D. and Freeman, Y. Bilingual Learners:
How Our Assumptions Limit Their World.
Paper presented at the Annual Meeting of
the Teachers of English to Speakers of
Other Languages, Anaheim, California,
March, 1986.

The authors maintain that five common
assumptions are held by teachers about
learners: (1) adults should choose what

children need to learn; (2) oral language
must be mastered before written language
can be introduced; (3) real, whole language
is too difficult for students learning
language; (4) language learning is
different in different languages, and
simultaneous learning will be confusing;
and (5) specifically for bilinguals,
teaching in English is essential to school
success and acculturation. According to
the authors, there is research to dispute
each of these assumptions. Describes the
whole language approach, the one
instructional approach that incorporates
recent research and rejects the
assumptions. This approach, according to
the authors, integrates all four skills
(listening, speaking, reading, and
writing); exposes children to language in
real, functional contexts; encourages
language exploration; and builds on the
students' existing linguistic strengths.

Freeman, D.; Freeman, Y.; and Gonzalez, R.
"Success for LEP students: The Sunnyside
sheltered English program." **TESOL
Quarterly**, 21, 2, 361-367, 1987.

Describes the results of a sheltered
English program developed and implemented
for LEP high school students.

Froese, V. and Stanley, B.S. (Eds.) **Research in
the Language Arts: Language and Schooling.**
Baltimore: University Park Press, 1981.

Addresses the issue of language in relation
to schooling and the importance of
cognition in the language arts. It is
intended to address unresolved issues of
importance in oral language and literacy
development.

Gonzalez, J.R. **Guide to Multicultural
Educational Resources.** Albuquerque:
University of New Mexico, 1987.

An annotated bibliography of materials currently available in the field of bilingual bicultural education.

Green, J. M. "Learning modes and language teaching methods: The search for the right mix." **NABE News**, 10, 1, 3-7, 1986.

Describes four learning modes: concrete experience, active experimentation, reflective observation, and abstract conceptualization with practical applications for the classroom.

Halsall, S.H. An Ethnographic Account of the Composing Behaviors of Five Young Bilingual Children (ED 273 967). Paper presented at the Annual Meeting of the American Educational Research Association, April, 1986.

Examines bilingual children's composing behaviors during classroom writing and their perceptions of writing. Students' descriptions of what occurred in their day to day environment were analyzed using ethnographic methods.

Hernandez, N.G. and Descamps, J.A. Review of Factors Affecting Learning of Mexican-Americans. Paper presented at the National Association for Chicano Studies, El Paso, Texas, April 1986.

Describes a review of more than 500 empirical studies conducted since 1970 on the achievement of Mexican Americans. The review found widely accepted stereotypes about Mexican Americans lack of internal locus of control, reluctance to compete, depressed intelligence, field dependence orientation in learning, and failure to acculturate to be false. Factors found to be associated with increased achievement included language usage, bilingualism, bilingual education, positive self-concept, home independence training, and school/classroom affective climate. Findings indicated that teacher warmth and enthusiasm and absence of authoritarianism and punitiveness significantly impact academic achievement of Mexican American students; cooperative learning environments produce greater academic gains than competitive or individualistic learning environments for all students; and students in low-track high school classes receive less educational opportunities than students in heterogeneous groups.

Kessler, C. Mathematics and Language Intersections for Hispanic Bilingual Students. Paper presented at the Annual Meeting of the National Council of Teachers of Mathematics, Washington, D.C., April, 1986.

Examines intersections between mathematical and language performance in light of data collected from Hispanic students at varying stages of acquiring English as a second language in school. The study focused on aspects of the developing linguistic system as it affects underlying metacognitive processes related to mathematical performance. Analyzes metacognition and bilingual learners; cognitive/academic language proficiency; and cognitive, analytic, mathematical proficiency intersections; the language of mathematics and metacognition; and the learning of mathematics in terms of person, task, strategy, and the regulation of cognition. Implications for mathematics education are presented.

Krashen, S. **Inquiries and Insight.** New York: Alemany Press, 1985.

Discusses topics in second language learning, bilingual education and literacy in the primary language.

Lantolf, J.P. and Labarca, A. (Eds.) **Research in Second Language Learning: Focus on the Classroom.** Norwood, NJ: Ablex Publishing, 1987.

Discusses the second language learning process and implications of research for classroom language learning. Some of the topics included are: second language learner's acquisition of description and explanation; psychological aspects of pedagogical grammar in foreign language teaching; cognitive processes in learning a second language; the optimal age hypothesis; the role of language and cognition in second language awareness; improving oral comprehension through intonation and kinetics; and a comparison of native and second language discourse.

Low, G. "The need for a multi-perspective approach to the evaluation of foreign language teaching materials." **Evaluation and Research in Education**, 1, 1, 19-29, 1987.

Drawing on research conducted in a number of countries, the article examines the program and material evaluations likely to be performed by language teachers. It is argued that these evaluations are frequently not independent.

Maldonado-Guzman, A.A. "Theoretical and Methodological Issues in the Ethnographic Study of Teachers' Differential Treatment of Children in Bilingual Bicultural Classrooms." In Saravia Shore, M. and Arvizu, S. (Eds.) **Communicative and Cross Cultural Competencies: Ethnographies of Educational Programs for Language Minority Students in Community Contexts**. In press.

A study of teachers' differential treatment of children in two first-grade Chicano bilingual-bicultural classrooms in Chicago.

Marcum, K. L. **Teaching to Enhance Acquisition of Pragmatic Competence** (ED 274 206). WATESOL Working Papers, 1986.

Identifies some of the problems of acquisition of pragmatic competence in speech experienced by language learners and the implications of selected literature to enhance pragmatic competence through second language instruction.

Mohan, B. **Language and Content.** Reading, Mass.: Addison-Wesley, 1986.

Presents a model for the integration of language and content learning. Provides a summary of strategies to coordinate language objectives with content area objectives.

Morley, J. "Current directions in teaching English to speakers of other languages: A state of the art synopsis." **TESOL Newsletter,** 21, 2, 16-20, 1987.

A brief overview of English language teaching and language learning in the last twenty years. Focuses on some of the current directions in second language learning and teaching.

National Association of State Boards of Education (NASBE) and the National Clearinghouse for Bilingual Education (NCBE). **A Guide to Special Language Services for Minority Language Students.** Rosslyn, Va.: National Clearinghouse for Bilingual Education, 1986.

Examines the development of English language skills and describes programmatic options for the education of LEP students.

New Levine, L. "Language learning and academic success in multi-lingual classrooms." **NABE News,** 9, 3, 7-16, 1986.

Discusses a grouping model for application in classes of children with mixed language ability, reading ability, and learning style.

Nieto, C. "The California challenge: Preparing teachers for a growing Hispanic population." **Action in Teacher Education**, 8, 1, 1-8, 1986.

   Addresses issues raised in developing programs and strategies to serve Hispanic students. Discusses the following issues: (1) the demographics of California and educational implications; (2) the role of culture in the home-school relationship; and (3) the significance of language for linguistic and cognitive development of language minority students.

Omagio, C. **Teaching Language in Context**. Boston: Heinle & Heinle, 1986.

   Discusses issues in second language learning and approaches to listening and reading. Outlines strategies for cultural understanding.

O'Malley, J. M. and Chamot, A. U. "What will happen to Tran and other LEP children?" **PTA Today**, 11, 6, 8-10, 1986.

   According to the authors, the inability of LEP children to profit from instruction in English can lead to nonacademic courses, failure, and dropping out. The two basic types of educational programs, bilingual programs and English language programs, are described.

Ovando, C.J. and Collier, P. **Bilingual and ESL Classrooms: Teaching in Multicultural Classrooms**. New York: McGraw-Hill, 1985.

   Combines theory and research with practical classroom applications. A good source for teacher training courses in teaching methods, curriculum development, language acquisition, and content area instruction.

Pena, A. Implementation Procedures in Bilingual Education: The Difference between Success and Failure. Paper presented at the Conference of the National Association for Bilingual Education, Chicago, Illinois, April, 1986.

Argues that rather than abandon bilingual education programs that have not met expectations, there is a need to assess implementation procedures in bilingual programs to determine whether or not they foster success or failure. Describes areas that need to be examined for insights and improvement of programs.

Rigg, P. and Hudelson, S. "One child doesn't speak English." Australian Journal of Reading, 9, 3, 116-125, 1986.

Describes general guidelines for diagnosing students' strengths and integrating the student into the class. Presents four principle of language development and shows how they translate into practice.

Rorsch, E.G. The Effects of Reader Awareness: A Case Study of Three ESL Student Writers. Unpublished doctoral dissertation, New York University, 1986.

A case study was conducted with three advanced ESL college students enrolled in basic writing courses to examine how audience awareness influenced their revisions.

Stevick, E. Teaching Languages: A Way and Ways. Rowley, Mass.: Newbury House, 1985.

Discusses detailed teaching language strategies for the development of communication skills.

Terrell, T.D. "Acquisition in the Natural Approach: The binding/access framework." Modern Language Journal, 70, 3, 213-227, 1986.

Explores second language acquisition theory in the context of language teaching in a classroom using the Natural Approach. Focuses on the acquisition process and describes the functions and interaction of acquisition and learning for the Natural Approach class. Analyzes the Natural Approach process for students learning Spanish, French, Dutch, German, Greek, Japanese, and Mandarin Chinese as a second language.

Ulloa, Y. "Language, culture and self-esteem." **Equity and Choice**, 3, 1, 54-56, 1986.

A discussion of schools use, reinforcement, and enhancement of the dominant culture at the expense of the culture of minority students. The author argues that if schools recognize the importance of language and culture, they will see improvement in minority children's academic growth, self-image and economic future.

United States General Accounting Office. **Bilingual Education: A New Look at the Research Evidence.** Washington, D.C.: United States Department of Education, 1987.

A report sponsored by the United States General Account Office to help assessment statements made by Department of Education officials concerning their interpretation of research evidence in bilingual education. The report addresses the following issues: (1) the native language requirement and the learning of English; (2) the native language requirement and the learning of other subjects; (3) the merits of alternative approaches; (4) long term educational outcomes; and (5) targeted vs. generalized answers about approaches to teaching students whose English proficiency is limited.

Valdes, J. M. (Ed.) **Culture Bound: Bridging the Cultural Gap in Language Teaching.** Cambridge: Cambridge University Press, 1986.

A collection of essays intended to introduce teachers of language to the interaction between language and culture. The papers explore the difference between interacting with another culture and actually entering into it. Includes discussions on language, thought, and culture; cultural differences and similarities; and classroom applications.

VanPatten, B. "Second language acquisition research and the learning/teaching of Spanish: Some research findings and implications." **Hispania,** 69, 1, 202-216, 1986.

Discusses recent findings in second language acquisition research and implications for the teaching/learning of Spanish.

Violand de Hainer, E; Bratt, T; Kim, S; and Fagan, B. "Learning styles: A new approach to teaching limited English proficient students." **NABE News,** 9, 3, 3-12, 1986.

Describes a learning style model and its applications bilingual classrooms.

Wei, D. "The Asian American success myth." **Interracial Books for Children Bulletin,** 17, 3-4, 16-17, 1986.

A discussion of the stereotypes about Asian American students and their need for bilingual education programs.

Wong Fillmore, L. and Valadez, C. "Teaching Bilingual Learners." In Wiltrach, M.C. (Ed.) **Handbook of Research on Teaching.** New York: McMillan, 1986.

Presents a summary of the research
background to consider in assessing the
appropriateness of instructional methods to
be used with LEP students. The chapter
includes the following sections: (a)
assumptions and definitions of bilingual
education; (b) language use in bilingual
classrooms; (c) language learning and
teaching through bilingual instruction; and
(d) cognitive and social effects of
bilingualism.

Chapter 10

TECHNOLOGY AS A PARTNER IN DEVELOPING LITERACY COMPUTER-ASSISTED LANGUAGE LEARNING (CALL) FOR ESL AND BILINGUAL EDUCATION

Dennis Sayers

INTRODUCTION

An important document concerning computer-assisted language learning (CALL) with bilingual and ESL program students was published this year. The U.S. Congress Office of Technology Assessment issued a staff paper entitled, <u>Trends and Status of Computers in Schools: Use in Chapter 1 Programs and Use with Limited English Proficient Students</u> (Roberts, 1987). This OTA Report is based on a comprehensive review of the academic literature, a survey sent to all State Education Consolidation Improvement Act (ECIA) Chapter 1 Directors, and the 1985 National Survey of Instructional Uses of School Computers conducted by Henry Becker of Johns Hopkins University. The scores of interviews with practitioners contained in this publication provide a fascinating overview of perhaps the most rapid introduction to date of a technological innovation into the U.S. educational system.

> Between 1981 and 1986, the percentage of American schools with computers intended for instruction grew from about 18% to almost 96%. There are now more than one million computers in public schools alone, and over 15 million students and 500,000 teachers in public and private schools who make use of computers (stand-alone microcomputers) and related technologies (Roberts, 1987, pp. 1-2).

This rapid implementation of a largely untested technology has been accompanied by major discrepancies in equity and access. While the majority of students in bilingual and ESL programs are concentrated in pre-secondary schools, OTA finds that "generally, students in relatively 'poor' elementary or middle schools have significantly less potential access than their peers in relatively 'rich' schools. At the high school level, however, this trend disappears" (OTA, p.3.). Yet merely securing access to a school's computers does not assure a balanced exposure to computer-based instructional approaches. According to the OTA Report, "students in poorer (low socioeconomic status) schools typically spend more time with drill and practice than students in richer (high socioeconomic status) schools" (p.5).

Teachers who work with students in bilingual and ESL programs are less likely to employ computer-based approaches in their teaching strategies, since "among regular classroom teachers who teach limited English proficient (LEP) students, 22% use computers. This is even lower compared to the proportion of all regular classroom teachers (50%) who use computers" (OTA, p. 7). Only 1% of the software programs available commercially were designed for ESL classes (OTA Report, Table 1, facing p. 16).

To date, little quantitative research has been completed on the effectiveness of computer-assisted language learning (CALL) as compared with traditional methods of instructional delivery for students in ESL and bilingual programs. Inferences must be drawn from evaluation studies not specifically concerned with LEP students. For example, local district evaluation studies of Chapter 1 computer use, which in some cases include high percentages of LEP students, generally show improved achievement test gains in mathematics and reading through computer drill and practice; yet these many studies are difficult to compare "due to lack of standardized data among various programs" (OTA, p. 8) and are of limited utility since

> none of the Chapter 1 program evaluations compared the benefits of drill and practice with other types of computer based instruction, such as use of simulation or problems

approaches, or to other nontraditional
approaches.   Future   research   might
consider these issues...
Research studies on uses of technology
with LEP students   are   not extensive;
few studies have   been conducted   and
more   are   needed.   Several   projects
exploring use of computers   with   LEP
students   show   promising results: for
these   students,   word   processing
and   computer   networking   provide
vehicles   for   students   to   function
effectively   in   both   their   native
language   and   in   English   (OTA, pp.
8-9).

In   the   conclusions   detailed   in its
"Summary   and Implications   for Federal Policy,"
the OTA Report reiterates these   two key points:
a)   that more research is urgently   needed since
current   research has not   concerned itself with
"defining the problem of adequately serving this
growing   percentage   of   American [LEP] students
and identifying possible solutions;" and b) that
educational   computering   holds   the   unique
potential for promoting   writing skills with LEP
students.

There   is   one   particular   area where
computers seem to be   making a special
impact   on   language   development   --
that is in the field of writing. Word
processing   capabilities   and   in some
instances,   local   or   long-distance
networking capabilities of computer-
based technology,   are   being used   to
encourage LEP students   to   write and
communicate   more   effectively   in
highly functional   contexts, both   in
their native language and in   English.
When   used   in   this   context,   the
computer   can   provide   a   means   for
students   to   break   out   of   the
traditional   mode   of   thinking,   to
enhance their sense of mastery, and to
enrich   the   learning   experience   by

providing access to role models and speakers from their native culture (p. 96).

A number of educational researchers, speaking largely from anecdotal experience gathered in a variety of educational settings, have suggested that "the functional writing environment" provided by these three computer applications may promote the development of writing skills both in the students' mother tongue and in English, their second language (Cummins 1986a; Cummins 1986b; Rosa & Moll, 1985; Sayers 1986; Sayers & Brown 1987). These researchers are thus in substantial agreement with the OTA Report's finding that "some of the most promising avenues of computer use for ESL students are in the area of language development through writing" (p. 86). The focus of Computer-Assisted Language Learning (CALL) in bilingual and ESL education will, therefore, be on promoting literacy through 1) word processing, 2) interactive writing prompters, and 3) computer writing networks. However, these technological innovations can only be understood in the context of the radical re-examination which the teaching of writing has undergone during the last decade.

DISCUSSION

Writing process approaches

The teaching of writing has experienced a profound transformation during the last decade, due in large part to the impetus provided in the research of James Moffett (1968), Janet Emig (1971), James Britton and his British colleagues (1975), and Donald Graves with his associates in New Hampshire (1983). A "process approach" to writing instruction --stressing purposeful writing on student-selected topics for real audiences, with many opportunities for revision, peer feedback and teacher conferencing-- has been embraced by a number of teachers very enthusiastically. A process approach to teaching writing can be distinguished from the more product-oriented approaches which prevailed

in most schools during the first three-quarters
of this century --that is, where writing was
taught at all.

Product-oriented approaches are teacher-
centered and prescriptive. The teacher usually
determines the topic and is the only audience
for any drafts and the final text. The
instructor is placed in the role of sole arbiter
of a difficult-to-define standard, usually
embodied in some "model" text, a polished piece
of professional writing the student is
encouraged to imitate. Every student draft,
where drafts are permitted, is an attempt to
attain a final product approximating the
teacher's high standard. Failure to do so
results in the teacher marking up the paper and
the student re-writing it, until the teacher is
satisfied with the text. While some students
learn to write in this manner, many learn to
hate writing, in some cases for life.

A process approach to composition
instruction, as its name implies, stresses the
phases through which an effective piece of
writing will pass. While adherents may use
differing terminology, most descriptions of
writing process approaches make reference to
planning, composing, sharing, revising, editing
and publishing as essential stages through which
several drafts will pass in the creation of the
final text. However, advocates of a process
approach are careful to underscore the recursive
quality of composition, namely, that every text
is unique in its circuitous path from conception
to publication, with much looping back to
"earlier" moments in the process, and
considerable leap-frogging to "later" stages.
The shaping of every text is individual
precisely because each writer is unique, and
writing process approaches most definitely place
the student at the center of a creative activity
the purpose of which is to generate and
communicate meaning. Thus process approaches
often state as one of their primary goals the
honing of thinking skills through writing.

I have been careful to use the indefinite
article in describing "a" process approach to
teaching writing. Using "the" would impose a
homogeneity on a pedagogical movement which has

been distinguished by vital discussion and, at times, by healthy disagreement. Indeed, in this period when writing instruction is undergoing such a profound shift, it is very easy --too easy-- to overstate the dichotomy between a process and a product approach to writing. Recently, there has even been much talk at professional conferences stressing the "complementary" relationship between process and product at various stages in the shaping of a text.

Yet there can be no doubt that writing instruction in our schools has taken a new direction, one that is moving into the mainstream. Where only five years ago many teachers were unacquainted with or had only a passing familiarity with the process approach to writing instruction, now we are observing a rebirth of interest in effective strategies to promote written expression in the classroom.

Educational Word Processing

At the same time that the teaching of writing has entered a welcome phase of renovation, a sweeping innovation is being integrated into the curriculum of today's schools: interactive technology, particularly microcomputers. Word processing (using the computer as a dynamic typewriter allowing the writer to revise without recopying) has shown the most promise for language learning for three reasons.

First, word processing has served as the entry point for countless teachers into the seemingly arcane world of interactive technology. In the first wave of educational computing, way back in the early 80's, many teachers were told that programming "courseware" (computerized lessons) was the principal use of these new machines in their classrooms. Most hesitated to invest the time to acquire the programming skills needed to produce their own software. When straightforward educational word processing became available with the Bank Street Writer, many teachers found a writing tool that was helpful to them, both for personal writing and for managing the remarkable amount of paperwork that crosses their desks. From their new vantage point as "insiders," teachers began to see the potential of word processing for students and became more receptive to other computerized "writing tools."

The second and third reasons word processing has shown such promise in the bilingual and second language classroom are inter-related. The context for writing made possible by word processing responds both to "the developmental needs of the learner" and to "shifting cognitive demands placed on the writer at each stage of the writing process" (Dalute 1985).

For younger students, the act of forming letters is taxing both at a physical level, with children often complaining of their hands being tired after a writing session, and at a cognitive level, where handwriting consumes much of the available "mental energy" in short-term memory. The ability to make a well-formed letter with a single keystroke and to immediately delete errors lowers a major threshold to fluency in writing for very young writers. By the time students reach the upper elementary grades, they have, in Piagetan terms, "de-centered" sufficiently in their psychological development that they can appreciate a reader's point of view, and are thus better prepared to employ teacher and peer feedback in order to improve texts through revision. With a word processor, young authors can easily print multiple copies of drafts for teacher and peer comments; once suggestions have been offered, a word processor facilitates the incorporation of improvements without recopying the entire text. Adolescent and young adult writers are often asked to produce extended texts, such as term papers, on detailed topics. These writers welcome the power of word processing to "divide and conquer" a complicated piece of writing, that is, to elaborate the parts of a text and to "cut and paste" these parts electronically into a coherent whole.

This past year saw two major developments associated with educational word processors: the perennial favorite "Bank Street Writer" was released in a much improved 128K format, and

"FrEdWriter" ("Fr\ee\Ed\ucational\Writer") continued to proliferate in classrooms across the
country. The "Bank Street Writer" had
previously been difficult to use for younger
writers. If a student wished to make a
correction in her text, she had to leave that
part of the program where writing took place and
then move to a different area where corrections
could be made. To resume writing, she would
then retrace her path. The new "Bank Street
Writer" has shed this cumbersome structure and
now allows students to write and edit in the
same area, a change welcomed by writing teachers
everywhere.

"FrEdWriter" is the free, public-domain
word processor for Apple II computers developed
by Al Rogers of the San Diego County TECC
(Teacher Education and Computer Center). Based
on a simplified version of AppleWriter, "FrEd"
may be copied legally and given away which
has resulted in its rapid acceptance in
schools. Everything a writer needs to get
started with "FrEd" is on the disk itself:
documentation, on-line lessons and sample files.
The "FrEd" program disk can also double as a
storage disk for student writings, simplifying
classroom management of word processing, since
a teacher can provide each student with a
single program/text disk of his own. While
not a full-powered "adult" word processor,
"FrEd" has been used successfully in elementary
and secondary writing classes. Particularly
important for bilingual and ESL teachers is
the publication of "Spanish FrEdWriter." While
"Spanish FrEd" is not free, it is cheap for
a word processor with the ability to display
accented letters on the screen and print them
out on most printers. The $40 pays for the
cost to produce a special computer chip
containing the accented letters which a teacher
inserts in an Apple II+ or IIe. "Spanish FrEd"
has provided a tremendous impetus for
educational word processing in Spanish bilingual
classes and in Spanish as a foreign language
instruction.

This year has also witnessed the
introduction of educational versions of several
popular "adult" programs by software publishers.

Of   particular   interest   are   integrated
applications   programs,   that is, programs which
tie several useful computer tools, usually a
word processor, a database and a financial
spreadsheet, into a single, functional unit.
These programs permit students to experience
first-hand the types of computer software they
will quite likely encounter in the world of
work.   Addison-Wesley   has   introduced   a
streamlined, cheaper version of "Lotus 1-2-3,"
the biggest selling integrated software program
for IBM computers, while an educational version
of   "PFS:Write,"   ":File"   and   ":Report,"
distributed   by Scholastic for a range of
computers, continues to do well in schools. The
flexible but expensive "WordPerfect," fast
becoming the word processor of choice for
professional writers, is now available for
Apples as well as IBMs and has been marketed at
special rates for educators associated with
universities.   However, as of this writing,
"AppleWorks" remains the most widely-used of the
integrated software packages for the Apple II
family of computers, the machine which continues
to dominate the educational computing scene.
     In a class by itself is "LogoWriter,"
introduced this year for Apples, Commodores and
IBMs.   With "LogoWriter," any teacher familiar
with the Logo programming language can create
custom-tailored writing environments which blend
graphics and word processing capabilities.

Interactive Writing Prompters

     A prompted writing program is nothing more
than a series of suggestions designed to
stimulate an internal dialogue within student
writers at various stages of the writing
process, usually the pre-writing, sharing and
revision phases. For example, a prompting
program might cause the computer to ask a
writer:

     How was your topic viewed in the past?
     In what way is your topic viewed today?
     How would someone argue against your topic?
     Can you tell me more?
     Could you offer an example?

After each question, the computer pauses
for the student to respond and finally provides
a printout of the session which can be used as
a memory jog for later stages in the writing
process. Hugh Burns, a pioneer in the use of
prompted writing to encourage pre-writing,
suggests that

> the resulting interaction [between
> student and writing prompter] thus
> raises to the conscious level what
> writers "already know" about their
> subjects and makes them write down
> their ideas. Also, the programs have
> an uncanny ability to ask questions
> that writers "don't know" the answers
> to yet. Thus such dialogues, by
> generating some dissonance, prompt
> writers to articulate problems which
> the computer-cued interaction uncovers
> (Burns, 1980).

Many writing prompts lead students through
a series of composition "rules of thumb,"
often called writing heuristics. "Aristo" by
John Harwood of Pennsylvania State University
and "Create" by Valerie Arms of Drexel
University employ Aristotelian heuristics, while
a tagmetic approach is used in "TAGI" by Hugh
Burns and available in William Wresch's
"Writer's Helper" from Conduit. Another
popular set of pre-writing heuristics are the
journalistic "Wh-" questions seen in
InterLearn's "Computer Chronicles." Some
prompters ask the writer to draw novel
conclusions by comparing her topic to an
unrelated concept: "Think about how your topic,
nuclear waste disposal, compares to an ocean"
(Rodrigues & Rodrigues, 1984). Stickland (1985)
has defined good computer prompters as programs
which

> offer individuality through branching
> capabilities, uniqueness through op-
> tions not available with traditional
> pen and paper, and interactivity
> through responses to the user, which

simulate   human   dialogue.   [Bad
prompters]   focus   on   surface-level
concerns before higher order concerns,
work   on   a   linear   model   of   writing
...., focus on small chunks of writing
behaviour based on a stimulus-response
model   of   learning,   rather   than the
whole   writing,   [and]   teach   the
strategies   as   content   rather   than
techniques to be used in the writer's
own work (pp. 70-71).

Writing   prompters   can   be   as   useful
during revision as during pre-writing, causing
authors to literally "re-view" their draft and
perhaps re-examine the direction the text is
taking.
Because   writing   prompters   can   help
authors   at   various   stages   in   the   writing
process,   pre-defined   writing   prompters   have
begun to appear as part of a   "systems approach"
to   writing   software.   These   are   sets   of
prompting   programs sold as   a unit with a word
processor,   comprising   a   package   designed   to
offer   support for every   stage   of   the writing
process.   The most prominent examples of these
writing systems include "Quill"   from D.C. Heath
for Apple II's.   "Writer's Helper" from Conduit
and "HBJ Writer" from Harcourt Brace Javonovitch
runs on both   Apple II's and   IBM's.   The latter
programs also offer computer analysis of texts,
displaying graphic visualizations of patterns of
pronoun   use and word   frequency. However, with
all these programs it is quite difficult to move
between   the   word   processor   and   the   various
writing   prompters   and   analyzers;   indeed, the
word   processor   and   prompting   programs   are
completely   separated.   Moreover,   the
possibilities   for teachers   to   move beyond the
pre-defined   hueristics   and   create   their   own
writing prompts are limited or non-existent.
Because   of   these   limitations,   the   most
significant development   of   the   past   year has
been   the appearance   of   the 128K "Bank Street
Writer"   and "FrEdWriter,"   since   both of these
programs allow teachers   to   create "boxed text"
"inside"   a word   processing   file itself.   This
means that teachers can make their own writing

prompters based on local curricular needs, rather than depend on software developers to market pre-defined prompters. Just as important, the student can write directly into the word processor while responding to the teacher's prompts. "FrEd" comes with the following sample prompter, in which a teacher's prompts are protected within boxes while the student writes outside the boxes just as she normally would using "FrEdWriter."

A DESCRIPTIVE PARAGRAPH

the first draft

Answer each question with at least one sentence. Print out your text and use your clusters to help you think of ideas

---

WRITE A TOPIC SENTENCE LIKE:
My special place is_____.
                    OR
The place I remember best is_____.

My favorite place is the beach.

DESCRIBE HOW YOUR PLACE LOOKS.

The cold water splashes on the sticky sand. The birds dive through the water.

DESCRIBE THE FIRST THING OR PERSON YOU SEE WHEN YOU ENTER YOUR PLACE

I see a lifeguard on a high school. I also see people taking their dogs for walks along the shore.

DESCRIBE TWO OTHER THINGS OR PEOPLE YOU SEE AT YOUR PLACE.

There are little children playing in the sand.

DESCRIBE ANY PARTICULAR SMELLS AT YOUR PLACE

It smells like sour fish and burned hot dogs on the barbeque.

DESCRIBE ANY SOUNDS AT YOUR PLACE

I hear children splashing in the cold water and radios blasting rock and roll music.   .

DESCRIBE ANY ACTIVITIES YOU DO AT YOUR PLACE

I like to play in the cool wet water.

DESCRIBE HOW YOU FEEL WHEN YOU'RE AT YOUR PLACE

When I get in the frozen water I feel excited!

GOOD WORK! NOW HOLD DOWN THE CONTROL KEY AND PRESS P TO PRINT.

In this example, when the student prints out her text, the teacher's prompts disappear. The student sees only

My favorite place is the beach. The cold water splashes on the sticky sand. The birds dive through the water. I see a lifeguard on a high stool. I also see people taking their dogs for walks along the shore. There are little children playing in the sand. It smells like sour fish and burned hot dogs on the barbeque. I hear children splashing in the cold water and radios blasting rock and roll music. I like to play in the cool wet water. When I get in the frozen water I feel excited!

Plenty of copies can be made immediately of this first draft and distributed for comments and suggestions from peers and the teacher, leading to timely, effective revision. The ability to create prompts "directly" within a simple word processor lets teachers provide a range of dynamic support to novice writers. In the case of students in ESL and bilingual classrooms, that extra measure of linguistic "scaffolding" offered by prompted writing can allow students to benefit from teacher-provided models while encouraging students to experiment and take risks with their developing language competencies. As students become more competent as writers, the teacher can design new prompts to foster more advanced composition skills, eventually removing the "scaffolding" altogether. The easy-to-use "boxed text" feature found in "Bank Street Writer" and "FrEd" brings prompted writing within the reach of more teachers concerned with language development.

COMPUTER WRITING NETWORKS

On March 23, 1987 this public statement, drafted by a group of ESL professionals and bilingual educators, was read at a press conference in Hartford, Connecticut.

International Computer Writing Network
Takes a Stand
Supporting Bilingual Education
and Against "English Only" Legislation

"To be really successful, you will have to be trilingual: fluent in English, Spanish, and computer."
-- John Naisbitt, in "Megatrends: Ten new directions transforming our lives" (p. 78).

As educators, researchers and students from Argentina, Canada, Mexico, Puerto Rico, Arizona, California, New York and Connecticut gathered at the New England Conference on Writing and Computer Networks in Bilingual Education Programs, we wish to affirm our support of bilingual education and our strong opposition to recent "English Only" legislative initiatives in the United States. We participate in a bilingual writing network which uses computers and telecommunications to link up student writers in Spanish-speaking countries and elsewhere with bilingual classrooms in the United States and Canada. Everyday, students send writings via computers and modems to sister classes across an ocean or across a continent. Thus, our goal is to promote biliteracy, or literacy in another language <u>and</u> English. We see our work as an important step in using computers to help ALL students --including those from English- speak ing backgrounds-- become bilingual. This goal is <u>in direct opposition</u> to "English Only" initiatives which seek to denigrate and restrict the rich linguistic and cultural resources of the Americas --with grave economic and political implications for the "global village" of today's world and the world of the future. Instead of "English Only," we support "English Plus" and the strong bilingual education programs that make English Plus a reality for all children. We emphasize: in 1987, "a person who speaks only one language is a disadvantaged minority."

The signatories to this statement ranged from researchers, including Jim Cummins (Ontario Institute for Studies in Education), Esteban Diaz (University of California-San Diego), Luis Moll (University of Arizona) and Pedro Pedraza (Center for Puerto Rican Studies, Hunter College-CUNY); to teachers, such as Ivelisse Druet and Michelle Gonsalves (San Diego County Schools), Nelly Bonilla and Andres Menendez (University of Puerto Rico Laboratory Schools), Luly Saldana (Academia RaSal, Tijuana, Baja California), and Arturo Solis (New Haven Public Schools); and teacher educators, like Kristin

Brown (San Diego State University), Enid
Figueroa (University of Turabo, Puerto Rico),
Jorge Migliarini (Page Schools, Los Angeles) and
Dennis Sayers (University of Hartford). That
these educators felt moved to take such a strong
public stand reveals much of their commitment to
employing technology in the service of an
empowering pedagogy. This commitment to the use
of computers in promoting first and second
language literacy deserves our attention.

Computer writing networks are difficult to
define, since they may range from a simple
message system within a single classroom on one
computer to much more elaborate linkages using
phone lines to connect classroom computers in
several schools, sometimes in other cities,
states, or nations. But teachers involved in
these writing networks share a common
assumption: that computers can be used as a
powerful medium of communication in educational
settings and thus can encourage the development
of literacy, both in the student's mother tongue
and in a second language.

Simple Message Systems Within Classrooms

The simplest form of computer writing
network is the electronic bulletin board system
(BBS) for a single classroom computer. A BBS is
a rudimentary mail system that turns a computer
into a post office. The teacher and every
student has a mail box where they can fetch and
read messages that have been addressed to them.
Messages can be sent to any other "user," or
member of the mail system. In fact, copies of a
single message can be automatically sent to a
group of users who are working on a special
project. In addition to allowing users to send
mail to individuals or groups, most BBSs have
two other features: a public message board which
everyone on the system can use as an open forum
and a library of files, such as back issues of
the class newsletter or the latest drafts of
students' writings, which any user can "check
out."

Even this most rudimentary form of
computer networking can help achieve powerful
instructional goals when used in the service of

a process approach to teaching writing. While
such networks ought never to replace
face-to-face teacher and peer conferencing, they
do provide yet another context within which
students can offer and receive suggestions on
drafts. Indeed, the simplest of networks can
generate a strong impetus for joint authorship
and other forms of collaborative writing.

Dodge and Dodge (1987a) offer the most
comprehensive description of networking
alternatives for schools on a "shoestring
budget." Their suggestions include: a) setting
up a computerized database filing system to
simulate an electronic BBS; b) using BBS
simulators such as "Electronic Village,"
"Electronic Mailbag," "Kidmail" and "SimuComm"
as in-class message systems; and c) modifying a
full-fledged BBS like the Computer Mail System,
usually designed to be used with phone lines, so
that it works on a single computer.

A hybrid program which blends the features
of prompted writing with a single-classroom BBS
is the "Dialog Maker" in English (Sayers 1985)
and "El Dialoguista" and "Le Dialoguiste" in
Spanish and French (Sayers 1986). These
computer programs help a teacher keep dialogue
journals with a large group of students. A
dialogue journal is a written exchange between
a teacher and each student, usually kept in a
bound notebook. Studies have shown that
dialogue journals can help bilingual and ESL
students learn to read and write by building a
bridge from conversational abilities to
literacy skills; moreover this kind of
interactive writing encourages teachers to use
many of the same proven strategies which parents
use to "teach" the first language (Staton 1984).
However, most teachers balk at the huge time
commitment involved in writing unique entries in
each student's journal.

The "Dialog Maker" programs help make this
process considerably easier and more
interactive. The teacher and the student use
the program in different ways. First, the
teacher writes a series of prompts, one after
another, to her students. These comprise her
half of the written conversation. Then, as a
student reads the first in the chain of

teacher-generated prompts, the program pauses and allows the student to write his response. When he has finished, the "Dialog Maker" presents the student with the second teacher prompt and pauses for him to read it and then write a response. The conversational give-and-take continues. As soon as he answers the entire string of messages, the computer makes a printout that looks just like the script of a play, with that student and his teacher as the principal actors.

What makes this interactive process easier for the teacher to manage is the ability of the "Dialog Maker" to blend both GENERAL and PERSONAL messages into a single chain of prompts. For example, the teacher can write a personal "opener" to all twenty students; next, she might write a general prompt for all the students about, say, a class field trip; and then she could close with a single brief general message to all the students. By writing 22 short prompts she has allowed all 20 students to have three conversational "turns" at the computer. To each student, the general prompts are indistinguishable from the personal messages as they appear one after another on the screen, inviting a written response.

"Real-time" Networks Within Classrooms

An excellent example of a "good fit" between a general-purpose technology and efforts to encourage the language development of a special needs group is the ENFI (English Natural Form Instruction) Laboratory at Gallaudet College, where computers are linked in a local area network --LAN-- similar to those that are becoming common in offices. Hearing-impaired students write at computers which are arranged in a circle, and the group's conversation appears like a playscript on each screen. The rationale is that by "talking English" through writing, deaf students will increase their fluency in this language which is the coin of the realm of the larger society in which they live. Research has shown that this type of

computer-mediated "live" conversation translates
into better writing for academic purposes
(Peyton & Batson 1986).

Once more, there are valuable lessons to
be learned by teachers everywhere who are
concerned with language development. At present
this is a promising but costly technology,
requiring at least $10,000 to create a classroom
like the ENFI. However, as LANs are employed
more extensively in business settings, educators
can expect costs to descend and we should be
prepared to exploit the immense potential for
advancing literacy through real-time computer
networking.

Communication Between Classrooms

A modem is a small device which connects a
computer to a phone jack. Used with a disk
called a telecommunications terminal program, a
modem can link a classroom with a vast
universe of electronic information services.
Though the scale of operations is much grander,
using a modem to "telecommunicate" is similar to
using the simplest BBS. With a BBS, a student
reads and answers mail from her teacher and
classmates directly at a desktop microcomputer.
Occasionally, she might leave a message in the
public forum or read a document that was put on
reserve by the teacher in the computer
"library." Using a modem, the student types at
the computer and the modem connects her via
phone lines to a distant, giant computer post
office where she might read correspondence from
a classroom in Mexico. At times, she joins in
public message forums with participants from all
over the world, or she might get information for
a school project "on-line" from databases run
by professional news organizations or the
National Weather Service.

The InterCultural (IC) Network is the
oldest such project, centered at the University
of California-San Diego, with sites in Japan,
Israel, Mexico, Spain, Puerto Rico as well as
Alaska, Connecticut, and Hawaii. Writings are
composed by students on word processors and then
sent through modems (devices which connect
computers with telephones) to a giant "computer

post office," ominously called The Source (not to worry --it's owned by **Reader's Digest**). There, copies of a message are placed in the mailboxes of each participant in the IC Network, and are later read when other sites use a modem to check their electronic mailbox (Sayers 1986a, 1986b). Studies show that as students develop a broader sense of audience, their writing improves (Cohen & Riel 1986).

Each site is comprised of a university researcher and a classroom teacher who develop and respond to projects on the network. Examples of collaborative projects have included

- .making astronomical observations from different points on Earth and comparing results with distant sites;
- .constructing and sharing surveys on controversial issues such as student suicide and nuclear arms; and
- .researching and comparing local solutions to water shortages around the world.

These experiences have led teachers and investigators to assert that when students use writing to pose and solve problems of intrinsic interest, their literacy skills will improve significantly (Riel 1983), and that increased literacy from networking experiences will transfer across students' languages (Rosa & Moll 1985).

Cost is a serious limiting factor in any network using commercial telecommunication services like "The Source." Charges for "The Source" are still prohibitive --at $8 to $20 per hour-- for most school budgets. And there is another substantial "hidden price" to be paid. The "turn-around" of messages between schools is far from instant, as researchers must often carry disks back and forth between computers at universities and those in the schools. The more gatekeepers there are, the longer a student must wait for a response and the greater potential for high levels of frustration when messages are not answered in a timely fashion.

This past year, teachers and researchers have experimented with new kinds of "non-real time" networks that are within the reach of more school budgets. Their search has brought them back to a simpler technology, electronic BBS's running on microcomputers like Apples or IBM's, but this time with a new twist added. These more powerful BBS's use modems to plug into a phone line. During the daytime, students may use them directly. Indeed, other students at nearby schools may call up the BBS and read or leave messages. But late at night when phone rates are lower, these bulletin boards can automatically call distant bulletin boards and exchange packets of messages.

"De Orilla a Orilla" (From Shore to Shore) is the multilingual "special interest group" of a large and growing confederation of Apple bulletin boards called "Computer Mail System-SchoolNet". CMS--SchoolNet was founded by Al Rogers of the San Diego TEC Center. Project Orillas began by linking up classes in Mexico and Puerto Rico with Latino students in the United States. From the outset, Orillas classes joined two at a time, creating partnerships between distant teachers whose classes became "sister classes."

Now Project Orillas includes many pairs as more bilingual and second language teachers in the United States and educators in other nations participate. Typically, sister classes have included collaborations between two United States bilingual classes, or between a bilingual class here and a class from the "mother" culture. Recently, however, students who study Spanish as a foreign language at a California high school have been paired with a class in Puerto Rico. Another fascinating exchange occurred between deaf high school students in San Diego, most of Mexican heritage, and a secondary class of hearing students in Rio Piedras, Puerto Rico. Thus students from two language backgrounds, American Sign Language and Spanish, learned about their sister class through their shared second language, English.

How have the messages been exchanged? The local electronic bulletin boards communicate by passing boundless messages through an

interlocking network of similar boards. In
bulletin board jargon, there are a few "hub"
computers surrounded by many "node" computers.
The hubs serve as relay points for the exchange
of mail between nodes. Most participating
schools pay nothing for the local call that
connects their node to the closest hub computer.
The hub computers share costs over the entire
system as each relay point pays the phone bill
--usually under a dollar-- for just one leg of
the overnight mail delivery service. The result
is next-day delivery to each participating
classroom of large batches of student writings.

Using the technology, students write much
more than electronic pen-pal letters. The most
successful projects have been those which have a
life of their own away from the computer, and
can be amplified by the participation of the
sister class, such as the production of local
newsletters mentioned earlier. Teachers discover myriad ways to exploit the learning
potential of computer writing networks, some of
which employ other media and even the
"old-fashioned" postal service. The steady
stream of student writings is often supplemented
with culture packets --"time capsule" packages
including photos, maps, items of local interest,
and audio tape recordings or videotapes.
Teachers have found that both the number and
quality of texts shared over the computer
increases as culture packets are regularly
exchanged between sister classes.

Project Orillas is expanding, especially
with the merging of the entire InterCultural
network, mentioned earlier, with the CMS-
SchoolNet and Orillas networks. This means
that ESL students can communicate with peers who
are also learning English in Japan, Israel,
and Mexico. Soon more countries (Argentina,
Canada, and Cape Verde) and language groups
(Cape Verdean Creole, French, Jamaican Creole,
Portuguese, and Puerto Rican Sign Language)
will "log-in." Efforts are also underway to
involve visually-impaired students in Orillas
through the use of speech synthesizers which
voice the bulletin board messages. Yet the
underlying rationale has not changed. The
goal of Project Orillas --for bilingual educa-

tion and second language students in the United
States as well as for their colleagues in
other nations-- is to promote literacy by
linking novice writers to a wide world of
language learners. Computers are but one means
to this end.

CONCLUSION

While using computers to develop writing
skills in Limited English proficient students
is just one of a range of computer applications
to enhance language learning, it is an area
which has attracted much attention from
educators concerned with bilingual and ESL
program students, as exemplified in the
previously cited OTA Report. In this and other
areas of computer-assisted language learning,
carefully executed research studies, both
quantitative and qualitative, are needed to
build sound pedagogical theories to aid
policymakers and educators in making wise
decisions for allocating scarce dollars.

Both forms of research can play a useful
role in this regard. Quantitative approaches
must be complemented by ethnographic case
studies, since qualitative research can prove
invaluable in giving accurate, "recognizable"
portraits to educators and policymakers of
specific computer applications, particularly in
an area of technology that changes quite rapidly
and in which longitudinal and survey studies
with many subjects are impractical.

REFERENCES

Britton, J.; Burgess, T.; Martin, N.; McLeod, A. and Rosen, H. **The Development of Writing Abilities.** London: Macmillan Education, 1975.

Brown, K. and Sayers, D. "World Class Correspondent." In **Technology in the Curriculum: Foreign Language Resource Guide: A Guide to the Instructional Use of Computers and Video in Foreign Languages.** Sacramento, Calif.: CSDE, 1987.

Burns, H. A Writer's Tool: Computing as a Way of Inventing. Paper presented at New York College English Association Conference, October, 1980. (ERIC ED 193 693)

Cohen, M. and Riel, M. **Computer Networks: Creating Real Audiences for Students' Writing.** Technical Report No. 15. La Jolla, Calif.: Interactive Technology Laboratory, 1986.

Cummins, J. "Cultures in contact: Using classroom microcomputers for cultural exchange and reinforcement." **TESL Canada Journal/Revue**, TESL du Canada, 3, 2, 13-31, 1986a.

Cummins, J. "Empowering minority students: A framework for intervention." **Harvard Educational Review**, 56, 1, 18-36, 1986b.

Dalute, C. **Writing and Computers.** Reading, Mass.: Addison-Wesley, 1985.

Dodge, J. and Dodge, B. "Readiness activities for telecommunications." **The Computing Teacher**, 14, 7, 7-8, 22, 1987.

Emig, J. **The Composing Processes of Twelfth Graders.** Urbana, Ill.: National Council of Teachers of English, 1971.

Graves, D. **Writing: Teachers and Children at Work.** Exeter, N.H.: Heinemann Educational Books, 1983.

Naisbitt, J. **Megatrends: Ten New Directions Transforming Our Lives.** New York: Warner Books, 1984.

Peyton, J. and Batson, T. "Computer networking: Making connections between reading and writing." **ERIC/CCL News Bulletin,** 10, 1, 1, 6-7. 1986.

Riel, M. "Education and ecstasy: Computer chronicles of students writing together." **The Quarterly Newsletter of the Laboratory of Comparative Human Cognition,** 5, 3, 59-67, 1983.

Riel, M. "The computer chronicles newswire: A functional learning environment for acquiring literacy skills." <u>Journal of Educational Computing Research</u>, 1, 317-337, 1985.

Roberts, L. Trends and Status of Computers in Schools: Use in Chapter 1 Programs and Use with Limited English Proficient Students. Staff Paper. Science, Education and Transportation Program, Office of Technology Assessment, United States Congress Office of Technology Assessment, Washington, D.C., 1987.

Rodriguez, D. and Rodriguez, R. "Computer-Based Creative Problem Solving." In Wresch, W. (Ed.). **The Computer in Composition Instruction.** Urbana, Ill.: National Council of Teachers of English, 1984.

Rosa, A. & Moll, L.C. "Computadoras, comunicacion y educacion: Una colaboracion internacional en la intervencion e investigacion educativa." **Infancia y Aprendizaje,** 30, 1-17, 1985.

Sayers, D. **The Dialog Maker.** Cardiff-by-the-Sea, Calif.: InterLearn, 1985.

Sayers, D. _El Dialoguista and Le Dialoguiste_. Cardiff-by-the Sea, Calif.: InterLearn, 1986a.

Sayers, D. "'Interactive' writing with computers: One solution to the time problem." **Dialogue**, 3, 4, 10-11, 1986b.

Sayers, D. "Dialogue journals: A literacy 'close encounter' of the first kind." **New England Bilingual Literacy Correspondent**, 2, 2, 4-5, 1986c.

Sayers, D. "Sending messages: Across the classroom and around the world." **TESOL Newsletter** (Supplement on Computer-Assisted Language Learning), 20, 1, 7-8, 1986d.

Sayers, D. "From journals to journalism: ESL writers." **Puerto Rico TESOL-Gram**, 13, 3, 7-8, 1986e.

Sayers, D. and Brown, K. "Bilingual education and telecommunications: A perfect fit." **The Computing Teacher**, 17, 7, 23-24, 1987.

Strickland, J. "Prewriting and Computing." In Collins, J.L. and Sommers, E.A. (Eds.) **Writing On-Line: Using Computers in the Teaching of Writing.** Upper Montclair, New Jersey: Boynton/Cook Publishers, Inc., 1985.

ANNOTATED BIBLIOGRAPHY

This section includes: (a) a summary of periodicals which center on CALL in bilingual and ESL education, or in general and computer-based education; (b) an annotated bibliography of relevant books and articles not cited in the body of the chapter; and (c) a list of suppliers of computer programs described in this chapter.

A. Periodicals

C.A.L.L. Digest. Published eight times a year by the International Council for Computers in Education, University of Oregon, 1787 Agate Street, Eugene, Oregon 97403-1923. Subscriptions are $18.50 per year ($25 outside North America).

Since 1985 this journal has provided its readership, described in its masthead as "computer-using ESL teachers", with current information on computer applications to promote language learning. Of particular interest have been the special issues devoted to word processing (March 1987) and telecommunications (July 1987). Regular features include columns on "Trends", "Product News", "Model Applications" and "Research".

The Computing Teacher. Published nine times during the academic year by the International Council for Computers in Education, 1787 Agate Street, Eugene, Oregon, 97403-1923. Subscriptions are $21.50 per year.

This journal is the most widely-read periodical dedicated to educational applications of computers. Each issue is devoted to special themes which often become standard reference materials, such as the indispensable April 1987 issue on telecommunications. Regular departments include columns of perennial interest, such as "Research Windows" with reviews of published scholarly investigations, and the updates

on software and hardware developments
provided in "What's New", "Software
Reviews" and "New Software Releases".

New England Bilingual Literacy Correspondent.
Published triquarterly by the New England
Multifunctional Resource Center, Weld
Building, 345 Blackstone Boulevard, Provi-
dence, Rhode Island 02906. No charge to be
placed on mailing list.

Many of the articles in this newsletter
are devoted to computer applications which
promote literacy in the mother tongue and
English. Every issue contains excerpts
from students' writings in the De Orilla a
Orilla writing network, with an update on
computerized exchange of writings between
sister classes.

TESOL CALL-Interest Section Newsletter. Pub-
lished several times a year by the CALL-
Interest Section of TESOL for members.
Membership information available from
TESOL, 201 D.C. Transit Building, George-
town University, Washington, D.C. 20057.

This journal links ESL teachers with an
interest in computer-assisted language
learning who are members of the largest
international professional organization
devoted to the teaching of English as a
second language.

B.   Articles, Books and Resource Materials.

Balesse, L. and Freinet, C. (1973). La lectura
en la escuela por medio de la imprenta.
Barcelona: Editorial Laia.

Celestin Freinet and his colleagues were
the first to link classroom technology (in
this case, printing presses) with
correspondence networks between schools,
beginning in the 1920's in France and
continuing to this day in thousands of
European schools. This book, originally
published in 1961, remains the most

thorough attempt to elaborate a pedagogical
theory that can guide the use of technology
in developing literacy.

Bogard, J. and Postman, J. (1986). Using Word
Processing in the Classroom: For Bank
Street Writer on the Apple. Reading, MA:
Addison-Wesley.

These curricular materials exemplify the
kind which are needed to adequately support
teachers in their attempts to integrate
word processing into the writing
curriculum. A loose-leaf binder includes
teacher resource materials, overhead
transparencies masters and student
worksheets on all aspects of teaching
"process writing" with one popular
educational word processor.

Cummins, J. (1986). Cultures in contact: Using
classroom microcomputers for cultural
exchange and reinforcement. TESL Canada
Journal/Revue, TESL du Canada, 3, 2,
13-31.

Reviews the literature on computer-based
writing networks, describes several
promising projects in Canada and the United
States and attempts to place these efforts
within a theoretical framework which
promotes bilingual literacy.

Dalute, C. (1985). Writing and Computers. Reading, MA: Addison-Wesley.

Offers a comprehensive review of the
scholarly literature on computer-based
writing instruction. She contextualizes
her discussion of technology both in terms
of (a) the relationship of various computer
tools to different stages of the writing
process and (b) the appropriateness of
various computer writing aids for different
stages of students' psychological development.

Dutra, I. (Ed.) (1986). CALL: Computer-assisted language learning (Special Issue). TESOL Newsletter, 20, 1.

A special supplement containing fourteen articles on various topics, most of which stress the value of computer-based writing instruction for ESL programs. Of particular interest is the lead article by Michael Canale and Graham Barker of the Ontario Institute for Studies in Education, "How Creative Language Teachers Are Using Microcomputers". This article concludes with thoughtful recommendations for teachers and policy makers which stress the need to reflect critically on educational practice both with and without the computer's mediation.

Mehan, H., Miller-Souviney, B.; Riel, M.; Souviney, R.; Whooley, K. and Liner, B. (1986). The Write Help: Resources and Activities for Word Processing. Glenview, IL: Scott, Foresman & Co.

The authors of this helpful teacher resource manual draw on their unparalleled experience both as developers of software to promote writing and as coordinators of the first international computer writing network. While examples refer to materials designed by InterLearn (see below), this compendium of classroom activities can be adapted to any word processor. Especially useful is the section on the classroom logistics of managing computer-based writing instruction.

Parson, G. (1985). Hand in Hand: The Writing Process and the Microcomputer, Two Revolutions in the Teaching of Writing. Juneau: Alaska Department of Education.

An introduction to current theories of "process writing" instruction, an orientation to word processing, and a record of writings by teachers and teacher trainers during the Alaska State Writing Consortium

Summer Institute. Offers secondary teachers a thorough manual for integrating word processing into their writing curriculum.

Peyton, J. and Batson, T. (1986). Computer networking: Making connections between speech and writing. ERIC/CCL News Bulletin, 10, 1, 6-7.

The most detailed description yet published of the English Natural Form Instruction Laboratory at Gallaudet College which uses the Local Area Network to link computers in a language laboratory that relies exclusively on written, real-time (simultaneous) exchange of text between deaf students and their teachers.

Roberts, L. (1987). Trends and Status of Computers in Schools: Use in Chapter 1 Programs and Use with Limited English Proficient Students. Staff Paper. Washington, D.C.: Science, Education and Transportation Program, Office of Technology Assessment, U.S. Congress Office of Technology Assessment.

Gives the preliminary findings of a task force investigating computer use with two groups of students in programs receiving Federal funds. Computer applications which stress writing instruction and telecommunications are cited as promising. A final report, to be released by mid-1987, will detail the most complete investigation of educational computer utilization ever undertaken by a Federal agency and will contain recommendations to Congress for future funding.

Rosa, A. and Moll, L.C. (1985). Computadoras, comunicacion y educacion: Una colaboracion internacional en la intervencion e investigacion educativa. Infancia y Aprendizaje, 30, 1-17.

Published in Spain's leading educational
research journal, this article is a
pioneering effort to describe the potential
of computer writing networks for encouraging language development and to situate
this educational enterprise within a
Vygotskian perspective stressing interactive learning.

Sayers, D. and Brown, K. (1987). Bilingual
education and telecommunication: A perfect
fit. The Computing Teacher, 17, 7, 23-24.

Describes the De Orilla a Orilla (From
Shore to Shore) computer writing network as
a vehicle for promoting mother-tongue
literacy for students in bilingual programs
and second language learning for secondary
level foreign language students. The
authors also provide specific information
on how to connect with existing computer
writing networks.

C. Computer Programs and Interface Cards

The following annotated listing is by no
means exhaustive. It represents the reviewer's
impressions of promising software and "firmware"
(interface cards which extend the capabilities
of off-the-shelf computers). Authors and
designers are not listed individually since
this information is either unavailable or the
program is the result of wide-ranging efforts
by large teams. Prices quoted, when available,
are given for July 1987. All programs require
printers.

AppleWorks. Apple Computer Company, Inc., 20525
Mariani Avenue, Cupertino, Calif. 95014;
$250.

The best-selling program for the Apple II
computer, this package is really three
integrated application programs (wordprocessor, database and spreadsheet)
designed to share information. Many

educators have designed files to promote
writing which take advantage of AppleWork's
integration (see Immigrant below).

Bank Street Writer III. Scholastic Software,
730 Broadway, New York, N.Y. 10003; $99.95
for Apple and $124.95 for IBM; requires
128K.

This version overcomes the deficiencies of
the earliest BSW programs because it is
"non-modal": the program is ready to write
or delete wherever the cursor is located
without switching to a different editing
function. Versions are provided for viewing
writing on the screen in primer, large and
regular type sizes (and if your computer
has a graphics card, for printing out the
larger type). Moreover, the addition of
"frozen text" to help teachers create
prompted writing files will be welcomed by
teachers seeking to integrate writing
skills instruction with their particular
curriculum area. The manual is clearly
written and helpful, and a well-designed
tutorial disk is provided.

BIT Program Computer Software. CUE Softswap,
P.O. Box 271704, Concord, Calif. 94527.

Twenty-two programs were designed by
bilingual teachers who learned programming
in the Bilingual Instructional Technology
Program funded by Title VII (1983-1987).
These programs are now public-domain
software, available for a nominal handling
charge.

Computer Mail System. CUE Softswap, P.O. Box
271704, Concord, Calif. 94527.
See description in text of chapter.

Dialog Maker. InterLearn, Box 342, Cardiff-by-
the-Sea, Calif. 92007; $60.
See description in text of chapter.

For Comment. Broderbund Software, Inc., 17
Paul Drive, San Rafael, Calif. 94903-2101;
$147.

An IBM program that requires DOS 2.0 (or
later), 256K and either two floppy disk
drives or a single floppy drive and a hard
disk, or a Local Area Network (LAN).

This program   represents   the   first
successful attempt to create a computer-
based writing environment that can help an
author receive and incorporate   feedback
from multiple readers on a   draft text.
Up to 16 reviewers can comment or revise an
author's draft.   These readers can rewrite
passages, offer comments, or   comment on
other reviewers' comments, all in the
lower window of a divided   screen where
each suggestion is organized   within a
clear outline format.   Only the author,
however,   can   incorporate   suggested
revisions into the original   text in the
upper window.   Documents can be printed
out with comments and rewrites incorporated
as endnotes or footnotes.   While the
commands appear in English, the   program
could organize reviewers' comments offered
in   any   language written in   Roman
characters.

FrEdWriter and FrEdLessons. CUE Softswap, P.O.
Box 271704,   Concord, Calif. 94527; nominal
handling charges.   Spanish chip: Hands-On
Training, 4021 Allen School Road, Bonita,
Calif. 92002; $40.

English and Spanish versions of FrEdWriter
are   described   in   the   chapter above.
FrEdLessons are well-designed prompted
writing files which were authored and
classroom-tested by teachers at a TEC
Center Summer Institute in San Diego,
California, in 1986.

HBJ Writer. Harcourt Brace Jovanovich, College
Department, 1250 Sixth Avenue, San Diego,
Calif. 92101; requires IBM's with 256K.

Conceived as a comprehensive package which
provides computer-based support at every
stage of the writing process, this cluster
of programs is most useful at the
pre-writing and text evaluation stages.
Thus, this program is similar to <u>Writer's
Helper</u> and <u>Write Start</u>, reviewed below.
However, unlike these programs, <u>HBJ Writer</u>
is limited in its "portability" since it
will only work with files created in the
HBJ word processor itself, an awkward,
hard-to-learn editing environment. A
unique feature of <u>HBJ Writer</u> permits
readers to leave comments on an author's
draft.

<u>Hide and Sequence</u>.   Sunburst Communications, 39
Washington Avenue, Pleasantville, N.Y.
10570; $99; for Apple II and Commodore.

This program contains pre-packaged stories
which offer a new twist on traditional
"scrambled sentences" programs. Up to
three story characters can be the
"storyteller" in one story, and the game
involves finding the most logical order for
a story part <u>as well as</u> the most reasonable
storyteller to say that part. Teachers or
students may enter their own stories with
an elementary word processor. This program
provides a rich context for language
development of bilingual/ESL program
students since writing done in a mother
tongue using the Roman alphabet can be
typed into the program.

<u>Immigrant: The Irish Experience in Boston,
1840-1870.</u>   Educational Technology Center,
337 Gutman Library, Appian Way, Cambridge,
MA 02138.

Developers have created a disk filled with
wordprocessor, database and spreadsheet
files which can be used with <u>AppleWorks</u>
to promote creative writing. Students
"adopt" an Irish immigrant family described
in a passenger list database and then

complete writing assignments based on their
study of information in the Immigrant files
and other support materials which are based
on historical documentary evidence. Immigrant can thus serve as a model for a
class-designed product exploring the
history of immigration from other
countries.

InterLearn interactive software for students.
Box 342, Cardiff-by-the-Sea, Calif. 92007.
Most programs, $60; for Apple II computers.

Each InterLearn disk contains several
programs which provide a range of support
for helping novice writers create the first
draft of a particular genre of writing,
such as a letter, an expository essay, or a
newspaper article. Every program is an
interactive word processor designed to ask
the student questions and pause for him or
her to respond in writing. Once the first
draft is completed, revision can be
accomplished in most educational word
processors. Computer Chronicles Newswire
is a bilingual (English/Spanish) program.

LogoWriter. Logo Computer Systems, Inc., 555
W. 57th Street, Suite 1236, New York, N.Y.
10019. Package includes disks which run on
various computers; $250.

An extension of the original Logo computer
programming language to permit word
processing capabilities, LogoWriter offers
many possibilities for creative language
learning, but requires extensive teacher
training, a need which developers are
meeting through well-designed teacher
support materials and regional workshops.

Magic Slate. Sunburst Communications, 39
Washington Avenue, Pleasantville, N.Y.
10570. For Apple II; $99.95.

The first of the educational word
processors to allow students to view text
on the computer monitor in 20-, 40- and 80-

columns, and to print out this text on most printers connected with the proper graphics card. This "expandable" word processor lets schools choose one program for use from primary through secondary school and is supported by an excellent manual.

M-ss-ng L-nks. Sunburst Communications, 39 Washington Avenue, Pleasantville, N.Y. 10570. For Apple II and IBM; Spanish and English versions; $99.95.

This program permits teachers to enter text and then creates a variety of "cloze procedure" games, in which every other word, every other letter, all vowels, all consonants, or even all letters (!) are deleted and students are encouraged to predict the missing letters. The program may be purchased with prepared texts provided by the publisher, but the versions which allow teachers and students to type in their own writings are more versatile.

PFS-Write, -File, -Report. Scholastic Software, 730 Broadway, New York, N.Y. 10003. Described in chapter above.

SlotBuster. RC Systems, 121 West Winsesap Road, Bothell, WA 98012. For Apple II+, IIe and IIgs computers; $150-$300.

SlotBuster can be purchased with a built-in speech synthesizer that adds "voice" to most software programs and comes programmed with English and Spanish pronunciation rules. Developers have also designed a software program that can be employed with AppleWorks, so that for the first time a popular integrated program is available for visually-impaired learners, who in the past had to purchase expensive machinery and/or customized programs. This single computer card can be inserted into a slot inside an Apple II to serve as the connection with a serial printer, a parallel printer and a modem, simultaneously.

<u>Talking Text Writer.</u> Scholastic Software, 730
    Broadway, New York, N.Y. 10003. Requires
    Apple IIe or IIc with 128K and the ECHO+
    for the IIE or Cricket speech synthesizer
    for the IIC; $199 with synthesizer.

An elementary word processor which speaks
    letter names or words in English as or
    after they are typed, either by letter,
    word, line or page. The teacher or student
    can improve the synthesizer's performance
    by teaching it new pronunciations.
    Especially significant in its potential for
    use with visually-impaired students in
    bilingual/ESL programs. See, however, the
    comments on the <u>SlotBuster</u> card, above.
    Very well designed manual with much
    practical information on classroom
    activities to promote writing.

<u>Writer Rabbit.</u> The Learning Company, P.O. Box
    2168, Menlo Park, Calif. 94026-2168.
    Requires Apple II with 64K.

A sequence of six games for second through
    fourth graders designed to improve
    awareness of English language mechanics in
    context, and thus to improve writing
    skills. Interestingly, grammar study is
    contextualized through the use of question
    words as the unit of analysis for sentences
    in stories. In some games, students are
    permitted to add their own story parts with
    a limited editor. All games allow for
    printing of texts produced. The low level
    of English and the functional orientation
    of grammar analysis make this a promising
    program with bilingual/ESL program
    students.

<u>Writer's Helper, CONDUIT.</u> The University of
    Iowa, Iowa City, IA 52242. Requires Apple
    II or IBM; $120.

Designed as a comprehensive package which
    provides computer-based support at all
    stages of the writing process. The program
    is particularly helpful at the pre-writing

and text evaluation steps. Pre-writing
modules are pre-programmed prompts which
facilitated open-ended activities like
brainstorming and freewriting or more
structured prompts such as "debating an
issue", "three ways of seeing" or "the
five-paragraph theme". Evaluation modules
check for homonyms, flag "be" verbs or make
word frequency lists. Files from most
common word processors can be evaluated
with this program. Most appropriate for
secondary or college level students.

Write Start. MECC (Minnesota Educational Computing Corporation. $60.

A cluster of modules that combine a word
processor with (a) a number of ways to
share writing or react to drafts by members
of a class; and (b) several pre-writing or
"experimenting" activities, including
modules for freewriting, sentence expansion
and "word play" activities like poetry
writing. All activities take place within
the word processing context, thus encouraging an easy flow from "experimenting" and
"sharing" to actual writing.

Chapter 11

BILINGUAL EDUCATION AND ESL INSTRUCTION:
AN OVERVIEW OF FINDINGS AND A RESEARCH AGENDA

Alba N. Ambert

An Overview

In the preceding overview of recent
research in bilingual education and ESL, the
salient area of consistent examination was
language. This is understandable, since
language is at the core of any discussion on
bilingual education and the acquisition of a
second language. Specifically, the process of
acquisition of English as a second language and
the role played by the native language in this
process have been emphasized. Most of the
recent research, then, has focused on language
and literacy in language minority populations.
      A second outstanding strand in reviewing
current studies, in the United States as well as
in other countries, deals with the differential
treatment accorded to linguistic minorities in
educational settings. It is clear that programs
intended for language minorities differ from
those of language majority children. Ideology,
politics, educational philosophies, attitudes,
and values are at the core of program
implementation in bilingual education and second
language instruction. These issues transcend
actual research findings and program evaluation
results and are at the basis of the current
debate on bilingual education.
      Current government opposition to native
language instruction and the official-English
provisions vigorously promoted by certain groups
in the United States, necessitate careful
scrutiny of recent legal developments that apply
to language minorities. The protection afforded
to LEP students under Title VI of the Civil
Rights Act of 1964 is declining. However, as a
result of recent court decisions, the Equal
Educational Opportunities Act is at present the
legal provision which best protects the
educational rights of language minority
students.

Reauthorization of Title VII funding, and possible amendments to the law, will be taken up in 1988. Although proposed amendments reflect a desire to maintain current federal funding levels for native language instruction, there is also a proposal to increase federal funds for English-only programs for language minority students. Congress' debate and resolutions on these issues must be carefully monitored.

Another legal debate of considerable interest and concern for language minorities concerns the official-English provisions promulgated in many states. According to informed legal opinion, the legality of provisions declaring English to be the official language of a state, are subject to challenge under the Equal Protection Clause of the Fourteenth Amendment.

A Research Agenda

Although a substantial body of research exists on bilingual education and the acquisition of English as a second language, the preceding chapters underscore the research needs that still exist. There are some areas that have barely been touched, such as bilingual vocational education, bilingual science and mathematics, the bilingual/ESL language arts curriculum, to name some. The following are the research needs found in the specific areas addressed in this volume.

LANGUAGE

Native Language Development

Further research is needed on the native language development of children who are growing up in bilingual settings. The linguistic characteristics of these children will allow us to identify differences in native language development (as compared to the language development of children in monolingual settings) and avoid the designation of "language delayed or deficient" placed on children who may be acquiring a different variety of the native language because they are exposed to language in a bilingual environment. The role of language minority parents as linguistic models requires further research, especially in light of recent findings on the importance of child directed speech in the development of language. We need a better understanding of the cognitive processes involved in language acquisition. We need more data on how language is processed.

Native language loss should be of particular concern to researchers because recent research findings confirm the importance of a strong native on second language acquisition. At the same time the subtractive effects of most bilingual education programs is consistently noted by researchers in the field of bilingualism and second language acquisition. It appears that native language maintenance is rarely a goal in bilingual programs and, as a result, LEP children are losing an important part of their selves, as well as the asset of bilingualism, in the process of acquiring English. In addition, they are losing an important tool in the acquisition of a second language. What happens to a lost language in the brain? Can it ever be retrieved?

Continued research needs to be done on the role of the native language in second language acquisition. Longitudinal studies are needed to determine the long-term effects of a strong native language base on general cognitive development, literacy skills development and the acquisition of other languages.

It would also be useful to know what happens to the native language during the second language acquisition process. How does the native language change, regress, progress? What conditions result in native language regression or progression? What conditions need to exist to maintain a strong native language and develop true bilingualism?

The hemispheric lateralization of the brain for language function is still of great interest to psycholinguists and neurolinguists. To what extent are some language functions processed in the right hemisphere? What can brain studies tell us about the optimal age for language acquisition?

Second Language Acquisition

Although researchers today tend to conclude that older children acquire a second language more efficiently than younger children, further research is needed to determine the role of motivation, cognitive maturity, and stronger native language skills in this matter. Do older learners appear to learn the second language quicker and easier because of more sophisticated cognitive and general linguistic skills? Is the question of relative proficiency between young and older learners an issue? That is, we can assert that older children and adolescents are simply more proficient language users than young children, since we know that language becomes more complex with age. Does this mean that older learners of a second language learn in a qualitatively different way?

Further investigation into the individual differences in second language acquisition is important in practical applications in the classroom. ESL teachers could use more information on the linguistic characteristics of children acquiring English as a second language. The importance of this is evident in the number of LEP children referred for special education because school personnel do not understand the linguistic and behavioral characteristics of children acquiring a second language. There are also have fixed expectations on the rate of second language acquisition.

We need more information on the intermediary stages of language development in children acquiring a second language to gauge the changes in competence in the native and second languages as a child's exposure to the two languages varies in quantity and content.

We also need to know more about the specific strategies children use in learning a second language. The research points to many differences in strategies between native and second language acquisition. What are these differences? Are there more effective strategies? How dependent are these strategies on individual children's learning styles? Can

teachers assist children in developing a set of
effective strategies in second language
acquisition?

The research suggests that many interrelated factors affect a child's language
development and second language acquisition.
More ethnographic studies are needed to
describe the characteristics of effective
learning environments in bilingual education and
ESL classrooms, including teacher-student
interactions.

Bilingual teachers note the ease and
apparent automaticity of skills transfer from
one language to the other. We need more
information on the transfer of skills process.
Does it occur from the second to the native
language in the same manner as from the native
to the second? Do some linguistic skills
transfer more readily than others? Can we
facilitate the transfer process by manipulating
certain conditions? In other words, are there
specific conditions which propitiate transfer?

Furthermore, does the transfer of skills
from one language to another occur solely in
contexts with heavy linguistic content, such as
social studies, or does it occur as well in
areas not as linguistically laden, as visual
arts?

Evidence has emerged that bilingual persons
perform better than monolinguals on certain
areas of intelligence tests. Researchers have
concluded that bilinguals have greater cognitive
flexibility than monolinguals. Other researchers
have criticized the methodologies in these
studies. Further research in this area is
needed to confirm these very important
findings.

We need more studies on the effects of
attitudes and educational philosophies of
program administrators on the implementation of
bilingual and ESL programs.

The consensus on bilingual education and
ESL instruction research seems to be the need
for methodologically sound program evaluation
studies. Yet, the issue of proper program
implementation is critical in evaluation
studies. All too often evaluation studies are
conducted on bilingual education/ESL programs

not implemented according to sound educational
theory and practice. It is not surprising,
then, that results show little positive impact.
To evaluate bilingual/ESL programs effectively,
it is necessary to select true bilingual/ESL
programs, properly developed and implemented. A
biologist would not select diseased cells in a
study of normal cell development. Neither
should improperly implemented programs, which
are often only nominally bilingual, be selected
for program effectiveness studies.

LITERACY

Reading and writing are linguistic
functions, therefore most of the issues relevant
to language development and second language
acquisition apply to literacy and biliteracy
development. An important development in
literacy research in general, which applies to
LEP populations as well, is the interrelated
nature of reading and writing with the other
communication skills of listening and speaking.
For the purposes of this discussion, we have
separated the categories of reading and writing,
but would like to point to the unity of the two
processes in the practice. A theme that emerges
frequently in the literature is that reading
affects writing and writing affects reading.

Reading

As in second language acquisition, the role
of the native language in literacy development
is of critical importance. It appears that in
language minority children literacy development
is best achieved in a child's stronger language.
In addition, it is clear from the research that
literacy skills in the native language transfer
readily to the second language. Yet, we need
further research to determine how to proceed
with children whose native languages do not have
a written tradition. Is it more appropriate to
introduce literacy in the second language?
Should research efforts concentrate on the
development of phonetic alphabets for those
languages without written tradition, so the

literacy development of these children can proceed more efficiently? We also need further research on the transfer of literacy skills from the native to the second language when the two languages do not share the same type of alphabet (Roman and Chinese script, for example).

More information is needed on the transfer of skills phenomenon in reading to identify effective techniques teachers can use to facilitate the transfer. Further research is needed on the role of literacy in oral language development. It appears that it is not necessary to wait for a child's full oral language development (in the native language or English) to introduce literacy. Does literacy have a subsequent impact on the child's oral language development, then?

Teachers would benefit from an understanding of the differences which exist between a student's native and second languages in facilitating biliteracy development. Differences in the cultural, lexical, and discourse forms of the two languages are known to affect the literacy development of LEP students.

Writing

Reading and writing skills are interrelated and development of one affects the other.

More case study, ethnographic and descriptive studies are needed to study the nature of the writing or composing behaviors in LEP children, both in the native language and in ESL. How do children use the native language when writing in the second language? For example, do they "think" in their native language before they actually write in the second language? What are the orthographic, spelling, vocabulary, punctuation, syntactic differences between native languages (Spanish, Greek, Chinese, for example) and English that affect LEP children's composing behaviors in ESL? How can teachers facilitate transfer of writing proficiencies from the native language to English? Does the development of writing skills in the native and second languages affect oral language development?

EARLY CHILDHOOD

The research described in this volume categorically confirm the linguistic strengths of young bilingual children. This is evident in research studies that have looked at young bilingual children's language development from different perspectives. Further research is needed to establish the differences in linguistic development between monolingual English-speakers and LEP children.

Self regulatory private speech appears to be an important cognitive strategy used by bilingual young children. Practitioners would benefit from further research in this area to determine whether this natural learning strategy can be developed. The relationship between native language development and cognitive development in LEP young children needs to be studied, as well as effective strategies to develop thinking and problem-solving skills in LEP young children.

Research questions are still to be answered on the appropriate time to introduce English as a second language to LEP children. Results such as the Carpinteria Early Childhood Program described in this volume indicate that in young children more native language development and less English is more effective in the eventual acquisition of English. More research is needed to confirm this view. The immediate cognitive effects of learning a second language in early childhood also need to be studied.

Longitudinal studies must be conducted to evaluate the long term effects of preschool programs that emphasize bilingualism and multiculturalism, since the effects may not be apparent until six or seven years after participation (as in the Head Start programs).

SPECIAL EDUCATION

Perhaps one of the most urgent issues in the field of special education is that of language development. It is evident from the studies reviewed that LEP children's placement in special classes is determined by their second

language proficiency. Teachers, school psychologists and other school personnel are not
familiar with the linguistic and behavioral
characteristics of children acquiring a second
language. They confuse limited language
proficiency (which is often only evident at
higher level academic tasks) with learning
disabilities or intellectual limitations.

Referral and Assessment

More research is required on the linguistic
and behavioral characteristics of LEP children
(especially when performing in English) and
results must be disseminated to teachers in
mainstream classes. More appropriate language
assessment techniques need to be developed for
language minority children who are functioning
in two languages to determine the true level of
their language proficiencies. It appears that
after two years in the host country, native
language testing may not suffice in determining
a child's true abilities. Alternative methods
must be devised in the assessment process of LEP
children referred for special education
evaluation.

LEP Children with True Learning Problems

More empirical studies are needed to
establish the differences between second
language learners and LEP children with true
learning and language disorders. We also need
to identify the behaviors characteristic of LEP
children in all-English classes and the
behaviors of children with learning problems,
since very often both populations exhibit
similar behaviors in the classroom (inattenti-
veness, distractibility, etc.).
We also need to learn more about the
learning process in LEP children with true
learning problems. How can we teach LEP
children in bilingual special education programs
more effectively? How and when do we introduce
English as a second language? Is the process of
second language acquisition the same in LEP
children with handicaps as it is for normally
developing LEP children? If not, what are the

differences?   How effectively can LEP children
with handicaps   learn   a   second   language?   Can
they   function   bilingually?   More evidence is
warranted   on   the   transfer   of   skills between
languages in LEP children with different types
of learning problems.   For example, does the
process differ between LEP learning disabled and
LEP   mentally   handicapped   children?   More
research evidence is needed on the advisability
of providing instruction to LEP handicapped
children in the native language before or while
they acquire a second language. More curriculum
based studies are needed in developing effective
programs for LEP handicapped students.

LOW INCIDENCE LANGUAGE GROUPS

        More focused research needs to be done on
LEP children from low incidence language backgrounds.   Basic research questions, such as the
nature of second language acquisition, interaction   between   first   and   second   languages,
relationship   between   language   and   cognition,
individual   differences   in   second   language
acquisition,   literacy   and   biliteracy development,   relationship   between   second   language
acquisition and cognitive style; would benefit
from closer scrutiny in low incidence language
populations.   Are these issues the same or
different when applied to members of low
incidence language groups?   What   are the
differences among the low incidence language
groups in language (first and second) and
literacy/biliteracy development?   What is the
best method for the special situation of Native
American children who are considered LEP, yet do
not   speak   their   native   languages?   How   can
educational programs be modified to address the
special needs of low incidence language groups?

ASSESSMENT OF LANGUAGE MINORITY STUDENTS

        Biases built into tests used to assess the
proficiencies   of   language   minority   students
continue   to   be   a source   of   concern.   Tests
which are not standardized on the populations

tested; translated, but not adequately adapted; and the use of set batteries of tests administered to all children regardless of their specific difficulties are all too frequent. It appears from a review of the recent research that a trend exists towards less reliance on standard tests and more reliance on criterion-referenced measures to assess language minority students. There still exists a great research need to develop these informal measures in the areas of language dominance, language proficiency, reading and writing, and academic performance, as we move away from inherently biased standardized tests. In addition, use of other informal measures, such as interviews and objective observations, needs to be further explored in the research efforts exploring alternative assessment techniques for language minorities. More research in the assessment process must focus on language minority children's environment and their interactions within it.

LANGUAGE ARTS

The area of bilingual/ESL language arts encompasses learning skills in the areas of listening, speaking, reading and writing. While researchers have dealt with specific areas, especially in linguistic performance, there is still a great need for research which integrates the language arts. No research could be found in the area which dealt with in-depth theory on structuring language activities in language arts programs. In order to develop and implement more effective language arts programs, we need information on the characteristics of a success-ful language arts classroom, the characteristics of a successful language student, learning and teaching strategies that are conducive to effective native and second language acquisi-tion, and how to group children in the language arts classroom (according to language proficiency, cognitive maturity, or other criteria). We require more data on auditory processing skills, especially in listening; non-verbal communication strategies of second

language learners when they cannot produce
language; and more research is needed on
large-scale, longitudinal studies of effective
bilingual/ESL language arts programs.

COMPUTER TECHNOLOGY

Although computer use has proliferated in
the past few years to promote language
development and literacy skills, the research is
still not clear on the best uses of computer
technology in bilingual and ESL education.
Quantitative and qualitative research is
recommended to evaluate the results of computer
use, specific computer programs, and to develop
the most effective educational programs to
enhance language minority children's language,
literacy, and general cognitive development.
Because of the high cost of computer use in the
classroom, and the rapidly changing nature of
computer technology, it is important to
disseminate research results in this area.
Teachers may then be in a better position to
select the most cost-effective, as well as
educationally effective, computers and computer
programs for their students.

A P P E N D I X   I

Multifunctional Resource Centers   (MRC)

o Service Area 1 : New England MRC
                             Brown University - Weld Bldg.
                             345 Blackstone Blvd.
                             Providence, R.I. 02906
                             (401) 274-9548
   Specialty Area : English Literacy for LEP
                             students

o Service Area 2 : New York Multifunctional
                             Resource Center
                             Hunter College
                             645 Park Avenue, Box 367
                             New York, NY
                             (212) 772-4764
   Specialty Area : Bilingual Adult Education

o Service Area 7 : Southwest Education
                             Development Laboratory
                             (SEDL)
                             211 East Seventh Street
                             Austin, TX 78701
                             (512) 476-6861
   Specialty Area : English as a Second Language
                             and Other Alternatives

o Service Area 14: Northwest Regional
                             Educational Laboratory-MRC
                             1164 Bishop Street
                             Suite 1409
                             Honolulu, HI 96813
                             (808) 533-1748
   Specialty Area : English Literacy for Persons
                             of Languages with non-Roman
                             Alphabets

o Service Area 15: University of Guam - MRC
                    Project BEAM
                    College of Education
                    UDG Station
                    Mangilao, GU 96913
                    Cable: Univ-Guam.
                    TELEX: 721-6275
  Specialty Area : Literacy for Persons of
                    Languages with New or
                    Developmental Orthographics.

A P P E N D I X I I

ORGANIZATIONS

o Center for Applied Linguistics
   1118 22nd Street, NW
   Washington, DC 20037

o English Plus Information Clearinghouse
   (EPIC)
   Joint National Committee for Languages
   20 F Street NW, Fourth Floor
   Washington DC 20001

o National Association for Bilingual Education
   1201 16th Street, NW, Room 407
   Washington, DC 20036

o National Clearinghouse for Bilingual
   Education
   11501 Georgia Avenue, Suite 102
   Wheaton, MD 20902

o Teachers of English to Speakers of Other
   Languages (TESOL)
   1118 22nd Street, NW Suite 205
   Washington, DC 20037

A P P E N D I X   I I I

INFORMATION RESOURCES

o   Betty H. Seal
    Southeast Asian Learners Project
    Long Beach Unified School District
    Instruction Department
    701 Locust Avenue
    Long Beach, CA 90813
    (213) 421-9336
    Contact for: information on consultative
                 services to schools and
                 district   offices, staff
                 development and bilingual
                 materials development for
                 Indo-Chinese programs.

o   Van Khoa Bookstore and Distributors
    9393 Bolsa Avenue, Suite E
    Westminister, CA 92683
    (714) 531-6591
    Contact for: information on Indo-Chinese
                 ESL and bilingual materials,
                 information on employment
                 opportunities, retraining and
                 certification concerns,
                 upgrading and inservice needs
                 of Indo-Chinese educators.

o   Do Dinh Tuan
    Office of the Los Angeles County
    Superintendent of Schools
    Office of Bilingual Education
    9300 East Imperial Highway
    Downey, CA 90242
    (213) 922-6469
    Contact for: information on obtaining a
                 copy of the annotated
                 bibliography of Indochinese
                 materials.

o   Lexuan Khoa, Executive Director
    Indochina Resource Action Center
    1424 Sixteenth Street, NW - Suite 204
    Washington, DC 20036
    (202) 667-7810

Contact for: newsletter, list of
            publications and general
            information on Indochinese.

o   Siri Vongthieres
    Colorado Department of Education
    201 East Colfax Avenue
    Denver, CO 80203
    (303) 573-3281
    Contact for: information on Laotians.

o   Puthsarak Mum
    2838 Linden Lane
    Falls Church, VA 22041
    Contact for: information on Cambodians.

o   Je Xiong
    1015 North Broadway, Apt. A
    Joliet, IL 60435
    Contact for: information on Hmong.

o   Samsak Saythongphet
    Iowa Refugee Services
    4626 9th Street, SW
    Des Moines, IA 50315
    Contact for: information on Laotians.

o   James B. Tumy, Director
    Refugee Materials Center
    US Department of Education
    324 East 11th Street, 9th Floor
    Kansas City, MO 64106
    Contact for: bibliography of refugee
                materials.

o   Sithinary Kim
    1401 South Edgewood, Apt. 501
    Arlington, VA 22204
    (202) 265-6565
    Contact for: information on refugee
                resettlement.

A P P E N D I X   IV
SOURCES FOR STUDENTS*

o   Hi, World! A childrens' journal
     Multifunctional Resource Center
     University of Hartford
     Hillyer 226
     West Hartford, CT 06117
     (203) 243-4773

o   International Friendship League
     PEN PALS, Box 106
     22 Batterymarch Street
     Boston, MA 02109
     (617) 523-4273
     Ages 7 - 10

o   Letters Abroad
     209 E. 56th Street
     New York, NY 10022
     (212) 752-4290
     Age 16 - Adult

o   Students Letter Exchange
     910 Fourth Street, SE
     Austin, MN 55912
     (Elementary, High School)

o   World Pen Pals
     1690 Como Avenue
     St. Paul, MN 55108
     (617) 647-0191
     Ages 12 - 20

* Source: The State New York Education
          Department
          Center for Multifunctional and
          Comparative Education
          Newsletter - July, 1987
          Albany, NY 12234

A P P E N D I X   V

Journals and Newsletters of Interest to Bilingual and English as a Second Language Educators

o <u>Bilingual Review/La Revista Bilingue</u>
Office of the Graduate School, SUNY
Binghamton, New York 13901.

o <u>Bilingual Special Education Newletter</u>
University of Texas
Department of Special Education
Education Building, 306
Austin, Texas 78712-1290.

o <u>ELT Journal</u>
Journal Subscriptions Department
Oxford University Press
Walton Street, Oxford OX2 6DP
England.

o <u>Findlay College Newsletter</u>
Center for Bilingual Multicultural Studies
1000 North Main Street
Findlay, Ohio 45840

o <u>IDRA (Intercultural Development
Research Association) Newsletter</u>
5835 Callaghan, Suite 350
San Antonio, Texas 78228

o <u>Journal of Multilingual and
Multicultural Development</u>
Multilingual Matters, Inc.
Bank House, 8a Hill Road
Clevedon, Avon 8521 7HH, England

o <u>NABE Journal</u>
1201 16th Street, NW
Washington, DC 20036

o <u>TESOL Quarterly</u>
Suite 205, 1118 22nd Street, NW
Washington, DC 20037

AUTHOR INDEX

SUBJECT INDEX